CLASSIC EXPERIMENTS IN PSYCHOLOGY

CLASSIC EXPERIMENTS IN PSYCHOLOGY

Douglas Mook

GREENWOOD PRESS
Westport, Connecticut • London

Library of Congress Cataloging-in-Publication Data

Mook, Douglas G., 1934-
    Classic experiments in psychology / Douglas G. Mook.
      p. cm.
    Includes bibliographical references and index.
   ISBN 0-313-31821-2 (alk. paper)
    1. Psychology—Experiments. I. Title.
BF198.7.M66 2005
150'.72'4—dc22   2004023845

British Library Cataloguing in Publication Data is available.

Library of Congress Catalog Card Number: 2004023845
ISBN:0-313-31821-2

First published in 2004

Greenwood Press, 88 Post Road West, Westport, CT 06881
An imprint of Greenwood Publishing Group, Inc.
www.greenwood.com

Printed in the United States of America

The paper used in this book complies with the
Permanent Paper Standard issued by the National
Information Standards Organization (Z39.48-1984).

10 9 8 7 6 5 4 3 2

Every reasonable effort has been made to trace the owners of copyright materials in this book, but in
some instances this has proven impossible. The author and publisher will be glad to receive information leading to a more complete acknowledgments in subsequent printings of the book and in the
meantime extend their apologies for any omissions.

To the memory of Eliot Stellar, who could have done it better.

CONTENTS

Contents

ILLUSTRATIONS

FIGURES

TABLES

PREFACE

When I told a colleague that I had undertaken to write a collection of classic experiments in psychology, his first reaction was, "Have you any idea how many friends you'll lose?" He has a point, and I can only hope my friends—many of whom could well have been included here—will understand and forgive. And there are many "friends I haven't met" whose omissions I regret: "He didn't include Curt Richter? Jean Piaget?" Even some Nobel laureates are not included—Karl von Frisch, Konrad Lorenz, Eric Kandel.

There were a number of criteria for inclusion of an item. First, only experiments through 1980 were considered. This policy allowed an experiment about a quarter of a century to establish itself as "classic," and considers roughly the first century of psychology as an experimental discipline. Second, the experiment should be cited in the introductory texts I skimmed, so that students and instructors would have heard of it before. Third, the experiment could not be too technical to be described both clearly and briefly. Fourth, entries should not be too similar to each other (that is why, for example, Nikolaas Tinbergen is included but Konrad Lorenz is not). That way, those that did get included would reflect the diversity of interests, problems, and approaches that nonetheless are linked to each other by their use of the experimental method.

One or more of these criteria were relaxed in some cases (for example, Vincent Dethier's work on feeding in the fly is not considered in most introductory textbooks, but it should be). So the final selection resulted simply from my decisions, for which I am solely responsible. To the many readers who will feel that I have done injustices to many fine investigators, I can only say that I agree.

ORGANIZATION

The book is organized into seven sections after the two introductory chapters. There was necessarily arbitrariness here too (does the work of Teitelbaum and

Epstein on the lateral hypothalamic syndrome go under psychobiology or motivation?). Within each section, the entries, with one exception, appear in roughly chronological order—only roughly, first, because careers overlap, and second, because there was also some attempt to put related chapters adjacent to each other, for the convenience of readers who wish to read blocks of chapters together.

The exception is Benjamin Franklin's foray into experimental psychology with the investigation of Anton Mesmer's claims. That chapter is put last, for dessert.

CITATIONS

Each chapter ends with a list of references and further reading. To keep the book from getting too long, I have tried to keep citations to a minimum. Works referred to directly are cited, as are book-length biographies of the investigators where available (brief biographies are readily available online). Added to these are one or two secondary sources, usually college-level textbooks dealing with the general topic in question (cognition, social psychology, etc.). It is assumed that these will (a) be more accessible to the general reader than technical papers, (b) provide more context for the individual experiments, and (c) refer in turn to primary sources for readers who wish these.

Finally, I will surely have made mistakes. I shall be grateful to readers who take the trouble to point them out to me.

ACKNOWLEDGMENTS

This book and its author owe much to Marcie Ewasko, who agreed to "help" with graphics and surely ended up doing most of them. I also was fortunate to have the guidance of three wise and patient editors at Greenwood Press: Emily Birch, who remembered a course in experimental psychology with enough fondness to want to do a book on it; Debra Adams; and Marie Ellen Larcada. Each of them saved me from many blunders, and I thank them all.

My thanks also to Bridget M. Austiguy-Preschel, who steered the book through production; and Marcia Goldstein, who steered the author patiently and pleasantly through the perils of permissions. The book itself was produced by the team at Apex Publishing, LLC; and James Duncan added the final touches as copyeditor.

Among my friends, Marcia Ewasko and Scott Parker read through parts of the book and saved me from other blunders. And my best friend, Melody Browning-Mook, read all the chapters—some more than once—and made them better. She makes many things better.

1 INTRODUCTION

1 ABOUT EXPERIMENTS

Stop 100 people on the street and ask them to name a psychologist, either living
or dead . . . If we leave out the media and pop psychologists, . . . there would be
no question about the outcome of this informal survey. Sigmund Freud would
be the winner hands down. B. F. Skinner would probably finish a distant second.
No other psychologist would get enough recognition even to bother about.

Keith Stanovich

Thus Keith Stanovich (2001, p. 1) begins his excellent book *How to Think Straight
about Psychology*. The present writer's view is similar. B. F. Skinner is the only experimental psychologist who would be mentioned, and then not for his experiments.
Names such as Hermann Ebbinghaus, Edward Thorndike, Solomon Asch, and
Amos Tversky—the experimental psychologists whose work has led to the large
body of solid scientific findings we now possess—are not household names. A
majority of the people we ask, chances are, will never have heard of any of them.

Not only the names are unfamiliar, but the findings too—and the methods. Much
of what psychology has learned is unknown by most people, or is not distinguished
from the pseudoscientific claims that surround us on every side. There is not, in
other words, an appreciation of what is meant by *solid scientific findings*, largely
because there is little or no appreciation of what makes a finding solid. In particular, the power of the experimental method, as applied in the social and behavioral
sciences, is not widely understood.

The typical introductory course in psychology will attempt to develop such an
understanding, but it faces difficulties in doing so. There is a tremendous amount
of material to cover, so that any single investigation can only be discussed briefly,
and its background and implications—and the thinking that went into it—more
briefly still.

Hence this book, which attempts to show the research process by selecting just
a few classic experiments for more leisurely examination. The book shows where

an experiment comes from, how it is done and why it is done that way, and how its findings combine with others to enhance our understanding—and the excitement and adventure of the whole process.

Not that there is any one "right way." Indeed, the examples are deliberately selected to emphasize the great diversity of the problems in psychology that have been investigated by experiment, and the further diversity that attends the nuts and bolts of experimental procedures.

However, it will also attempt to show that all this diversity consists of variations on a single theme. This theme is the first of several that will recur throughout this book.

Theme 1: However the specifics vary from one experiment to another, the underlying logic remains the same.

Let us look at the logic.

WHAT IS AN EXPERIMENT?

The word *experiment* tends to call up an image of a laboratory, with glassware and people in white coats. This is much too limited an image. As shown in the following chapters, experiments can be done in classrooms, or underwater in scuba gear, or in a liquor store—or even in a laboratory.

An experiment is a way of establishing causal relations—of specifying, in other words, what causes what. It consists of making something happen—causing something to vary—and observing its effects.

We do experiments all the time in daily life. Suppose a light won't light. We ask why not, and we test the various possibilities one at a time.

Is the lamp unplugged? We may be able just to look and see if it is; this much does not require an experiment. Such "looking and seeing" (sometimes called *naturalistic observation*) can answer questions and provide valuable information, and it can lead to experiments—as here.

For if the lamp is unplugged, then we turn to experiment. We plug it in (we make something happen), and note the effect of this: Does the lamp work now?

If it does not, then we will look to other possibilities, and also check those by experiment. Is the bulb burned out? To find out, we again make something happen: Replace the bulb with a new one. And so on.

The point is that the logic of what we are doing is thoroughly familiar. Now let us extend that logic to some new cases—some examples of a more psychological kind.

Example 1: Social Pressure

The social psychologist Solomon Asch (chapter 56) asked, Suppose a person had to answer, publicly, a simple perceptual question—after he had heard a whole group of people give the same, clearly wrong answer? As it happened, these other people were assistants to the experimenter and were giving wrong answers on purpose, but the one real participant did not know that. What would he do when it came time to call out his answer? Would he give the answer that was obviously correct? Or would he "go along to get along," and call out the same wrong answer as the others?

Figure 1.1
**Results of one of Asch's conformity experiments. Many participants conformed to
the clearly wrong majority judgment if they had to call out their answers publicly
(left bar), but not if they wrote them down privately (right bar).**

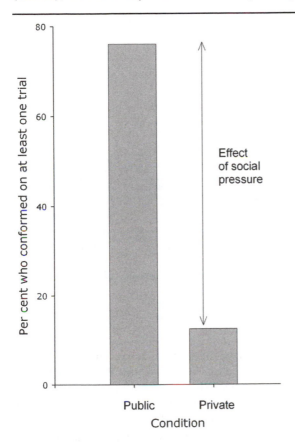

Source: Data from Asch (1951).

As it turned out, many people denied the direct evidence of their senses and went
along with the majority. They did, that is, if they were calling out their answers
aloud in front of the rest of the group. However, if the social pressure of the group
was removed, by letting the person write down his judgments privately instead of
calling them out publicly, then hardly anyone conformed to the majority opinion.
Therefore, social pressure, all by itself, is enough to make conformity more likely.

Example 2: Model Monkey Mothers

Baby monkeys, who are able to get around almost as soon as they are born, spend
much time clinging to their mothers. Why? Is it because they associate the mother
with food? That was the received view not long ago, for both baby monkeys and
baby people. Or, another possibility: Is it because she affords a warm, clingable
surface—what the experimental psychologist Harry Harlow called *contact comfort*
(chapter 13)?

Figure 1.2
Results of one of Harlow's "monkey mothers" experiments. Infant monkeys spent much more time in contact with the cloth mother (upper circles) than with the wire mother (lower circles), even though only the wire mother offered food.

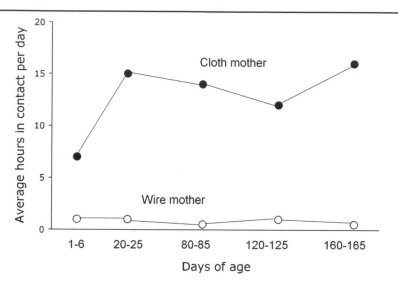

Source: From Harlow (1958, figure 6).

In nature, the two are inseparable, for a mother monkey offers both food and comfort at once. So, to separate the two possibilities, Harlow built two model monkey mothers of his own. One was made of wire mesh, but had a milk bottle mounted where the baby monkey could nurse. She offered food but not comfort. The other model mother had no milk, but she did have a warm, clingable surface made of terry cloth and warmed from inside. She offered comfort but not food.

Then Harlow allowed each baby monkey access to both models, so that the little participant could choose between them. And it was the comfortable mother with which the baby monkeys chose to spend their time. Since neither model responded to the baby monkey, and since the situation did not change, it was the difference between the two models all by itself that led the baby monkeys to choose one over the other.

This was strong evidence against the very powerful, but very wrong, food-based theories of mother-infant attachment that were current when Harlow's work began. It led to new questions about the attachment process in monkeys, and in humans as well.

Example 3: Behavior Therapy and Phobias

Based on Pavlov's work on conditioned reflexes (chapter 20), a new method of treating irrational fears, or phobias, was developed. Was it an effective method? To find out, Gordon Paul (chapter 26) selected some participants—college students who suffered from debilitating anxiety about giving speeches in a public-speaking course they were required to take. Some of these he arranged to be treated by the

Figure 1.3
Results of Paul's clinical experiment. The group treated with systematic desensitization therapy improved significantly more than the other groups.

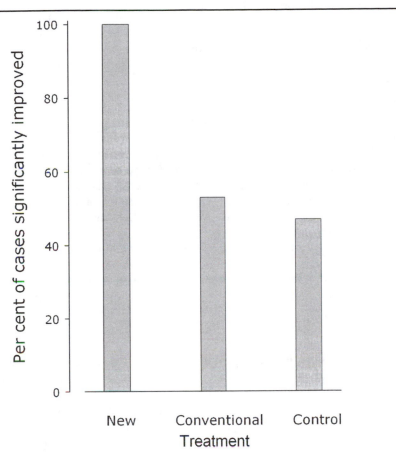

Source: Data from Paul (1966).

new method; others were treated by older methods; still others were not treated at all.

Those treated with the new method showed greater reduction in phobia than did those treated in either of the other ways. Since the groups were similar, and since the setting and measurements of anxiety were the same for all, we can be confident that it was the differences in treatment method all by itself that produced the differences in outcome. Based on this and other experiments, the new method is now considered an effective way of treating phobias, and an improvement on what was available before.

These three examples could hardly be more different on the surface. Yet the underlying idea is the same for all—and for the light-bulb experiment as well. Arrange for something to vary, and see what changes it causes. And the more we can arrange for everything else in the situation to be constant, the more confident we can be that what we vary is, all by itself, the cause of the effect we have seen.

THE ANATOMY OF AN EXPERIMENT

Researchers have developed a way of talking about experiments that we need to be familiar with, for the terms occur often.

Independent and Dependent Variables

An experiment causes something to vary. It does this independently of anything else that happens, or anything the participants do. So what the experimenter varies is called the *independent variable*.

Then we note the effect of this on something we observe or measure. These observations and measurements are the data we collect. In other words, we look to see how the data depend on the independent variable; what we observe or measure is therefore called the *dependent variable*. An experiment, in short, observes the effect of an independent variable on a dependent variable.

Thus we asked, Does changing the bulb cause the lamp to work? The independent variable was the difference between old bulb and new bulb. The dependent variable was whether the lamp worked or not.

Asch asked, Does varying the way participants' judgments were made—public versus private—cause differences in the judgments that they make? The difference in conditions, public versus private, was the independent variable. The judgment that each participant made was the dependent variable. Note that the setting, with the group of people making wrong judgments, was not an independent variable. It was not a variable at all but was constant under both public and private conditions.

Harlow offered his baby monkeys a choice between two model mothers, a comfortable one and a nutritious one. This was the independent variable: comfort versus nutrition. Which would they choose? That was the dependent variable.

Gordon Paul caused different groups of participants to be treated in different ways: the new way, the old way, or not at all. So type of treatment was the independent variable. Did this affect how much, and whether, they improved—the dependent variable? It did.

In any experiment, there will be at least one independent variable. There will be some difference among different experimental conditions—so there must be at least two conditions in any experiment. One compares these two (or more) conditions in order to see how, and whether, they affect the dependent variable that one observes.

So in all these cases, the independent variable is the cause. Its influence on the dependent variable is its effect—if it has one.

Experimental Control

An experiment tries to determine the effect of the independent variable on the dependent variable. Obviously, this effect will be easiest to see if nothing else affects what we observe. If there is something else that we do not consider, we may draw a wrong conclusion. Therefore, the ideal experiment will hold all variables constant that might affect the data, except for the one variable that is made to vary on purpose.

Return to our light problem for a moment. Notice that if we vary many things at once—we plug in the lamp, replace the bulb, replace the fuses, tear out and replace the wiring in the walls—then, even if the lamp works now, we won't know just what the problem was in the first place. It could have been any of these. These are referred to as *confounded variables*. *Confounded* means "confused," and here it could mean that we might be confused into thinking the wiring was responsible, when really the bulb was. That could be an expensive mistake! Hence the rule of thumb: An experiment varies one thing at a time, holding everything else constant.

Other control problems are more subtle, and depend on the specifics of the situation. Paul's experiment, in particular, took much thought and great care to assure that his groups of students differed in the variable of interest—type of treatment—and in no other way. The difficulties are discussed with his experiment in chapter 26.

There are many more questions to be faced and decisions to be made in conducting experiments. One must decide just how to vary the independent variable, how to measure the dependent variable, and what variables need to be controlled and how. One must decide how to recruit participants (the problem of sampling), whether to use different groups of participants for each condition or to impose them all on the same participants at different times (a problem of experimental design), how to equate groups if groups are used, and much besides. In addition, there are ethical questions that must be faced and that researchers take seriously. Some of these are discussed in chapter 58.

These technical matters, however, are beyond the scope of this book. They are discussed in books on experimental procedures (e.g., Kantowitz, Roediger, & Elmes, 2003; Shaughnessy, Zechmeister, & Zechmeister, 2002; Mook, 2001). This book is about how to understand experiments, not how to do them, though it is also true that the reader will develop a feel for these problems by seeing examples of how they have been solved—or, sometimes, have not been—in actual research.

For now, however, let us turn to another question: how experiments fit into the broader scheme of things.

THE SCIENTIFIC CONTEXT OF EXPERIMENTS

Although individual experiments are presented in this work, the author confesses a certain discomfort in presenting them that way. Experiments are done for reasons, and they have implications that extend beyond themselves. We may begin with the question, Why does one do research at all? We can distinguish two reasons.

Applied and Basic Research

In applied research, the researcher's interest is in a practical problem. An applied researcher in psychology might be concerned with designing the instruments and indicators in an airplane cockpit so they can be used most effectively, or finding a better way of training pilots or teaching children to read. He or she may seek more effective ways of treating a medical or psychological disorder—or preventing one, as when asking how best to persuade young people not to abuse drugs. Research like this is called *applied research*, because it is intended to be applied to a practical problem.

Gordon Paul's experiment with phobics was applied research. Pavlov's basic research on conditioning (chapter 20) led, by a series of historical developments, to a new, conditioning-based method for the treatment of phobias—irrational and troublesome fears. Now, having this method in hand, one needs to ask, Is it effective? Does it work better than the methods we already have? Does it work at all? Experiments can be designed to answer these questions, as in Paul's research (chapter 26), which showed that indeed the new method is effective.

Applied research can be contrasted with basic research, where the focus is not on a specific practical problem, but on the question, How does the system work? How does learning occur? How and how much do people influence each other? Why do infants form attachments to mothers? Enhanced understanding of these matters can come from the work of researchers who study learning, motivation, and the like, as things to be understood in their own right. Practical application will come later. The experiments of Asch and Harlow are examples of basic research; Pavlov's work on conditioning is another.

The motives of basic researchers are easy to misunderstand. To busy people facing problems, it may appear that basic researchers are wasting their time with trivia. Baby monkeys prefer comfortable to nutritious monkey mothers. Who cares?

Basic researchers may not worry much about these questions, but this does not mean they do not care about making the world a better place. They do. But they would point out two things.

First, we are better able to repair or improve any system if we know how it works in the first place. We can better combat disorders of (say) memory if we understand how memory works—how the brain receives, stores, and retrieves information. All knowledge will be useful in the long run, perhaps in very direct ways.

Second, the understanding that comes from basic research may turn out to be useful in indirect ways, often ones that could never have been foreseen when the research was done. Who could have known in advance that a new method of treating phobias (chapter 26) could have arisen from Pavlov's studies of salivation in dogs (chapter 20)? Yet it did.

Richard Nisbett (1990) has given an excellent example of the unforeseen and unforeseeable application of knowledge. Of all the people in history, who has done most to cure diseases? Nisbett points out that a strong case could be made for the Greek geometer, Euclid (129–210?). Euclid? A geometer? Yes. Euclid systematized geometry, which made possible the science of optics, which made possible the invention of the microscope, which made possible the discovery that germs cause diseases.

And that is what basic research can offer us—an understanding of what is going on, which we then find useful in all sorts of unforeseen ways.

Small Experiments, Big Questions

Any experiment is a modest thing. It may arise from a very big question, such as, How does the brain work? Or, how do we learn? But these questions are too broad to be addressed by any single experiment. A researcher must narrow the question down until it becomes specific enough that an experiment can answer it.

So in practice, experimenters will manipulate some specific independent variable in some specific way, and measure some dependent variable in some specific way. Other variables are held constant (for now), not because the experimenter thinks they are unimportant, but because at the moment she is studying something else. No experiment can study everything at once.

Because of this, an experiment seen in isolation can seem downright trivial. What makes it nontrivial is that its findings will bear on more general issues. This leads us to two ideas that will also be recurring themes in the chapters that follow.

Theme 2: Small Experiments Can Bear on Big Questions

Not by "answering" them once and for all—few experiments can do that. Rather, experiments contribute to a body of knowledge that helps us understand them better.

Paul Broca (chapter 4) studied intensively just two patients who had suffered brain damage. The damage had left them unable to speak. By a series of modest little experiments, Broca showed that the problem was specific to the production of speech—the patients were not cognitively impaired in other ways.

A small finding? Yes. But it bore on a much broader question: How does the brain work? Specifically, does the brain work as a unit, or does it have separate parts that do different things? The answer to that very big question will have implications for our whole understanding of brain function. Broca's findings came down on the "separate parts" side of this controversy, and they helped encourage the search, by other experimenters, for other separate parts within the brain that perform other functions. And these were found (see, e.g., chapters 8, 9, and 31).

Theme 3: No Experiment Stands Alone

Even a classic experiment does not stand alone. General conclusions come from the convergence of findings from many experiments, by many investigators.

When Pavlov discovered the conditioned reflex using the salivary reflex in dogs (chapter 20), his experiments were repeated in laboratories all over the world using different specific procedures. His findings held up across these variations. Different laboratories, different experimental procedures, and even different species all gave equivalent results. Such repetitions, or *replications*, of the original experiment show not only that the original finding was sound, but also that it holds up under all the differences from one experiment to another.

Then again, some other experiments gave results that were quite different from Pavlov's—in particular, the research on conditioned taste aversion (chapter 24). Those findings too have been replicated many times, and they too have held up. It is now clear that Pavlov's findings apply to some conditioning experiments, but not all. And the difference itself can be pinpointed, and it is so instructive that it just might revolutionize how we think about the learning process. That story—or its beginning, for research on the matter is very much still in progress—is told in chapter 24.

Finally, it is worth noting that this process of replication provides a safeguard against the mistakes a single investigator may make—or against fraudulent findings, which do occur and which may be announced with great fanfare in the popular media. Mistaken or fraudulent findings will quickly be discovered, for other researchers will be unable to confirm them. "In the long run, fraud and incompetence will out, because every statement is open to verification" (Dethier, 1962, p. 65).

In summary: A researcher begins with an interest in a very general question, but must narrow it down to a much more specific question in order to perform an experiment. However, after this is done, it all opens out again! The findings, together with other findings, all combine to advance our understanding of the much more general questions with which we began.

We might compare a single experimental finding to a single stone. Then we can consider that from many single stones, a beautiful and very useful house can be built.

FREQUENTLY ASKED QUESTIONS

There are a few questions that are raised quite often by those learning about experiments in psychology. A sampling of these follows.

But What If . . . ?

Any experiment must make some specific decisions: how to manipulate the independent variable, how to measure the dependent variable, what variables to control and how. It is natural and legitimate to wonder, What if the decisions had been different?

Asch set up just *this* particular setting in his studies of conformity. What if the situation had been different? What if a different task had been used? If an experiment used male college students as participants, what if it had used female students or homemakers? What if the room had been painted a different color? And so on for a thousand what-ifs. No single experiment can be expected to answer all these what-if questions at once.

Instead of being frustrated by this, we should remember that no experiment stands alone. Conclusions rest not on single studies, but on the convergence of many studies, among which the specifics vary. Asch himself went on to study different questions in different experiments: What if the majority were a different size? What if it were not unanimous? He himself did not ask, What if it were done in a different country? But other investigators did (for discussion see Aronson, Wilson, & Akert, 1994).

Part of the problem may be a perceptual one. Many what-if variables will be held constant in an experiment, and this may give the impression that the experimenter thinks they are unimportant. Quite the opposite is true: if he thought them unimportant, he wouldn't bother to control them! He recognizes their potential importance. He is just choosing to study something else—right now.

In short, the what-if questions will be answered sooner or later, not by any single experiment but by the convergence of many. What experimenters do not study today, they will study tomorrow. Or if they do not, they can be sure that someone else will.

But Aren't Experiments Artificial?

Many experiments occur in artificial settings, far removed from natural ones. They are designed that way, to permit control over the situation. In such cases, though, one may ask, Will these results generalize to more natural settings—the "real world"? For some purposes, one does indeed need to worry about this (for discussion, see Aronson, 1999). It has even been called the experimenter's paradox: a tightly controlled, simplified situation may make the effect of a variable easier to see, but will also make it less generalizable to real-world situations.

Three considerations, however, make the issue less problematic. First, experiments can be conducted in real-life settings. An independent variable can be manipulated in a natural setting that otherwise is left to vary as it normally would do. Such an experiment is called a *field experiment*. Where this can be done, the applicability of the findings to the real world is guaranteed, for they occur in the real world.

Second, what one wants to generalize is not the findings of a laboratory experiment, but the processes those findings reveal. Asch's conformity experiment took place in a highly artificial situation, yes. But his participants' reactions, during the experiment and in interviews after it, made clear that his participants were fully engaged by the scenario. "They're all giving the same wrong answer! What is going on? Are they all crazy? Am I?" The dilemma was real enough for them.

In fact, in this case, the conclusion was all the stronger *because* of the unnaturalness of the situation. The correct answer was perfectly clear and apparent; it was directly before the person's eyes. In most real-life situations, the information on which we base our judgments is fragmentary, obtained a little at a time, and may be trustworthy or may not—very different from the very clear case that Asch's experiment presented.

But many of his participants conformed anyway! They succumbed to group pressure and called out the wrong answer, despite the fact that its wrongness was unmistakable. The artificiality of the situation makes Asch's findings all the more dramatic, not less. All this clarity—and yet there was conformity.

Finally, for many experiments the question simply does not arise. Generalizing the findings to real life may not be what the researcher is trying to do.

Take Harlow's monkey-mothers experiment, for example. Harlow did not intend to generalize his findings to monkeys in their natural habitats. If he had, he would not have offered them wire and cloth mothers! When would they ever encounter these, in real monkey life?

Do Harlow's findings generalize to real life? They do not. His situation had no real-life counterpart. However, that is not a drawback to his experiment, but its great strength.

In real life, real monkey mothers offer both food and comfort; the two always occur together. To see which is more important, one has to separate the two, and no amount of observing under natural conditions will do that. The only way to do it is to build one's own mothers. The artificiality, in other words, was necessary in order to answer his question at all.

That does mean that Harlow could not generalize his findings to real life, but then he never intended to do that. His question was about a theory, or a pair of theories. One of these (the popular one at the time) predicted that the monkeys—these monkeys, in this setting—would choose the nutritious mother. The other predicted that they would choose the comfortable mother. They did the latter. And Harlow concluded not that monkeys in the wild would do the same, but that a theory of attachment—it depends on the association of mother with food—had trouble accounting for his findings.

In summary: Before dismissing laboratory findings as "not like the real world," we might do well to ask ourselves three things. First, was the artificiality required in order to ask the question at all? Second, are the findings really intended to apply directly to the real world? Or are they being applied to a theory instead, which predicts what the participants, in this setting, ought to do? And third, if the setting is different from real-world ones, does this really challenge the experiment's conclusions? Or might it actually strengthen them instead? (For further discussion, see Mook, 1983; Stanovich, 2001.)

How Can We Generalize from Animals to Humans?

A number of the experiments that follow use animals. A question that often arises is, "What do such findings tell us about human beings? How can you generalize from monkey behavior, much less rat behavior, to human behavior?" There are several answers. First, scientists do much less generalizing than is popularly supposed. If one said, "Monkeys do it, therefore people do it," that would be generalizing. Few of us say any such thing. We may instead say, "Monkeys do it. Let's see if people do it." Here we are not generalizing an answer, but rather asking a new question. Harlow's work on monkeys raised a host of questions about human behavior, to be answered by research with human beings.

Second, if we get a clear answer to a question in an animal experiment, we can at least say, "Here is how one system does it." That too may lead us to ask questions—not necessarily the same question—about human beings, perhaps with quite different methods. Here what is generalized is not the finding, but the more general question. Chapters 48 and 52, showing how new questions about human vision arose from the study of crab and frog vision, give good examples.

THE BEAUTY OF RESEARCH

One final note, and we will move on.

In the chapters that follow, it is the author's hope that the reader will not only reach a broader and deeper understanding of research, but also catch some of the sheer aesthetic pleasure of investigating and discovering. A scientist who speaks of a "beautiful experiment" means the phrase literally.

This applies even to the simple experiments readers can conduct for themselves. Chapter 7 describes how one can locate the taste receptors on the feet of a fly. Take a nonthirsty fly (because it has just drunk its fill of water). Dip the fly's feet—just its feet, and nothing else—in plain water, and nothing happens. Dip the feet in sugar water, and feeding reflexes are triggered, for sugar water is fly food. One can flip the little participant back and forth between two states: water on the feet, no feeding; sugar on the feet, feeding. Who can doubt (*a*) that the fly tastes with its feet, giving us a whole new worldview to consider, and (*b*) that by this simple experiment one can show that this is so?

Asch's experiment has the same beauty. If the participants write down their answers privately, there is little conformity. If they must call them out publicly, there is much more. And because nothing else differs between the two conditions, this beautiful experiment is able to tease out the effect of one variable—social pressure—from all the staggering complexity of human behavior and the things that influence it. And it shows that such pressure, all by itself, is enough to influence conformity dramatically.

Sir Isaac Newton once said that he felt like a small boy who had managed to pick up a few pebbles of knowledge from a vast beach. Here then, in the chapters that follow, are some pretty pebbles. Enjoy.

BIBLIOGRAPHY

Aronson, E. (1999). *The social animal* (8th ed.). New York: Worth Publishers.

Aronson, E., Wilson, T. D., & Akert, R. M. (1994). *Social psychology: The heart and the mind.* New York: Harper Collins College Publishers.

Asch, S. (1951). Effects of group pressure upon the modification and distortion of judgments. In H. Guetzkow (Ed.), *Groups, leadership and men.* Pittsburgh, PA: Carnegie Press.

Dethier, V. G. (1962). *To know a fly.* San Francisco: Holden-Day.

Harlow, H. F. (1958). The nature of love. *American Psychologist, 13,* 673–685.

Kantowitz, B. H., Roediger, H. L., & Elmes, D. G. (2003). *Experimental psychology: Understanding psychological research* (7th ed.). St. Paul, MN: West Publishing Company.

Mook, D. G. (1983). In defense of external invalidity. *American Psychologist, 38,* 379–387.

Mook, D. G. (2001). *Psychological research: The ideas behind the methods.* New York: Norton.

Nisbett, R. E. (1990). The anticreativity letters: Advice from a senior tempter to a junior tempter. *American Psychologist, 45,* 1078–1082.

Paul, G. L. (1966). *Effects of insight, desensitization, and attention placebo treatment of anxiety.* Stanford, CA: Stanford University Press.

Shaughnessy, J. J., Zechmeister, E. B., & Zechmeister, J. S. (2002). *Research methods in psychology.* New York: McGraw-Hill.

Stanovich, K. E. (2001). *How to think straight about psychology* (6th ed.). Boston: Allyn & Bacon.

2 A BRIEF HISTORY OF EXPERIMENTAL PSYCHOLOGY

Psychology, Hermann Ebbinghaus (chapter 29) once said, has a long past but a short history. Its past goes farther back than history does, for it seems very likely that psychological questions—questions about why we think and act as we do—were being asked long before writing was invented. Its history as a science, however, begins much later.

THOUGHT EXPERIMENTS: THE BACKGROUND IN PHILOSOPHY

Our science can be seen as a fusion of two lines of investigation: the philosophical investigation of the mind, and the physiological investigation of the body. It began as an application of physiological methods to psychological questions. And we can pick up both of these lines of thought in the early 1600s, with the work of a single remarkable man.

Descartes and the Primacy of Consciousness

This man was the Flemish philosopher René Descartes (1596–1650). Descartes ("deh-*cart*") was a philosopher, scientist, mathematician (he invented analytic geometry and the Cartesian coordinates that bear his name), and professional soldier, who fought as a mercenary in the wars of religion that were sweeping across Western Europe at the time. Between battles, he would find someplace warm and secluded, retire from the world for a while, and think. In what amounts to a series of psychological thought experiments, he asked the following question: What can we know for sure?

"Knowing" is a psychological phenomenon. But what knowledge can we trust? What, if anything, can we say that we really know without any doubt? In tackling the problem, Descartes' method was to force himself to doubt everything that he knew, and see if he could get to some item of knowledge that he could not doubt. Let us follow his thinking.

At present, your author believes that he is sitting in a chair in front of a computer keyboard, moving his fingers to type out words. Can he doubt that these things are true? Of course. Many times he has dreamed that he was someplace where in fact he was not, doing things that he was not doing. Perhaps he is dreaming, or in a delirium, at present. It is even possible for him to doubt that he has fingers, or any body at all, or that anything like computers really exist. He might be dreaming it all.

Not that Descartes believed any of this. He was not a madman. He was only pointing out that it is logically possible to doubt any or all of these things.

But now, asked Descartes, can I also doubt that I am doubting? No. That is logically impossible: if I doubt that I am doubting, then I am doubting! More generally, if I inspect my inner mental states, I can be absolutely certain that they are as they are. Even if I am wrong in thinking that I have fingers, still the fact is undeniable that I do think that I have them. If the computer I see is a hallucination, that just means that there's nothing "out there" to correspond to what I see. The fact that I see it, however, is beyond dispute. This means in turn that I can be absolutely certain of my existence as a thinking, seeing, doubting mind. All the outer world, including my own body, may be an illusion, but not my mind. Hence Descartes' famous summary: *Cogito ergo sum*. I think, therefore I am.

Even this much was enough to set in motion a line of thought that was enormously influential on subsequent philosophy and psychology. If you want knowledge, look within. Examine your own consciousness—or, as later writers put it: introspect. This was to be the starting point for experimental psychology itself.

Locke: The Mind as Blank Slate

For the next step, we turn to the English philosopher John Locke (1632–1704). Descartes had asked, What knowledge can we depend on? Locke asked a prior question: Where does knowledge come from in the first place? How do we know anything? He looked within himself, invited friends to do the same, and published his conclusion, which was as follows:

> Let us suppose the mind to be, as we say, white paper, devoid of all characters, without any ideas; How comes it to be furnished? Whence comes it by that vast store, which the busy and boundless fancy of man has painted on it with an almost endless variety? Whence has it all the materials of reason and knowledge? To this I answer, in one word, from *experience*. In that all our knowledge is founded, and from that it ultimately derives itself. (Locke, 1959/1690, p. 121)

All knowledge, in other words, comes into the mind through experience—that is to say, it comes in by way of the senses. Hence another of Locke's famous dicta: There is nothing in the mind that was not first in the senses.

In this, he took issue with Descartes. The latter, searching his mind, found ideas there that he did not believe he could have learned from experience. There were, in other words, innate ideas. These included, besides the idea of his self, the ideas of God, of the truth of mathematics, and of the truths of morality. But, Locke pointed out, different societies have very different conceptions of both God and morality (an early use of anthropological data in psychology). And if knowledge of mathematics is innate, why is this the very topic so many schoolchildren have most trouble with (an early use of developmental data in psychology)? No. There are no innate ideas; all of the "furniture" of the mind comes in by way of the experiences to which our sensory apparatus gives rise. This point of view—there are no innate ideas—is called *empiricism*. It is contrasted with *nativism*, which holds that some ideas are innate. Descartes was a nativist.

Now, it is true that we can see, or imagine, things that are wholly new. We can imagine, for example, a creature with the head and torso of a man, joined to a horse's body. True, but although we have never seen a centaur, we have seen all the parts. We are just making new combinations from those parts.

Then it follows that our experiences do break down into more elementary parts. This seems quite reasonable: if we look around the room, we can break down what we see into little patches of light, darkness, and various colors. I know that I am sitting at a desk in part because of the pressures I feel on various parts of my body— again, relatively simple sensations that, when joined together, form part of the total experience of sitting in a chair. But joined together how? How is our experience organized, so we don't perceive just the buzzing confusion of colors, touches, and so on? Locke's answer is that sensory elements are joined together to form complex ideas, and they are joined together by a process called *association*.

The various sensations that attend sitting at a desk become associated with each other—mental bonds are formed between them so that the sight of some of them calls to mind the others. In this way they become joined into a more complex idea that we call "sitting at a desk."

We get to what is going to be a very powerful idea: the mind is made up of elements that either are "in the senses" now (sensations) or were so in the past (memories), and these are joined together by learned associations. It has been called the Tinkertoy theory of mind: the mind is made up of many little elements (like the disks of a Tinkertoy), and they form structures that are held together by the bonds of association (like the little dowels that hold a Tinkertoy construction together).

Theories of this general type have been with us ever since and are with us still. So is the question, Is this enough? Can we explain the human mind with only elementary sensations as building blocks, and the dowels (or glue) of association to hold them together? Locke thought so, but not everyone agreed. We turn to the most influential of the dissenters, the German philosopher Immanuel Kant (1724–1804).

Kant and the Organization of Mind

Kant took issue with Locke's fundamental assumption: Nothing is in the mind that is not first in the senses. On the contrary, Kant said that there are many things in our minds that were never in our senses and never could have been.

Consider this example. A few moments ago, the author got up from his chair, left the room where the computer was resting, walked around for a bit, and came back. When he came back and saw the computer again, he did not say, "Hello! There's an object on my desk that looks just like the object that was there before." Instead, if he had spoken of the matter at all, he would have said, "Hello! There is that same computer, right where I left it."

Now what makes him so sure? How does he know that the computer did not wink out of existence when he left the room, and wink back into existence when he came back to it? How does he know that someone didn't substitute another computer while he was away? How does he know that the room itself kept existing, when no one was there to perceive it?

If these strike the reader as silly questions, Kant would have agreed. That is exactly his point. We somehow know that there are such things as objects. They have permanence; unless something very drastic happens, they stick around even when no one is there to have them "in his senses." But how do we know that there are such things? Indeed, how could the very idea that there *might* be such things ever once occur to us? Sensory information cannot tell us that there is any such thing as a permanent object. So where does the notion of a permanent object come from?

Well, if our senses did not give us that idea, then we must have supplied it ourselves. Our minds must go beyond the sensory input, to organize and categorize it.

There are many other examples. Suppose we watch a billiard ball roll across the table and strike another billiard ball, which then begins to move. In describing the sequence we do not say, "One billiard ball moved and came in contact with a second billiard ball, which then moved." Rather, we say, "The first billiard ball *caused* the second billiard ball to move." And yet causation is not anything that we have ever perceived as such. We see one event followed by another event, but the whole notion of a causal relation goes beyond that information. We have to supply it ourselves, for the sensory input does not provide it. There are other ideas, concepts, and categories that we apply to the sensory input, making it into the kind of experience (of substance, of causality, and of many other types) that it is.

Looking over these examples, we begin to understand Kant's method. We look at what we experience, and we ask how much of that experience can be provided by sensory input. If not all of it can, the difference must be supplied by the observer; we ourselves as perceiving, thinking beings must put that information there. Very similar logic was used by writers who came much later. For example, the Gestalt psychologists worked that way, as discussed later. Here, they said, is what our experience is like; here is what the sensory information provides us with; and any difference must be supplied by our own perceptual apparatus. Kant's views, like Locke's, are influential even among those who have never heard of either philosopher.

Let us now compare the three points of view we have considered: Descartes', Locke's, and Kant's. Locke thought of the mind as a blank sheet of paper at birth, on which sensory experience writes everything we know. Descartes also realized that we need sensory information, of course; much of what we know, we know through experience. He held, however, that there are certain ideas that we know, but not through experience: the fact of our own existence, the concepts of God and morality, and the truths of mathematics. For him, the mind was in part a blank sheet, but it was not wholly blank. There were things already written on it—innate ideas.

Kant's view was not like Descartes'. We use sensory information, yes, but in the process the mind does things to it, classifying and elaborating it. If we want to stay with the sheet-of-paper metaphor, we might think of the mind as a blank form, like an application form, in which sensory experience provides information that fits into certain places in the form. There will be a space for our name, a different space for our place at birth, and so on. And the mind is set up so that only certain kinds of information will fit in each blank. If what we perceive meets certain criteria (and only then), we classify it as an object, or as a causal sequence, and so list it in the corresponding place on the form. We do this, not arbitrarily or because we want to, but simply because our minds work that way. They have to. If they didn't, we could not even recognize our computer as being the same old computer as before.

So these are not innate ideas so much as innate operations the mind performs. (William James spoke of the Kantian mind as not a sheet of paper but a machine shop.) What our experience is like, therefore, is a result of the input as classified and identified by the active mind. What is "in" our consciousness is the result of these operations. Modern cognitive psychology presents a very similar picture.

THE BACKGROUND IN PHYSIOLOGY

However the mind works, it controls action, or at least some actions. Actions are movements of the body's parts. How does movement of the body take place? Once again, an important early insight came from the remarkable René Descartes.

The Reflex Concept

How do we move our bodies? In Descartes' time, even artificial objects could be made to move in humanlike ways. Dolls and mannequins were being made that were moved around—seeming to move themselves—by means of hydraulic systems in which fluid was forced through tubes. Something similar may happen, Descartes suggested, in living bodies: fluid may be forced through hollow tubes, which Descartes considered the nerves to be.

Suppose a child touches a hot stove. She will at once jerk her hand away. Perhaps, Descartes suggested, the touch of the hot surface exerts pressure on the skin, forcing fluid to move through the nerves into the central nervous system—the brain and spinal cord. The fluid pressure may then be reflected back into the muscles of the arm, causing them to swell and therefore shorten, moving the hand away. Hence the term *reflex*.

Thus Descartes introduced the concept of the reflex into physiology—and thence into psychology. Though the details needed correcting, it has remained there ever since, as a cornerstone of the body's adjustment to its circumstances. Such simple reflexes are the building blocks of such actions as standing, walking—and, yes, withdrawing from painful stimuli.

The Mind-Body Problem

Descartes suggested that perhaps all animal action was of this reflexive kind. But what about voluntary, willed action in humans? What about freedom of the will? How can we act freely if our actions are triggered by stimuli in such an automatic way?

To this question, Descartes' dualism offered an answer. Descartes, remember, held that mind is absolutely certain and is known directly; physical objects, like chairs and computers and even fingers, are not. It is an easy step from there to conclude that they are separate "kinds" of reality—made of different "stuff," as it were.

The universe therefore contains two kinds of "stuff": the physical and the mental. This contention is known as *mind-body dualism*.

And that idea in turn suggested a solution to the free-will problem. If one moves one's finger, that is a mechanical event—it is matter in motion. So it ought to be subject to the same laws of cause and effect as any other mechanical event. Yes, but mind is not matter. There is no reason to think that mental events are subject to the same laws of cause and effect as physical events are. The mind can escape such causal laws. Then if we make one further assumption—that the immaterial mind can somehow cause movement of the material body—we can see how free will is possible! Action can be freely chosen because it can be *willed* by the mind, rather than *caused* by the pokes and prods of physical inputs.

The details of this theory need not concern us, for unlike the reflex concept, it did not last long. The problem with it, and with any theory like it, is that it entails a physical impossibility. If it were true, then the total amount of mass-energy in the universe must increase any time anybody even wiggles a finger voluntarily. Moving the physical finger requires energy, and if there is no physical energy to produce it, then energy must be added to the universe on every such occasion. And the conservation-of-mass-energy principle, which is about as well established as any physical principle we have, tells us that this cannot happen.

As this became apparent, most physiologists—not all—turned away from Cartesian dualism in favor of a *materialistic* conception of the body and its workings. Matter and energy are the only "realities," says the materialist. What we call voluntary action is just action going on in the brain, where physical causes are difficult to pinpoint. But they must be there.

Helmholtz and the Nerve Impulse

The controversy between materialists and dualists provides the context for the enormous impact of the work of Hermann von Helmholtz (1821–94). This much was known: nerves provide communication between one point in the body and another. If you stimulate a nerve here, for example, a muscle over there will contract—provided that the nerve connecting the two is intact. Obviously, a "message" is transmitted from the point of stimulation to the muscle.

But causing a muscle to contract is also something that the mind does. If nerves are the "agents" of mental events, and if mental events are nonphysical, the nerves too should partake of the nonphysical. But Helmholtz showed that, in fact, nerve tissue is matter like any other. Its action generates heat, for example, and its action takes time. Prior to Helmholtz, some writers assumed that the nerve message moved instantaneously from its origin to its destination. But Helmholtz showed, in a classic experiment examined in detail later (chapter 3), that in fact the conduction of the message takes time, and a fairly long time at that. The "organ of mind" is a physical structure, and the nerve's "message" is a physical event.

Brain Physiology and Localization of Function

Throughout the nineteenth century, understanding of the nervous system was undergoing explosive development along other lines as well. Many investigators contributed to this enterprise, and the cast of characters could easily become unmanageably large. Here we will consider only a few of the most important ideas.

First, some reflexes do in fact seem like fixed, automatic, almost mechanical responses to stimulation. Correspondingly, some such reflexes do not require the brain at all. A frog whose head has been removed, for example, may still jerk its foot away in response to a pinprick on the foot. But whereas the brain is not required for this, the spinal cord is: damage the spinal cord and these reflexes disappear, even though there has been no damage to the skin or the muscles. The spinal cord seems to act as a kind of switchboard: excitation comes in from the skin and is "switched" in the spinal cord to the appropriate output, which activates the right muscles.

These experiments represent what we now called the method of *ablation*, or removal. To study how the nervous system works, remove part of it, and see what the system can still do without that part. Later, the method of ablation was applied to the brain, and a controversy sprang up: Does the brain have many independently acting parts, or only a few parts with more global actions? Certainly there is some separation, or localization, of function; ablating the entire brain abolishes voluntary movement, but as we have seen, it leaves some reflexes intact. Clinical studies of brain damage in human patients sometimes suggested an even more precise localization. An example is the work of Broca (chapter 4) in patients with aphasia, an inability to speak even though the muscles are not paralyzed and the mind seems to be otherwise intact. This seems to be caused by damage to just one localized area of the brain.

Complementary to the ablation method is the method of *stimulation*. Since the end of the eighteenth century, it had been known that nervous-system tissue will respond to electrical stimulation; Helmholtz took advantage of this property in his studies of nerve-impulse conduction (chapter 3). Later, it became possible to stimulate the surface of the brain itself. Such stimulation in certain parts of the brain can be shown to produce movement of the muscles, suggesting that the "commands" for movement may normally originate in those areas of the brain.

These are the kinds of findings that point to a rather strict division of labor within the central nervous system, with different parts doing different things. Other kinds of experiments, however, suggested that the brain, or at least large parts of it, may act as a single unit for some purposes. This conclusion was argued partly on philosophical grounds (we perceive our own mind as unitary; we speak of our mind, not of our minds), but also by some experimental investigators, in particular by the Gestalt psychologists (chapters 21 and 46) and by the physiological psychologist Karl Lashley (chapter 5). We will defer discussion of this issue until later.

THE FOUNDING OF EXPERIMENTAL PSYCHOLOGY

By the second half of the nineteenth century, it was clear that a new science was emerging—a science of mind to set alongside physiology, the science of body. Thus the two lines of investigation that Descartes had set asunder were ready to be put back together again. The major developments here are close enough—or closely enough related—to contemporary research that we will consider them in more detail in later chapters of this book. Here we will only list a few of them.

Ernst Weber (chapter 44) and Gustav Fechner (chapter 45) were investigating the properties of sensations and how to measure those sensations—how to measure the mind! Hermann von Helmholtz (chapter 3) was studying, among many other things, vision, hearing, and the speed of the nerve impulses—using the methods of physiology in frogs, and the methods of psychology in humans. And, as Helmholtz was showing that we could learn about the nervous system by measuring how long it took to react to certain stimuli, so F. C. Donders (chapter 36) was showing that we could learn about the operations of the mind by measuring how long they took under different conditions.

It only remained for someone to give the emerging science a name, a journal in which results could be published, a laboratory, and textbooks—many textbooks. The German physician-physiologist-philosopher-psychologist Wilhelm Wundt ("voont"), did all of these. His psychological laboratory at Leipzig was the first major psychological laboratory to be called that, and he gathered around him a whole generation of eager young investigators.

Wundt saw that an experiment involved a manipulation—one does something to a system, and observes how the system reacts (chapter 1). Well, the mind reacts to inputs. One can do things to the mind—present something to see, for example, or something to hear. The study of sensation fits in naturally here, and it did indeed occupy much of the attention of the Leipzig laboratory.

However, there was much more. A simple but instructive example of Wundt's work may give the flavor of what introspective methods can do. The reader should borrow a metronome, and try to replicate the following experiments.

Set the metronome going at a moderate rate—say, one per second. Listen to the clicks with closed eyes. You will hear them fall into a rhythmic pattern, probably an alternation: tick, tock, tick, tock. Now, the ticks and the tocks seem to have a difference in quality: they sound different, but the difference is in the mind, not in the clicks. One can show this by experiment. After the rhythm takes form, reverse it in your mind, so that the sounds that were ticks now are tocks and vice versa. You will have no trouble doing this. The tick-or-tock qualities are the mind's addition to the input.

Conclusion: the mind does not just register the incoming clicks. It adds something to them, organizing them into a pattern that simply is not there in the clicks themselves. The mind does not just receive inputs, but transforms and organizes them.

This may seem like a modest finding. It is. But it is an experimental finding, and, like many experimental findings, it invites us to explore further. For example: How many clicks can our mind organize into groups like that? What is the limit on what has been called our *span of apprehension*? Can one organize the clicks into groups of three: tick, tick, tock; tick, tick, tock? Most can. What is the limit to this grouping? For most of us, the limit is about six clicks, plus or minus two (compare chapter 39).

Does the limit depend on the number of items, or on how long it takes to present them? We can find out easily—by experiment! We just vary the rate of the clicks. If the limit is time-dependent, we should be able to lump more clicks into a group if the presentation rate is faster. Can we? Probably not, unless the rate is very slow (compare chapter 32). Questions are still being asked that began here.

There is yet more—all in this simple case of "doing something to the mind." As we form various rhythmic groups, we will surely find that some are more pleasant than others. Even pleasure and displeasure can be evoked experimentally—and simply. So can the feeling of excitement at fast rates, or calmness at slower ones. At slow rates, we can even observe in ourselves a kind of tension, a waiting anticipation, as the next click comes due. Here then are *feelings*, not just sensory events, that we can produce in the laboratory. We might want to describe these feelings more carefully, and see what other things they are related to—physiological reactions, for example. Perhaps we begin to see why the prospects Wundt raised were exciting to those who heard about them and came to learn more.

Thus Wundt and his students, like Descartes, began with the examination of consciousness—by introspection. But Wundt's method was not like Descartes'. It was not a matter of looking inside one's mind and making deductions from what one found there. Nor did it mean the kind of casual, perhaps rather gloomy self-examination that the term *introspection* suggests today. Rather, it was a matter of noting and describing exactly what is in one's mind and looking to see how this is affected in turn by precisely controlled changes in experimental conditions. By doing this, Wundt proposed, we pursue the fundamental task of psychology. We identify the elements of consciousness; determine what compounds they form; and then determine how they do it, what processes are involved. This was Wundt's research program for the newborn science.

Wundt's historical importance was enormous. His students spread his approach, and his goal of founding an actual science of the mind, to other laboratories in Europe and America. They met with opposition, too, and many researchers explicitly rebelled against Wundt's approach to psychology. But even the opposition can best be understood if we see what it was in opposition to. Let us look at some of the controversies to which Wundt's program gave rise.

DEVELOPMENT AND CONTROVERSY

First, introspective methods have a problem when introspectors disagree with each other. Boring describes a poignant case in point: "that famous session of the Society of Experimental Psychologists in which [Professor X], after a hot debate with [Professor Y], exclaimed: 'You can see that green is neither yellowish nor bluish!' And [Y] replied: 'On the contrary, it is obvious that green is that yellow-blue which is just exactly as blue as it is yellow' . . . When two distinguished experts could disagree [about] so basic a matter as the nature of [color], some other method of approach was needed" (1942, p. 176).

The problem is not that two scientists disagreed with each other; that happens all the time. The problem was that there was no way of resolving the dispute. There is no way an outside referee, or anyone else, can determine who is right and who is wrong. Since science depends on replication and cross-check by different experimenters, this was a highly disturbing situation.

There was another source of doubt about introspection as a method. In 1859, Charles Darwin published his catastrophic theory of evolution. It was a theory about why living animals had the characteristics they had—mental as well as physical. Much oversimplified, the idea came down to this: Animals have the characteristics they have because, over long ages, animals that had those characteristics (or approximations to them) left more descendants than those that did not. And the animals we see today, ourselves included, are those descendants.

Characteristics evolve, then, because they confer advantage in reproductive success—number of descendants. But this idea applies, as Darwin saw clearly, to behavior as well as to wings, claws, and teeth—and, therefore, it applied to the fine structure of the interconnections of the brain that controls behavior. Tigers have evolved teeth and claws for grasping and devouring prey. Chickens have evolved beaks with which to peck at grain. But these structures would be useless without the brain mechanisms that control them and direct their use toward appropriate objects—imagine a tiger trying to peck at grain and the point will be clear. But then, finally, if the mind is controlled by the brain, then the mind itself must have evolved.

Recognition of this had many ramifications, but only two will be mentioned here. First, it led to questions about animal behavior and the animal mind. Descartes had made a firm division—humans have minds, animals have instincts. The division could no longer be maintained. Perhaps animals have minds, too. But if they do, their minds cannot be studied by asking them to introspect! Their minds must be studied in other ways—in particular, by observing their behavior. Edward Thorndike's studies of problem-solving behavior in animals (chapter 19) pointed the way.

Second, an evolutionary perspective leads us to wonder just how important it is to know what is going on inside an animal's—or a human's—mind. After all, from an evolutionary point of view, it is what the human or animal does that matters, not what it thinks about before doing it.

In short, consciousness may simply be less important than we have supposed, at least some of the time. Some writers spoke of consciousness not as a step in the chain of events that leads to action, but as a kind of "readout" of what action has already been selected. It is the difference between a computer monitor and a computer program: consciousness may be the monitor, rather than part of the program.

As a specific example, take the theory of emotion developed independently by William James and Carl Lange at about the same time, and so known as the James-Lange theory of emotion. Our commonsense conception of emotion treats it is a link in a causal chain of events leading to action: we see a danger, we are afraid, and we run. But if we look at what actually happens, James argued, we see a different sequence. Our hearts beat faster, we begin to sweat, our digestive system shuts down, and perhaps we begin to run. Now, we feel all these changes in our bodies, and our perception of these changes is what we call the emotion of fear. To oversimplify: We do not run because we are afraid. We are afraid because we run.

The purpose of this example is not to argue for the James-Lange theory (but see chapter 16), but rather to point out where it leaves the experience of emotion. As James and Lange see it, emotion is not a link in the chain of events that leads to some action, such as running away. Rather, it is a kind of after-the-fact reflection of an adaptive reaction that has already occurred.

These considerations led many psychologists—not all—to shift from studying the mind itself to studying the behavior to which mental events give rise. This became a self-conscious school of thought with the writings of John B. Watson.

THE BEHAVIORIST REFORMATION

A number of lines of thought are converging. Consciousness is not observable, so disagreements about it may be difficult to resolve. It may not be the most important thing to study anyway: it may follow the relevant action rather than precede it, and from a Darwinian point of view, what matters is what the organism does, not what it thinks about before doing it. And we have learned a great deal by objective methods as opposed to introspection; objective methods allow us to study interesting things in cases where introspection is simply not possible—animal psychology, for instance.

It only remained for someone to put these ideas together and make them the cornerstone of a new approach to psychology. That someone was John B. Watson (1878–1958), who, in an address to the American Psychological Association in 1913, laid out the change of direction he proposed. We cannot observe what is in an animal's mind, or even another human's. But we can observe what animals and humans do. And their actions are taken in a particular situation—a particular set of stimuli in the environment—and they adjust their behavior to that environment. In short, behavior consists of stimulus-response relationships, and it should be the task of psychology to specify those relations. "In a system of psychology completely worked out, given the response the stimuli can be predicted; given the stimuli the response can be predicted" (Watson, 1913, p. 158).

Psychology, in other words, is not to be the study of mind of all. It is to be the study of how humans and animals behave in situations—the study of relations, in other words, between observable stimuli and observable responses.

On first encounter with behaviorism, many feel that it leaves much too much out of account. What about emotions, for instance? And what about thought? Surely these are too important to be left unstudied; yet doesn't Watson's program for psychology ignore them entirely?

Not really. What we must do, said Watson, is not ignore these processes but demystify them. Take emotion, for instance. We can tell when a child is angry even before he can tell us. His face reddens, the corners of his mouth turn down, his eyes squeeze shut, and he is likely to make a great deal of noise. Now, we cannot look inside his mind and tell what he is feeling. We never could! So when we say he is angry, we are really describing his behavior, and always have been. Similarly for other emotions: They are not mental states that cause behavior. They are behavior. What about thinking? Well, we often "think out loud," and sometimes we talk out loud to ourselves. Later we make less sound (most of the time), but the talking persists as internal speech. As Watson says, we don't think it's mysterious when we talk to another person. Why make a mystery of it when we talk to ourselves? In short, thoughts, like emotions, are not something that is added to behavior. They are behavior.

Even so, there was an omission in Watson's plan. It seemed restricted to cataloging reflexes and their eliciting stimuli. It did not provide for the modification of our responses, their adjustment to situations as the result of experience. Then the other shoe hit the floor: there became available in English translation the work of the great Russian physiologist Ivan Pavlov (1849–1936), who showed that we are not limited to the stimulus-response connections we are born with. We can form new ones.

Everyone surely has heard of how Pavlov, by presenting food along with (say) a bell, or the clicking of a metronome, could produce dogs that salivated at the sound in question. But note what this means. A new connection had formed in the dog's brain. We might call it an association—not between two ideas in the mind, but between a stimulus reaching the brain and a response triggered from there. Let us look at another example, to see both the generality of the idea and the adaptiveness of this capability the brain has.

Consider again a child who touches a hot stove and reflexively jerks her hand away, thus minimizing damage. But now take another step. Sensations arising from the sight of the stove, and the act of reaching and touching, become associated with a painful consequence—or perhaps with the act of withdrawal. Later, the child approaches the stove again. But now the same set of sensations is associated with the act of withdrawing the hand, or perhaps with the remembered pain that in turn causes withdrawal. The child then withdraws her hand before it touches the stove and so avoids the pain entirely. In other words, a learned, seemingly foresightful action can be understood much more simply: it is a conditioned reflex of withdrawal.

This is speculative, yes, but Watson himself, with his associate Rosalie Raynor, went on to show directly that conditioned responses of fear or avoidance can be formed in human beings. Thus the conclusion is a general one: The brain does not just react to what is present now. It modifies its reactions in light of what has happened before—that is, its history of conditioning. And this provides the link that Watson's developing theory had been missing: to our repertoire of innate or unconditioned reflexes: we can add learned or conditioned ones. The stimulus-response framework incorporates both.

With Pavlov, we again find ourselves talking about associations—not between one idea and another this time, but between a response (like salivation) and a stimulus (like the bell). And such associations could go well beyond this example. Much more significant responses, like fears, can be established by conditioning, and in human beings.

We begin to see wide vistas here. If conditioning can produce fears, could it also be used to eliminate troublesome fears? And if fears are products of conditioning, why not also skills, attitudes, perhaps even thoughts? If these really are the products of our conditioning histories, and if we knew enough, might it be possible to explain even such complex actions as career choices in terms of conditioning? No wonder early behaviorists were intrigued by Pavlov's work!

Looking over this sketch, we realize that we are on familiar ground. We can see in Watson's developing theory of behavior some striking parallels to the theory of mind that the philosopher John Locke had put forth over two centuries earlier. Let us review both of them by listing the similarities.

Locke: The mind is made up of elementary sensations.

Watson: Behavior is made up of elementary reflexes.

Locke: The sensations are elicited by stimuli.

Watson: The reflexes are elicited by stimuli.

Locke: New connections among sensations may be formed and strengthened by association.

Watson: New connections between stimuli and responses may be formed and strengthened by conditioning.

Locke: Therefore, if present stimuli do not account for what is in our minds, we can consider past stimuli—that is, our learning histories.

Watson: Therefore, if present stimuli do not account for what we do, we can consider past stimuli—that is, our conditioning histories.

Some ideas in psychology are remarkably persistent.

Was this enough? Watson thought so. Emotions were nothing but patterns of conditioned and unconditioned reflexes; thought was nothing but internal speech, which could (Watson believed) be seen as chains of conditioned reflexes. As for instinctive urges, drives, talents, and the like—these he dismissed as mythical beasts, just as Locke had dismissed innate ideas. There were no instincts—aggression, sex, mother-infant attachment, and the like were again nothing but conditioned responses. And, as it happened, this view drew support from outside psychology. At around this time, anthropologists such as Franz Boas and his student Margaret Mead were concluding from cross-cultural observations that the ways in which sexuality, aggression, and attachment were triggered and expressed were highly variable from one culture to another. It appeared that these reflected cultural "conditioning," rather than any fixed "human nature." This concept of cultural relativism again triggered controversy that is still with us today (Pinker, 2002), but, right or wrong, it fit wonderfully well with Watson's radical environmentalism: conditioning is all. Watson summed it up in his famous boast:

> Give me a dozen healthy infants, well-formed, and my own specified way to bring them up in and I'll guarantee to take any one at random and train him to become any type of specialist I might select—doctor, lawyer, artist, merchant-chief and yes, even beggar-man and thief, regardless of his talents, penchants, tendencies, abilities, vocations, and race of his ancestors. (Watson, 1924, p. 82)

(In fairness to Watson, here is his next remark, which is less often quoted: "I'm going beyond my facts and I admit it, but so have the advocates of the contrary and they have been doing it for thousands of years.")

In the years following, behaviorists modified and extended the original ideas in a number of ways. To the original program—knowing the response, identify the stimulus; or, knowing the stimulus, predict the response—behaviorist writers added Thorndike's law of effect, or the reinforcement principle, which Watson had rejected (chapter 19). The consequences that follow a response are important, not just the stimuli that precede it. Other investigators found that behavior was affected by internal drive states such as hunger, thirst, and specific nutritional needs, as well as by stimuli (chapter 10).

Behaviorist writers continued to insist, however, that all of these processes referred to events that were directly observable, or if they were not, at least they followed the same principles as processes that were. In a word, the behaviorists continued to insist on directly observable, objective data—data that anyone could see and confirm for him or herself. Later developments, however much they might diverge from behaviorist explanations, accept the necessity of this methodological principle.

Even so, not everyone thought that the Watson-Pavlov theory of behavior—the modern Tinkertoy theory—would work. The most forceful and influential dissent was that of Gestalt psychology, to which we now turn.

GESTALT PSYCHOLOGY

The German word *Gestalt* has no exact translation. (It is not a proper name; there was no Professor Gestalt.) It means something like "whole," as in "the whole thing." The Gestalt researchers insisted that mental and behavioral events are not made up of elementary parts. It is the other way around: the parts are embedded in wholes, which give the parts their properties.

If we take behaviorism to be the modern incarnation of John Locke's philosophy, Gestalt psychology could be treated as an incarnation of Kant's. Though there were many differences, the Gestalt psychologists argued forcefully for his fundamental principle: There is more in the mind than sensory elements—and there is more to behavior than responses to stimuli.

Their method, too, was recognizably Kantian: (1) Look at what experience (or behavior) is like, (2) see what it would be like if it consisted only of sensory elements (or reflex elements), and (3) the difference is the perceiver's (or behaver's) own contribution. This argument runs through Wertheimer's studies of apparent movement (chapter 46) and productive thinking to Köhler's experiments on problem solving in apes (chapter 21).

Wundt's experimental program took for granted that the mind consists of elements, so our task is to identify the elements and find out what combinations they form, and how. But what if we have chosen the wrong path at the outset? What if the mind—and the behavior it controls—does not consist of elements at all?

Gestalt psychology's research program began with the discovery of apparent movement by Max Wertheimer (chapter 46). He showed that if two lights flash in alternation, and if the spatial separation and time intervals between them are exactly right, what the observer will see is a single light jumping back and forth. Here is a case in which the experience simply does not match the stimulus: there are two lights, not one; movement is seen where there is none; and the "light" is seen as passing through the intervening space, which it does not do. Something is contributed by the observer. And the contribution is not just a matter of adding to the elementary experiences. Rather, the experience depends upon the whole sequence of events. It is this that makes the experience what it is.

Demonstrations of this sort of thing had preceded the emergence of Gestalt psychology with Wertheimer's research. Consider, for example, our perception of a melody. We may present the same melody in a different key, such that every single one of its elements is different from what it was before. But the whole thing is recognized as the same melody; indeed, the listener may even be unaware of the key change.

Further examples came in a flood. Look, for example, at figure 2.1. We see very clearly a cube that isn't there—the famous Necker cube. We have some options as to how we will perceive the figure. We can see it with the northwest corner toward us, or with the southeast corner toward us. What we cannot do, at least not without great effort, is to see it as a two-dimensional array of lines with nothing toward us—which is what it is. It snaps irresistibly into three dimensions in our mind's eye.

A more complex example is shown in figure 2.2 (from Boring, 1930). The figure can be seen as a young woman (the "wife"), or as an old woman (the "mother-in-law"). Most viewers see one or the other, and the figure is stable; we may even

Figure 2.1
A reversible figure: the Necker cube. The figure can be seen as a cube in either of two ways, but not as a two-dimensional array of lines, though that is what it is.

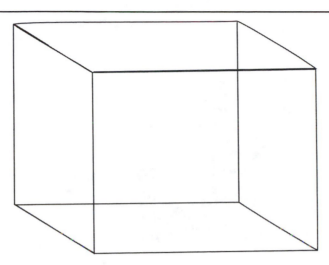

have difficulty seeing the alternative organization. However, once we do see it, we cannot "un-see" it. The figure becomes unstable, like the Necker cube; our perception flips back and forth between the two organizations. Even then, it remains one or the other; never both at once, and never a meaningless black-and-white array. Throughout all these vicissitudes, the stimulus—the pattern of black ink on white paper—never changes at all. (Hint if needed: the old woman's eye is the young woman's ear.)

In each of these cases, what we see is a very complex and busy set of stimuli perceived as a unit—as a whole thing. It forms a coherent, meaningful unit. Our perceptual apparatus, we might say, is "wired up" so as to make the complex look simple, and the arbitrary look meaningful.

To account for these and many other phenomenon, the Gestalt psychologists turned their backs on the whole project of analysis into elements. Instead, they took as their model what the physicists of the time were calling *fields*. A magnet produces a field in the space surrounding it, and that field is capable of doing work—affecting the movement and the final configuration of iron filings, for example. The iron filings do not produce the field; rather, they are affected by the field—the whole thing—in which they are embedded.

The Gestalt principles, and the related notion of fields, began as a revolt against the program of Wundt, but they did not end there. As behaviorism gained ground, the Gestalt psychologists turned their guns on that school of thought in turn, and for the same reason: they saw these writers too as trying to analyze into Tinkertoy elements something that simply could not be understood that way. The elements now were reflexes rather than sensations, but the mistake was the same. However, we are now moving into modern times, and elaboration of these controversies must be deferred to later chapters (e.g., chapter 21).

Figure 2.2
Another reversible figure: the "wife" and the "mother-in-law." This one can be seen as a young woman or as an old woman, but not both at once.

Source: From *American Journal of Psychology*. Copyright 1930 by the Board of Trustees of the University of Illinois. Used with permission of the University of Illinois Press.

Where does Gestalt psychology stand now? First, no one can doubt the force of Gestalt demonstrations like the ones above. These are reprinted in every introductory psychology textbook. And the vocabulary of Gestalt psychology—closure, contrast, perceptual barriers, pathways in mental space—appears in the writings of many research psychologists, and laypersons as well. Surely they refer to something important, though they are not linked specifically to Gestalt psychology anymore.

Finally, it is surely no accident that many of the founders of experimental social psychology—Solomon Asch (chapter 56), Muzafer Sherif (chapter 54), and Kurt Lewin (chapter 55)—were heavily influenced by Gestalt psychology. It does seem natural to consider a person in a social situation as embedded in a field, where he or she affects, and is affected by, everything that is going on—the whole thing—including the actions of others.

The Gestalt psychologists were less effective in specifying just how these perceptual phenomena work. What are the mechanisms underlying them? In recent years, we have made great advances on that problem, but that is for later chapters (chapters 48 and 52).

THE COGNITIVE COUNTERREFORMATION

In the years following Watson's manifesto, behaviorism broadened. His program was to establish relations between the response and the stimuli that triggered it, but it soon became clear that more had to be considered. Thorndike (chapter 19), and later Skinner (chapter 23), emphasized that one had to consider the consequences of a response—rewards and punishments—as well as the stimuli that preceded it. Internal states, such as hunger and thirst, also had to be taken into account.

All these, however, were still things that were external to the animal, or at least external to its brain, and could be specified objectively. So the task could still be seen as relating behavior to its external circumstances. The behaviorists could say what John Locke might have said: behavior (or the mind) is complicated, not because the way it works is complicated, but because the environment is.

Though there were dissenters (notably the Gestalt psychologists), this view became the dominant one within experimental psychology until about the 1950s. During the next two decades, however, this orthodoxy received a series of hammer blows that sent the research enterprise into new territory—or, better, led it to explore some old territory with new ideas. These blows took the form of a series of books, each of them challenging received views and offering new perspectives.

First came Nikolaas Tinbergen's *The Study of Instinct* (1951). Behaviorists writers had thrown the concept of instinct out the window. There are no instincts, they argued, only reflexes—responses to stimuli. However, while behaviorism became the dominant force in experimental psychology, investigators known as *ethologists* were studying behavior in its natural environment. Tinbergen's book presented a survey of this research and showed how it challenged the orthodox view in psychology. Animals showed complex patterns of behavior, not just isolated reflexes. And they showed these patterns in appropriate situations, when it could be shown by direct experiment that they could not have learned to do so. The complexity must come from within the animal—how it is "wired up" to respond to internal and external states.

In short, even animal behavior exhibited complexities that were not put there by the environment. An example from Tinbergen's own research is treated in more detail in chapter 14.

Then in 1957, a linguist, Noam Chomsky, published a book titled *Syntactic Structures* that said many of the same things about human language. Language has a structure, he argued, that neither present nor past stimuli can account for. So we ourselves must make up the difference—for Chomsky as for Tinbergen, and Kant.

For one thing, our fluency in language cannot be accounted for by our learning all the necessary responses. If we had to learn to speak only by imitation of what we hear, or by speaking sentences and being rewarded for doing so, simple arithmetic shows that there are not enough seconds in a century for us to hear, or speak, all the sentences that we might generate by the time we are six years old. What we must learn does not consist of specific responses or stimulus-response connections; rather, we must learn the underlying rules of language, so we can generate new sentences as well as repeating old ones. Once again, our use of these rules bespeaks a complexity that could not have been put there by the environment.

Yet another challenge came in 1960, with *Plans and the Structure of Behavior* by George A. Miller, Eugene Galanter, and Karl Pribram. During and following World War II, information-processing technology had made great strides, and psychology could learn much from these. Miller and his colleagues explored some possibilities.

Consider how chess is played. (This is not their example.) We look at the board, consider each reasonable move, what the reply might be, how we would respond to each reply in turn, and select the move that we think will be most to our advantage. We are planning—thinking ahead, constructing scenarios in our imagination, making decisions.

Now these processes—planning, thinking, imagining, deciding—were ones that behaviorists thought could not be studied scientifically. We cannot observe them. But after all, if we can understand them well enough to program a machine to do them, then they cannot be all that mysterious. And we can: chess-playing computers nowadays can give human world champions a run for their money! In short, processes once dismissed as mental could be performed by a very physical machine. Moreover, to understand how a machine does these things, it will not suffice to consider only what the inputs are or have been. Once again, we need to look inside at the organization of the computer's actions—its program.

The parallels between machine and human information processing gave psychologists a new way of talking and thinking about the things the mind does—storing information, retrieving it, foreseeing consequences and planning how to deal with them. It is true, as many behaviorists pointed out, that knowing how machines do these things does not tell us how living beings do them. No, but if nothing else, it may give us some ideas about how humans and other animals *might* perform these feats, ideas that we can then check by experiment. No one thinks that the mind is just like a computer. But many are working on the hypothesis that the mind is enough like a computer to give us useful hints. We use the computer, whose workings we understand so well that we can build our own, as a guide to thinking about the mind, whose workings we do not understand—yet.

Finally, at the end of the 1960s, came Ulrich Neisser's *Cognitive Psychology* (1967). This was a summary and synthesis of research on mental images, perceptual organization, memory encoding and retrieval, and thinking, and it was filled with experimental findings. It was not a polemic against the behaviorists, but it was a pretty compelling answer to them anyway: "We can't study the mind scientifically, you say? But we are doing so—and look at all we've discovered!" Holdouts remained in the behaviorist camp, notably the influential B. F. Skinner, but in the following years the focus of psychological research has shifted toward the cognitive. Cognitive concepts continue to influence social psychology, as they had done all along, and in clinical psychology, a kind of fusion took place to produce *cognitive-behavioral* methods of therapy (chapter 26). Clearly, if one had to choose a school of thought as dominant in contemporary psychology, a cognitive, information-processing approach would be the strongest candidate.

And yet the new cognitive psychologists also recognize that the behaviorists had a point. If experimental participants are asked to describe their experience, they may or may not be able to do it, and there is no way that another observer can check what they say. One needs objective data—data that are "out there" for anyone to see. And today, most experimenters seek ways to ask and answer their questions with objective data: How long does it take to solve this kind of problem? How many errors are made, and of what kinds? The objective answers to questions like these can lead to solid inferences about what kind of mental operations are being performed. We will see many examples in later chapters.

Today, the arguments about psychology's subject matter have pretty well died down. We seldom hear the objection, "You can't study that!" The reply, "We can't? Just watch us!" is too strong. As a result, psychological research on cognition, social processes, psychological problems and their treatment, and the way these processes are controlled by the brain are all proceeding explosively.

What ties these diverse areas together is a method—the scientific method, and in particular the powerful method of experiment. The remaining chapters will explore this idea.

BIBLIOGRAPHY

Boring, E. G. (1930). A new ambiguous figure. *American Journal of Psychology, 42*, 444–445.

Boring, E. G. (1942). *Sensation and perception in the history of experimental psychology*. New York: Appleton-Century-Crofts.

Boring, E. G. (1950). *A history of experimental psychology* (2nd ed.). New York: Appleton-Century-Crofts.

Chomsky, N. (1957). *Syntactic structures*. The Hague, The Netherlands: Mouton.

Heidbreder, E. (1933). *Seven psychologies*. New York: Century.

Leahy, T. H. (1987). *A history of psychology: Main currents in psychological thought* (2nd ed.). Englewood Cliffs, NJ: Prentice-Hall.

Locke, J. (1959). *An essay concerning human understanding, vol. 1*. New York: Dover (original publication 1690).

Miller, G. A., Galanter, E., & Pribram, K. H. (1960). *Plans and the structure of behavior*. New York: Holt, Rinehart & Winston.

Neisser, U. (1967). *Cognitive psychology*. New York: Appleton-Century-Crofts.

Pinker, S. (2002). *The blank slate*. New York: Penguin.

Tinbergen, N. (1951). *The study of instinct*. London: Oxford University Press.

Watson, J. (1924). *Behaviorism*. Chicago: University of Chicago Press.

Watson, J. B. (1913). Psychology as the behaviorist views it. *Psychological Review, 20*, 158–177.

2 | PSYCHOBIOLOGY

3 | HERMANN VON HELMHOLTZ AND THE NERVE IMPULSE

Often the most important experiments are elegantly simple. They may be technically difficult to perform; it may take special apparatus, and much skill and much labor, to manipulate some variable (the independent variable), and measure another (the dependent variable). But the question being asked is simply, How does the one affect the other? And if the *question* is well chosen, the simple answer may be a conclusion of fundamental importance. Surely there is no better example than Helmholtz's measurement of the speed of the nerve impulse in 1850.

Hermann Ludwig Ferdinand von Helmholtz (1821–94) was not a psychologist. Indeed, the term itself was not in use through most of his career. But if Helmholtz was not a psychologist, that was about the only thing he was not. He towered over the middle-to-late nineteenth century as a physicist, physician, optician, acoustician, mathematician, nerve physiologist, muscle physiologist, metabolic physiologist, philosopher, and lecturer on popular science. One wonders when he slept.

Helmholtz was born in Potsdam, near Berlin. He began his career as a surgeon in the Prussian army, but his primary interest was in research, and he formed close friendships among the academic physiologists at the University of Berlin. While still a surgeon, he began publishing scientific papers on the conservation of energy and on the nervous system; as one writer puts it, he was "still being the physicist within physiology" (Boring, 1950, p. 299), for he also showed that the conservation principle applied to living tissue.

In 1849, Helmholtz left the army to join the faculty as a physiologist at the University of Königsberg, though later he became a professor of physics at Berlin, thus realizing what his first desire had always been. It was at Königsberg that he performed the experiment discussed here—a classic experiment if there ever was one. It is one of the most famous experiments in the history of psychology and of physiology.

By the mid-1800s, it was recognized that the nervous system formed the organ of mind. Mental operations depend on the workings of the physical brain. On the other hand, many people then believed (as some still do today, though few scientists do) that mental events are nonphysical, taking place in a mental or spiritual world that is separate from the world of physical objects and events. If that is so, then the nervous system, the organ of mind, ought to have special properties that distinguish it from other physical systems.

Thus the sensation of (say) a touch on the foot depends on messages carried by nerve cells from the foot up into the spinal cord and then to the brain. If those nerve cells are severed, no touch is felt. Moving a limb (as when we flex an arm) likewise depends on neural messages, this time ones that are passed down from the brain into the spinal cord and relayed to the nerve cells that run to the muscles involved. If the nerves to a muscle are severed, the muscle is paralyzed. In short, registering a sensation (a mental event) and willing the movement of our bodies (another) both depend on messages carried by nerves.

But what are the properties of these nervous-system messages? For instance, do they take time? It does not seem so. When something touches one's foot, one seems to feel it instantly. When one wills a foot to move, it seems as if it moves instantly. Thus, before Helmholtz's experiment, many scientists believed that the messages within the nervous system traveled instantaneously, or perhaps at the speed of light.

However, what seems instantaneous is not. In 1850, Helmholtz showed that the conduction of nerve impulses from place to place does take time, and a fairly long time at that.

To show this, Helmholtz worked with an isolated nerve-muscle preparation from a frog—that is, a nerve with the muscle attached, dissected out from the rest of the frog, so that one sees the muscle itself and the long, threadlike nerve attached to it. With proper care, such an isolated part of the system will remain alive for some time. If one then stimulates the nerve with a brief pulse of electric current (the stimulus), the muscle will shorten, or contract, though it is some little distance away from the stimulus. Clearly, a "message" has passed from the point of stimulation to the muscle, causing it to contract.

Using such a procedure, Helmholtz applied a brief pulse of electric current to the nerve and arranged for that pulse to also start a timing device. When the nerve impulse reached the muscle, the muscle contracted, and its movement ended the timed interval. Thus Helmholtz could measure, quite precisely, how much time went by between the stimulation of the nerve and the resulting contraction of the muscle some little distance away.

Now, that time interval does not, by itself, give the speed of the nerve impulse per se. The total time between timer-on and timer-off included the time it took the message to reach the muscle, but it also included the mechanical events of the muscle contraction itself. How can one separate the two?

Helmholtz saw how it could be done. Just move the stimulator: if he now stimulated the nerve again, farther from the muscle, the events at the muscle itself take the same amount of time as before. But now the nerve impulse has farther to travel on its way to the muscle. So—if the message travels at a measurable speed—the total time between stimulus and muscle contraction should be longer, now that the distance traveled is greater.

It was. Helmholtz took many measurements, in many frogs, under both conditions: stimulation close to the muscle, and stimulation farther from it. And the total time for conduction-plus-contraction was reliably longer for the more distant stimulus. Then, knowing the distance between the two points of stimulation, and knowing the difference in response time, Helmholtz could simply divide distance by time to get speed, as in miles per hour (or in this case, meters per second). Helmholtz measured this speed at about 30 meters per second. This really is not very fast, as fast things go. Far from being instantaneous, the nerve message travels more slowly than sound.

But the important point is that the speed of the nerve impulse is measurable.

More modern methods have greatly enhanced our understanding of what is happening. The threadlike nerve is not a nerve cell, but a cable of even tinier cells—much finer threads—running along together. And the message, the nerve impulse, does run along each of these threads, not like electric current flowing through a wire, but like a spark running along a fuse (though the nerve cell, unlike the fuse, restores itself to its former state after conducting an impulse, ready to conduct another). The cell does not send an instantaneous message from here to there. On that fundamental matter, Helmholtz was quite correct.

Perhaps this idea is so familiar that it is difficult to get excited about it now. But it would be hard to exaggerate the impact of Helmholtz's findings when they were first announced. The nervous system is the "organ of mind," yes. But it is still a biological organ, and a physical one, subject to physical constraints. Its actions take time.

BIBLIOGRAPHY

Boring, E. G. (1950). *A history of experimental psychology* (2nd ed.). New York: Appleton-Century-Crofts.

Brazier, M. A. B. (1988). *A history of neurophysiology in the 19th century*. New York: Raven Press.

Koenigsberger, L. (1965). *Hermann von Helmholtz*. New York: Dover.

4 | PAUL BROCA AND THE SPEECH CENTER

Science, its methods and its discoveries, deals in small, researchable questions. As we get immersed in these, we should bear in mind that even small questions, and their small, restricted answers, may bear on questions that are very broad indeed.

Consider this question: What is the relation between the brain and the mind? Clearly there is one. We know that if the brain is damaged, the mind may not work properly; vision, or memory, or foresight, may suffer. Similarly, if the functioning of the brain is altered by drugs, the result may be mental alterations—in mood, for example. We often think of the brain as the "organ" of mind, the part of the body that does our perceiving, thinking, willing, and so on.

Further questions then arise. Does the brain have parts? Do different parts of the brain have different tasks to perform? If so, does the *mind* have parts? Is it all *one* mind, or is "the mind" just a name for an assembly of different operations, produced by different mechanisms within the brain?

Many students of brain function doubted this, and there were logical—and theological—reasons to doubt it. The brain is the organ of mind. Then, if a mind is single and indivisible—one speaks of one's mind, not of one's minds!—it would seem that the brain also must work as a unit. But the idea that the brain, and the mind, really do break down into parts gained support from some compelling lines of evidence. The discovery of the *speech area* of the brain, by Paul Broca, was early and prominent among these.

Paul Pierre Broca (1824–80) was born in Sainte-Foy-la-Grande. Precocious and brilliant, he entered medical school in Paris when he was 17 years old and graduated at 20, when most medical students were just beginning. He became a professor of surgical pathology at the University of Paris and, at 24 years of age, was already being showered with awards, medals, and important positions.

He was a prodigious worker, publishing both in neurology and in anthropology. It was he who identified the practice of trephining, a medical procedure dating back to the Stone Age in which an opening was made in a patient's skull, presumably to let evil spirits escape. His observations on fossilized skulls showed evidence of healing, indicating that patients could survive this procedure and live for some time after it.

In 1861, Broca was given charge of a patient called "Tan," who was given that name because that was the only word he could say. Except for that one word, the patient could not speak. He suffered from what is now called *expressive aphasia*—the inability to produce speech.

Tan died only six days after being placed in Broca's care. An autopsy showed that Tan had damage at a certain area (now called Broca's area) on the surface of the left frontal lobe of the brain (figure 4.1). In the little time he had, Broca studied Tan very intensively, trying to pinpoint just what his difficulty was. Broca knew that his patient had trouble *producing* speech, though he could *understand* speech perfectly well. Why should that be?

In seeking an answer to this question, Broca embarked on a series of neurological tests that we might call mini-experiments. In a sense, the damage itself could be considered an "experiment of nature," in that Tan could be compared with people whose brains had sustained no damage. That would be enough to show that something was wrong, but by itself it would not specify just what it was that Tan was unable to do. The answers would greatly affect the conclusions that could be drawn. If, for example, Tan's perceptual capabilities, control over his muscles, and general intelligence were all affected, there would be no reason to speak of a "center" *specifically* concerned with speech. Perhaps *all* aspects of mental functioning were being affected together, speech along with the rest.

So Broca would ask Tan various questions, different from one another (one independent variable), and he might vary the way in which Tan was asked to respond (another). Then he would note whether Tan could respond correctly (the dependent variable). Thus he was able to test, experimentally, various possible bases for Tan's speech disorder, and thus pinpoint the nature of that disorder.

Were the speech muscles paralyzed? No, for Tan could move his lips and tongue when asked to do so. There was some awkwardness in these movements, but Tan's voice quality was normal, and the sounds he made in pronouncing his name were perfectly clear. His hearing was apparently normal, for he could hear the ticking of a watch at about the normal distance, and, of course, his responding to questions showed that he could hear them. His vision was clear enough to allow him to tell time by looking at a watch. He understood what was said to him, but he could only communicate with gestures. He could tell Broca (correctly) how long he had been hospitalized by presenting the right number of fingers. When questions were repeated, and he realized he was being tested, he would become impatient, so he must have remembered the previous occasions and understood what was going on.

So Tan's general intelligence seemed unimpaired, and his speech apparatus was not paralyzed. Instead, Broca concluded, this patient suffered from a kind of memory failure. It was as if he could not *remember* how to use the speech apparatus to form the words he wanted to say.

Six months after the death of Tan, Broca had the opportunity to study another patient with expressive aphasia. This patient's symptoms were very similar to Tan's, and, it developed, so was the damage to the brain, though less extensive. Broca

Figure 4.1
Side view of the human brain, showing Broca's area

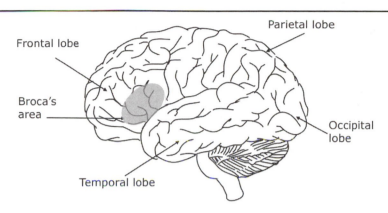

Source: From *Motivation: The Organization of Action* by Douglas G. Mook. Copyright 1987 by W. W. Norton & Company, Inc. Used by permission of W. W. Norton & Company, Inc.

concluded that he had located an area of the brain that was specialized for speech production—more specifically, the use of memory to select the words to express what the patient wants to say.

Since Broca's time, it has become clear that his patients' impairments were unusually severe. Patients with less severe aphasia may be able to speak and even to speak sentences, but their speech is slow and effortful. It often has a telegraphic quality, failing to include pronouns, conjunctions, helper verbs, and tense and number endings. It is tempting to relate these symptoms to Broca's idea of a specialized memory deficit. The patients seem to have trouble remembering how to put a complicated sentence together!

All told, it seems that a specific deficit in organizing and producing speech is associated with damage to Broca's area. Therefore, if we ask: Can one assign different functions to different areas of the brain? Broca's two cases and the many others that followed suggest very strongly that the answer is yes. Damage *just here* in the brain turned out to be associated with *just this* defect—difficulty in using the speech muscles for the specific purpose of producing speech.

Other scientists, in the decades following, sought—and found—other instances of such *localization of function* in the brain, and their search was much encouraged by Broca's convincing demonstrations. In our own time, the work on hemispheric specialization by scientists such as Roger Sperry and his collaborators (chapter 9) is but one of many examples of this research tradition.

Broca's observations, and the surrounding controversies, show how small findings can have implications for very large issues. They bear on questions such as the following: Does a person have one mind, or many? Does the mind have parts? If it does, does the *soul* have parts? (See Churchland, 1986, for discussion.) Questions about the very nature of humanity lie behind these limited, localized mini-experiments performed by a careful clinician.

BIBLIOGRAPHY

Boring, E. G. (1950). *A history of experimental psychology* (2nd ed.). New York: Appleton-Century-Crofts.

Brazier, M. A. B. (1988). *A history of neurophysiology in the 19th century*. New York: Raven Press.

Broca, P. (1960). Remarks on the faculty of articulate language, followed by an observation of aphemia. In G. von Bonin (Ed.), *Some papers on the cerebral cortex* (pp. 49–72). Springfield, IL: Charles C. Thomas (original work published 1861).

Churchland, P. S. (1986). *Neurophilosophy*. Cambridge, MA: MIT Press.

Kalat, J. W. (2001). *Biological psychology* (7th ed.). Belmont, CA: Wadsworth.

Sagan, C. (1974). *Broca's brain*. New York: Ballantine Books.

Schiller, F. (1979). *Paul Broca*. Berkeley, CA: University of California Press.

5 | KARL LASHLEY: BRAIN MECHANISMS AND LEARNING

Karl Lashley is sometimes classed with the behaviorists, sometimes with the Gestalt psychologists, but he cared little for affiliation with this or that school of psychology. He was a student of the central nervous system, and his work did much to show how one could study the functions of the brain by behavioral means.

Karl Spencer Lashley (1890–1958) studied with John Watson, the founder of behaviorism, while working on his Ph.D. (in genetics), which was awarded in 1915. His career following that took him to the University of Minnesota, the University of Chicago, and Harvard, where he remained until his death. During much of his time as a Harvard faculty member, he worked at the Yerkes Laboratory of Primate Biology in Florida.

Many of his experiments dealt with the role of the cerebral cortex—the outer covering of the cerebral hemispheres and the most complex part of the brain—in learning. In a series of classic experiments, he asked, what parts of the cortex are involved in learning by rats? Are there what he called *engrams*—specific places in the cortex where specific memories are stored (Lashley, 1950)? If so, then a specific memory or set of memories should be abolished by damage to a specific area.

These experiments all used the same underlying logic: train rats to perform some task, destroy or remove a part or parts of the cerebral cortex, and test the animal again to see what effects the cortical damage has on its performance. There were a number of variations on that theme, but they converge on this conclusion: The memory for a task does not reside in any single, fixed location in the brain.

In one series of experiments, three different mazes were used to test learning ability and memory (Lashley, 1929). Some rats were confronted with simple mazes, some with more complex ones. In each case, the rat's task was to learn how to get from the starting point to the goal box where food was located; Lashley could count how many trials it took before a rat could run the maze without entering any blind alleys. Before this training began, in different subgroups of rats, Lashley surgically removed varying parts of the cerebral cortex.

There were two independent variables, then, in this experiment. One was the ease or difficulty of the maze; the other was how much of the cortex was removed before learning began. It turned out that the results depended on both of these. If the task was simple, even a large amount of cortex removed—up to 50 percent!— had very little effect on maze performance. (As someone has said, it is remarkable how much brain a rat can get along without.) As the difficulty of the maze increased, the effect of cortical damage also increased (figure 5.1). The figure shows the average number of errors under each condition, so the higher the score, the worse the performance.

It is worth noting that the findings themselves include controls that allow us to rule out some possibilities. If rats with extensive loss of cortex had been unable to learn *any* maze, one would worry that the damage might have disrupted movement (the rats might have been too uncoordinated to run the maze) or motivation (they might have been no longer hungry). Neither of these was true. After even the most extensive removal, the rats could and did learn mazes—just not complicated ones.

What was perhaps most striking about these findings, however, was this: performance was affected by *how much* cortical damage there was, but not on *where* it was. A given amount of cortex removed from one location had about the same effect as a similar amount removed from a quite different location. This was what Lashley called *equipotentiality*: all parts of the cortex seem to be about "equally potent" in supporting the rats' ability to learn mazes. Still, it was also true that the *amount* of cortex removed mattered greatly; Lashley called this *mass action*. In short, what made the difference was the *amount* of cortical tissue that was removed (mass action), but not *where* it came from (equipotentiality).

All of these results were duplicated in another series of experiments, in which the brain damage was done prior to the original learning, rather than following it. The results were the same: deficits in learning, as in memory, depended on *how much* cortex was removed (mass action), but not *where* (equipotentiality).

Now, this is not at all the way matters should have been. Thorndike, Watson, and Pavlov all had conceived of learning as a matter of forming connections between situations and responses—or (for Pavlov) between sensory and motor systems in the brain. If that were so, there should be a specific pathway between just *here* and just *there* in the brain, and learning should be disrupted if just that pathway were interrupted—but only then. However, Lashley's equipotentiality finding is strong evidence that there is no *particular* pathway that has to be intact for maze learning to occur, or to be remembered after it occurs.

At first glance, then, these findings make trouble for any theory of learning that treats it as a matter of forming a specific Tinkertoy connection between *right here* and *right there* in the brain. Rather it seemed as if the cortex was operating as a whole—and this is why Lashley became interested in Gestalt psychology and is sometimes identified with it.

Yet there is another possible interpretation. Different parts of the maze look different, feel different, smell different, and perhaps even sound different if some parts of the maze are noisier than others. Maybe maze performance depends on associating *all* of the stimuli at each choice point with the correct response. And, if so, perhaps brain damage impairs performance because it removes some of these sensory cues. Then, the more cues are removed, the greater the effect should be

Figure 5.1
Results of Lashley's maze-learning experiment. Errors get more frequent (i.e., performance gets worse) as the difficulty of the maze increases (front to back) and as the amount of cortical damage increases (left to right).

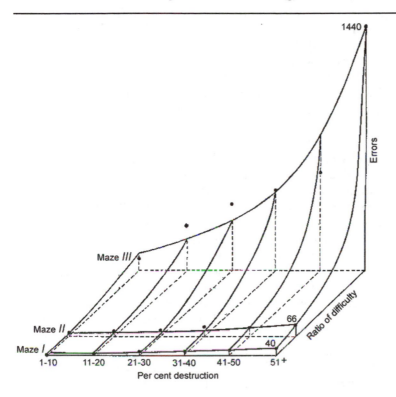

Source: From Lashley (1929, p. 74). Reprinted courtesy of Dover Press.

(mass action), and the equivalence of different locations (equipotentiality) might mean only that different sensory pathways are all about equally important.

However, another and quite different set of experiments shows the same things in a different way that avoids this problem. Rats might be trained, for example, to approach a white rather than a black card (or, of course, the reverse) in order to find food. If the rat can master this task—and it can—we know that it can discriminate differences in brightness; thus we zero in on *vision* specifically. And we know that the rat can remember, from one session to the next, which card to approach.

Now, what is the role of cortical tissue? In the brain, the receiving area for visual information is the visual cortex in the occipital lobe at the back of the cortex. Lashley showed that if it is removed, rats who had been previously trained in such a "brightness discrimination" task perform at chance level, as if they had forgotten the task. However, such rats can go on to learn the task again, and they learn it about as rapidly as they had the first time. This tells us, first, that the problem is probably not one of vision. The rats could see, or they could not have relearned the task. And delaying the retest did not improve relearning, so these results do not mean just that the brain was recovering after injury (another control!). Rather, it seems that the *memory for the task* is lost.

But it also tells us something more: the visual cortex is not fixed in its contribution to the memory for visual tasks. It does play a role, for if it is removed, the memory is lost. But whatever is lost is not connected to that bit of tissue in any fixed way. If that bit of tissue is missing, other parts of the brain take over the job, and the task can be relearned. In short, one part of the brain can substitute for another. In that sense, those two parts of the brain are "equi-potent."

What all this tells us is that we cannot think of the nervous system as a structure in which fixed pathways connect specific stimuli with specific responses, as Watson and Pavlov had supposed. So, like the Gestalt psychologists, Lashley was led to reject the whole notion of behavior as built up of small and stable building blocks of reflexes or conditioned reflexes. Again like the Gestalt psychologists, Lashley insisted that the brain is a structure in which the action of the *whole thing* is what matters, and not the actions of its parts taken in isolation.

All this does not mean that the brain is an undifferentiated mass, in which everything does everything. There is localization, as we know from Broca's experiments (chapter 4) and many others. Lashley suggested that different areas of the cortex may indeed have different functions in learning and memory, but that these functions may cut across particular tasks. In other words, the parts of the brain may do different *kinds* of things—generate words and sentences, for example, though there may be no single fixed location in which the ability to say "horseradish" is located.

Lashley was prescient in suggesting this, for much later research bears him out. As just one example, it has been found that there are certain areas of the brain that seem to be involved specifically in the recognition of faces—all faces, but just faces and nothing else (Farah, 1995). Damage to that area results in inability to recognize faces—all faces. This may be a rather specialized function for which a particular part of the brain is necessary. But that does not mean that the memory of a *particular* face is stored in any particular place in the brain. If it were, we might find cases in which a person was unable to recognize his grandmother's face, while recognizing other people's faces normally. As far as this writer knows, no such cases have been reported.

All told, there is no reason to think, and much reason to doubt, that specific memories—what *horseradish* means, or what Grandmother looks like—are located in just this or that area of the brain. These specific memories may instead reflect *patterns* of activation in networks of cells that may be widely distributed within the brain. In short, Lashley's critics were right—but so was Lashley.

Finally, we must note the careful way in which Lashley's manipulations of the brain were combined with techniques of behavioral observation. As one commentator says:

> The distinctive feature of the study is the experimental and quantitative determination of the animal's *behavior* throughout the investigation—a practice derived from psychology [as contrasted with physiology]. The point is an important one because in many of the older studies the investigators were content to rely on general observations for their accounts of behavior; to note, for example, that an animal seemed clumsy, or listless, or faltering. But in Lashley's studies, general observation was replaced by the experimental methods of animal psychology and by quantitative methods similar to those used in the objective measurement of intelligence . . . Through the definite mea-

surements of behavior throughout the research, it was possible to determine mathematically the relationships between loss or impairment of specified abilities and the location and extent of the correlated brain injuries. (Heidbreder, 1933, pp. 264–265)

So Lashley, often grouped with the Gestalt psychologists, was a behaviorist as well. The gap between these two schools seems great, but Lashley was great enough to bridge it.

BIBLIOGRAPHY

Farah, M. J. (1995). *Visual agnosia.* Cambridge, MA: MIT Press.

Heidbreder, E. (1933). *Seven psychologies.* New York: Century.

Lashley, K. S. (1929). *Brain mechanisms and intelligence.* Chicago: University of Chicago Press.

Lashley, K. S. (1935). Studies of cerebral function in learning: XII. Nervous structures concerned in the acquisition and retention of habits based on reactions to light. *Comparative Psychology Monographs, 11*(52), 43–79.

Lashley, K. S. (1950). In search of the engram. *Symposium of the Society for Experimental Biology, 4,* 454–482.

Lashley, K. S. (1960). *The neuropsychology of Lashley: Selected papers of K. S. Lashley* (F. A. Beach, D. O. Hebb, C. T. Morgan, and H. W. Nissen, Eds.). New York: McGraw-Hill.

6 JAMES OLDS: REWARD SYSTEMS IN THE BRAIN

One of the most exciting discoveries of modern psychobiology is that the direct activation of certain cell clusters in the brain can act as a positive reinforcer. In a free-operant situation, animals will work away steadily for no other reward than direct stimulation of those parts of the brain that form the "reward system." This was first reported by James Olds and his associate Peter Milner (1954).

James Olds (1922–76) was born in Chicago. He took his B.A. at Amherst College in 1947, and his Ph.D. in 1952 in psychology. He then took postdoctoral training at McGill University, where he and Milner discovered the rewarding effects of brain stimulation. He followed up that discovery as an associate research psychobiologist in the anatomy department of the University of California–Los Angeles. He later moved to the California Institute of Technology, where he remained until his untimely death in 1976.

What does a brain-reward experiment look like? First, the rat is "prepared" by having a thin metal wire, or electrode, placed in its brain while it is deeply anesthetized. The electrode is electrically insulated with lacquer except at the tip. It is placed so that its tip ends within the reward system, and its shaft is cemented to the skull where it emerges. It remains in place after the rat wakes up. Having it there is not painful, for there are no pain-producing cells within the brain. After the rat recovers from the surgery, experimentation can begin.

For this kind of experiment, the rat's implanted electrode is connected to an electrical stimulating device through light, flexible wiring that leaves the rat free to move about. Then, to stimulate the brain, a series of pulses of electric current is delivered through the wires and the electrode into the brain itself. The effect of this is to activate, artificially, the brain cells that surround the tip of the electrode.

Like so many intriguing phenomena, such as Pavlov's classical conditioning (chapter 20), brain-stimulation reward was discovered quite by accident. Electrical stimulation of the brain can evoke signs of interest, attention, and arousal, and Olds and his colleagues' initial question was whether the arousal, seemingly produced by brain stimulation, might facilitate maze learning. Rats were "run" in mazes, with pulses of electrical stimulation applied at choice points. If the resulting arousal facilitated learning, then the rats should learn the maze faster if this was done.

Instead, a curious thing happened. Rather than running the maze more efficiently, the rats tended to stop running through the maze at all. They would instead hang around the choice points at which the stimulation was applied, rather than going on from there to collect their food reward. It is as if they came to *prefer* the places at which the stimulation occurred.

Could the brain stimulation be acting as a reward in its own right, more powerful than the reward of food? To find out, Olds and Milner changed the experiment, adapting the techniques of operant conditioning developed by Skinner (chapter 23). Rather than applying the electrical stimulation themselves, they let the rat do it. A lever that the rat could press was mounted on the wall of a little box in which the rat was placed. Whenever the rat pressed the lever, a brief series of electrical pulses was presented to the brain as before—only this time, the occurrence of the brain stimulation was under the rat's control. The rat could make it happen by pressing the lever.

The effect was dramatic. If the electrode was within the reward system, and if the current applied was within the effective range, there was a powerful reinforcing effect of this brain stimulation. The rat (or, in other experiments, the cat or monkey) would press the lever over and over, to deliver these pulses of activation to its own brain again and again.

The effect can be very powerful. In one experiment, the rat worked away at the lever, at a steady rate, from noon on one day to 2 P.M. the next day—26 hours—pressing the lever more than *50,000 times* in that period (Olds, 1955). Then the rat rested or slept for four hours and, after that, went back to work at the same high rate as before. Such findings have been repeated (or, as we say, *replicated*) many, many times in laboratories all over the world.

Not every place in the brain gives this effect. Olds and his colleagues followed up the finding. They varied the exact placement of the electrode in different rats, and mapped out a reward system running deep within the brain. Placement anywhere within these parts of the brain would be rewarding. There were neutral sites as well, where it had no effect, and a "punishment" or aversion system, within which stimulation was actively avoided (Olds, 1956).

It is natural to ask whether such effects occur in humans. They do. Sometimes in human patients, surgery must be performed deep within the brain, and it can be done under local anesthesia so that the patient feels no pain when a small opening is made in the skull and an electrode is passed through the tissue of the brain to a place deep within it. This may be done to locate, or even to destroy, an area of the brain whose abnormal discharges are producing troubling symptoms. On occasion, a patient undergoing such surgery has been asked to participate in experiments while the surgery is in progress. If the patient consents, parts of the brain may be stimulated, and the patient can then tell the experimenter what he or she experiences. And if the electrode is in the reward system, the patient may report warm, relaxing, "good" feelings, or relief of negative states, when this is done (Hooper & Teresi, 1986). (Science-fiction writers to the contrary, however, no wallops of unendurably delicious ecstasy have been reported to date.)

Finally, how is the reward of brain stimulation related to natural rewards, such as food to a hungry animal (Olds, 1958)? We know that stimulus-bound feeding can be evoked by brain stimulation; a series of electrical pulses within the brain can cause an otherwise satiated rat to eat. And sure enough, the effective site of stimulation is within the reward system, and at certain brain sites, the reward value of stimulation increases if the animal is hungry. If the electrode is placed a little bit farther back in the brain, stimulus-bound mating can be obtained in male rats. And, also in male rats, castration (which removes the source of sex hormones) reduces readiness to mate, and it also reduces the rewarding effects of posterior-hypothalamic stimulation. Maybe the brain's reward system underlies the pleasures of eating, sex, and so on, for both humans and animals (Hoebel, 1988).

Brain-stimulation reward, and the reward system in the brain, have led to a variety of jumping-off points for further investigation. Researchers have asked, for instance, whether drugs that produce pleasure (like cocaine) involve the activation of this reward system in the brain. (They almost surely do; see Carlson, 1995.)

Work on the relation between motives, rewards, drives and the pleasures of their satisfaction, and the brain is an active research area today. Whole new chapters in psychobiology are being written, based on the discovery that direct activation of brain cells can be its own reward.

BIBLIOGRAPHY

Carlson, N. (1995). *Foundations of physiological psychology* (3rd ed.). Needham Heights, MA: Allyn & Bacon.

Hoebel, B. G. (1988). Neuroscience and motivation. In R. C. Atkinson, R. J. Herrnstein, G. Lindzey, & R. D. Luce (Eds.), *Stevens' handbook of experimental psychology* (Vol. 1, pp. 547–625). New York: John Wiley & Sons.

Hooper, J., & Teresi, D. (1986). *The three-pound universe.* New York: Macmillan.

Olds, J. (1955). "Reward" from brain stimulation in the rat. *Science, 122,* 878.

Olds, J. (1956). A preliminary mapping of electrical reinforcing effects in the rat brain. *Journal of Comparative and Physiological Psychology, 49,* 281–285.

Olds, J. (1958). Self-stimulation of the brain: Its use to study local effects of hunger, sex, and drugs. *Science, 127,* 315–324.

Olds, J., & Milner, P. (1954). Positive reinforcement produced by electrical stimulation of septal area and other regions of rat brain. *Journal of Comparative and Physiological Psychology, 47,* 419–427.

7   VINCENT DETHIER: FEEDING IN A FLY

The black blowfly, *Phormia regina*, is one of the animal species whose feeding behavior is most clearly understood. Much of our understanding comes from the experimental research of Vincent Dethier and his associates. His research tells us much not only about the fly but also about the concepts and methods of research in the physiology of behavior.

Vincent G. Dethier (1915–93) was born in Boston. He took his undergraduate and graduate degrees at Harvard, graduating with a Ph.D. in 1939. After a stint in the Army Air Corps in World War II (during which time he still carried on an active research program), he taught briefly at Ohio State University and then at Johns Hopkins, where he began his investigations of taste and smell in the black blowfly. He later held a joint professorship in zoology and psychology at the University of Pennsylvania, moving from there to Princeton and then to the University of Massachusetts (1975). In addition to his major contributions to insect physiology and behavior, he published popular books on science for both adult and juvenile readers, including his classic book *To Know a Fly* (1962). This little book would well repay a careful (and delighted) reading by anyone interested in the biology of behavior.

The next time the reader has a fly for a lunch companion, it will be rewarding to watch the fly carefully. The fly will walk around the lunch table until its feet come in contact with the drop of sugar water that the reader will have made available on the table. The fly will then stop walking and will appear to stick out its tongue.

It does not actually stick out its tongue, for the excellent reason that it does not have one. It has what is called a *proboscis*, which looks something like an elephant's trunk and has the fly's mouth at its end. It is normally carried tucked up under the head. But upon encountering the sugar water, the fly will extend its proboscis down, until it is immersed in the sweet fluid. Then, though this cannot be observed easily, the fly will suck up the sugar water like a miniature vacuum cleaner. That is how it feeds, for sugar water is fly food.

Proboscis extension is a reflex, as fixed and invariable as the knee-jerk reflex in humans. It is evoked by the taste of the sweet water. Unlike mammals, the fly literally tastes with its feet. There are sensitive cells, or *receptors*, embedded in the hairs of the feet, which when activated trigger a barrage of nerve impulses up into the fly's brain. These have the effect (through way stations that we will ignore) of triggering in turn the extension of the proboscis. Then, once the proboscis is extended into the sugar water, another set of taste receptors in the mouth is activated, and these trigger more reflexes that drive the fluid up into the digestive tract.

Here we see a principle of nervous-system functioning: *excitation*. The sugar water excites sensitive elements in the feet, producing nerve impulses in one set of nerve cells (or a single one, if the experiment is set up so as to demonstrate this). These in turn can *excite* the next set of nerve cells, causing them to be active in turn, and finally, nerve cells excite the muscles that extend the proboscis. This is what causes the hungry fly to feed.

Even without electronic devices, one can learn something about the characteristics of this system by doing experiments—that is, by manipulating conditions. We might ask, for example, just how sensitive the fly is to sugar in water. The following experiment is one that a reader can easily perform, following Dethier's instructions (1962).

First, the most difficult part of the experiment: catch the fly. Then one can anesthetize the fly, by putting it in the freezing compartment of a refrigerator for 5 or 10 minutes. Then attach the sleeping fly to a handle, which might consist of a cotton swab with the cotton removed, or even a pencil. The fly can be attached to its handle with a drop of hot wax or fast-hardening glue, or even with a bit of adhesive tape joining the wings to the handle.

The experimenter will have prepared a little beaker of water. Carefully lower the fly toward the surface of water until its feet just touch the surface. If the fly is thirsty, proboscis extension will be seen and the fly will drink. Wait until the proboscis is retracted again (the fly is no longer thirsty), and then shift the fly to a beaker of water in which a small amount of sugar has been dissolved. Out will come the proboscis again, and the fly will feed. To be certain, one can again touch the fly's feet to the plain water (this is now a *control* for the effects of mechanical stimulation of the feet by fluid), and show that proboscis extension does not occur. Return the fly to the sugar water, and once again extension will occur. This experiment is enough to demonstrate that the fly can taste with its feet.

One can elaborate this experiment to ask, How sensitive to sugar is the fly? We can prepare a series of beakers containing different concentrations of sugar. We can then see at what point the fly refuses to extend its proboscis, and then we know that that concentration of sugar in water is below the fly's *sensory threshold*. It is also humbling to compare the fly's sensitivity with our own, taking an equivalent series of solutions and determining which one we can just barely taste. We will find that a hungry fly is much more sensitive—about 10 million times more sensitive—then we are.

But now comes a complication. Let the fly drink the sugar water until it stops. After a few minutes, we test the fly again. Does it resume eating? It does not. The proboscis does not extend. The fly is no longer hungry, or, as we say, it is *satiated*.

But what does this mean? Clearly, something is now happening to prevent the sweet taste from triggering the proboscis-extension reflex as it did before. Something must be blocking, or *inhibiting*, that reflex. Here is another principle of nervous-system functioning: a nerve cell, or group of cells, can *inhibit*, or suppress, the

Figure 7.1
The system controlling feeding in the blowfly. Shown by the experiments of Dethier and his colleagues.

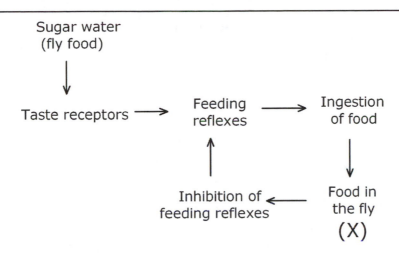

activity of other cells. Here, something is acting to inhibit the activity of the nerve cells that otherwise would cause proboscis extension.

This inhibitory mechanism must be triggered by something about the food that is now inside the fly's body. After all, the reflex was active before the fly had fed; but now that it has fed, the reflex cannot be evoked anymore. So the food it has ingested must be acting somewhere inside its body to cause the inhibition (figure 7.1). We do not yet know where, so we mark the unknown internal signal with an X, for "unknown," in the figure.

Where, and what, is this X? Dethier and his colleagues pinpointed it in a series of elegant experiments involving stomach loading, intravenous injections, the interruption of nerve pathways, and more—all this in the fly (Dethier, 1969).

When food is ingested by the fly, it goes first to a little storage sac known as the *crop*, somewhat analogous to the stomach in humans. Is that where the inhibitory signal arises? If it is, then surgically removing the crop in a recently fed fly should make the fly hungry again. But it does not. So the X is not in the crop.

Well, the ingested food passes from the crop into the gut—similar to the intestine in humans. Does food in the gut inhibit feeding? If it does, then placing food in the gut of a hungry fly should inhibit its feeding and make it hungry no longer. This must be done by the equivalent of rectal feeding in the fly, but it can be done. Does it inhibit feeding? It does not. A hungry fly, with sugar water placed in the gut, is hungry still.

So the inhibitory X is not in the crop and not in the gut. Is it in the bloodstream? Intravenous feeding in the fly can be done (very carefully), but even that fails to satiate a hungry fly. X is not in the blood.

As Dethier says, "There is not much fly left" (1962, p. 52). There are some other possibilities, but they too were ruled out, until the researchers were left with the one part of the digestive system remaining: a little place at the exit to the crop, where food passes on its way from the crop to the gut.

It proved impossible even for these experimenters either to remove that part of the digestive system or to load it with food. But there is another way of investigating the role that a structure plays, and that is to interrupt its nervous connection with the rest of the system. From this part of the digestive tract, a bundle of nerve cells—the *recurrent nerve*—runs up into the brain. Dethier and his colleagues made a very small incision in the neck of the fly, located the nerve, and severed it. As Dethier describes it:

> The results of this operation on a hungry fly were spectacular . . . it ate and ate and ate. It grew larger and larger . . . It became so big and round and transparent that it could almost be used as a miniature hand lens . . . We had pinpointed the mechanism controlling hunger in the fly. As long as there was some food in the region of the neck, the nervous system sent messages to the brain stopping further eating . . . By interrupting the pathway to the brain, we had made the fly chronically hungry. (1962, pp. 54–55)

The point of this experimental journey is not to teach the reader how feeding is controlled in the fly (though this can have some aesthetic value, as pointed out later). The point is twofold.

First, it illustrates especially clearly the use of the experimental method in psychobiological research. Each of these experiments asks a question about the role of some part of the complex system, varied all by itself. Does fullness of the gut inhibit feeding? The researchers filled it artificially, and showed that it does not. Does cutting the recurrent nerve take away the inhibition so that feeding resumes? It does. Dethier and his colleagues pinpointed the inhibitory control by testing the possibilities one at a time.

Along with the methods, this case study shows us some principles of nervous-system functioning. There is *excitation*, and there is *inhibition*. These give us the arithmetic of the nervous system: excitation is addition and inhibition is subtraction. And these are the only messages a nerve cell can send to other parts of the system: "be more active" (excitation) or "be less active" (inhibition). Think of a computer, which can write out payroll checks or guide a spaceship to the moon. Yet its working parts are tiny elements, each of which is "on" or "off." The complexity can come about because there are so many of them, and yet all that complexity breaks down into simple steps. So it is with the nervous system. The difference is that we built the computer and know how it works! The study of the nervous system is a study in reverse engineering. Here is what the system does. How does it do it?

Finally, the author's hope is that the reader has caught some of the sheer aesthetic pleasure of investigating and discovering. Again, there are two sources of this pleasure. First, a scientist who speaks of a "beautiful experiment" means it literally. This applies even to the simple ones readers can conduct for themselves. Dip a nonthirsty fly's feet in plain water, and nothing happens; dip them in sugar water, and feeding happens. Who can doubt (*a*) that the fly can taste with its feet, and (*b*) that the experiment *shows* that this is so? And then it stops and stays stopped, but if we make a tiny incision in the neck of the fly, locate the recurrent nerve, and sever it, it doesn't stop anymore. We have pinpointed the inhibitory control that keeps feeding in check.

And, secondly, there is the elegant simplicity of the feeding system itself, shown in figure 7.1. Taste receptors trigger mouth-parts extension, which brings the mouth into contact with the sugar solution. This activates feeding, and food moves into the fly. Once inside in sufficient quantity, the food activates the inhibitory control, which discourages further feeding. With just that much, we can understand how the fly identifies food, how it eats it, and how it keeps from eating too much. Dethier should have the last word here: "At this point one cannot help but wonder with awe and humility at the order, beauty, and complexity of the universe" (1962, p. 35).

BIBLIOGRAPHY

Dethier, V. G. (1962). *To know a fly*. San Francisco: Holden-Day.

Dethier, V. G. (1969). Feeding behavior in the blowfly. In D. S. Lehrman, R. A. Hinde, & E. Shaw (Eds.), *Advances in the study of behavior*. New York: Academic Press.

Dethier, V. G. (1976). *The hungry fly: A physiological study of the behavior associated with feeding*. Cambridge, MA: Harvard University Press.

Dethier, V. G., & Brodenstein, D. (1958). Hunger in the blowfly. *Zeitschrift für Tierpsychologie, 15*, 129–140.

8 S. P. GROSSMAN: CHEMICAL CODING IN THE BRAIN

The 1950s and 1960s were exciting times for students of the biology of behavior. A number of technical advances were converging to permit new insights as to how whole organized sequences of behavior were called into play by the brain. A number of these developments had to do with new methods of manipulating structures deep within the brain.

First, scientists had learned how to place thin wires, or electrodes, into structures deep inside the brain (chapter 6). By passing current through such an electrode, one could damage a small area within the brain and see what the effects of this were on behavior. For example, there was great interest in the *hypothalamus*, a collection of cell clusters near the base of the brain that is intimately involved in biologically important behaviors such as feeding, drinking, and sex. Damage to a certain sub-area within the hypothalamus in a laboratory rat or cat would produce an animal that failed to eat or to seek food (chapter 15).

Conversely, one could apply electrical stimulation through such an electrode. The procedure here is to place the electrode at the desired location and cement it to the skull—all this while the rat is deeply anesthetized (chapter 6). Once recovered from the anesthesia, the rat walks around with the electrode in place with no apparent discomfort. Then, for a stimulation experiment, the electrode is attached to flexible wires that allow the animal freedom of movement, and pulses of electric current can be applied through the electrode in the brain. No pain is produced by this; there are no pain receptors inside the brain.

Nerve cells are sensitive to electrical stimulation, so the effect of this is to activate the cells around the electrode tip artificially. Such artificial stimulation of the lateral hypothalamus could produce *stimulus-bound feeding:* if a series of pulses of current is applied through the electrode, the rat will stop whatever it was doing, go over to where the food is, and begin to eat. Current off, the rat will stop eating. Current on, it will resume (Coons, Levak, & Miller, 1965).

Putting these findings together—damaging that collection of cells in the brain abolishes eating, whereas stimulating those cells triggers it—we seem to get a coherent picture. That area of the brain, it seemed, must call up, organize, and direct feeding behavior. For a while, scientists called that area of the brain a *feeding center*, though no one does so today.

For it just was not that simple. In the first place, damage that abolished feeding also abolished drinking (chapter 15). Perhaps manipulations of this area were actually affecting two systems, not one. If so, perhaps there is a way of separating them so that they can be studied one at a time.

To see one way in which this can be done, we need to bring to bear yet another line of research. At about the same time, it was becoming increasingly clear that nerve cells communicate with each other by way of chemical messengers, or *neurotransmitters*. One nerve cell affects the next one by releasing a tiny amount of a chemical, the neurotransmitter, into the tiny gap between the two cells. This little packet of chemical then diffuses from the first cell over to the second, and causes that cell to become either more active (*excitation*) or less active (*inhibition*; compare chapter 7).

Now, even if different motivational systems are closely intertwined with each other in the brain, they might depend on different chemical messengers. If they do, it ought to be possible to stimulate them *selectively*. Suppose one were to stimulate the brain not with electric current that affects all the nerve cells indiscriminately, but with the chemical neurotransmitters themselves. If a certain chemical can affect one system without the other, one will have separated the two. But how can we stimulate structures deep in the brain with chemicals? S. P. Grossman saw a way to do it!

Sebastian Peter Grossman (1934–2003) was born in Coburg, Germany, and came to the United States in 1954. He took his B.A. at the University of Maryland in 1958 and his Ph.D. at Yale in 1961. He taught at the University of Iowa, then moved in 1968 to the University of Chicago, where he stayed until his retirement to Hawaii—turning, he says, to racing an outrigger canoe and other things for which he had never had time, until his untimely death in 2003.

Grossman began his research career with an interest in mental disorders and the possibility of chemical treatment of these. For this was yet another research area that was exploding at about the same time: the treatment of mental illness with drugs. After working at the new laboratory of psychopharmacology (the behavioral effects of drugs) at the University of Maryland, Grossman went to Yale to study with Neal Miller (chapters 10 and 11).

Because mental illnesses are themselves so complicated, Grossman decided to begin with the "simpler" problem of hunger and thirst. Another of Miller's students, E. E. Coons, was investigating stimulus-bound feeding and drinking in rats in response to electrical stimulation of the hypothalamus. If these were affected together by electrical stimulation, might they be affected separately by chemical stimulation?

At the time, only two neurotransmitters had been even tentatively identified (out of the hundreds that have been identified since). One was as acetylcholine (a-settle-*ko*-leen), mercifully abbreviated ACh, and the other was norepinephrine (*nor*-epi-*nef*-rin), abbreviated NE. So Grossman began with these. The procedure was to implant into the brain, in the lateral hypothalamus, not a thin wire this time but a very thin tube known as a *cannula*. Through this, it was possible to inject tiny amounts of a chemical neurotransmitter—NE or ACh—directly into the brain. There, the chemical so injected would affect any cells near the cannula tip that were sensitive to it as a messenger—and only those cells.

The effects of this in Grossman's experiment were quite dramatic. If NE were injected into the brain in minute quantities, the rat would eat but not drink. If tiny quantities of ACh were injected through the *same* cannula, the animal would drink, but not eat. So the pathways in the brain that control eating and drinking overlap anatomically in the brain, but can be separated by selective chemical stimulation.

These findings can be cross-checked in another way, too. There are drugs that block the effects of ACh elsewhere in the body, and sure enough, they blocked the effects on drinking of ACh in the brain. Other drugs have similar antagonistic effects on NE elsewhere in the body, and these drugs block the effects of NE on feeding (Grossman, 1960, 1962).

It is important to understand that even though the same cannula could be used to induce both feeding and drinking, this does not mean that the same cells are involved in the two cases. For injection of chemicals into the rat brain, a microliter of fluid is a typical quantity. Now, a microliter is a millionth of a liter, which sounds very small, but it is also a cubic millimeter, which sounds very large if we consider just how small nerve cells are, and how tiny are the gaps between them (the *synaptic clefts*). These gaps are only about 20 *billionths* of a meter wide.

Grossman's injections into the brain, in other words, were still affecting whole populations of cells, and different populations of cells may well have been involved in the feeding response on one hand, and the drinking response on the other. Even so, Grossman has shown how the two populations can be separated experimentally and so studied separately.

Since Grossman's pioneering studies, studies of neurotransmitters and their behavioral effects have given rise to the enormous research literatures, to which Grossman and many others contributed. As just one example, a male rat's interest in sexual behavior may be reduced or abolished by castration, which removes the body's source of the hormone testosterone. Interest can be restored, however, if testosterone is placed in minute quantities directly into the hypothalamus. Therefore, there must be cells in the hypothalamus that are sensitive to this chemical and respond with sexual interest to its presence in the brain.

Then too, there is yet another line of research that articulates with this one. A few years before this time, the rewarding effects of brain stimulation had been discovered (chapter 6). Reward systems in the brain ran through the hypothalamus and related structures. Are the pleasures of feeding perhaps related to the systems that control feeding behavior itself? Quite possibly. Bartley Hoebel and Philip Teitelbaum (1962) showed that one could obtain stimulus-bound feeding and rewarding self-stimulation of the brain with the same electrode in the same rat under different experimental conditions. Moreover, the rewarding effects of lateral-hypothalamic stimulation were affected by some of the same variables that affect food intake itself. In a recently fed rat, for example, the tendency to feed was reduced, and the rewarding value of lateral-hypothalamic stimulation also was reduced. If the rat were made hungry, both were enhanced. In a different part of the reward system, parallel effects with sexual motivation were observed; as it was made to rise or fall, the reward value of electrical stimulation in that part of the brain also rose and fell.

In more recent times, an important neurotransmitter in the reward system has been identified as *dopamine*, a member of the same chemical family as NE. Some data suggest that release of dopamine as a transmitter in rewarding circuits of the brain may produce the rewarding effect. This may occur not only with biological rewards but also with mood-altering drugs, and even such "rewards" as the excitement of gambling or videogames (see Kalat, 2001, for discussion).

Studies of "chemical coding," and the role of neurotransmitters in evoking and organizing motivated behavior, are writing whole new chapters in our understanding of the control of behavior by the brain.

BIBLIOGRAPHY

Coons, E. E., Levak, M., & Miller, N. E. (1965). Lateral hypothalamus: Learning of food-seeking response motivated by electrical stimulation. *Science, 150,* 1320–1321.

Grossman, S. P. (1960). Eating or drinking elicited by direct adrenergic or cholinergic stimulation of hypothalamus. *Science, 132,* 301–302.

Grossman, S. P. (1962). Direct adrenergic and cholinergic stimulation of hypothalamic mechanism. *American Journal of Physiology, 202,* 872–882.

Hoebel, B. G., & Teitelbaum, P. (1962). Hypothalamic control of feeding and self-stimulation. *Science, 135,* 376–377.

Kalat, J. W. (2001). *Biological psychology* (7th ed.). Belmont, CA: Wadsworth.

Miller, N. E. (1958). Central stimulation and other new approaches to motivation and reward. *American Psychologist, 13,* 100–108.

9 ROGER SPERRY AND THE BISECTED BRAIN

Does the brain have parts, or does it function as a whole? And if the former, what does this imply for our conception of mind? If the brain has parts, does the mind have parts too? This sounds very strange, if we think about it. We are accustomed to thinking of our minds as unitary entities; after all, we speak of our *mind*, not of our *minds*. Are we mistaken?

Broca's work on the speech center (chapter 4) strongly suggested a "parts" approach to the workings of the brain: speech was disrupted by damage just *here* in the brain, while other kinds of mental functioning apparently remained intact. More recently, even more dramatic evidence for a "division of labor" within the brain has come from the experiments of Roger Sperry and his associates on the capabilities of "split-brain" patients.

Roger Wolcott Sperry (1913–94) was born in Hartford, Connecticut. He received an A.B. in English at Oberlin College, having distinguished himself as an athlete as well as a scholar. After receiving his Ph.D. at Chicago in 1941, he worked at Harvard University with Karl Lashley (chapter 5). In 1954 he moved to the California Institute of Technology, where he remained until his death.

To understand the split-brain experiments, it will be necessary to digress briefly for an overview of our visual pathways.

Figure 9.1 shows part of the layout (much oversimplified) of the human visual system. The part of the external world that is seen (called the *visual field*) is projected onto the receptive surface, the *retina*, of each eye—though the image on the retina is backwards and upside down, because the light rays must pass through the tiny pupil of the eye on their way to the retina. Those light-sensitive cells communicate through a series of stages (not shown; see chapters 48 and 52) with cells whose axons are gathered together to form the *optic nerve*, which sends information up into the brain. Curiously enough, however, some of those cells, but not all, cross over from one side to the other on their way to the brain. The system is organized such that information from the left half of each retina is sent to the left hemisphere

Figure 9.1
Overview of the human visual system. The corpus callosum is severed in split-brain patients, thus preventing the two cerebral hemispheres from communicating with each other.

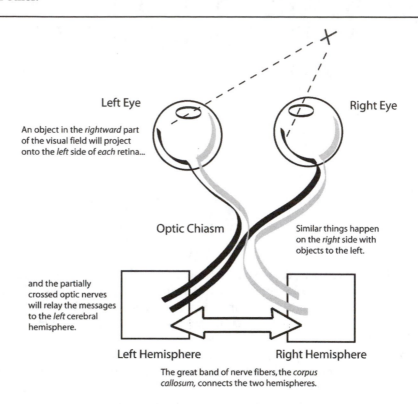

Left Eye

Right Eye

An object in the *rightward* part of the visual field will project onto the *left* side of *each* retina...

Optic Chiasm

Similar things happen on the *right* side with objects to the left.

and the partially crossed optic nerves will relay the messages to the *left* cerebral hemisphere.

Left Hemisphere

Right Hemisphere

The great band of nerve fibers, the *corpus callosum,* connects the two hemispheres.

Source: Drawing by Marcie Ewasko. Copyright © 2004 by Marcie Ewasko. All rights reserved. Used by permission.

of the brain. Information from the right half of each retina is sent to the right hemisphere of the brain. The result of all this is that each hemisphere sees just half of the visual field. The left hemisphere sees information coming from the left side of the retina—which is looking at the right side of the visual field—and conversely for the right hemisphere.

If we ask, then, how visual input guides action, we find that there is yet another reversal. The *left* hemisphere controls movements on the *right* side of the body, and conversely. Thus, if there is an object in the right half of the visual field, to which we must point with our right hand, here is what happens: visual information from that object crosses over to be delivered to the left cerebral hemisphere, and the output that moves the hand starts in the left hemisphere, but then crosses over to control the right hand. It might help visualize this if we consider that the object is to our right; the layout is reversed so that the left side of the brain sees it; but then the motor output reverses the layout again, so that everything is put back on the side where it all began. We point with the hand that is nearest the object we see.

In the cat, the layout is a bit different. The cat has a completely crossed visual system, rather than a partially crossed one as humans do. The left hemisphere sees everything that the right eye sees; the right hemisphere sees everything that the left eye sees. Thus each hemisphere sees the entire visual field. Yet they remain separate hemispheres, and that makes a difference, as we will see.

Now comes a vitally important point. In both humans and cats, the two cerebral hemispheres are connected by a very large band of nerve fibers, some running in one direction and some in the other—the *corpus callosum*. This is what permits the brain to transmit information from one hemisphere to the other. Thus the brain, with its two hemispheres, can act as a single coordinated whole—provided, that is, that the corpus callosum is intact and functioning. If it is not, then it can be as if we had two brains rather than one.

Using cats as subjects, Sperry and his colleagues showed that under experimental conditions, the two hemispheres could function independently to a surprising degree. For example, cats can be trained to discriminate between two patterns, using the techniques pioneered by Karl Lashley (chapter 5). A square and a circle might be presented to the animal, and the rule might be that if it approached the square, it would be rewarded with food. Using a hood that covers one eye and leaves the other one exposed, one can restrict the visual input to one or the other hemisphere.

And if one does that, and also severs the corpus callosum, one finds that there is no transfer of learning from the trained to the untrained half of the brain. It is even possible to train one half of the brain to approach one of the stimuli (say the square), and the other half to approach the other (the circle). A cat with an intact brain would find that situation hopelessly confusing, but the split-brain cat would make the one approach or the other with no hesitation, depending on which eye, and therefore which hemisphere, was now seeing the pair of patterns.

Now, cutting the corpus callosum was also being done in humans, as a desperate, last-ditch attempt to control intractable epileptic seizures. Seizure activity typically begins in one half of the brain and spreads to the other. Severing the corpus callosum restricts the abnormal brain activity to the one side of the brain where it originated. This procedure—which, of course, is tried only after everything else has failed—permits many patients to live normal lives, whereas they had been incapacitated by repeated seizures before.

Many such patients offered themselves for experimental study, and in any case their ability to get around in the world was of course monitored. What was the effect of such radical surgery on the patients' sensory, motor, and cognitive functioning? At first, the amazing answer was, none. The behavior of the patients was indistinguishable from that of unoperated people; they could see normally, move normally, think normally. Yet a very large pathway within their brains had been severed. If doing this had no effect, what was that very large pathway *for*? To keep the brain from sagging, as Lashley suggested tongue-in-cheek? Surely not.

A group of physicians who had been doing split-brain surgery and studying its effects on patients invited Sperry and his associates to join the team and devise behavioral measures that might pick up more subtle effects of the damage to the brain. This they did. They realized, first of all, that the patients were able to move their eyes. This meant that visual input from any source could be directed anywhere within the visual system as the patient moved his eyes around. To prevent this, stimuli were presented *very briefly* at various places within the subject's visible world. That way, the input could be restricted to specific parts of the patient's brain—*experimental control!* In particular, they could be restricted to the left or the right hemisphere.

More specifically, such an experiment might look like this: Patients are instructed to fix their eyes on a point in front of them. Some visible stimulus will be presented to the left, or to the right, of that fixation point. It will be presented very briefly—less than 200 milliseconds, which is how long it takes the eye to begin to move in response to such stimulation—and than the patients will be asked what, if anything, they had seen.

Under these conditions, the results are quite dramatic. In split-brain patients, visual information that is presented to one half of the brain simply is not available to the other half. If the image of an object is presented in the left half of the visual field (remember, the visual field is that part of the world that the subject can see), the visual information is sent to the right hemisphere. And when this is done, the patient cannot identify or describe what is shown. If asked, "What did you see?" the patient says a revealing thing: not "I saw something, but I can't tell you what it was," but "I didn't see anything."

In contrast, if the information is sent to the *left* hemisphere, the patients can name and describe it without difficulty. As a matter of fact, this is also true of touch: patients could name and describe objects that were placed in their right hands (which send their information to the left half of the brain), but could not name or describe objects placed in their left hands (which send information to the right half of the brain).

Does this mean the patients cannot see or feel with their right hemispheres? No. They can indeed see things that are presented there (even if they say they cannot), for they can, for example, identify these by picking them out from among others, by touch, using their left hands. They can see them. They just cannot tell us anything about them, not even that they *have* seen them.

These curious findings actually make eminent sense, for Broca's work (chapter 4) showed that the apparatus for generating speech is located in the left hemisphere for most people. If the information is restricted to the right hemisphere, *and* if the lines of communication between hemispheres is disrupted, then the information does not get to that speech generator. The patient cannot, by speaking, tell us anything about it.

This remains so even after an object has been identified. If a picture of a spoon was shown to the right hemisphere, patients were able to pick out a spoon, by touch, from among other objects using the left hand (controlled by the right hemisphere). But when told that they were correct, they might say something like, "What? I was right? How can I pick up the right object when I don't know what I saw?" The left, speaking hemisphere knew nothing about what the right hemisphere had seen.

In short, it seems that visual or tactile input to the right hemisphere is not relayed to the left hemisphere in split-brain patients, because the channel has been severed by which such information normally would be conveyed. The speech apparatus cannot generate a name for what the right hemisphere sees, because it is not told about it. The left hemisphere no longer knows what the right hemisphere is doing—or seeing or feeling.

The separation of the two halves of the brain can be dramatic in its effects. A split-brain patient can easily rearrange blocks to match a drawing with the left hand (directed by the right hemisphere). Using the right hand (directed by the left hemisphere), they do not do nearly so well (it's the right hemisphere that does better at spatial tasks of this kind). The right hemisphere, watching this bumbling performance, will sometimes direct the left hand to reach over and interrupt the inept right hand when it is about to make a mistake! It knows what is going on even though it cannot talk about it. Even outside the laboratory, a few such patients report that while their left hand was unbuttoning their shirt, the right hand would follow along behind and button it again. It is as if the two hands were controlled by two different purposes, each controlled in turn by the two different halves of the brain.

Since the original observations, much further work has been done, as investigators have asked what specific structures transmit information from one hemisphere to another, and precisely what it is that is transmitted (for discussion, see Gazzaniga, Ivry, & Mangun, 1998). In addition, the findings are an invitation to philosophical exploration. Looking over these patients' symptoms, we feel an "inescapable inclination to infer that they have two of something where the rest of us have only one. But two of *what*? Two minds perhaps, or two souls, or two selves, or two persons, two centers of consciousness, two centers of cognition, two centers of control, two wills, or what?" (Churchland, 1986, p. 321) However we describe the symptoms, the separation into parts, where we would have expected unity of a whole, is undeniable.

In 1981, Roger Sperry shared the Nobel Prize in physiology and medicine with two other students of brain function, David Hubel and Torsten Wiesel.

BIBLIOGRAPHY

Churchland, P. S. (1986). *Neurophilosophy*. Cambridge, MA: MIT Press.

Gazzaniga, M. S. (1970). *The bisected brain*. New York: Appleton-Century-Crofts.

Gazzaniga, M. S., Ivry, R. B., & Mangun, G. R. (1998). *Cognitive neuroscience: The biology of the mind*. New York: Norton.

Sperry, R. W. (1964). The great cerebral commissures. *Scientific American, 219*, 42–52.

Sperry, R. W. (1969). A modified concept of consciousness. *Psychological Review, 76*, 532–536.

Sperry, R. W. (1981). Some effects of disconnecting the cerebral hemispheres [Nobel lecture, December 8, 1981]. Retrieved October 17, 2004, from http://nobelprize.org/medicine/laureates/1981/sperry-lecture.html

Sperry, R. W. (1982). Some effects of disconnecting the cerebral hemispheres. *Science, 217*, 1223–1226.

3 MOTIVATION AND EMOTION

10   NEAL MILLER: FEAR AS A LEARNABLE DRIVE

In the years following Watson's founding of behaviorism, the movement grew and broadened. A new generation of experimenters and theorists arrived on the scene who, while remaining behaviorists—psychology was to be the objective study of behavior—placed that study in a broader context, recognizing that there were more influences upon behavior than Watson had supposed. Prominent among these "neobehaviorists" was the extraordinarily energetic Neal E. Miller—the only person who appears in two chapters of this work.

Neal Edgar Miller (1909–2002) was born in Milwaukee, Wisconsin. He earned his undergraduate degree at the University of Washington and his Ph.D. at Yale, where he later became a researcher in the university's Institute of Human Relations. He was appointed professor at Yale in 1950 and taught there until 1966, when he became a professor at Rockefeller University. During the early 1970s, he taught at Cornell University Medical College. He returned to Yale in 1985 as a research affiliate.

Miller's contributions to psychology began with his research on fear as a learned drive and its role in conflict, the two lines of research considered here. Later, however, his active mind turned to the study of brain mechanisms in motivation (Miller, 1958). For example, that feeding could be elicited by electrical stimulation of the brain in rats was discovered by E. E. Coons in Miller's laboratory. Later, Miller focused on behavioral medicine, in particular the technique known as biofeedback, now used widely in a variety of medical conditions including high blood pressure, epilepsy, and migraine. The Academy of Behavioral Medicine Research established the Neal E. Miller New Investigator Award in his honor, and the American Psychological Association established a distinguished lectureship in his name.

The original program of behaviorism, as laid down by Watson, was very simple. It was to determine the relations between stimuli coming in from the environment and the responses they evoke—so that, knowing the stimulus, we would know what response to expect, or, knowing the response, we would be able to say what stimulus gave rise to it.

It soon became apparent that that program would not work, on two counts. First, the behavior of even relatively simple animals was affected by influences from within as well as from the environment. The experiments of Curt Richter (1922) showed this especially clearly. For example, rats increased their spontaneous running activity dramatically if they were deprived of food. Since the external situation had not changed, the rats must have been responding to some *internal* influence. Moreover, the effect of food deprivation was not to enhance food-getting behavior only; it enhanced a behavior (running) that was not related to food in any obvious way. It did not, in other words, call forth any particular response. Rather, it seemed to exert a general, nonspecific activating or arousing influence on behavior.

Second, it became clear that the effects of *reinforcement*—events that follow an action—were important, as well as events that precede it. If hungry rats ran the correct route in a maze and were rewarded with food for doing so, then they would learn the maze.

These considerations led researchers to begin talking about *drives* as factors motivating behavior. Hunger was a drive, thirst was a drive, sexual deprivation produced a drive, and shock or other painful stimuli also produced drives: these aroused the animal, just as hunger or thirst would. They also provided the conditions for reinforcement. Turning a painful shock off, like giving food to a hungry animal, made the preceding response more likely to occur in the future.

But then yet another problem emerges. People often do things when no biological drives motivate them. A writer may work at writing a book, or a reader at studying from one, when neither is hungry or thirsty or in pain. Other, more complex motives are at work. As Miller puts it:

> People are not born with a tendency to strive for money, for the discovery of scientific truths, or for symbols of social status and security. Such motives are learned . . . A learnable drive or reward is one that can be acquired by a previously ineffective cue as a result of learning. Thus, if a child that has not previously feared dogs learns to fear them after having been bitten, it shows that fear is learnable. (1951, p. 436)

"Fear," in this case, sounds very much like a *conditioned response* in Pavlov's sense: the stimulus (the dog) comes to elicit a response (fear) that it did not elicit before. Indeed, Miller sees it that way: fear *is* a conditioned response, which becomes attached to the stimulus situation in which painful events have taken place. Then, having become conditioned in that way, fear may have the properties of a drive: "Fear is called *learnable* because it can be learned as a response to previously neutral cues; it is called a *drive* because it can motivate the learning and performance of new responses in the same way as hunger, thirst, or other drives" (Miller, 1951, p. 436). In the research discussed here, Miller set out to demonstrate experimentally that fear does in fact have these properties (Miller, 1948).

The procedure was as follows. Rats were tested in a box that was divided into two compartments, one with walls painted black, the other with walls painted white. The two compartments were separated by a door through which the rat could run. The floor of the box on one side consisted of metal rods through which electric current could be passed to deliver a mild electric shock to the rat's feet.

When the rats were permitted to explore the apparatus, they showed no particular preference for either of the two compartments into which the box was divided. Then, however, they were taught to be afraid of the white compartment. Each rat was placed in that compartment, the shock was turned on, and the rat was allowed to escape the shock by running through the door into the other, safe compartment. Each rat received 10 such conditioning trials. This was the first phase of the experiment.

Following this, the shock apparatus was turned off—permanently. *The rats were never shocked again.* Each rat was then placed in the formerly dangerous compartment. Each time it was placed there, the rat would run promptly through the door and into the other compartment. Since there was no longer any shock, it seems that the rat was motivated by nothing but the *fear* of that place, produced by having been shocked there before.

There is, however, another possibility. Perhaps the rats had simply formed the habit of running from one compartment into the other. The real question was whether this acquired drive of fear would motivate the learning of *new* responses, ones that the rat had not made before. So, in the next phase of this experiment, the door between compartments was locked. The rat could unlock it by turning a little wheel that was mounted on one wall of the compartment in which the rat was placed; the door would then open and the rat could escape to the "safe" compartment. When this was first done, the rats showed behavioral symptoms of fear such as tensing, crouching, and apparently random movements. The acquired drive of fear had an arousing, energizing function, just as hunger does. Eventually, the rat would turn the wheel by accident, whereupon the door fell open and the rat could escape into the safe compartment. On successive trials, the rats would go to the wheel and turn it more and more promptly. Then, as a final check, the wheel was made inoperative, but the door could be unlocked if the rat pressed a little lever. When that change was made, wheel turning dropped away, to be replaced by lever pressing. Escape from a threatening place, therefore, would motivate the learning of new responses—again, just as hunger or thirst would do.

In short, fear has both the defining properties of a drive state. It energizes behavior, and it can motivate new learning.

Now we are accustomed to thinking of fear as an internal, unobservable, mental state. In speaking of fear, was Miller backing off from the behaviorists' emphasis on observable stimuli and responses? Not really. The reactions to shock or other painful stimuli are just that—reactions. These may include freezing, tensing, an increase in heart rate, an increase in breathing rate, and so on. All of these are *responses* that can either be observed directly, or measured by appropriate apparatus. Thus we can show that they occur without making inferences about what, if anything, the animal's mental state is.

Moreover, we recall that when the trained animal was placed in the dangerous box, it would do many of the same things. It would freeze or tense up, and later experiments showed that in fact its heart rate and breathing rate would increase. Now, all these changes in what the body was doing would produce stimuli—internal stimuli, but stimuli nonetheless. Miller suggested that what we experience as fear is actually our experience of these conditioned responses—or, more precisely, experience of the stimuli to which they give rise. In short: We can think of fear as simply the *conditioned form of the pain reaction* and the stimuli produced by this. It is these self-produced stimuli, Miller suggested, that are the real drive: Their presence energizes behavior, and their removal (when the animal reaches safety and is no longer afraid) reinforces a new response such as wheel turning or lever pressing.

Now, this is a simple demonstration experiment, but the underlying idea might have ramifications that go well beyond it. Let us return to the examples we began with: someone studying for an exam, or writing a book. We have agreed that this very hard work may occur in the total absence of hunger, thirst, or pain. But what might be present, and very important, is the state of fear or anxiety that would be evoked if these behaviors did not occur.

The author who stops working may become anxious about impending deadlines. The student who stops studying may become anxious about the prospect of poor exam performance. In both cases, resumption of the activity would be accompanied by reduction in anxiety or fear, and therefore reinforced.

Or consider the person who, having been bitten by a dog, is afraid of dogs. The sight of the dog now triggers the conditioned reaction that in turn provides the internal stimuli that we call *fear*. The person's fear of dogs, by this theory, is a conditioned response.

We are led to wonder whether a similar history of conditioning might underlie the fear of vastly different stimulus situations in different individuals. It might help explain some troublesome human problems as well. A little fear or anxiety might be a good thing if it keeps us writing, studying, and being careful in traffic. But clearly it is not always such a good thing.

Some people become so anxious during examinations that they cannot do themselves justice, even if they are thoroughly familiar with the material they are being examined on. Some people are so afraid of rejection that they tense up in social situations, so they are unable to function smoothly, and thus invite rejection. In each case, we could think of the anxiety as a conditioned response, which the person makes habitually under certain stimulus conditions. In fact, Miller later wrote a book in collaboration with a colleague, John Dollard, titled *Personality and Psychotherapy* (1950), based on the application of conditioning principles to complex human behavior—ineffective or self-defeating behavior in particular.

We cannot pursue these ideas here. However, another chapter looks at another line of research that Miller pursued: the closely related topic of *conflict* (chapter 11). And the concept of fear as a learned motivational state has been an extraordinarily fruitful one, one that is touched upon in other chapters in the present book (e.g., chapters 11 and 26).

BIBLIOGRAPHY

Bower, G. H., & Hilgard, E. R. (1981). *Theories of learning* (5th ed.). Englewood Cliffs, NJ: Prentice-Hall.

Dollard, J., & Miller, N. E. (1950). *Personality and psychotherapy: An analysis in terms of learning, thinking, and culture*. New York: McGraw-Hill.

Miller, N. E. (1948). Studies of fear as an acquirable drive: I. Fear as motivation and fear-reduction as reinforcement in the learning of new responses. *Journal of Experimental Psychology, 38*, 89–101.

Miller, N. E. (1951). Learnable drives and rewards. In S. S. Stevens (Ed.), *Handbook of experimental psychology* (pp. 435–472). New York: John Wiley & Sons.

Miller, N. E. (1958). Central stimulation and other new approaches to motivation and reward. *American Psychologist, 13*, 100–108.

Miller, N. E. (1978). Biofeedback and visceral learning. *Annual Review of Psychology, 29*, 373–404.

Miller, N. E. (1983). Behavioral medicine: Symbiosis between laboratory and clinic. *Annual Review of Psychology, 34*, 1–31.

Richter, C. P. (1922). A behavioristic study of the activity of the rat. *Comparative Psychology Monographs, 1*(2), 1–55.

11 | NEAL MILLER: CONFLICT

A *conflict* is a situation in which a human or animal is motivated to perform two or more actions at the same time where the actions are incompatible. One might want to do well on tomorrow's examination, and therefore be motivated to study this evening, but one might also want to spend the evening with friends. Assuming one must do one or the other, that is a conflict situation. Or one might want to start a conversation with some stranger to whom one is attracted, but also want *not* to do so for fear of rejection. That too is a conflict.

Obviously, both these cases consider conflict between two rather complex motives. The processes might be made easier to study by simplifying both the organism and the situation, thus making a model of the conflict in which fewer variables act to complicate matters. This is what Neal E. Miller set out to do (1944). Miller's biography is presented in chapter 10.

Miller's experiments placed laboratory rats in conflict situations. The experimental situation consists simply of a narrow alley on which a rat is placed. The alley is raised high off the floor, to prevent the rat from escaping. Now one may set up conflict in a variety of ways.

APPROACH-APPROACH CONFLICT

First is the case where the rat must choose between two incompatible actions or goals, both *positive*. A human example of this kind of conflict might be selecting a dinner from a menu. Shall one have the steak or the lobster? Each is attractive, and neither, we assume, is dangerous.

We can model such a conflict in the rat. Suppose that the rat is hungry and is placed in the middle of the alley, and that there is food available at each end of the alley (figure 11.1). The rat is attracted to the food at the left end of the alley (from our perspective), but also is attracted to the food at the right end. This is the case

Figure 11.1
Approach-approach conflict. A positive stimulus (food) is at each end of the alley.

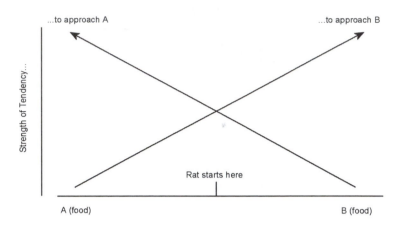

of *approach-approach* conflict. There will be a tendency to approach the one bit of food, but also to approach the other, and the rat cannot do both.

The figure also shows two sloping arrows, representing the tendency to approach the left-hand goal (the arrow sloping up toward the left) and to approach the right-hand goal (the arrow sloping up toward the right). The slopes of the lines represent the idea that as the rat moves closer to a food source, the tendency to approach it further become stronger. In other words, the closer the rat is to the food, the stronger is the tendency to move closer still. The arrows are called the *gradients* of these two behavioral tendencies. These gradients, by the way, are not hypothetical. Actual measurements of running speed show that a rat runs faster the closer it is to a positive goal. Or one can equip the rats with little harnesses and measure how hard they pull against a weight as they run; in this way, too, the gradients can be measured. The results are the same.

The conflict, then, is between two tendencies to approach an attractive goal. Conflicts like this are normally easily resolved. If the rat is placed squarely at the center of the alley where the two gradients intersect, the animal may hesitate for a brief period, but random movements of its head or body will soon move it at least slightly toward one goal or the other. And once that happens, then the tendency to make a further approach toward that goal will become stronger; that will bring the rat even closer to that goal, so the tendency to approach it yet further will become stronger still—and before long the rat will be happily scampering the rest of the way to the food that it first began to approach. The conflict will have been resolved.

Parallel cases in human behavior are easy to identify. Steak or lobster? This highly rated movie, or that one? Such a conflict usually does not detain us for long.

AVOIDANCE-AVOIDANCE CONFLICT

Other kinds of conflict, however, are not so easily resolved. Suppose again that the rat is placed in the center of an alley, but this time, each end of the alley pro-

Figure 11.2
Avoidance-avoidance conflict. A negative stimulus (shock) is at each end of the alley.

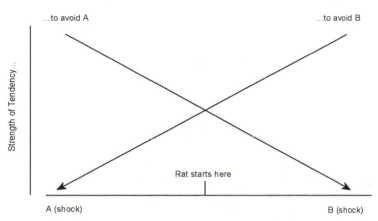

duces electric shock if the rat goes there. This is an *avoidance-avoidance* conflict—the rat will try to get farther from each shock place, but moving away from one only moves the rat closer to the other.

Again we have two intersecting gradients, but this time they represent tendencies to run away from each end of the alley: these are *avoidance gradients* (figure 11.2). Presumably they are motivated by the *acquired fear* that has been conditioned to each end of the alley (chapter 10).

What should happen? The rat placed in the middle of the alley, where the gradients intersect, may begin to run away from (let us say) the left-hand end of the alley. But that moves the animal toward the right, so that the tendency to avoid the right-hand end of the alley becomes the stronger tendency. Then the rat turns and begins to move back toward the left, but then the tendency to avoid the left-hand end becomes the stronger, so the animal turns back toward the right-hand one again . . . and so on. The rat is trapped in the middle of the alley. A movement toward either end of the alley results in a stronger tendency toward a movement in the opposite direction. The rat should vacillate somewhere around the middle of the alley. Observation shows that this is exactly what happens.

All of this is certainly an unpleasant situation from the rat's point of view. Movement in either direction increases the fear of further movement in that direction, so the rat will remain trapped in the middle indefinitely, unless rescued by the experimenter. Notice, however, that this will be true only if the animal is confined between the two alternatives. Instead of an alley, suppose the rat is placed between two shock sources on a broad tabletop—no alley connects the two. In that case, the rat could express both avoidance tendencies at once simply by taking off along a path at a right angle to where the alley would be if there were one. Such an action would move the rat away from *both* sources of discomfort. In other words, faced with two alternatives, both of which are unpleasant, a person or animal may be trapped in hesitation for a long time—but only if matters are arranged such that escape from the whole situation is not an option.

Parallels in human behavior are easy to find. A child does not want to clean her room, but neither does she want to be punished for not doing so. "Movement" in either direction increases her discomfort. Is there some way of avoiding both, and getting out of the conflict situation altogether? The child might pretend to be sick, perhaps. Or she might run away from home. Either way she would escape the whole conflict situation.

APPROACH-AVOIDANCE CONFLICT

Finally, consider the case in which both a pleasant event and an unpleasant event are associated with the *same* place. We would then have an *approach-avoidance* conflict (figure 11.3). In Miller's rat model, the rat would be placed at one end of the alley (not the middle). At the other end, of the alley, the rat has already learned that there is food (good), but also shock (bad).

There will be a tendency to approach, but also a tendency to avoid, the far end of the alley. As before, each of these tendencies will grow stronger as the rat moves toward the far end. As the rat approaches the food, the tendency to go on to eat the food gets stronger (the approach gradient), but so does the tendency to turn back and run from the shock (the avoidance gradient).

One final consideration: *The slope of the avoidance gradient will be steeper than the slope of the approach gradient.* This makes sense. Hunger, which motivates approach toward the food, is an internal state that the animal carries with it; wherever the rat may be, its hunger is the same. But fear, which motivates avoidance, is a conditioned response to the *particular* place associated with shock. So as the rat moves away from that place, fear, unlike hunger, diminishes.

The resulting conflict is diagrammed in figure 11.3, which also shows the likely result. Placed at the far end of the alley, the rat should run toward the food until its hunger, which motivates approach, is balanced by its fear, which motivates avoidance. It should then turn to run away from the food, but then hunger becomes the stronger motive, so it turns back toward it.

From the far end of the alley, therefore, the rat should run toward the food until, at some point short of the end of the alley, the point of balance is reached. Again the rat should vacillate at some point along the alley. Closer to the food, fear is stronger and the rat moves away. Farther away, hunger is stronger and the rat turns back toward the food source again. As before, the rat is trapped somewhere in the middle by the conflicting motives to approach and to avoid.

At first glance, approach-avoidance sounds like a less unpleasant situation than avoidance-avoidance conflict. At least there is something good in it! But in another sense, this kind of conflict is even worse than avoidance-avoidance conflict.

Avoidance-avoidance conflict, described earlier, leaves the rat trapped somewhere in the middle of the alley, unable to go very far either one way or the other. In approach-avoidance conflict, the animal again is trapped at the equilibrium point, unable to move closer to the food because of its fear, unable to move farther away because of its hunger. In the avoidance-avoidance case, the rat can reduce both avoidance tendencies at once, running away from both shock sources at once. To prevent this, the rat must be confined.

But with approach-avoidance conflict, no such confinement is necessary. Suppose again that the rat is free to move around on a large tabletop, but also that there is still a place where both food and shock await. The rat will then be trapped somewhere close to that place, not by walls but by the very terms of the conflict. The

Figure 11.3
Approach-avoidance conflict. At the far end of the alley is a positive stimulus (food) but also a negative one (shock).

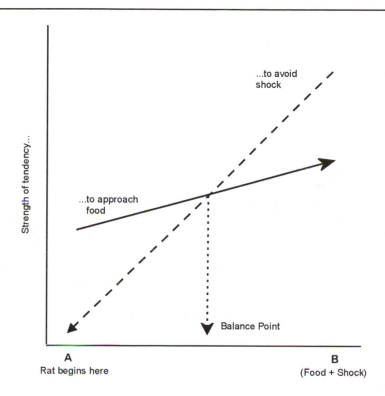

tendency to approach extends out *in all directions* from the place where the food is, and so does the tendency to avoid. If the rat close to the food/shock runs away from it *in any direction*, the tendency to avoid will soon grow weaker until it just balances the tendency to approach. If the rat starts far away from the food/shock and runs toward it, the tendency to avoid will grow stronger, again until it just balances the tendency to approach. On the tabletop, the point of vacillation (where the rat comes to a halt) will sweep out a *circle* some fixed distance in all directions from the food/shock. No walls are needed; the tendency to approach is enough by itself to keep the animal hovering not far away from where the food is located.

Parallels in human situations are easy to find. A shy person might like to strike up a conversation with an attractive person (approach), but might also be fearful of being rejected (avoidance). As he approaches the attractive person, fear grows stronger, until it balances attraction and the approach stops. But then if he turns and walks away (in any direction), fear grows weaker and, once outside the circle of equilibrium, his attraction to the other person becomes stronger than his fear and he turns back to begin another approach, which may then be aborted in turn. A person may be trapped like that for quite some time.

Finally, returning to the experiment, one can test some predictions specifying what should happen as conditions are changed. Suppose it has been determined, under a given set of conditions, where the rat will come to rest at its vacillation point, somewhere around the middle of the alley. How could one get the rat to approach the food more closely—perhaps even to go ahead and eat it? Clearly, there are two ways one might go about this: increase the hunger, or decrease the fear. If the rat is made hungry enough, the approach gradient will be raised so high that the avoidance gradient will not intersect it. In such case, the rat may indeed go on to eat the food, but the fear that is evoked may remain very high—remember, the food place is also the shock place! The rat may eat, but fearfully and unhappily.

It would be much better if instead we can manage to reduce the fear. Then the rat may be able to eat the food, without having to endure intense fear in order to do it.

As a matter of fact, this idea has been put to use in therapeutic contexts. Suppose that a person is unable to make friends or establish relationships because of her intense fear of rejection. She is in an approach-avoidance conflict: She wants to *approach* people and make friends, but she also wants to *avoid* people because of her fear. A behavior therapist might focus on the fear that social situations evoke in this person and try to reduce it. One way might be to try to *condition* a response other than fear to social situations or the prospect of them—a therapeutic technique known as *systematic desensitization*. An experimental evaluation of it is presented elsewhere in this book (chapter 26).

For that matter, antianxiety drugs may also be used with this aim in mind. We would like to reduce anxiety, not only because it is unpleasant, but also because it interferes with our doing things we want to do—like making friends or establishing relationships or giving an effective speech. In fact, Miller has suggested that one important effect of alcohol is just this: it reduces anxiety, and so enables us (for good or ill) to do things that the anxiety would normally hold in check (see Miller, 1959).

As we examine conflict situations in daily life, we may well find ourselves impressed with how often Miller's analyses of such situations will come to mind. Even if we do not accept the behavioristic orientation that gave rise to Miller's models, the models themselves still give us a way of thinking about a wide variety of human dilemmas.

BIBLIOGRAPHY

Miller, N. E. (1944). Experimental studies of conflict. In J. M. Hunt (Ed.), *Personality and the behavior disorders* (pp. 431–465). New York: Ronald.

Miller, N. E. (1959). Liberalization of basic s-r concepts: extensions to conflict behavior, motivation, and social learning. In S. Koch (Ed.), *Psychology: A study of a science: Vol. 2. General systematic formulations, learning, and special processes* (pp. 196–292). New York: McGraw-Hill.

Other readings are listed at the end of chapter 10.

12 | DAVID McCLELLAND ON ACHIEVEMENT MOTIVATION

Some motives operate over the short term. An animal or human may be hungry, thirsty, or fearful, right now. But there are other motives that operate over much longer times; indeed, over a whole lifetime, one's actions may be guided by desires for success and achievement, or for rewarding relationships, or for wealth or power over others. David McClelland was a pioneer in the study of long-term motives.

David Clarence McClelland (1917–98) was born May 20, 1917, in Mount Vernon, New York. He received his B.A. degree in 1938 from Wesleyan University and his Ph.D. from Yale University in 1941. He taught at the Connecticut College for Women and Wesleyan University, then moved to Harvard University in 1956. After 30 years at Harvard, he moved to Boston University in 1987 as Distinguished Research Professor of Psychology. He remained at Boston University until his death.

To study a long-term motive such as, for example, the desire for achievement—what McClelland called "need for achievement," or nAch—one will want to know what sorts of things affect it and are affected by it. To do that, one must measure its strength. How can that be done?

Well, motives of the sort we're considering have to do with goals that lie far in the future and that we are *imagining* now. Therefore, *imagined states of affairs* can act as goals. This means in turn that our goals can literally be as complicated, and as far in the future, as our imaginations permit. It also suggested to McClelland a possible way of measuring how important to us an imagined goal might be.

If we are seeking such an imagined goal, then that goal should be "on our minds," and readily brought to the front of our minds. If we take steps to evoke some motive, and if it in turn affects what is on our minds, then it ought to affect the imagery that we report. McClelland therefore tried out the use of *projective tests* as measures of motivation.

A projective test presents a series of ambiguous stimuli—blobs of ink, as in the Rorschach test, or pictures showing scenes. Such a blob or picture is purposely made ambiguous so that it could mean any of a number of things, and the participant is asked to say what it suggests to him or her.

Specifically, McClelland used a variation of the thematic apperception test, a well-known projective test. The participant is shown a series of pictures, one at a time, and is asked to tell a brief story about it: What are the people in the picture doing? What are they thinking? What will happen?

One picture, for example, shows a man at a work table with a family photograph at one side. One participant's story about this picture went as follows:

> The engineer is at work on Saturday when it is quiet and he has taken time to do a little daydreaming. He is the father of the two children in the picture—the husband of a woman shown. He has a happy home life and is dreaming about some pleasant outing they have had . . . He plans on the following day, Sunday, to use the afternoon to take his family for a short trip. (McClelland, 1964, p. 18)

In this story, the person's talk centered around family and family activities. It has little to do with achievement. In this, it contrasts sharply with the following story about the same picture, told by another person:

> The man is an engineer at a drafting board. The picture is of his family. He has a problem and is concentrating on it. It is merely an everyday occurrence—a problem which requires thought. How can he get that bridge to take the stress of possible high winds? He wants to arrive at a good solution of the problem by himself. (McClelland, 1964, p. 18)

Here, the focus is on a problem that the engineer wants to solve by his own efforts. Such an answer reflects concern with personal achievement—it suggests that achievement is on that person's mind. A participant who told many stories like that would be scored high in achievement motivation.

But is this method a valid way of measuring motivation? How can it be tested? McClelland reasoned this way: if it is a valid measure, then a motive that is *made* to be prominent in the participant's mind should affect the way he or she responds to the pictures.

One of McClelland's early experiments, conducted with Richard Atkinson (Atkinson & McClelland, 1948), asked simply, If participants are made hungry, so they have food on their minds, will there be more hunger- or food-related imagery in their responses to the pictures? To find out, hungry and nonhungry participants were compared. All of them responded to the same pictures, and their responses were scored by "blind" scorers who did not know who was hungry and who was not—a control for the possible effect of scorers' expectations.

Sure enough, hungry people produced more food-related imagery. Therefore, having food on one's mind can indeed affect the images one has in response to the test pictures.

What about more complex human motives? What about the motivation for personal achievement? Can it be measured in a similar way? We can find out by a similar logic: activate the motive, and see if it affects the stories people tell.

Suppose, for example, that some participants are led to believe that they are about to take an important test. They should—right then—be concerned with doing well; they should have achievement on their minds. Would their responses to ambiguous pictures contain more achievement-related themes, as compared with participants for whom the test was presented as unimportant? Again the answer was yes (McClelland, Atkinson, & Clark, 1949).

These experiments—classic in their own right—show that short-term motivational states do indeed influence the images that come readily to a person's mind. They build a bridge between the study of motivation and the study of cognitive processes, such as mental imagery.

McClelland's original interest was in long-term motives and long-term goals. So his later research returned to these, focusing on the consequences and determinants of achievement motivation as a *long-term* motivational state, operating over the life span of individuals and in whole societies. Some of this research was necessarily correlational rather than experimental, but some brief examples will give its flavor (see Weiner, 1989, for discussion).

Is the long-term strength of achievement motivation reflected in the kinds of tasks one chooses to undertake? In one investigation, for example, participants played a ring-toss game, trying to throw a little plastic ring over an upright post from some distance away. They were free to choose how far away they stood when making their tosses. Some of these were high in achievement motivation, or *need for achievement* (nAch); others were not, as measured separately. It turned out that participants who were high in nAch chose to stand an intermediate distance away, so that success was not impossible, but was not guaranteed either. There was no such consistency in the choices made by those low in nAch.

Why? One interpretation is that high-nAch people seek challenges. Tasks that are too easy or too difficult do not interest them. Or perhaps they seek information about their own skills—they wish to evaluate their performances. In that case, too easy a task would provide little information; the participant can do it, but so can everyone else. Too difficult a task would be no better; if the participant fails, again, so would anyone else. A task of intermediate difficulty is most informative.

Is achievement motivation reflected in career choice? McClelland and his collaborators showed, for example, that business executives scored higher in nAch than people in the number of other occupations—for example, technicians and students in professional schools. This was true in the United States, in Italy, and in Poland.

But these are correlational data, so it is hard to know whether businesspeople go into business because they are high in nAch, or whether they develop a high nAch later because their professions demand it. So McClelland and his colleagues measured nAch in college students, and looked at the jobs they held 10–14 years later. The jobs themselves were divided into entrepreneurial ones, with individual responsibility and individual risk, and other, nonentrepreneurial ones. It turned out that people who were high in nAch early, while in college, were more likely than others to be found in entrepreneurial jobs later on. So the difference in nAch shows up *before* the occupational choice is made, and may contribute to that choice.

One can go further—much further. McClelland's method depended on diagnosing motivation based on imaginative productions. There is no reason why these have to be responses to ambiguous pictures. What is on one's mind can affect many other kinds of imagery. Therefore, the preoccupations of a person—or a whole society—could be diagnosed from any kind of imaginative productions.

Consider works of fiction, for example. There are children's stories that are filled with achievement-related imagery, like *The Little Engine That Could*. There are others that lack such imagery, like *Snow White and the Seven Dwarves*. Might the differences among stories be related to differences in how (and how much) different people—or perhaps different whole societies—think about personal achievement, and how important they think it is? Will *The Little Engine That Could* be more popular—or more likely to be written in the first place—in a society that has achievement on its mind?

Moreover, will a society's preoccupations, as they change over time, be related to changes in the fiction it produces? McClelland's reasoning was as follows. If a society emphasizes personal achievement, then entrepreneurship should be valued, and be more frequently sought by members of that society. The society as a whole should have entrepreneurship on its mind. This in turn should be accompanied by industrialization and high productivity—*and* by a high level of achievement imagery in its fiction!

By taking stories from different periods of history, and having them scored for achievement imagery (again by blind scorers), he was able to show that a measure of industrialization in England rose and fell with variations in the frequency of achievement imagery in fiction over the period from 1500 to 1850—from before the time of the Spanish Armada, through two revolutions in England and one in America, to just past the Napoleonic wars. Three and a half centuries! All these other events, and all the other influences on industrialization free to operate, and *still* the relationship was visible (see McClelland, 1955).

We can take it further still. If the achievement motive is a way of thinking about challenges, problems, and enterprises, perhaps those ways of thinking could be *taught*. McClelland and his associates have developed training programs intended to do just that—to teach people to think like high need-achievers. And there have been some impressive successes. In one study, program participants showed a higher rates of advancement within their companies than a control group (Aronoff & Litwin, 1971). In another, an achievement-motivation training program for small-business owners enhanced performance as measured by sales, profits, personal income, and number of employees. A cost-benefit analysis of this government-sponsored program showed that it more than paid for itself by the net increase in tax revenues, due to the increased profitability of the businesses. After two years, the cost-benefit ratio was over 5 to 1 (Miron & McClelland, 1979).

Much remains to be learned, of course, and McClelland's conclusions—like any other scientific conclusions—may have to be modified in light of further investigation. Nevertheless, he has shown us how a complex motive, operating over the lifetime of an individual and over centuries in the history of nations, can be investigated by the methods of science. Surely this is a stunning achievement in its own right.

BIBLIOGRAPHY

Aronoff, J., & Litwin, G. H. (1971). Achievement motivation training and executive advancement. *Journal of Applied Behavioral Analysis, 7*, 215–229.

Atkinson, J. W., & McClelland, D. C. (1948). The projective expression of needs: II. The effect of different intensities of the hunger drive on thematic apperception. *Journal of Experimental Psychology, 38*, 643–658.

McClelland, D. C. (1955). The psychology of mental content reconsidered. *Psychological Review, 62,* 297–302.

McClelland, D. C. (1961). *The achieving society.* Princeton, NJ: Van Nostrand.

McClelland, D. C. (1964). *The roots of consciousness.* Princeton, NJ: Van Nostrand.

McClelland, D. C., Atkinson, J. W., & Clark, R. A. (1949). The projective expression of needs: III. The effect of ego-involvement, success, and failure on perception. *Journal of Psychology, 27,* 311–330.

McClelland, D. C., Atkinson, J. W., Clark, R. A., & Lowell, E. L. (1953). *The achievement motive.* Princeton, NJ: Van Nostrand.

Miron, D., & McClelland, D. C. (1979). The impact of achievement motivation training on small businesses. *California Management Review, 21,* 13–28.

Weiner, B. (1989). *Human motivation.* New York: Holt, Rinehart & Winston.

13 HARRY HARLOW: A TALE OF TWO MOTHERS

In the 1930s and 1940s, a widely accepted theory of motivation, human and animal, ran like this: The motives for all our actions are derived from a short list of simple biological needs—hunger, thirst, sex, and the like. This was Sigmund Freud's view of human motivation. It was also a theory of motivation held by many behaviorist writers. Granted, we do many things even when we are not hungry, thirsty, or lustful, but in such cases, our motives could be considered *acquired drives*, like fear, that in turn were based on basic drives, like pain (chapter 10).

In short, it was once a popular idea that all motives are ultimately based on internal drive states. In addition, drive was seen as providing the conditions for *reinforcement*. A hungry rat makes the correct response and is given food, a thirsty rat makes the correct response and is given water, a rat receiving a shock makes the correct response and the shock goes off, and in each case the response is reinforced. This gives us the *drive-reduction theory* of reinforcement: reinforcement is reduction of drive (chapter 10).

There were always difficulties with this idea (Mook, 1996). But it was the work of Harry Harlow that put spikes in the coffin of this inadequate theory, while also helping turn around our conception of mother-infant attachment.

Harry F. Harlow (1905–81), born in Fairfield, Iowa, was nothing if not a determined investigator (see Blum, 2002). Having obtained his B.A. and Ph.D. from Stanford, he moved to the University of Wisconsin to take his first academic job. There he discovered that the space promised for his research with rats had not been provided. The medical school offered him one room to use for research, which was so small that he kept tripping over the cages. Later, he was given two small rooms near his office in the basement of the administration building to use for his research. Within this windowless basement, Harlow's room turned out to be directly below the office of the Dean of Men. Odors from Harlow's rat room floated straight up, and students waiting for a conference with the dean could be found leaning out the windows. Like Thorndike's landlady of half a century earlier (chapter 19), the dean chose serenity over science; Harlow's rats had to go.

Harlow decided to go to the animals instead of bringing the animals to him. Near Madison was a zoo in which some apes were housed. The rest is history: Harlow was able to do experiments on the animals' home ground, dealing with concepts, memory, social relations, and much besides. Later, he was given an entire building to house his primate research—though he had to renovate the building himself, aided by some football players recruited from his undergraduate classes.

Harlow never did think much of either drive or drive-reduction theory (Harlow, 1953). His research showed that in addition to internal drive states, there were powerful *external* motives for behavior. Indeed, a series of experiments that were classic in their own right showed the power of these.

Baby monkeys that were neither food- nor water-deprived were given access to a simple mechanical puzzle that they could take apart. Harlow found that as often as he would assemble the puzzle, a monkey would take it apart, though the monkey never received any reward for doing this. The monkeys never did master the skill of putting the puzzle together, but they would take it apart, over and over. Apparently, the simple fact that it was *there* was enough to arouse a motive to explore and manipulate it. It provided, in other words, an *external* source of motivation, in contrast to the internal states.

The later and more famous "two mothers" experiment, the one described here, addressed another instance of drive-reduction theory. An infant monkey spends a great deal of time in contact with its mother, clinging to her fur. It forms what we now call an *attachment* to the mother. Why does it do this?

At the time, the received view of mother-infant attachment was the one held by drive-reduction theorists, and also by Freud and his influential followers. Harlow calls it the "cupboard" theory—the mother, like Mother Hubbard, has (or is) a cupboard from which food is available. The infant comes to associate the sound, sight, and feel of the mother with the pleasure (Freud) or the reduction in hunger (the drive-reduction theorists) from the food she provides.

An alternative, however, was suggested by Harlow's observation that laboratory-raised baby monkeys showed strong attachments to the cloth pads that covered the floors of their cages, clinging to them and reacting angrily when they were changed. Perhaps the infant's reaction to the mother is similar. Maybe the infant seeks the *comfort* that contact with the mother provides—again an external, rather than internal, source of motivation, based on what the infant *likes* rather than on what it *needs*.

The trouble is that real mothers, monkey or human, provide both food and comfort. To find out which is the more important, the two must be separated from each other. So Harlow built a pair of artificial monkey mothers (figure 13.1). One of the two was a cold, bony structure based on a cylinder of wire mesh. Mounted on this mother's body was a bottle of milk with a nipple from which the baby monkey could nurse. This mother provided *food, but not comfort*. The other mother had no milk, but in her case the wire mesh was covered with a layer of terry cloth, and her body was made warm by a light bulb mounted inside. She provided *comfort, but not food*. Thus Harlow separated the two commodities, food and comfort. Which would the baby monkeys prefer?

Figure 13.1
An infant monkey with two "mothers." An infant monkey takes a snack from the
wire mother (note the milk bottle) while clinging with both feet to the cloth mother,
to which it will shortly return. The different heads on the models were just for fun;
they were reversed for half the infant monkeys, so it could be shown that they made
no difference.

Source: Photo courtesy of Harlow Primate Laboratory, University of Wisconsin.

Clearly, they preferred comfort (Harlow, 1958; Harlow & Zimmerman, 1959).
They would cling to the warm terry-cloth mother for long periods. When they
got hungry, they would go over to the wire mother and have a snack, but then they
would immediately go back to the warm terry-cloth mother and cling there. In
other words, when food and comfort were pitted against each other, comfort won.

There was more. The comfortable terry-cloth mother seemed to offer a certain security as well as comfort. If a baby monkey were shown something new and

frightening (like a toy teddy bear), it would rush to the terry-cloth mother and cling to its surface. From that secure "home base," the infant appeared to draw courage as well as comfort, and would watch the teddy bear carefully and, indeed, might then venture forth to explore it.

But all this happened only if the terry-cloth mother was there. If she was not, the frightened baby monkey was likely to huddle in the corner of the cage, head hidden under its arms, until the frightening object went away.

The "comfortable" mother seemed, in other words, to offer a secure home base to which the little monkey could retreat in times of danger, and from which it could then explore. And this was so not because she offered food when hungry—an internal source of motivation—but because she offered comfort, an external one.

These experiments, and Harlow's many others, had a number of ramifications. On the theoretical side, they were powerful evidence against the simplistic drive-based theories of motivation that had been popular before.

Then, too, these findings (along with other observations) encouraged students of human development to reconsider some of their own ideas. It was not uncommon at the time—and in some places, unfortunately, it is still not uncommon—for adult caretakers to be concerned only with the basic physiological needs of infants: they must be fed and cleaned, but that should be enough. In addition, minimal contact with caretakers was desirable because it minimized risk of infection.

Infection was a valid concern, to be sure. But a hands-off attitude was also encouraged by some popular but poorly supported psychological theories. John Watson, the founder of behaviorism (chapter 1), had some stern advice for parents: "When you are tempted to pet your child remember that the mother love is a dangerous instrument," and "Once a child's character has been spoiled by bad handling, which can be done in a few days, who can say that the damage is ever repaired?" (1928, pp. 81–82). In effect, Watson was asking caretakers to act as if made of wire.

This advice was very influential for awhile, strange as it now seems (see Blum, 2002, for discussion). It seemed to have "science" on its side, though in fact it was based on no science at all. But most advisers today, and most parents, realize that it was very bad advice. Harlow's "contact comfort" is something babies need and parents are right to enjoy, babies deprived of it often do not thrive, and modern students of child development freely acknowledge their debt to Harlow and his colleagues for showing its importance (e.g., Bowlby, 1969).

There is much more to infant development than contact comfort, and Harlow and his students and colleagues discovered much more about it. The work continued after his death, extending it to the effects of social factors on emotional development, and the genetic and biochemical mechanisms of these effects. Some researchers believe, as did Harlow, that models of human emotional disorders may come from this work (e.g., Suomi, 1991). Harlow set in motion an active and vigorous research program that continues today.

One final comment about the two-mothers experiment is appropriate. This issue was touched upon in chapter 1, but it bears repeating here. One often hears—even in psychology textbooks—that a drawback of experiments in psychology is their artificiality. One cannot be sure that the results will "generalize" to "real life."

Sometimes that concern does arise, but there are many cases where it is wide of the mark, and so one has to think it through case by case. Harlow's experiment is an excellent example.

In the "real life" of infant monkeys, the real monkey mother will offer both food and contact comfort. They are inseparable. So if we ask which of the two is more important, no amount of observing under natural conditions will tell us. The only way to find out is to build our own artificial mother, as Harlow did. Creating an artificial setting was the only way he could answer his question at all.

Is this a drawback to his experiment? Harlow's findings cannot be generalized to real life, because the artificial setting has no real-life counterpart. But that was not his intention. He did not conclude, "Monkeys in the wild would probably make the same choice if it were offered them." It will not be offered them, and in any case who cares?

What Harlow did conclude was that the prevailing theory of attachment—association of the mother with food—could not be right. It is this *theoretical* conclusion, not the "generalization" of his findings, that challenged prevailing views and has led to new outlooks on mother-infant attachment. He has changed the way we think about mother-infant attachment, and that is what counts. (For further discussion, see Mook, 1983; Stanovich, 2001.)

BIBLIOGRAPHY

Blum, D. (2002). *Love at Goon Park: Harry Harlow and the science of affection*. Cambridge, MA: Perseus Publishing.

Bowlby, J. (1969). *Attachment and loss*. New York: Basic Books.

Harlow, H. F. (1953). Mice, monkeys, men, and motives. *Psychological Review, 56*, 51–65.

Harlow, H. F. (1958). The nature of love. *American Psychologist, 13*, 673–685.

Harlow, H. F., & Zimmerman, R. (1959). Affectional responses in the infant monkey. *Science, 130*, 421–432.

Mook, D. G. (1983). In defense of external invalidity. *American Psychologist, 38*, 379–387.

Mook, D. G. (1996). *Motivation: The organization of action* (2nd ed.). New York: Norton.

Stanovich, K. E. (2001). *How to think straight about psychology* (6th ed.). Boston: Allyn & Bacon.

Suomi, S. (1991). Primate separation models of affective disorder. In J. I. V. Madden (Ed.), *Neurobiology of learning, emotion, and affect*. New York: Raven Press.

Watson, J. B. (1928). *Psychological care of infant and child*. New York: Norton.

14 NIKOLAAS TINBERGEN: THE STUDY OF INSTINCT

Experimental psychology around 1950 was dominated by behaviorism. Behaviorist researchers emphasized the study of behavior under laboratory conditions, with the study of *learning* a major emphasis. However, biologists and naturalists continued to investigate behavior in its natural setting, emphasizing observation before experiment. Watching what animals did in the natural world, scientists identified patterns of action that characterized the members of a species, and the patterns of stimulation that triggered these actions.

A direct challenge to behaviorist orthodoxy was the publication in 1951 of *The Study of Instinct*, by Nikolaas Tinbergen—a book that summarized much of this work. Even the title was a challenge.

Behaviorists had thrown the concept of *instinct* out the window. There were several reasons for this. First was the belief that learning could account for all the complexity of behavior. Second, instincts were unobservable, and sounded like mysterious driving forces for which science had no need. Third, it was objected that the concept was circular. Why does an animal do this or that? It is instinctive. How do we know it is instinctive? Because the animal does it. Not very helpful.

Meanwhile, however, observations of behavior in its natural setting were being made by scientists, most of them biologists and many of them European, known as *ethologists*. Their observations convinced them that there are complex actions that are not learned. These action patterns—or the interconnections within the nervous system that control them—have evolved in a given species, just as its fur or feathers have evolved. We might as well call them *instinctive*. This is not intended to explain them—no modern ethologist will ever say that an animal does this or that *because* it is instinctive to do so—but only to distinguish them from complex actions that do result from learning.

The work of ethologists was brought to the attention of English-speaking psychologists during the 1940s and 1950s, and a landmark event during this period was the publication of Tinbergen's *The Study of Instinct*.

Tinbergen (1907–88) was born in The Hague, Netherlands. As a young boy, he spent much of his time just observing the abundant wildlife of Holland (and the stickleback fish that lived in an aquarium in his backyard) rather than at his studies. He did decide to study biology at Leiden University, after which he organized a course in animal behavior for undergraduates. It was in connection with this that he made his famous observations of courtship and mating in the stickleback fish. Tinbergen later joined the faculty at Oxford University, where he published many books on ethology—the study of behavior in its natural environment.

Tinbergen's curiosity about nature led him to take observations on a wide variety of species, from digger wasps to herring gulls (Tinbergen, 1961). Of necessity, we will focus on his observations dealing with the reproductive behavior of a fish, the three-spined stickleback *Gasterosteus aculeatus*, a fish about three inches long as an adult and found in fresh- or saltwater shoals.

In the spring, the male three-spined stickleback is brought into reproductive condition by hormonal changes. These have effects on its behavior, and also on its appearance: they give the male fish a characteristic red-colored underbelly (more on this later). The male fish builds a tube-shaped nest under the water and then patrols the territory around the nest entrance.

What happens when another stickleback approaches? It depends. If another fish with a red underbelly approaches, the male treats it as a rival male and attacks it. The attack is quite constant in its form. It begins with a head-down posture and spread fins—the threat display (figure 14.1). When so threatened, the intruder usually gives up and swims away. If he does not, a full-blown biting fight is likely.

This threat pattern is so characteristic of the species that early ethologists referred to it (and other stereotyped actions like it in many species) as a *fixed action pattern*. The *fixed* was later dropped, because the actions turned out not to be as fixed as all that, but the term *action pattern* remains a handy way of referring to species-typical patterns of movement and posture.

Having identified this pattern, Tinbergen and his colleagues turned from observations to experiments. They made models of male sticklebacks, omitting or adding different features for different models. In this way, they were able to show that the male's threat display is elicited, or *released*, by a specific characteristic of the intruder—the red underbelly. Even very crude models, if lowered into the water near the male, will be threatened if their undersides are red, but only then. This one specific aspect of a male fish's appearance is a *releasing stimulus* for attack.

If it is a female fish that comes along, then the homeowner male behaves quite differently. Instead of attacking, he courts. Here the action pattern is a peculiar back-and-forth swimming pattern, a zigzagging dance. Again, experiments with models can identify the releasing stimulus for this action pattern as well, It is the swollen underbelly of the female fish heavy with eggs. Even crude models with swollen undersides will be courted with the zigzag dance; good models without them will not be.

If mating occurs, it will be with a meticulously choreographed series of releasing stimuli and action patterns in response to them. The male leads the female to the nest. If she follows, he points to the nest entrance with his nose. If she swims into the nest, he nuzzles her, causing her to release her clutch of eggs. He then swims after her, depositing sperm to fertilize the eggs (fertilization takes place outside the body in this species). Experiments with models have shown that every stage of the

Figure 14.1.
Threat display by a male stickleback fish. A male stickleback near its nest (left)
makes the head-downward "threat display" at an intruding male (right).

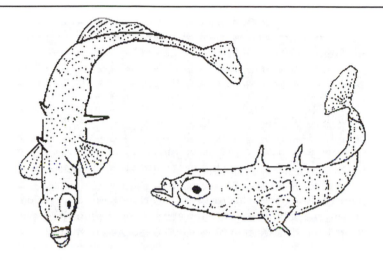

Source: From Tinbergen (1951). Reprinted by permission of Oxford University Press.

sequence is an instinctive pattern of responses—an action pattern—triggered by certain releasing stimuli provided by the partner's appearance and/or behavior.

Finally, experiments show that the actions, and the coupling of these to releasing stimuli, are unlearned. Male sticklebacks that have been raised in isolation, never having seen another fish, nonetheless threaten or court in the normal way when the appropriate releasing stimuli are encountered for the first time. This does *not* mean that learning cannot modify these actions—a frequent source of confusion. It does mean that no specific learning experiences were required to put them there.

One more important concept came from this research. The actions of an animal are produced not just by the external stimulus situation, but also by the internal organization of a species' behavior. Only thus can we understand why a red underbelly releases attack behavior in one species of fish but not in another—and why, for that matter, it will release attack only if the internal hormonal state of the animal is right. Internal as well as external influences must be identified and understood. Watson's original program—given the stimulus, to predict the response—will not work. We need to know more than the stimulus.

All this is just one of the many analyses of instinctive behavior reported by ethologists—most of them in relatively simple animals such as fishes, birds, or insects (for it makes sense to begin with simpler cases). The impact of these ideas was severalfold. First, they did resurrect the concept of instinct from the behaviorist tomb. Second, they affected the way we study behavior. And third, they affected the way we think about it.

Most experimental psychologists studied behavior in tightly controlled environments, as Pavlov (chapter 20) and Skinner (chapter 23) did. This has the advantage, first, that the tighter control makes it easier to see the effects of experimental manipulations, and second, that it allows us to see interesting effects of conditions that might never occur in nature. (Will a male stickleback learn to make a lever-pressing response, or equivalent, in order to gain access to a female? It will [Sevenster, 1968].) This would not have been discovered in the fish's natural environment, where there are no levers (or equivalents) that have that consequence.

On the other hand, important aspects of a species' behavior might never be seen in a controlled setting, if the experimenters did not happen to impose the right conditions. Suppose experimenters placed a male stickleback in a controlled environment and imposed various changes in conditions one at a time. They might never see the threat display. Why? Because they might never happen to present an object with the red underbelly required to elicit the action. Even if they did, they would not know what to make of the reactions they saw if they did not already know that this is *how* a male stickleback threatens an intruder. In short, there is much to be said for looking carefully at what happens in nature before experimental variations are imposed.

The arguments about these matters have largely died down. It is clear that the two approaches to research are not antagonistic but complementary. In recent years, scientists from the two traditions have cooperated in fruitful ways (see, e.g., Rozin & Schull, 1988).

Finally, the terms and concepts of ethology led us to ask whether they might apply to more complex creatures—monkeys, perhaps (chapter 13), or even humans. Notions like action patterns, releasing stimuli, and behavioral hierarchies have been useful concepts in thinking about human behavior. After all, our bodies are products of evolution, and this includes the fine-grain wiring of our brains. Why should we not, like the stickleback, have evolved certain patterns of action and their connection to appropriate stimuli?

Here is just one example. In humans, certain facial expressions have some of the properties of action patterns. Facial expressions for certain emotions, like anger, sadness, or happiness, are the same in cultures that have been separated from each other by many thousands of years. In that sense they are characteristic of the human species, just as the stickleback's attack and courtship patterns are characteristic of that species. And they are, at least initially, unlearned (though learning can modify them). The typical facial expressions of emotion are displayed by people who could not have learned them in any obvious way—for example, children born both blind and deaf. It appears that indeed we are not Lockean blank slates! (For discussion, see Pinker, 2002.)

Questions about the evolution of behavior, including human behavior, have led to the rapidly developing field of *evolutionary psychology*. It is a direct descendant of the work of the early ethologists.

For his scientific and theoretical work, Tinbergen was awarded the Nobel Prize in 1973. Two other ethologists, Konrad Lorenz and Karl von Frisch, were also awarded the prize in that year. These three were the first behavioral scientists to win that prestigious award.

BIBLIOGRAPHY

Buss, D. M. (1998). *Evolutionary psychology: The new science of the mind.* Boston: Allyn & Bacon.

Eibl-Eibesfeld, I. (1970). *Ethology: The biology of behavior*. New York: Holt, Rinehart & Winston.

Pinker, S. (2002). *The blank slate*. New York: Penguin.

Rozin, P., & Schull, J. (1988). The adaptive-evolutionary point of view in experimental psychology. In R. C. Atkinson, R. J. Herrnstein, G. Lindzey, & R. D. Luce (Eds.), *Stevens' handbook of experimental psychology* (Vol. 2, pp. 503–547). New York: John Wiley & Sons.

Sevenster, P. (1968). Motivation and learning in sticklebacks. In D. Ingle (Ed.), *The central nervous system and fish behavior*. Chicago: University of Chicago Press.

Tinbergen, N. (1951). *The study of instinct*. London: Oxford University Press.

Tinbergen, N. (1961). *The herring gull's world: A study of the social behaviour of birds*. New York: Basic Books.

Tinbergen, N. (1973). Autobiography [Nobel lecture, December 12, 1973]. Retrieved October 17, 2004, from http://www.nobelprize.org/medicine/laureates/1973/tinbergen-autobio.html

15 TEITELBAUM AND EPSTEIN: HUNGER, THIRST, AND THE BRAIN

We get hungry, we eat, and when we have had enough, we stop. We get thirsty, we drink, and when we have had enough, we stop. Feeding, and drinking in land-dwelling animals, are vitally important biological functions; they are also model cases of motivated behavior. Both humans and laboratory rats will work hard for something to eat or drink when they need it. We do know this much: hunger and thirst are controlled by the brain. This is shown clearly by the effects of damage to the brain. The careful experiments of Philip Teitelbaum and Alan Epstein showed how a detailed investigation of these effects can tell us much, not only about the brain, but also about how hunger and thirst are organized as motivational systems.

Philip Teitelbaum (1928–) was born in Brooklyn. He attended City College in New York, then went to Johns Hopkins for graduate study, taking his Ph.D. with Eliot Stellar in 1954. After teaching at Harvard, he moved to the University of Pennsylvania, where the work discussed here was conducted, then went to the University of Florida, where he is today.

Alan Epstein (1932–94) also worked with Stellar, as an undergraduate research assistant. He then took an M.D. at Johns Hopkins, but decided that a research career was what he wanted. He too moved to Pennsylvania, first as a postdoctoral fellow, then as a faculty member in the biology department. He continued his research on ingestion until his untimely death in 1994.

When scientists learned to make manipulations deep in the brain, something they learned early on was that an important focus of the control of behavior was found in the collection of cell groups deep in the brain known as the *hypothalamus*. Interference with this area could cause disturbances in a wide variety of motivated actions—eating, drinking, and sex. The effects on feeding were especially dramatic and caught the attention of a large number of investigators.

Damage to one part of the hypothalamus, in laboratory rats, gave rise to overeating and gross obesity. It is as if an inhibitory control (compare chapter 7) had been disrupted by the brain damage, so that the animal did not know when to stop eating. A few years later, the converse case was discovered: with damage in the *lateral hypothalamic area*, the rat would refuse to eat at all, and would have to be force-fed to be kept alive. Otherwise it would starve, with food freely available.

Putting these findings together led scientists to the *dual-center* theory of hunger and satiety. One area (the "feeding center") started feeding; another (the "satiety center") stopped it. In 1954, Eliot Stellar published an influential theoretical paper in which these ideas were put together as a general theory of motivated behavior: hunger, thirst, sex, and other biological motives might each reflect the balance of activity in "excitatory centers," which started the behavior, and "inhibitory centers," which stopped it. This theory is no longer held in its original form, though it remains a useful way of reminding us of the multiplicity of influences, excitatory and inhibitory, to which motivated behavior is subject (Mook, 1996).

Now, very often, one will see some recovery from the effects of brain damage. Disruptions that may be very severe often become less so over time. Just why this happens is a focus of research in its own right, and there may be multiple reasons for this too. Philip Teitelbaum collaborated with Stellar in asking, What would happen if a rat with lateral hypothalamic damage (an LH rat for short) is kept alive by force-feeding for a considerable period of time? Will there be some recovery from the failure to eat?

There was indeed substantial recovery (Teitelbaum & Stellar, 1954). It occurred over weeks or months in a series of definite stages, each reflecting the recovery of some parts or parts of a complex control system. By watching the system reassemble itself after the initial damage, one could see the various parts individually, and see what part they played in the control of food and water intake. A detailed experimental analysis of this *lateral recovery syndrome* was undertaken by Teitelbaum and Epstein (1962). They identified four distinct stages of recovery of feeding and drinking.

Stage I: Aphagia and adipsia. Following surgery, the rat refuses to eat food (*aphagia*) or to drink water (*adipsia*). It has to be force-fed, or it will simply accept a life-threatening starvation and dehydration. This is so even though experiments showed that the rat is fully capable of moving around, licking, and chewing. It can make the necessary movements. It just does not.

This is important, for it shows that the rats were not too sluggish or uncoordinated to seek and eat food. If they had been, there would be no reason to speak of a specific problem with feeding behavior. The rats might have had problems with *all* behavior. In a similar way, if Broca's patient had been deficient in all cognitive functioning, there would be no reason to speak of a problem specifically with speech (chapter 4). But this was not true of Broca's patient, and it was not true of the LH rats.

Stage II: Anorexia and adipsia. After days or weeks, the rat will begin to nibble on wet, highly tasty food; it will accept things like eggnog, chocolate-chip cookies soaked in milk, or baby pablum. But *nibble* is the right word. The rat does not eat enough to keep itself alive; it still has to be force-fed. It seems to be "pulled" to the attractive food by its attractiveness; it is not "pushed" to the food by an internal hunger state. In other words, it feeds in response to external stimuli, like an attractive food, but not in response to internal ones, like hunger. It still will not drink water.

Stage III: Adipsia and dehydration aphagia. The transition from Stage II to Stage III may be very abrupt. One morning the experimenters may find that the animal's body weight has bounded up. They then know that the animal has entered Stage III and does not have to be force-fed anymore. It will now eat enough of a *liquid* diet to maintain its body weight, and it will regulate its caloric intake, for if the diet is diluted with water, the rat will promptly increase the amount that it eats so as to hold caloric intake constant.

However, the rat still refuses to drink water. This persisting adipsia can mask the substantial recovery that has occurred if one only offers the rat dry food and water. It does not drink water, and because it does not drink water it becomes dehydrated. And the dehydrated rat has great difficulty eating dry food, partly because its mouth is dry. However, a rat at this stage will eat dry food and regulate its caloric intake *if it is kept hydrated.* This can be done by delivering water directly into the rat's stomach. If the rat is not permitted to become dehydrated, then it will thrive on ordinary dry rat food. The internal control of food intake—regulation of caloric intake—has recovered, but water intake still has not.

Stage IV: "Recovery." The word *recovery* is in quotes because, although the rat now looks normal, it is not. It may never be normal again; some controls may never recover. Once again, however, it takes careful experimentation to reveal the deficiencies that remain.

The rat continues to regulate its caloric intake, but now, for the first time, it is seen to drink water. It drinks enough to hydrated itself and is able to eat dry food. But its drinking is highly abnormal. This is apparent when one examines the pattern of feeding and drinking using electronic sensing devices to detect and record episodes of feeding and of drinking. In an intact rat, water intake occurs in prolonged drafts prior to, and especially following, a prolonged meal. Not in the Stage IV LH rat. This rat will nibble a bit of food, take a few licks of water, nibble a bit more, lick a bit more, and so on throughout the meal.

It seems that the rat is drinking water not to satisfy thirst, but to wash down dry food. Later, this was shown by experiment (see Epstein, 1971). If one arranges for a bit of water to be delivered into the rat's mouth along with each small pellet of food, then the rat does not drink spontaneously anymore. It already has the water in its mouth that it requires. But if the same amount of water is delivered into the stomach instead, then the rat drinks just as much water *by mouth* as it did before. Therefore, it must be drinking to wet its mouth, not to hydrate its body. True thirst is still absent. A striking example of how easily one can confuse one cause for another! A rat may drink for many reasons.

At this point Teitelbaum and Epstein published their classic paper, identifying these four stages in recovery from LH damage. They continued to investigate, however, and found that the "recovered" LH rat had yet other instructive deficits. For example, one way to produce ravenous hunger in both rats and humans is to make blood sugar unavailable to the cells of the brain. In fact, it often been suggested that such unavailability of blood sugar was the normal stimulus for hunger.

But the "recovered" LH rat does not eat in response to *this particular stimulus* for feeding (Epstein, 1971). And yet the very same LH rat does eat at other times. So we can say two things: (1) unavailability of blood sugar is a separate control for feeding, because normal rats show it where LH rats do not, and also, (2) it cannot be the *only* such control, for LH rats, in which it is lacking, nevertheless eat. So they must be eating for some other reason.

There is much more, but this is enough! Let us review what this series of experiments has taught us about hunger, thirst, and the brain.

1. Hunger and thirst, and feeding and drinking, are controlled by systems in the brain that are separate, but adjacent or overlapping (compare chapter 8).

2. The different systems recover at different rates following damage. It is this that allows us to identify them; where one has recovered and another has not, we see that the two are separate.

3. The act of feeding is one thing; regulation of food intake is another. Similarly, the act of drinking is one thing; true thirst is another. A rat may eat, but not enough to maintain itself. A rat may drink in order to wash down dry food, while drinking in response to dehydration of its body is lacking.

4. Feeding is responsive to both internal and external influences. Early in recovery, the LH rat can be coaxed to eat by a highly attractive diet—an *external* influence. Only later does it become responsive to its *internal* requirements, so that it eats enough to meet its nutritional needs. Indeed, this is true of motivational systems generally: they are responsive to influences both from within and from without (compare chapter 13).

5. Even with respect just to *internal* controls over feeding, there must be more than one. The LH rat, even if "recovered," may not eat when its cells are deprived of blood sugar, though the normal rat does. Yet such a rat does eat at other times, and regulates its body weight, so there must be other controls that can do the job even if that particular one is damaged.

Exactly how each of these things happens, and just where in the brain they happen, is still under intensive investigation. These investigations cannot be pursued here. However, even if we leave the matter here, we will have learned a great deal about the organization of hunger and thirst. And the careful, insightful experiments by which the lateral recovery syndrome has been analyzed give us a model case of how the complexities of the brain can be teased apart and investigated one or a few at a time.

BIBLIOGRAPHY

Carlson, N. (1995). *Foundations of physiological psychology* (3rd ed.). Needham Heights, MA: Allyn & Bacon.

Epstein, A. N. (1971). The lateral hypothalamic syndrome: Its implication for the physiological psychology of hunger and thirst. In E. Stellar & J. M. Sprague (Eds.), *Progress in physiological psychology* (Vol. 4, pp. 263–317). New York: Academic Press.

Epstein, A. N., & Teitelbaum, P. (1967). Specific loss of the hypoglycemic control of feeding in recovered lateral rats. *American Journal of Physiology, 213,* 1159–1167.

Hoebel, B. G. (1988). Neuroscience and motivation. In R. C. Atkinson, R. J. Herrnstein, G. Lindzey, & R. D. Luce (Eds.), *Stevens' handbook of experimental psychology* (Vol. 1, pp. 547–625). New York: John Wiley & Sons.

Mook, D. G. (1996). *Motivation: The organization of action* (2nd ed.). New York: Norton.

Stellar, E. (1954). The physiology of motivation. *Psychological review, 61,* 5–22.

Teitelbaum, P., & Epstein, A. N. (1962). The lateral recovery syndrome: Recovery of feeding and drinking after lateral hypothalamic lesions. *Psychological Review, 69,* 74–90.

Teitelbaum, P., & Stellar, E. (1954). Recovery from the failure to eat produced by lateral hypothalamic lesions. *Science, 120,* 894–895.

16 SCHACHTER AND SINGER: COGNITION AND EMOTION

Stanley Schachter is particularly difficult to characterize as any one kind of psychologist. His active imagination has led him to do research on topics ranging from the study of food intake, body-weight control, and nicotine addiction (so he was a psychobiologist and a health psychologist), to the role of cognition in emotion (so he was a cognitive psychologist), to the psychology of affiliation—when and why people want to be together, and how friendships form (so he was a social psychologist too).

As so often, we can focus on only a small part of an illustrious career. Here we consider Schachter's *two-factor* theory of emotion—an enormously influential one—and the experiment that he performed with Jerome Singer to test it (Schachter & Singer, 1962).

Stanley S. Schachter (1922–97) was born in New York City. He received his B.S. and M.A. from Yale in 1942 and 1944, respectively. After working on vision in the Aero-Medical Laboratory of the Armed Services during World War II, Schachter went to MIT in 1946 to work with Kurt Lewin (chapter 55), who had just set up his Research Center for Group Dynamics. The young social psychologists attracted to the center included Leon Festinger, with whom Schachter collaborated in the study of the Seekers (chapter 57) and with whom he did his dissertation research. He received his Ph.D. in social psychology from the University of Michigan in 1949. He later went to Columbia University, where he remained until his retirement.

Jerome E. Singer (1957–) took his B.A. in social anthropology at the University of Michigan in 1957 and his Ph.D. in psychology in 1961 at the University of Minnesota. In 1977, when the Department of Medical Psychology was founded at Uniformed Services University in Bethesda, Maryland, Singer was made chairman. He remained there and is now a professor emeritus.

The theory is that our experience of an emotional state depends on two processes—two *factors*. First, there must be a state of physiological arousal; this is the first factor. But then comes the second factor: perceiving that arousal, we look for its cause. The emotion we then experience is shaped by what we perceive the cause to be—that is, how we *explain* the arousal to ourselves.

Consider how we judge another person's emotional state. We observe his or her behavior—including, perhaps, such involuntary behavior as blushing. Based on what we see the person do *and* our knowledge of the situation, we infer what his or her emotional state must be.

Schachter proposed that we identify our own emotional states in very much the same way. We observe our situation and our reactions, and infer our emotions from these. The only real difference is that we have access to cues from within our own bodies; for example, if our hearts begin to pound or the palms of our hands begin to sweat, we can perceive these bodily changes in ourselves better than we can perceive them in someone else. We still must infer, from the cues we receive, what emotion we are experiencing.

At first sight, this idea seems very strange. Cannot we just look inside ourselves and see directly what we are feeling? But it is clear that at least sometimes, the answer is no. Consider how we say, "Look how much I ate! I must have been hungrier than I thought." Here we are saying, first, that we can be mistaken about so simple a matter as how hungry we feel, and second, that we infer the true state of affairs from what we observe ourselves doing.

Schachter's two-factor theory of emotion extends these ideas to emotional experience generally. The theory says this: The emotion we experience depends on how we interpret our own external and internal reactions. So, first of all, there must be something to interpret: a state of internal arousal, for example, that might cause us to breathe a bit harder, our palms to sweat a bit more, our heart rates to increase. Second, we look for an explanation of our aroused state, and, from whatever explanation we settle on, we infer what emotion we must be feeling.

Schachter and Singer's experiment was a test of this idea. The experiment is complicated, and it will be easier to visualize it if we follow a partial flowchart (figure 16.1).

First, some participants, but not others, were placed in a state of physiological arousal by injection of a drug. (Actually, it was the hormone *epinephrine*, but we will call it just a drug for short.) This drug produces the signs of physiological arousal, and the participants feel their hearts pounding, hands shaking a bit, palms sweating, and the like. Other participants received placebo injections instead, so these signs of arousal did not occur. Thus the first of the two factors was varied as an independent variable: some participants, but not others, were placed in an aroused state.

Now, the participants who received the drug did not know what they had been given (the purpose of the experiment was disguised throughout). When the reactions occurred, how would the participants explain them to themselves? Here is where the second factor—interpreting one's bodily reactions—should come into play.

Some of the participants were given an explanation for what they were experiencing. They were told (correctly) that the drug they had received would produce the symptoms. So, when the symptoms appeared, these participants could attribute them (correctly) to the drug, and so they should not interpret them as *emotional* arousal.

Figure 16.1
Sequences of events in the Schachter and Singer experiment

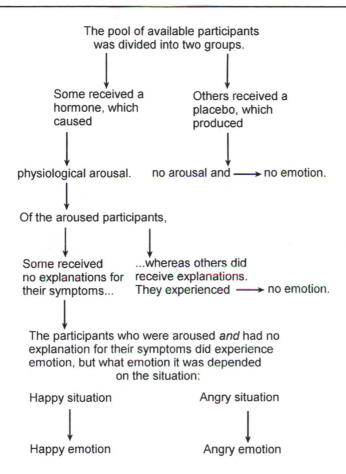

The other members of this group, however, were not given an explanation for the symptoms that the drug produced. Then, the theory says, they should seek an explanation; if internal state does not provide one, they should look to the situation for an explanation. Therefore, the *kind of explanation* the situation provides should affect how the symptoms are interpreted, and therefore what emotion is experienced.

So the situation also was varied. After receiving the injections, each participant was put in a room, supposedly to fill out a questionnaire. In the room there was another person, pretending to be another participant but actually an assistant to the experimenter. At this point, each participant encountered one of two conditions.

In one condition, this fake participant acted happy and giddy, laughing, making paper airplanes out of the questionnaire sheets, and generally being full of fun. What happened? Hormone-treated participants were likely to join in the fun—

more likely than the control participants who had received no hormone. And they were more likely to report themselves as in happy moods, when asked.

In the other condition, the stooge portrayed anger rather than happiness. He scowled, griped about the experiment, and swore at the questionnaire, finally tearing it to pieces. What happened? These participants themselves were more likely to act angry than control participants (without hormone treatment) were, and more likely to report themselves as in an angry mood.

In short, in a happy situation, the participants were happy; in an angry situation, angry. However, this was so *only* in participants who experienced physiological arousal *and* were given no explanation for it. Other participants, as noted earlier, were led to expect the tremors, the pounding heart, and so on, as an effect of the injection they had received. These participants were much less affected by the stooge's giddiness or anger.

Schachter and Singer interpret the findings as follows. If participants feel themselves in an aroused state, they seek an explanation for it. If they have been told to expect these symptoms, then they have their explanation. They can say, "My hands are shaking and my heart is pounding. Well, that's the drug; they told me it would have that effect." They do not *interpret* the aroused state as an emotion, and so they feel no emotion.

But if the participants feel this arousal *and* have no explanation for it, then they will seek an explanation, and the situation provides one. They may say, "That guy is really in a good [or angry] mood. And my heart is racing, and I'm breathing a bit hard . . . Perhaps I'm in a very good [or angry] mood too!" Having interpreted the state of arousal one way or the other, they feel and act accordingly.

To summarize, the emotion did not depend *only* on the physiological arousal. That was the same for happy-situation and angry-situation participants, and it was the same for those who were and were not told to expect their symptoms. The emotion depended also on how the arousal was interpreted. The emotional experience was not the physiological state per se, but the result of an interpretation of that state.

This experiment itself remains somewhat controversial (see Mook, 1996, for discussion and references). Not all of these differences met the usual criteria of statistical significance, and Schachter and Singer discarded some of their data on grounds that were reasonable (at least to this author), but unorthodox. However, it is now pretty clear that the idea was correct even if the evidence for it was flawed. Since the experiment was published, a very large number of other studies support its main conclusion: we can misinterpret a state of arousal as an emotional state (see Fiske, 1991; Mook, 1996).

In one of these studies, male participants were required to ride an exercise bicycle vigorously enough to induce physiological arousal. A little later, they rated the attractiveness of pictures of women. Their ratings were higher under conditions of arousal than under nonaroused conditions!

Another particularly ingenious experiment took the finding another step (Valins, 1966). Each participant, a male college student, looked at a series of pictures of women. He did this while listening to what he *thought* was the sound of his own heartbeat, fed back through earphones. In fact, the heart-rate sounds were controlled by the experimenter, but the participant did not know that. Then, with some slides but not others, the participant was made to hear an increase in "his" heart rate. And those were the slides that the participants tended to rate as most attractive—the pictures they *thought* had made their hearts go pitty-pat, though in fact they had not.

This study, then, further supports the earlier conclusions: we can mistake one source of arousal for another, just as we can mistake drug-induced arousal for emotional arousal. But it also adds something new: the physiological arousal need not even be there. If we *think* it is there, that is enough. We go on to make inferences about that, drawing conclusions about why our bodies are reacting the way we think they are.

This line of research has both practical and theoretical implications. On the practical side, we can see that if we are about to have an argument with our colleague or mate, and if we expect the other person to be angry, then right after a vigorous game of tennis might not be the best time to raise the issue. The arousal produced by the exercise could easily be mistaken for greater anger directed toward a person—ourselves, for example.

On the theoretical side, these findings seem quite surprising. Certainly they go against much common sense. As noted earlier, we feel that we ought to be able to just look inside ourselves and *see* how angry we are, or how attracted, but in fact we can mistake one source of arousal for another, quite different one.

We are sometimes told, "Trust your feelings. Your feelings are never wrong." Not true. We can be quite wrong about what we are feeling. Just as we can be mistaken about how hungry we are, so we can be mistaken about how angry we are, or happy, or attracted. That is because we do not just *feel*, we *interpret* our feelings—and the interpretation can be wrong.

Finally, there are some parallels between this view of emotion and other ideas that at first seem far removed. Consider Bartlett's work on memory (chapter 30). Remembering, he found, is not just reading an internal record of what happened; it consists largely of making inferences about what *must have happened*. Similarly for emotion. Perhaps we do not just feel our feelings; we interpret them, making inferences about what we *must be feeling* and why. In both cases, too, our inferences and interpretations leave room for error; they may simply be wrong. As one writer (Wilson, 2002) put it, we may be "strangers to ourselves" to a greater extent than we suppose.

BIBLIOGRAPHY

Fiske, S. (1991). *Social cognition*. New York: McGraw-Hill.

Mook, D. G. (1996). *Motivation: The organization of action* (2nd ed.). New York: Norton.

Schachter, S. (1982). *Emotion, obesity and crime*. San Francisco: Academic Press.

Schachter, S., & Singer, J. E. (1962). Cognitive, social, and physiological determinants of emotional state. *Psychological Review, 69*, 379–399.

Valins, S. (1966). Cognitive effects of false heart-rate feed-back. *Journal of Personality and Social Psychology, 4*, 400–408.

Wilson, T. (2002). *Strangers to ourselves: Discovering the adaptive unconscious*. Cambridge, MA: Harvard University Press.

17 | HERMAN AND POLIVY: HUMAN HUNGER AND COGNITION

Even simple biological motives involve cognition. Consider hunger and feeding, for example. Physiological controls are there, of course, but so are cognitive controls. We may refuse even a delicious food for religious reasons, or because we are allergic to it and it would cause hives, or—the present focus—because it contains more calories than we allow ourselves.

Stanley Schachter proposed an influential idea about cognition and feeding (Schachter, 1971; Schachter & Rodin, 1974): perhaps we have to *interpret* internal cues for hunger and satiety, just as we must interpret a state of emotional arousal, as he and Singer had shown (chapter 16). Perhaps those of us who eat too much do so in part because we either do not attend to internal cues for hunger and satiety, or do not interpret them correctly. The effect of this would be to weaken the internal controls over our eating. And, as in the Stage II lateral-hypothalamic rat (chapter 15), a weakening of internal control could leave feeding more responsive to *external* stimuli—such as the wide variety of very attractive and readily obtainable foods that abound in our society. An "obesity epidemic" could well result from this.

This idea remains controversial, but right or wrong, its exploration has taught us much. The work on *counter-regulation* by Herman and Polivy is an example.

C. Peter Herman (1946–) was born in Toronto. He took his B.A. at Yale in 1968 and his Ph.D. in 1972 at Columbia with Schachter. He taught at Northwestern, then returned to Toronto, where he became professor in 1983.

Janet Polivy (1951–) was born in New York City in 1951. She took her undergraduate degree at Tufts University in 1971 and her Ph.D. with Herman at Northwestern in 1974. She and Herman, now married, continue their productive scientific collaboration at Toronto.

It was while Herman was at Northwestern that his work on counter-regulation began, with a senior thesis by an undergraduate student, Deborah Mack.

By that time, Schachter's idea had given rise to an extensive research literature, most of it comparing obese with normal-weight people. There is a difficulty, however, in making such a comparison. Most overweight people consciously limit their food intake, or try to, in an attempt to lose weight. In effect, many of them walk around chronically hungry. So if one sees differences between one group and another, is it because the overweight people are overweight, or is it because the overweight people are hungrier? To find out, one can compare "restrained eaters" with "unrestrained eaters," where both are of normal weight—where, that is, voluntary restraint has succeeded in keeping weight within normal bounds for the restrained eaters.

So Herman and Mack (1975) compared two groups of normal-weight college women: a group of restrained eaters who were consciously restricting their food intake (as determined by questionnaire) and a group of unrestrained eaters who paid little attention to how much they ate.

The two groups were further subdivided at random into three subgroups each. The experiment was conducted as follows: When a participant came to the lab, she was first asked to drink down two big, rich milk shakes (for one subgroup), only one (for another), or none (for the third). Then each participant was offered a dish of ice cream and invited to eat as much as she wanted. What was of interest (though the participant did not know this) was how much ice cream she would eat. The design of the experiment is summarized in table 17.1.

The experimenters were quite unprepared for what happened.

First, consider what should have happened. The more milk shake a subject had just drunk, the less hungry she should be, and the less ice cream she should eat. As figure 17.1 (the solid line) shows, this is exactly what happened—for the unrestrained eaters.

Now, if restrained eaters are less responsive to their internal states, one might expect them to be less affected by the amount of milk shake they had drunk just before. This is what the experimenters expected. But in fact, the amount eaten by these participants was affected by the milk shakes—in the wrong direction (the dashed line). They ate *more* if they had just had one or two milkshakes than if they had not!

This *counter-regulation* makes no physiological sense at all. The effects of the milk shake should have reduced hunger, and reduced hunger should have led to less ice-cream intake, for both groups. For one it did; for the other it did the opposite. However, it might make good *cognitive* sense. If a restrained eater has just drunk down a lot of high-calorie milk shake, she may feel that her diet has already been violated. She may say, in effect, "Well, I've already blown my diet, so I might as well go ahead and enjoy myself and eat as much as I like." Hence this phenomenon has also been called the "what-the-hell effect."

There is another possibility, however. Perhaps the milk shake(s) had the effect of whetting the appetite, so that the restrained eaters were hungrier now. To check that possibility, Polivy (1976) did a follow-up experiment, this time comparing two groups of restrained eaters. In this case, both groups received the same food initially (pudding this time), but one group was led to believe that it was rich in calories; the other, that it was very low in calories. The first group showed the counter-regulation effect, but the second did not.

Since in fact the pudding itself was the same for all participants, any physiological appetite-whetting effect should have been the same. The difference between

Table 17.1
Design of the counter-regulation experiment

Status of participant	Number of milk shakes before ice cream		
	Zero	One	Two
Unrestrained	Unrestrained, no milk shake	Unrestrained, one milk shake	Unrestrained, two milk shakes
Restrained	Restrained, no milk shake	Restrained, one milk shake	Restrained, two milk shakes

groups, then, was a purely cognitive effect. It is the thought that counts: what mattered was what the subjects *thought* they had ingested.

This counter-regulation effect has now been seen many times (Herman & Polivy, 1980). There are limits. If participants have already taken in a *very* large amount of food before being tested, counter-regulation is not seen; both restrained and unrestrained eaters will then say, "I've had enough, thank you," and eat little or nothing. The very large meal seems to trigger a physiological control that affects both groups.

Putting these findings together, we get the image of a dual-control system. There are physiological controls that say, "I've had all I want," and cognitive controls that say, "I've had all I'm allowed." In restrained eaters, the cognitive control is set more restrictively, so it kicks in first. But that control also has a certain fragility to it. If the restrained eater believes her diet to be already violated, the cognitive control may collapse like a punctured soap bubble (a very Lewinian image; compare chapter 55). A large bout of further eating may then occur—the counter-regulation effect.

A strikingly similar account of the relapse process in alcohol abusers was put forward independently (Marlatt & Gordon, 1985). And recovering addicts of many kinds are warned against the dangerous idea that they can safely "have just one." Recovering alcohol abusers are warned, "First drink, then drunk," and ex-smokers are reminded, "You're one puff away from a pack a day."

In a later paper, Polivy and Herman (1985) relate these ideas to the feeding disorder known as *bulimia nervosa*. In this condition, periods of restrained eating are punctuated by binges in which control collapses and eating runs riot. The amounts eaten during a binge can stagger the imagination: as much as *seven pounds* of food have been eaten at one sitting!

Clearly, in such cases, voluntary control has indeed popped like a soap bubble, but even physiological controls may simply be ignored. A bulimic patient may

Figure 17.1
Counter-regulation in restrained eaters. From Herman & Polivy (1980).

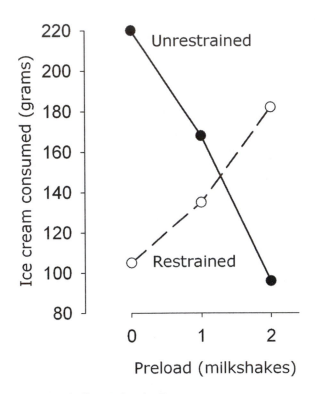

Source: Reprinted courtesy of Albert J. Stunkard.

say things like, "When I would binge, my stomach would get so full I would feel stuffed. I'd say, 'So what?' and go on eating anyway." Thus feeding behavior in bulimics may become nearly independent of the cognitive *and* the physiological controls that would otherwise keep ingestion within reasonable bounds. A possibility—though this idea is speculative—is that having learned to ignore internal hunger cues that say, "I want more!" the bulimic person also ignores physiological satiety cues that say, "I've had enough!"

If so, then these ideas, like Schachter's, underscore the central role of cognitive processes—perception, attention, and inference—in human motivation. To understand even "simple" motivated actions such as eating, it is not enough to know what the person's internal state is. We must also consider whether the person attends to the internal cues, how she interprets them, and what she decides to do about them.

BIBLIOGRAPHY

Herman, C. P., & Mack, D. (1975). Restrained and unrestrained eating. *Journal of Personality, 43*, 647–660.

Herman, C. P., & Polivy, J. (1980). Restrained eating. In A. J. Stunkard (Ed.), *Obesity* (pp. 208–225). Philadelphia: Saunders.

Marlatt, G. A., & Gordon, J. R. (1985). *Relapse prevention: Maintenance strategies in the treatment of addictive behaviors.* New York: Guilford Press.

Polivy, J. (1976). Perception of calories and regulation of intake in restrained and unrestrained subjects. *Addictive Behaviors, 1*, 237–243.

Polivy, J., & Herman, C. P. (1985). Dieting and bingeing: A causal analysis. *American Psychologist, 40*, 183–291.

Rodin, J. (1981). Current status of the internal-external hypothesis for obesity: What went wrong? *American Psychologist, 36*, 361–372.

Schachter, S. (1971). Some extraordinary facts about obese humans and rats. *American Psychologist, 26*, 129–144.

Schachter, S., & Rodin, J. (1974). *Obese humans and rats.* Potomac, MD: Lawrence Erlbaum Associates.

18 | WALTER MISCHEL AND SELF-CONTROL

> Understanding the transition from the young infant, who has virtually no impulse control and delay ability, to the adult who must have at least some self-control to survive, is one of the greatest challenges for students of human development.
>
> O. Ayduk and W. Mischel

We have motives to do, or to obtain, this or that, over the short term or the long. But very often, we must suppress or inhibit the direct expression of our motives, desires, or wishes. How do we do it? And can we learn to do it better?

There is a tendency in this society to think of self-control as a personal trait, something that people have or do not have to varying degrees. Thus, foolish or short-sighted actions are often attributed to "weakness of will" as a trait that some people carry around with them. Thus, Hillary Clinton's explanation for her husband Bill Clinton's infidelity was that it was a "sin of weakness," an inability to control himself.

However even if this is true, it would tell us little about the processes involved. First, how does "strength" or "weakness of will" work? Second—even if it is true—it cannot be the whole story. The "ability" to delay gratification turns out to depend very strongly on the specifics of the *situation* in which waiting occurs. This is enough to produce large differences among groups of participants formed at random—which means that there should be about as many strong- and weak-willed people in one group as in another. Yet the groups turn out to differ as the conditions of the situation—the independent variable—is manipulated. Something else is going on.

Walter Mischel, and his collaborators over the years, have shown this dependence on situational factors (see Mischel, 1996). Their findings suggest that self-control may depend upon a set of *skills* that can be taught.

Walter Mischel (1930–) was born in Vienna, Austria, and moved to New York when he was 10 years old. He took his Ph.D. at Ohio State in 1955. He was at Stanford from 1962 to 1983, then returned to New York at Columbia University, where he teaches at present.

In his early experiments on self-control, the procedure was as follows: Participants, usually young children, were told that they could have a highly valued reward, if they would wait before getting it. They could also have a reward right away, but the reward would be less desirable.

In such experiments, the rewards can be varied in age-appropriate ways, but for young children, something as simple as marshmallows or pretzels sticks will do. The children are told that they can wait until the experimenter returns and have two of the desired treats, or they can ring a bell and the experimenter will come back right away—but then they will get only one of the treats, not two. The children thus face a persisting dilemma. They prefer the larger reward and undertake to wait for it. As they wait, however, the delay becomes increasingly difficult and the children increasingly frustrated. They may give it up and settle for the smaller reward now.

In an early experiment (Mischel & Ebbeson, 1970), children four years old were given a choice of that kind, but under one of several conditions. In one, both the delayed and the immediate rewards were left exposed where the children could see both. In the second, both rewards were covered so that the children could not see them. And in the third and fourth conditions, one reward was covered while the other was left visible.

We would expect that if there were differences at all, leaving the large reward visible should be most effective in encouraging the children to wait. There is the large reward, visible for them to focus on, and a reminder of the big treat they can soon have. We might expect that thought to be a kind of temporary reward in itself, and that this would make waiting easier.

Quite the opposite happened. The children were able to wait much longer when both the immediate and the delayed rewards were hidden from view. Children under the other conditions (where they could see the immediate rewards, the delayed rewards, or both) only waited for very short times before yielding to temptation, calling in the experimenter by ringing the bell and accepting the immediately available reward.

In these experiments, what was varied was the physical presence of the desired objects during the period of waiting. It was expected that it would help the children anticipate, by *imagining*, the large reward they could have for waiting. Well then, suppose that what is varied is the *thought* of the objects—the images of them that the children have in their heads? In follow-up experiments (Mischel & Moore, 1973), the children waited (or failed to do so) in the presence not of the objects themselves, but of pictures of the objects shown by a slide projector. In other words, the rewards were not visible, but images of them were. The results of these experiments were the opposite of the previous ones: whereas the presence of the desired objects had made delay more difficult, the presence of pictures of the objects actually made delay easier!

Why should there be this reversal? In a further experiment, children were shown the actual rewards, but were told to imagine them as pictures, with frames around them; this was one condition. In the other, they were shown pictures but were asked to imagine them as real. This simple manipulation made a great difference. Whether the children were looking at real rewards or pictures, *thinking* of them as real made delay more difficult. Thinking about them as pictures made delay easier. Once again, it is the thought that counts.

But why should this be so? One possibility is that real objects, or stimuli thought of as real objects, may intensify the desire for those objects by emphasizing their desirable features. But thinking of the objects as pictures may have shifted the emphasis to the pictures (or objects) simply as thoughts, or as things to look at rather than as objects of desire. As one child said, "You can't eat the picture."

That idea too was tested, in another study. In this one, children were able to see the rewards (marshmallows), but here, again, different children were instructed to think about them in different ways. Some were told to think about the abstract, emotionless qualities of the objects—for example, thinking of the marshmallows as puffy white clouds. Others were told to think about the desirable qualities of marshmallows as things to eat—how, for example, the marshmallows would taste and feel in their mouths. Again, this purely cognitive manipulation made a great difference. When children thought about the pleasantness of the marshmallows, they were able to wait for only five minutes on average. But when they thought about their more abstract properties, their shape and color and the like, the average delay increased to a full 13 minutes.

Already the results suggest that there may be certain *strategies* for delaying gratification and taking the long view. This would involve shifting the focus of thoughts and images from the pleasures of the delayed reward to its less emotion-laden properties. If so, the effective strategies, if taught and practiced, might stand the participants in good stead in delay-of-gratification situations later in life.

In other writings, Mischel puts these ideas in broader context. Metcalfe and Mischel (1999) distinguish between a "hot" emotional system and a "cool" cognitive system. The former is a "go" system, disposed to react immediately to positive and negative emotion-provoking stimuli. The latter is a "know" system, tuned to the information that stimuli provide for cognitive processing. Thus, in the experiments described earlier, focusing on the good taste and feel of a marshmallow in the mouth is likely to activate the hot system, which fosters immediate gratification and so brings delay to an end. Focusing on the "cool" properties of a marshmallow, its color or the cloud its appearance suggests, calls up the cool system and makes delay less difficult.

If this is so, it follows that anything that calls up the hot emotional system should interfere with delay, even if it has nothing to do with the rewards. This strange-seeming prediction was in fact supported. In one experiment, some children were told to think *sad* thoughts while trying to wait for their bigger rewards. They were told, for example, to think about the last time they fell off a swing. Now, falling off a swing has nothing whatever to do with marshmallows, but it should call up the hot system concerned with emotional reactions, and so, like thinking about good tastes and textures, it should make waiting more difficult. And that is exactly what happened: children who were thinking of sad things, like those who were thinking of the yumminess of the rewards, were not able to wait as long as those who were steered to "cooler" thoughts.

Ayduk and Mischel (2002) go on to apply these ideas to other "hot" cognitive states, such as fear of rejection, that situations may trigger. The notion of "keeping our cool" thus takes on new meaning.

Finally, it is quite obvious that delay of gratification is only a part of what we call self-control. "A life goal like getting a college degree, for example, requires more than just waiting four years; it calls for studying, taking and passing courses, and resisting the diverse distractions and temptations along the route" (Ayduk & Mischel, 2002, p. 93). It can make a great difference, too, what one's beliefs are; whether, for example, one thinks that one *can* attain the goal in question and, therefore, whether control of one's impulses will be of any help in attaining it. Here Mischel's ideas make contact with Bandura's *self-efficacy* (chapter 25), and those of Seligman and his colleagues on *learned helplessness* (chapter 27).

So Mischel's group is studying a small part of a complex set of beliefs, habits, and strategies. But that is how science progresses: we take small bites, examining complex systems a few at a time. If we understand the pieces more clearly, then later we can better see how they fit together.

In any case, we have learned this much. In contrast to the popular view, self-control is not simply a trait that one has (or lacks) to varying degrees. Or if it is—if some are better at self-control than others—it may be because they have acquired certain skills that make them more competent at controlling their impulses so as to benefit in the longer term. These simple experiments make a very general point: there are strategies that one can adopt, and that one can be taught, that greatly affect one's mastery of the important skill called *delay of gratification*.

BIBLIOGRAPHY

Ayduk, O., & Mischel, W. (2002). When smart people behave stupidly: Reconciling inconsistencies in social emotional intelligence. In R. J. Sternberg (Ed.), *Why smart people can be so stupid* (pp. 86–105). New Haven: Yale University Press.

Metcalfe, J., & Mischel, W. (1999). A hot/cool system analysis of delay of gratification: Dynamics of willpower. *Psychological Review, 106,* 3–19.

Mischel, W. (1996). From good intentions to willpower. In P. M. Gollwitzer & J. A. Bargh (Eds.), *The psychology of action: Linking cognition and motivation to behavior* (pp. 197–218). New York: Guilford Press.

Mischel, W., & Ebbeson, E. R. (1970). Attention in delay of gratification. *Journal of Personality and Social Psychology, 16,* 329–337.

Mischel, W., & Moore, B. (1973). Effects of attention to symbolically presented rewards on self-control. *Journal of Personality and Social Psychology, 28,* 172–179.

Mischel, W., Shoda, Y., & Peake, P. (1988). The nature of adolescent competencies predicted by preschool delay of gratification. *Journal of Personality and Social Psychology, 54,* 687–696.

4 | LEARNING

19 EDWARD THORNDIKE AND THE LAW OF EFFECT

Darwin's theory of evolution implies that there is no sharp line of demarcation between humans and other animals, either in their gross physical structures or in the fine structure of the nervous system that control their behavior. If humans are able to solve problems in intelligent ways, we would expect at least the rudiments of such capabilities in other animals as well. Of the many who set out to investigate this possibility experimentally, Edward Thorndike was one of the earliest and most influential.

Edward Lee Thorndike (1874–1949) was born in Williamsburg, Massachusetts. After taking his B.A. at Wesleyan University 1895, he developed an interest in psychology from reading William James's *Principles of Psychology*, so he went to Harvard to study with James, taking a second B.A. in 1896. He set about studying the learning abilities of animals, beginning with chicks, which he incubated and hatched in his room in Cambridge. Unfortunately, as anyone who has worked with chicks knows, their tiny bodies can generate a formidable amount of sound. Thorndike's landlady could not tolerate the noise they made. So James took Thorndike, chicks and all, into the cellar of his own home, "much to the glee of the James children" (Boring, 1950, p. 562).

Shortly after that, Thorndike was offered a fellowship at Columbia under the auspices of James M. Cattell, a student of Wundt. So Thorndike and some of his more educated chicks moved to New York. There, dogs and cats could be accommodated, though Thorndike also continued to test the learning ability of chicks, using mazes made of books stood on end. Thorndike began a series of studies that were published in the year he got his degree, 1898. What he found was that animals were indeed able to solve the problems that he set them, doing things that would be called intelligent if humans did them. So he titled his book *Animal Intelligence*.

After taking his degree, Thorndike taught for a year at Western Reserve, then returned to Columbia in 1899, then joined the faculty at the Teachers College, where he remained until his retirement in 1940.

For his most famous animal experiments, Thorndike invented what he called a *problem box*. A cat might be confined uncomfortably in a little box, from which it could escape by making some response that was designated as correct—pulling a loop of string, for example, that would trip a latch, allowing a door to fall open so that the cat could escape confinement and, as a bonus, collect a bit of fish that been placed outside the door. (Or it could just take off, and have to be recaptured for the next trial.)

Thorndike measured the *latency* of the correct response—that is, from the time the door was closed on the cat, how long did it take the cat to make the correct response and escape from the box? What typically happened was that, when confronted with the problem for the first time, the cat would flounder around aimlessly, scratching and grooming and exploring, until by chance it happened to perform the act that was correct. Then, on successive trials, the response was likely to appear more and more promptly until the cat had mastered the task, and would make the correct response immediately upon being shut up in the box.

By measuring these latencies, Thorndike was able to plot learning curves, showing how long it took the cat to escape on the first trial, the second trial, and so on. Latency gradually declined over successive trials—that is, the correct response occurred more and more promptly. What struck Thorndike about these data was the *gradualness* of the change. We might expect that after an initial period of confusion, the cat would suddenly "make the connection," understand what it had to do to escape the box, and do it promptly thereafter. There should, in other words, be a sudden drop in its latency that should remain low thereafter. But that is not what happened. Instead, the time to escape diminished slowly and gradually over many trials.

It was as if the correct response were *gradually being strengthened* by the *reward* of escape from confinement (and fish). Unrewarded responses gradually dropped out. This was Thorndike's view, and he laid it down in his famous *law of effect*. Rewarded responses are gradually "stamped in," becoming stronger and stronger with successive rewards. We need not talk about what the animal "knows" or "comes to realize," but only about the *effect* that its action has in bringing about reward. Thorndike saw this as a process of forming and strengthening a connection between the stimulus situation *(S)* and the response *(R)*. As he put it, a response that is followed by a pleasant or satisfying consequence becomes more strongly connected to the situation in which it occurs. The more often the response is rewarded in that situation, the stronger the connection becomes.

He also stated the converse—if a response is followed by an unpleasant consequence, its connection to the situation is weakened—but he later discarded this idea. Finally, there was his *law of exercise*, to account for the effects of practice: the more often a response occurs in a situation, the more strongly it is connected to that situation. "Practice makes perfect," we say, but Thorndike would have corrected us: No, practice makes *habits*—that is, connections. It may be better, far better, not to practice at all than to practice wrong responses.

The law of effect, which we now call the *reinforcement principle*, has been either a fundamental principle or a target of intense criticism ever since Thorndike's day. Some behaviorists objected to it on the grounds that it speaks of subjective states such as satisfaction or annoyance, but Thorndike was careful to define these terms behaviorally: a satisfying state of affairs is one that an animal will work to bring about, and an annoying state of affairs is one that the animal will work to terminate.

Then, however, we encounter another difficulty: The principle begins to sound circular. Why will the animal work to achieve this or that? Because it is a reward. How do we know it's a reward? Why, because the animal works to achieve it! However, we can escape the circularity this way: if we identify an event as a reward in one experiment, we can predict that it will be a reward in another one as well. Thus, if we show that food for a hungry animal will reinforce, say, latch pulling in one situation, we can predict it will reinforce lever pressing in a different situation. Unfortunately, all this turns out not always to be true (chapter 24), but that became clear only much later.

These difficulties, however, did not seriously deter the acceptance of Thorndike's law of effect, at least by second-generation behaviorists. That actions are sensitive to their *rewarding and punishing consequences* is so clearly evident that it seems perverse not to accept it. But how does it work? And how important is it? Does it apply only to cats in boxes or chicks in mazes?

Thorndike titled his monograph *Animal Intelligence*. However, looking over his interpretation of his experiments, we see that he is really not assigning his animals much intelligence at all. A cat, while "learning" to escape from a problem box, is not really *doing* anything except making responses. It is the environment—the rewarding consequence of action—that "stamps in" the correct response over successive trials.

What then of the continuity between animal and human, the question with which we began? There would seem to be two possibilities: (*a*) perhaps animals are more intelligent than Thorndike gave them credit for, which was the view of Köhler (chapter 21) and Tolman (chapter 22); or (*b*) perhaps the human mind is simpler than we have supposed. "Connections" between situations and responses sound very much like the "associations" of Ebbinghaus (chapter 29) and, for that matter, of John Locke (chapter 2). Perhaps the human mind looks complicated only because there are so many associations, formed by experience of various situations, responses, and consequences. Its actual workings might be quite simple. Indeed, what we call intelligence in humans might actually be *measured* by the richness of connections with which the adult human is equipped. This was Thorndike's view. It put him in opposition with other students of intelligence, such as Charles Spearman, who contended that there was something like a faculty, or capability, that ran through a very wide variety of specific tasks. That controversy is still with us (Sternberg, 1999).

When Thorndike joined the faculty at Columbia in 1899, he began applying his ideas to education. An enormously influential paper, in collaboration with Robert S. Woodworth, challenged a popular view of education—the concept of *formal discipline*. The idea was that the mind had "faculties" that could, like muscles, be strengthened by exercise. Schoolchildren memorized poetry, for example, in order to strengthen their memories; they studied mathematics not for its own value, but to strengthen their faculties for logical analysis. Thorndike and Woodworth performed a series of experiments asking whether practice at one sort of problem would transfer to other problems. They concluded that this could indeed happen, but if it did, it was not because a general "faculty" had been strengthened. Rather, it was because the new problems had elements in common with the old ones. Now, the notion of an *element*—a small part of a complex whole—again recalls the Lockean conception of mind in which complex ideas (and cognitive capabilities) are made up of smaller ones, connected to each other. Then, if a new problem has elements in common with an old one, this simply means that some connections required by the new problem have already been formed, through practice and rewarded success, with the old one. If this is so, then the notion of strengthening this or that "faculty" is unnecessary. What one strengthens are connections.

That controversy, too, remains alive today. Does training in statistics, for example, lead to a more logical approach to data and problem solving in general? Results have been somewhat disappointing, just as Thorndike would have predicted.

"Thorndike retired in 1940 after four decades of service to Teachers College, but he kept working. In 1942 he went back to Harvard as William James Lecturer, honoring the memory of the great man who had lent him his cellar for his chicks forty-four years before" (Boring, 1950, pp. 563–564).

BIBLIOGRAPHY

Boring, E. G. (1950). *A history of experimental psychology* (2nd ed.). New York: Appleton-Century-Crofts.

Bower, G. H., & Hilgard, E. R. (1981). *Theories of learning* (5th ed.). Englewood Cliffs, NJ: Prentice-Hall.

Clifford, G. J. (1984). *Edward L. Thorndike: The sane positivist.* Middleton, CT: Wesleyan University Press.

Sternberg, R. J. (1999). *Cognitive psychology* (2nd ed.). New York: Harcourt Brace.

Thorndike, E. L. (1898). *Animal intelligence.* New York: Macmillan.

Thorndike, E. L. (1928). *The Measurement of intelligence.* New York: Teachers College, Columbia University.

20 IVAN PAVLOV AND CLASSICAL CONDITIONING

Ivan Pavlov was not a psychologist. He was a physiologist, and one of the most prestigious scientists in the world even before his discovery of classical, or Pavlovian, conditioning.

Ivan Petrovich Pavlov (1849–1936) was born in Ryazan in central Russia, where his father was a village priest. He was educated first at the church school in Ryazan and then at the theological seminary there. But he decided to become a scientist, and in 1870 he enrolled in the natural science curriculum. During his first year thereafter, he conducted an experiment on the physiology of the pancreatic nerves that won him a gold medal.

He went on to study at the Academy of Medical Surgery, where he completed his studies (winning another gold medal for research on circulation) in 1883. In 1890 Pavlov was invited to organize and direct the Department of Physiology at the Institute of Experimental Medicine, where he remained. This institute became one of the most important research centers in the world, and here Pavlov did the research on the physiology of digestion that won him the Nobel Prize in 1904. From this work also came his accidental discovery of conditioned reflexes, which he saw as a way of investigating the higher functions of the brain.

Pavlov was passionate about his science. According to George Miller, "During the [Russian] revolution he scolded one of his assistants for arriving ten minutes late for an experiment; shooting and fighting in the streets should not interfere when there was research to be done in the laboratory" (1962, pp. 179–180). He could not have been an easy man to work with. Yet his clear sense of what was right extended beyond his high scientific standards. In 1927, when the sons of priests were expelled from the medical schools by the Soviet government, he resigned as a professor of physiology, saying, "I am the son of a priest and if you expel the others, I will go, too" (p. 185).

Pavlov's interest was in how the nervous system works. Such a big question cannot be researched all at once, so Pavlov narrowed his thinking down to the study of salivary secretions. When an assistant placed food in a dog's mouth, Pavlov would collect saliva (through a tube into the mouth), and measure the amount of salivation that occurred in response to the food under various conditions.

However, a difficulty soon arose. After a while, the dog would begin to salivate as the assistant approached, *before* any food was placed in its mouth. Clearly that was a problem. Pavlov wanted to study salivation as a response to food in the mouth. He could hardly do that if salivation begins when there *is* no food in the mouth.

Pavlov decided, however, that what was happening here was even more interesting than the original question. Pavlov realized that he was watching the brain form a new connection, or pathway. The sight of the assistant, who brought food, had become connected in the brain with the arrival of the food itself. Salivation occurred in *anticipation* of that food.

Pavlov set out to study the formation of such connections. But the assistant was an unnecessary complication, and the dog had had experience with him before. Pavlov wanted to study the formation of a brand-new association, from the beginning. Therefore, he would begin his experiments with a "signal" that, at the start, had *no association at all* with food. He would sound the clicks of a metronome (or it could be any of a number of stimuli, such as the famous bell). A very brief time after that, he would place some food in the dog's mouth, by way of a pneumatic system that would blow a measured amount of food directly into its mouth. (That way, there was no approach of an assistant to complicate things.)

After a few such pairings, what is called *classical* or *Pavlovian conditioning* occurs. Salivation now begins to occur to the metronome alone. (This can be shown by occasional test trials in which the food is omitted. Or, if the signal comes first by a brief period, we may see salivation in response to the signal before the food comes.) The salivary response has become a *conditioned response* or *conditioned reflex.*

Pavlov and his assistants went on to explore the effects of varying the kind of signal used. It could, it seemed, be almost anything that the dog could detect—a bell, the sound of a metronome, a light going on, a light going off, and so on. He could study the effect of varying the interval between the signal for food and the food itself, the effects of presenting the signal without the food *(experimental extinction)*, and much more. Meanwhile other researchers, following Pavlov's lead, were extending the findings to other reflexes and other species, humans included.

Human salivary conditioning, in fact, is quite easy to demonstrate. Salivation can be measured by weighing a small wad of cotton (the kind that dentists use), placing it in the subject's mouth, removing it after a carefully timed period, and weighing it again. The gain in weight shows how much saliva has been produced. But the response can be something quite other than salivation. A puff of air delivered to the corner of the eye will trigger a reflex blink. If the puff is signaled by some neutral stimulus such as a tone, after a while the blink will begin to occur as a conditioned response to the tone alone, before the puff of air occurs. Or the change in skin conductance that accompanies a state of emotion or arousal—the *galvanic skin response*, or GSR—might be measured. That too can be conditioned to a light, or a tone, or a picture of a particular person—any signal, presumably, can be used in this way.

All these findings, varied as they were, fit into a rather simple framework, shown in figure 20.1. Begin with some signal or stimulus—the *unconditioned stimulus*, or UCS—which already triggers some reflex reaction. The response is the *unconditioned response*, or UCR. These can be any of a number of specific things—food in

Figure 20.1
Pavlovian or classical conditioning

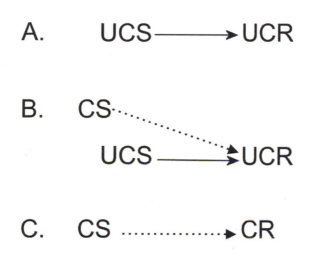

the mouth that evokes salivation, a puff of air on the eye that evokes a blink, a mild shock to the finger that elicits finger withdrawal, and so on. That signal is paired with another signal that initially does *not* trigger the response in question. This is the *conditioned stimulus*, or CS. It too can be different in different experiments: it might be a tone, the sound of a ticking metronome, a light going on, a light going off, or a touch on the skin—again, any of these will do. After a number of such pairings, we will begin to see the original response, the UCR, occurring in response to the CS alone. When that happens, we call it a *conditioned response* or *conditioned reflex* (CR).

Thus, figure 20.1 shows a summary picture of many such experiments in many species. Present any CS along with any UCS, many times, and we will see a "connection" forming, so that the CS comes to trigger the response (now a CR) on a greater and greater proportion of the trials.

Now, that conception of conditioning is too simple, and has had to be modified since Pavlov's day. Some reasons for this are discussed elsewhere (chapter 24). But the basic idea is still with us, and it extends far beyond saliva, and far beyond dogs.

First—and Pavlov made much of this—every variable in his conditioning experiments was *objective*. The tone, the food, the salivary flow—all are events that anyone can see and measure. For many centuries, philosophers had been talking about *associations* between one idea and another "in the mind" (chapter 2). But "ideas" *are* in the mind, locked up inside each person or animal where no one else can see them. In Pavlov's work, the association was between a stimulus and a response that anyone could observe. Anyone who doubted Pavlov's findings could repeat the experiments and see for him or herself. It is true that Ebbinghaus (chapter 29), a little earlier, had shown ways in which associations could be studied objectively in humans. But Pavlov showed how they could be studied objectively in *any* species. It's also true that the connection in the brain is hypothetical; we do not see it directly. But more modern methods of studying the brain have brought scientists much closer to seeing it directly, so that they can investigate how it works. Such research is still in progress today.

Apart from the question of how it takes place, the underlying *principles* of conditioning could shed some light on a number of real-life concerns, not just in dogs, and not just about salivation. Conditioning may well play a role in some of the *attitudes* we form. If a person has an emotional reaction (negative or positive) to members of certain groups, might this be a *conditioned* emotional reaction, occurring as a conditioned response to the mention of the group or to the presence of members of it?

Conditioning may play a role in the *fears* we acquire, and it might help explain the individuality and idiosyncrasy of these. One dog may salivate (or blink) at the occurrence of a tone, whereas another dog may ignore the tone but salivate (or blink) when a light goes off. The same response occurs to different stimuli in the two cases. This can be understood if the two dogs have different conditioning histories—that is, if salivation (or blinking) has been conditioned as a response to the tone in the one case, and to the light in the other.

Human behavior may include parallel cases. Perhaps John is afraid of dogs; James is not, but he is afraid of speaking before a group. The same response (fear) is evoked by different stimuli or situations. This too might result from differences in conditioning histories. Maybe James had been laughed at a number of times while giving an oral presentation, and perhaps the bad feelings associated with this became conditioned responses triggered by public-speaking situations. John may have had painful experiences with a dog. Or perhaps he has seen someone else react fearfully to dogs, and has picked up a conditioned fear reaction that way. Since Pavlov's time, we have learned that this sort of *vicarious conditioning* can and does occur.

Finally, if conditioning may play a role in the development of certain fears, it may also be used to eliminate them. In other words, it may be used as a *therapeutic* procedure (chapter 26).

Thus the concepts and methods of Pavlovian conditioning have very wide ramifications indeed. They may help explain some otherwise puzzling facets of human behavior.

BIBLIOGRAPHY

Babkin, B. P. (1949). *Pavlov: A biography*. Chicago: University of Chicago Press.

Boring, E. G. (1950). *A history of experimental psychology* (2nd ed.). New York: Appleton-Century-Crofts.

Bower, G. H., & Hilgard, E. R. (1981). *Theories of learning* (5th ed.). Englewood Cliffs, NJ: Prentice-Hall.

Miller, G. A. (1962). *Psychology: The science of mental life*. New York: Harper & Row.

Pavlov, I. P. (1927). *Conditioned reflexes: An investigation of the physiological activity of the cerebral cortex* (G. V. Anrep, Trans.). London: Oxford University Press, Humphrey Milford.

21 | WOLFGANG KÖHLER AND THE MENTALITY OF APES

Wolfgang Köhler (1887–1967) was one of the original Gestalt psychologists, along with Kurt Koffka and Max Wertheimer (chapter 2). Like them, he was convinced originally that for perception, but later for behavior too, the whole is not *made up of* its parts; rather, the parts are embedded in the whole, and their properties determined by it (chapter 2).

Köhler was born in Reval, Estonia. He took his Ph.D. at Berlin under Carl Stumpf, a contemporary (and intellectual rival) of Wundt. He then moved to Frankfurt, arriving there just before Max Wertheimer did (chapter 46), and the two, with Kurt Koffka, collaborated. Later he succeeded Stumpf at Berlin.

In 1913 Köhler became director of the Anthropoid Station of the Prussian Academy of Sciences on the Island of Tenerife, off the coast of Africa. He remained there through World War I. As to just why he was appointed, there may be an adventure story there; it is suggested that he was really there as a spy for the German government (Ley, 1990). In any case, his observations on chimpanzees led to his book *The Mentality of Apes*, published in German in 1917 and translated into English in 1925. Köhler came to America in 1934, moving to Harvard and then to Swarthmore College, where he continued to publish; his other books included *The Place of Value in a World of Facts*, published in 1938.

From his observations on apes in Tenerife, Köhler concluded that the Gestalt principles of perception (chapter 2) could also be seen in intelligent problem-solving behavior, and such behavior could indeed be intelligent, not just the mechanical "stamping in" or strengthening of successful responses, as Thorndike had argued earlier and as Skinner would argue later (chapters 19 and 23). It involves *insight*, which Köhler saw as a reorganization of the animal's perceptual field. This conclusion came from a variety of experiments, in particular the "box problems" and the "stick problems."

In the single-box problem, something attractive, such as a banana, is hung from the ceiling of the animal's cage, out of reach. It could be obtained by positioning a box underneath it and jumping from there. Once this problem was mastered, the chimp who was placed in a cage with a box and a banana would actually *turn away from the banana* first, in order to go get the box and position it. To Köhler, this initial "detour" was evidence that the whole sequence, leading to the desired outcome, was organized *as a whole* in the chimp's brain. There were other indications, too, of a reorganization in how the animal saw its world and the possibilities of the things within it. In one famous case, a chimp again turned away from the box, took Köhler by the hand, drew him over to where he would be useful, jumped up on his shoulders, and collected its prize—a solution that Köhler himself had not considered.

In the stick problem, the chimp had to use one or more sticks as tools to rake in food that was out of reach. Once the stick has been used successfully, Köhler reports, one can see the sudden reorganization of perception that occurs—the "Aha!" reaction.

The most dramatic of these experiments was conducted with a chimp named Sultan, an unusually gifted student. To get his reward, Sultan had to join two sticks together, one inside the other like a jointed fishing pole, and use the resulting long pole to get his food. Neither pole by itself was long enough. The solution to the problem came, apparently more or less by accident, when Sultan happened to line the two sticks up with each other end to end. Then the animal joined them and at once used the resulting long pole to draw in the food. Once having done the right thing, Sultan appeared to "see the point" and was able to repeat the solution promptly, over and over again, thereafter. From apparently random fiddling with the sticks, Sultan's behavior changed abruptly and lastingly to a purposive, well organized, and successful sequence of actions. It is as if Sultan's perceptual world had snapped into a new configuration, much as ours does when we see reversible figures (chapter 2).

Köhler argued, as Tolman would argue later (chapter 22), that purposiveness and insight of action are directly visible in the behavior. He quotes an observer as follows:

> [Sultan] first of all squats indifferently on the box, which has been left standing a little back from the railings; then he gets up, picks up the two sticks, sits down again on the box and plays carelessly with them. While doing this, if it happens that he finds himself holding one rod in either hand in such a way that they lie in a straight line; he pushes the thinner a little way into the opening of the thicker, jumps up and is already on the run towards the railings, to which he has up to now half turned his back, and begins to draw the banana towards him with the double stick. I call [Köhler]; meanwhile one of the animal's rods has fallen out of the other . . . whereupon he connects them again. (1927, p. 127)

This conception of problem solving was quite different from those of Thorndike's problem-box experiments (chapter 19). Thorndike was impressed with the *gradualness* of the change in the behavior of his animals; there was no evidence of any sudden insight. Köhler replied, Of course not! If a cat pulled on a loop of string to open the door of a problem box, this involved pulleys and latches that were hidden from the animal. There was no way that the animal could demonstrate whatever intelligence it had. And, in fact, when the conditions of the experiment are changed, even rats are capable not just of making responses, but of "seeing" the layout of a maze in a "cognitive map," and of taking "insightful" shortcuts when these are made available (chapter 22). These experiments, however, came later.

Köhler's conclusions were controversial and, indeed, remain so (see Bower & Hilgard, 1981). Writers in the behaviorist tradition have argued that, after all, Sultan had had extensive experience playing with sticks, so the response of extending a stick is well established. Where short sticks will not do, longer ones have often done the job before. When Sultan happens to line up the two sticks, he creates a stimulus situation that is very similar to the one provided by a single long stick. And that stimulus situation is already associated with the response sequence of extending the long stick and pulling in the desired object. The smoothness of its execution might only show that each segment of the response is already a well-established skill.

An insightful reorganization of perception, or the execution of a series of responses, the components of which are already available? That is the controversy, and it is interesting to note that the exactly analogous argument has arisen in connection with other claims for complex cognitive processes in apes—the question whether apes can use language, for example.

Other experiments, however, provide pretty convincing evidence that we do have to consider not just what the animal does and what has been rewarded, but also how it "sees" the situation. We know now that animals are quite capable of forming an internal *cognitive map* of a spatial layout (chapter 22), and of categorizing objects into complex internal *concepts* that they can then apply to new instances (chapter 42).

These more recent investigations provide more convincing answers than Köhler's experiments did. Nevertheless, his questions were surely right.

BIBLIOGRAPHY

Bower, G. H., & Hilgard, E. R. (1981). *Theories of learning* (5th ed.). Englewood Cliffs, NJ: Prentice-Hall.

Heidbreder, E. (1933). *Seven psychologies.* New York: Century.

Köhler, W. (1927). *The mentality of apes.* New York: Harcourt Brace.

Köhler, W. (1947). *Gestalt psychology.* New York: Liveright.

Ley, R. (1990). *A whisper of espionage.* Garden City Park, NJ: Avery Publishers.

22 EDWARD TOLMAN AND COGNITIVE MAPS

To early behaviorist writers, behavior was a matter of responding to stimuli—it consisted of stimulus-response, or S-R, relations. Learning was a matter of forming new stimulus-responds relations; this at least was the interpretation of Pavlov's experiments (chapter 20), and Thorndike's (chapter 19). And that was all one had to talk about; one need not consider cognitions, expectations, knowledge, or any other of the kinds of events that once had been called *mental.*

Not everyone thought it would work. The Gestalt psychologist Köhler insisted that even in apes, one had to consider how an animal perceives the situation (chapter 21). And even among behaviorists, some argued that one had to go beyond the visible stimuli and responses to make inferences about what was going on inside the animal's brain. Prominent among these was Edward C. Tolman.

Edward Chase Tolman (1886–1959) was born in Newton, Massachusetts, in 1886. He attended the Massachusetts Institute of Technology, studying engineering, but changed his career choice to philosophy after reading the works of William James, and later decided on psychology. In Germany he was introduced to Gestalt psychology. He received his doctorate at Harvard in 1915, then returned to Germany to learn more about Gestalt psychology. He became an instructor at the University of California in Berkeley in the fall of 1918, where he remained for the rest of his life. It was here that he conducted the many experiments that made him a founding father in the experimental study of animal cognition.

Tolman insisted that we must consider what is going on inside the animal, simply because we cannot make any sense of the behavior we see unless we do. Consider an animal that can, or could, press a lever for food. We observe that it does not press the lever now. Does that mean that it has not learned the lever-pressing response? Or does it mean that the animal is not hungry at the moment? Does it lack motivation, or does it lack the expectation that pressing the lever will produce food? These clearly are quite different, though the behavior is the same.

So, said Tolman, we have to consider internal variables such as motives and expectations. These processes intervene between the stimulus situation and whatever response occurs, so Tolman called them *intervening variables*. Perceptions, expectations, and the like are intervening variables of this kind.

That does not mean we cannot study them. Just as we can set up experiments that allow us to infer the properties of electrons, which we cannot observe directly, so we can set up experiments that allow us to infer the properties of internal cognitive operations. In other words, Tolman argued, we can study cognitive operations while remaining behaviorists, as long as we do the kinds of experiments that yield objective, observable data—and so allow us to make sound inferences about these operations.

Consider a rat that has mastered a maze. Placed in the start box, it now runs promptly to the goal box and collects its food reward. What has it learned? To make a series of *responses* in correct order? This would have been Thorndike's view (chapter 19). Or has it learned *where things are?* Does it represent in its head the spatial layout of the apparatus, forming what Tolman called a *cognitive map* of the situation and the objects, pathways, and rewards that were in it?

The way to find out is to pit the two possibilities against each other; in other words, to set up a situation where the two theories predict different outcomes. One early experiment by Tolman and his associates began with the apparatus shown at the top of figure 22.1.

It was an elevated maze, raised off the floor to discourage the rat from jumping down from it. A rat would be placed in the start box at point A, and it would learn to run across the circular arena to another alley at C, then to D, E, F, and finally G, where it would find a bit of food. Obviously, this was the long way around. A more direct route from the arena to the food box would have saved the rat time and energy, but no such shortcut was available. The rats were given five trials in this convoluted apparatus.

Then the animals were tested in a modified apparatus, shown at the bottom of figure 22.1. The original route was blocked, but instead there was a whole series of potential pathways radiating out from the central arena. The question was, would the rats choose the alley that pointed toward the original goal?

Notice how this second step separates the two possibilities: were the rats learning *to make responses*, or were they learning *where things were?* If the reinforcement had simply strengthened the responses that led to it, then the rats should choose one of the alleys adjacent to the original one; this was the closest possible *response* to the one that had been reinforced. On the other hand, if the rats had learned *where* the goal box was—if, in other words, they were able to represent the special layout as a cognitive map in their heads—then they should take the route that led directly to where the food was, even though they had never been reinforced for doing this.

And that is what happened. The numbers at the end of each alley represent the percentage of rats that choose that alley. We see that the shortcut was the overwhelming favorite. A little over a third of the animals chose it from among the 18 alternatives—far more than chose any other alley.

These and many other experiments, from Tolman's lab and those of others, made a strong case for a cognitive-map capability even in laboratory rats. They also revealed some properties of rats' mapmaking. If an animal is given too much training on the original problem, its behavior becomes more fixed and stereotyped;

Figure 22.1
A cognitive-map experiment. After training on a long-way-around route, will the rat take a pathway leading directly to the goal when offered one? If so, then rats can form a cognitive map of the spatial layout of the situation rather than just learning to make a series of responses.

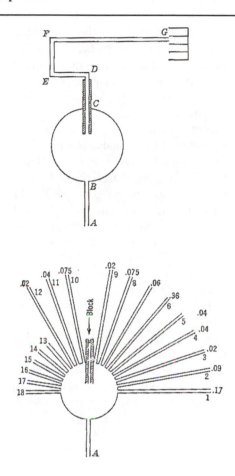

Source: From *Method and Theory in Experimental Psychology* by C. E. Osgood, copyright 1953 by Oxford University Press, Inc. Used by permission of Oxford University Press, Inc.

it is more likely to take the original route even if a shortcut is made available. As Tolman put it, the cognitive map becomes narrow and striplike (compare *mechanization*, chapter 38). The same may happen if the rat is too hungry; a moderate degree of hunger makes for better mapmakers. Thus, in addition to acquiring more evidence that cognitive maps exist even in rats, scientists began to learn something about the variables that affect them.

Since Tolman's time, his conclusion—even rats can learn where things are, and not just to make this or that response—has come to be generally accepted. Students of animal learning have gone on from there to ask other questions that build on that conclusion.

Just one example is the work on *radial mazes* as a tool for the study of memory (for discussion, see Kalat, 2001). In a radial maze, there is a central starting place, from which a number of alleys radiate outward. This time, however, each of the alleys is baited with a bit of food at the end (the food is recessed so that the animal cannot see it from the starting point). From the central starting place, the rat can run out to the end of any arm and collect its bit of food. It must then run back to the central place, and then it is free to choose another arm to run to. The original arm no longer has any food in it, for the rat has eaten it all.

After some exposure to the situation, the rat will run down one alley, pick up its bit of food and eat it, return to the central place, and then choose a *different* alley. An experienced rat, confronted with as many as eight arms of the maze, will visit all of them before returning to one it has already visited and which now has no food in it. In a word, the rat can remember *where it has been* and not go back there.

Rats with damage in the hippocampal area of the brain, a structure in the forebrain below the cerebral cortex, are not so good at this. They seem to remember the task itself; placed at the start, they will run promptly down one of the alleys and eat the food. The difference shows up on succeeding trials, where they are far more likely than normal rats to revisit an arm where they have already eaten all the food there is.

The structures damaged in these experiments are closely related to structures whose damage produced amnesia for recent events in the patient H. M. (chapter 31). And efficient food gathering in this situation requires the use of short-term memory: the rat must remember which arms it has already visited on this particular session. Thus this kind of experiment can be used to study the role of the brain in internal mapmaking, navigation, and memory.

That such studies can be conducted today owes a great deal to Tolman's pioneering experiments, which show not only that rats *have* cognitive maps, but also how to study them and learn what properties they have and what brain mechanisms underlie them. And he taught us that even the laboratory rat has rather impressive cognitive capabilities.

BIBLIOGRAPHY

Bower, G. H., & Hilgard, E. R. (1981). *Theories of learning* (5th ed.). Englewood Cliffs, NJ: Prentice-Hall.

Kalat, J. W. (2001). *Biological psychology* (7th ed.). Belmont, CA: Wadsworth.

Tolman, E. (1933). Sign-Gestalt or conditioned reflex? *Psychological Review, 40,* 246–255.

Tolman, E., Ritchie, B., & Kalish, D. (1947). Studies in spatial learning: V. Response learning vs. place learning by the non-correction method. *Journal of Experimental Psychology, 37,* 285–292.

Tolman, E. C. (1932). *Purposive behavior in animals and men.* New York: Appleton-Century-Crofts.

23 B. F. SKINNER AND OPERANT CONDITIONING

> The major problems of the world today can be solved only if we improve our understanding of human behavior.
>
> B. F. Skinner

B. F. Skinner became, and remained, by far the most influential spokesman for an uncompromising behaviorism: psychology is about behavior, not about the mind, and not about the nervous system. It deals only with variables that can be directly observed, and its task is to show how behavior is related to the variables that influence it. He and his students and collaborators amassed a formidable body of experimental findings.

He also caught the public eye with his ideas about how such findings could be put to use by society. In doing so, he drew intense criticism (and misunderstanding) from many quarters. Partly as a result of this, he is probably the experimental psychologist whose name is most familiar to the general public.

Burrhus F. Skinner (1904–90) was born in Susquehanna, Pennsylvania. After graduating from Hamilton College, Skinner decided to become a writer. But he wrote little. Moving to New York City, where he worked as a bookstore clerk, he came across the writings of Pavlov and Watson and was intrigued by them. So, to learn more, he enrolled in the Psychology Department of Harvard University. At Harvard he fell in with a physiologist, William Crozier, who was interested in studying the behavior of "the animal as a whole," as contrasted with the reflexes and conditioned reflexes of physiologists such as Pavlov. So Skinner began a program of experimental research that he never abandoned. The two departments, psychology and physiology, each assumed that the other was supervising the young student. But labels meant little to Skinner. He was happily studying behavior.

Skinner, like Thorndike (chapter 19), quickly became convinced of the great power that reward, or reinforcement, can exert on behavior. More or less by accident, he invented the *Skinner box* (though he himself never called it that, preferring the term *operant chamber*). This was a small enclosure in which there was a response to be made (a lever for a rat to press, or a disk mounted on the wall for a pigeon to peck), and a means of delivering a reinforcement (a bit of food, a sip of water, or anything else for which his animal would work). The reward having been delivered, the rat or pigeon was free to respond again. In this, the situation was a great improvement on Thorndike's. After Thorndike's cat had escaped its "problem box," it had to be caught and placed back in it again. Not so for Skinner. After reinforcement, the animal remained where it was, and Skinner could collect *his* reward of not having to catch and replace it (Skinner, 1956).

He also invented a mechanical device for automatically recording fine differences in the rate of response. Indeed, he was one of the pioneers of automation in behavioral research: responses could be detected, recorded, and followed up with reinforcements, all by automatic apparatus.

(Perhaps this is the place to note that after Skinner's first daughter was born, he, an enthusiastic gadgeteer, built a special crib that enhanced both her comfort and that of her parents. He made the mistake of sending an article about this crib to a popular magazine, which titled its story "Baby in a Box." The urban legend grew up that he raised his daughter in a Skinner box, and that she later became insane or committed suicide or both. None of this is true. The "box" was simply an improved crib, and Skinner's daughter is a successful artist who lives in England with her husband.)

Rather than focusing upon the things that happen *before* a response occurs, as with Pavlov's conditioned reflexes, Skinner found (as had Thorndike) that the events *following* the response had a great influence on its subsequent rate of occurrence. If food was presented to a hungry rat after it had pressed a lever, the rate of lever pressing would increase. This he called *operant conditioning*: if a response (the operant) is followed by a reinforcing stimulus, response strength is increased. And food, for a hungry rat, is a reinforcing stimulus. This is not circular. It means that an operant and a reinforcer are jointly defined by an experimental outcome. If we see this experimental outcome, then we say (*a*) that the lever press is an operant, and (*b*) that food is a reinforcing stimulus. The two are defined jointly by that outcome.

Other concepts are defined behaviorally in similar ways. If, for example, an animal is reinforced for lever pressing only if a light is on, and is never reinforced if it is off, then the animal will come to press at a much higher rate when the light is on than when it is off. This is *discrimination*. It is important to understand that for Skinner, that experimental finding is not a reflection of, or indication of, a process of discrimination going on somewhere inside the animal. It *is* discrimination. The term is used only to describe the behavior, and not to refer to any underlying process that cannot be directly observed or described.

In his later work, Skinner found that the pigeon had certain advantages over the rat as an experimental subject. Pigeons are not good a pressing levers, but they are quite good at pecking a little disk mounted on the wall of the box, known as a *pecking key* by analogy to a telegraph key. Skinner began a series of investigations of pigeon behavior, focusing on the effects of various schedules of reinforcement (described later). His classic book *Schedules of Reinforcement*, describing this work, was published with Charles B. Ferster (Ferster & Skinner, 1957).

A *schedule of reinforcement* is one in which reinforcement it is made available to the subject or participant only some of the time, according to certain rules; these rules define the schedule. And it turns out that different schedules give rise to character-istically different patterns of operant behavior. The simpler ones are as follows:

Fixed ratio. Every *n*th response is reinforced. Thus, for instance, every 10th response the animal makes may be reinforced; that would be FR 10. After receiving a rein-forcement, the animal must respond 10 times more to obtain the next reinforce-ment. The ratio, in other words, is the ratio of responses to reinforcements. On such a schedule, the animal will typically pause after each reinforcement, and then run off the next series of responses at a high rate (the "break-and-burst" pattern).

Fixed interval. A reinforcement becomes available after a fixed period of time (the "fixed interval") following the previous reinforcement. Thus with FI 10, after a reinforcement, no further reinforcement is available until 10 minutes have passed. The next response after that is reinforced. The reinforcement is not delivered automatically; the animal still has to make the response in order to receive it. On an FI schedule, the animal will come to make only a few responses immediately after reinforcement, but then will respond at a gradually increasing rate until the next reinforcement occurs.

Variable interval. In this case, a reinforcement is made available at variable intervals following a reinforcement. This means that reinforcement could become available any time, and there is no cue that tells the rat or pigeon when it is available. On a VI schedule, one will typically see a steady, moderate rate of response throughout the session.

There are other schedules, and they may be combined in various ways. Two things are worth noting about these schedules of reinforcement. First, they exert remarkably powerful control over the behavior of an organism in a controlled situ-ation. The various patterns just described are seen, not in group averages, but in the behavior of individual organisms (rats, mice, monkeys, or humans working for "points" that can be exchanged for something desirable). One can even show the change from one pattern to another within a single experimental section, in a single animal. One can arrange matters, for example, so that the pecking key is some-times colored red (by a colored Christmas tree lights that turns on behind it), and sometimes green. (Pigeons have color vision.) When the key is red, a fixed-ratio schedule is in effect. When it is green, a variable-interval schedule is in effect. Sure enough, as long as the key is red, one sees the break-and-burst fixed-ratio pattern; when it is green, one sees the steady response rate maintained over time. This is known as a *multiple schedule*, and this complex result, too, is seen in individual ani-mals—be they pigeons, rats, monkeys, or human beings working for points. Such consistent findings surely must mean that the conditions of reinforcement are of very great importance.

Convinced of this, Skinner, while continuing to experiment, wrote a series of books extending the idea to human behavior in society. He wrote a psychology text-book on the theme (Skinner, 1953), a utopian novel (Skinner, 1948; not all critics thought it utopian), and a critique of the concept of free will, which, like Watson, he thought a dangerous superstition (Skinner, 1971). It need hardly be said that the writings were controversial. Skinner was accused of wanting to "condition" a soci-ety of mindless automata. But this is a bad misreading. He was only arguing that behavior is controlled by reinforcement anyway, so we might as well arrange mat-ters so that the actions we all agree are desirable are the ones that are reinforced.

As a specific example: It used to be common practice to shower schoolchildren with praise and gold stars just for being there, in an attempt to raise their "self-esteem." It does seem that self-esteem is *correlated with* achievement, but the evidence is that the self-esteem is the result of achievement, not the cause. To present reinforcement no matter what a child does makes as much sense, to Skinner, as presenting food to a rat from time to time no matter what it does. We will not see much lever pressing.

On the other hand, most writers today feel that Skinner neglected too much in turning his back on cognition. The studies of cognitive maps and the work that came from these studies (chapter 22) show that we do need to consider not just the situation, but also what the organism (rat or human) makes of it—*and* that these internal events can be studied. Moreover, the use of external reinforcers can back-fire. Even if it is effective, it can undermine the *intrinsic* rewards of creating and exploring—that is, the rewards of performing these activities for their own sake (chapter 28).

That said, we must still acknowledge the very real accomplishments of Skinner's approach. One pair of authors (Wade & Tavris, 2000, p. 278) gives the following very partial list:

> Behaviorists have taught parents to toilet-train their children in only a few sessions. They have taught autistic children who have never before spoken to use a vocabulary of several hundred words. They have trained disturbed and mentally retarded adults to communicate, dress themselves, mingle socially with others, and earn a living. They have taught brain-damaged patients to control inappropriate behavior, focus their attention, and improve their language abilities. And they have helped ordinary folk get rid of such unwanted habits, such as smoking or nail biting, or acquire wanted ones, such as practicing the piano or studying. [References to these studies are given by Wade & Tavris (2000).]

At a meeting of the American Psychological Association 10 days before his death from leukemia, Skinner give a talk before a crowded auditorium. He then wrote a version of the talk for publication and finished the write-up on August 18, 1990, the day he died.

BIBLIOGRAPHY

Bower, G. H., & Hilgard, E. R. (1981). *Theories of learning* (5th ed.). Englewood Cliffs, NJ: Prentice-Hall.

Ferster, C. B., & Skinner, B. F. (1957). *Schedules of reinforcement.* New York: Appleton-Century-Crofts.

Skinner, B. F. (1938). *The behavior of organisms.* New York: Appleton-Century-Crofts.

Skinner, B. F. (1948). *Walden Two.* New York: Macmillan.

Skinner, B. F. (1953). *Science and human behavior.* New York: Free Press.

Skinner, B. F. (1956). A case history in scientific method. *American Psychologist, 11,* 221–233.

Skinner, B. F. (1971). *Beyond freedom and dignity.* New York: Knopf.

Wade, C., & Tavris, C. (2000). *Psychology* (6th ed.). Upper Saddle River, NJ: Prentice-Hall.

24 JOHN GARCIA: CONDITIONED TASTE AVERSION

By the 1950s, Pavlov's discovery, classical or Pavlovian conditioning, had been extensively studied in laboratories all over the world. The laws it followed seemed well established.

In classical conditioning, some neutral stimulus (or CS), which did *not* elicit the response in question, is paired repeatedly with another stimulus, the UCS, which does. One then sees the gradual development of a new reflex, such that the CS now triggers the response where it did not do so before. That is classical conditioning (figure 24.1).

Though dispute continued about just how it worked, three principles seemed so well established as to be beyond serious dispute. First, it doesn't seem to matter what CS, what UCS, or even what species is used. One can condition salivation in dogs (or humans) to the sound of bubbling water. One can pair a shock to the foot, or a shock to the finger, with a tone and see conditioned leg flexion in goats or conditioned finger flexion in humans. One can pair a clicking sound with a shock and see conditioned freezing in rats. Or one can pair a shock with the onset of a light and see a conditioned scrunching-up response in flatworms. It seems that *the specific choice of CS, UCS, and species is arbitrary.*

Second, *conditioning is a slow, gradual process.* Even in humans, it takes many pairings of CS and UCS before conditioning will be seen.

Third, *the interval between CS and UCS is quite critical, and must be short.* In many conditioning experiments, the procedure works best if there is an interval of about half a second between the onset of the CS (like a tone) or the UCS (like a shock). Let the interval be much longer than that, and conditioning will not occur.

Then, in the 1960s, came the catastrophic experiments of John Garcia and his colleagues, showing that all of these "principles of conditioning" were really only "principles of *some* conditioning." In other cases, it was quite possible in some species to get a strong conditioned response after only *one* CS-UCS pairing, with an interval between CS and UCS that was measured in hours! All of our "principles"

Figure 24.1
The early conception of classical or Pavlovian conditioning. It should not much matter just what the CS and UCS are, as long as the former is detectable and the latter calls forth a response. Garcia showed that matters are not so simple.

turn out to hold for only some cases, not for all—and those cases might turn out to be the exceptional ones.

John Garcia (1917–) was born in Santa Rosa, California. After working on farms and in shipyards, he earned his B.A. in 1948 (at age 31), his M.A. in 1949, and his Ph.D. in 1965, all at the University of California at Berkeley. He worked at the U.S. Radiological Defense Laboratory and has taught in the Oakland, California, public schools; at the State University of New York at Stony Brook; and at the University of Utah. He returned to Berkeley in 1973 as a professor of psychology and psychiatry, and is now a professor emeritus there.

It was while working at the U.S. Radiological Defense Laboratory that he noticed something strange. Radiation produces nausea in humans and behavioral signs of nausea in rats. Garcia noticed that after his rats got sick, they began rejecting their food—perfectly ordinary, harmless rat food. This was not just because they were feeling sick at the time. Even after they got better, they fed reluctantly. It was as if they blamed the food for the illness.

As a matter of fact, something very much like this is a quite common human experience, though neglected by learning theorists until recently. One psychologist realized that the rats' reactions closely matched his own on an occasion when he went out to eat, had steak with béarnaise sauce, and then got violently ill. He learned the next day that stomach flu was sweeping the department, so his illness was almost surely produced by the flu and not the sauce. It didn't matter. He now had a violent dislike for béarnaise sauce, a dislike that lasted for years.

Might rats—and other omnivores, like humans—be particularly quick to form an association specifically between *taste* and *illness?* Garcia and his collaborators decided to find out.

In one of the early experiments (Garcia, Ervin, & Koelling, 1966), the procedure was as follows. Rats were allowed to drink something novel and tasty—a saccharin solution. Saccharin apparently tastes sweet to rats, as it does to humans; they drink it with great enthusiasm when it is offered, and they did so here.

Then, a half hour after that, Garcia's rats were made sick by X-irradiation. A separate control group of rats was made sick in the same way, but without having drunk saccharin first. In both cases this was done only once.

Three days later, the rats in each group were simply offered the saccharin solution to drink. The control rats, whose illness had not been paired with saccharin, drank copious quantities of it now. But the experimental rats, who had been made sick *after* having drunk saccharin, now refused it, drinking very little.

In its framework, this conditioning experiment is analogous to Pavlov's experiments. The conditioned stimulus (CS) is the sweet saccharin solution; the unconditioned stimulus (UCS) is the illness-inducing agent. Then, if the animal later refuses the sweet solution, we say that it has formed a *conditioned aversion* to the sweet taste of the solution. So, in this case, the rats in the experimental group had formed such a conditioned aversion. The rats in the control group had not, because saccharin had not been paired with the illness. (That control group was necessary to rule out the possibility that illness, all by itself, might lead the rats to reject all unfamiliar solutions or foods. Clearly it did not, for the control rats did accept the saccharin solution.)

The finding encountered vigorous protest. This is not surprising, for it flew in the face of everything scientists thought they knew about conditioning. Suppose that Pavlov had sounded a bell to a dog, and then come back hours later and popped some food in the animal's mouth. Would he have seen conditioned salivation—after one such experience? Of course not!

But Garcia was showing that something very much like that could happen, if one chose the *right* CS-UCS combination. The conditioned aversion was formed with a *single* pairing of the saccharin taste with illness, even though they were separated by a full 30 minutes. Later experiments showed that they could be separated by many hours and conditioning would still occur—in one trial.

A typical reaction was that of a professor who, hearing of Garcia's findings, said to him: "Young man, that is completely impossible. The animal does not get sick from radiation until half an hour or more after it tastes the saccharin, and you cannot get any learning with such a big delay of the consequence, certainly not in one trial" (Bolles, 1993, p. 334). Conditioning just is not like that!

So strong was this kind of reaction that Garcia and his colleagues initially had a great deal of trouble getting their results published. Researchers in the field simply did not believe them. But Garcia persisted, and the experiments were replicated, and the results held.

Even so, one could have lingering doubts. Saccharin has a strong aftertaste that lasts for some time. It might last for hours, some argued; in which case maybe the aftertaste was still there when the illness came on. The reaction of aversion might be conditioned to the *aftertaste* of saccharin, and it might have generalized to the taste of saccharin itself when the test was conducted later. Or another possibility: perhaps nausea is such a very potent stimulus that a conditioned connection between nausea and *any* arbitrary CS would form especially rapidly.

But all this is not so, and was ruled out by a particularly elegant experiment, again by Garcia and his colleagues (Garcia & Koelling, 1966). To anticipate: What this experiment showed is that there is nothing special about saccharin as a CS or about illness as a UCS. It is the *combination* that counts: rats are particularly good at learning the *relation between* tastes and nausea.

Garcia and his colleagues reasoned as follows. A saccharin solution is really just water with a sweet taste added. One could add different stimuli to water just as well. So, in one group of thirsty rats, water was offered to drink, and an electronic sensing device was set up so that when the rat lapped at the water, lights flashed and bells rang. Instead of sweet water, these rats were drinking "bright noisy water." Under another condition, rats drink the saccharin-flavored "sweet water" as before. The point is that in both cases, something is being added to plain water: a sweet taste in one case, lights and noises in the other.

In addition to this, the investigators compared two different UCSs: illness and mild electric shock. In other words, some rats were made sick after they drank their fluid; but others were shocked instead. So we have four possible combinations of the two CSs and the two UCSs (table 24.1).

What happened? The conditioned avoidance response (refusal of the drinking fluid) depended on the combination of the CS and UCS that was used. If the rats were drinking sweet water, then nausea was much more effective than shock in producing a conditioned taste aversion. But if they were drinking bright noisy water instead, then the reverse was true: shock was more effective than nausea. In other words, nausea was not more effective than shock across the board; it was effective only if it was paired with taste. And the saccharin taste (sweet water) was not more effective than bright noisy water across the board; it led to rejection only if it was paired with nausea. Therefore, it is the *combination* that counts. Rats are particularly good at learning a connection between taste and nausea, but not so good at learning a connection between light-and-sound and nausea. With shock instead of nausea, the reverse is true.

A large number of studies have since been conducted in a number of species, including humans. In the human case, an elegant set of experiments by Ilene Bernstein (1978) took advantage of a kind of natural experiment. Teenage children who had cancer were receiving chemotherapy, which produces nausea. Bernstein arranged for them to taste a new and unfamiliar flavor of ice cream (Maple Toff) a few hours before the scheduled chemotherapy. After *one* such pairing of the novel taste with illness, the children rejected the new ice cream when offered it. Control groups, which had the ice cream without the illness or the illness without the ice cream, showed no such rejection.

What is most striking about these findings is this: The children *knew perfectly well* that what had made them sick was the chemotherapy, not the ice cream. They said so when asked. It didn't matter. They just didn't like that flavor of ice cream anymore! Apparently, here, as in the béarnaise-sauce phenomenon, conscious knowledge has very little to do with conditioned taste aversions.

The conclusion is now well established: a number of species, including rats and humans, are particularly talented at learning a connection *specifically between taste and illness.*

The implications of this are considerable. The Lockean "blank slate" conception of mind (chapter 2) implies the following: We should be able to learn that "*this* goes with *that*" for any pair of *this*es and *that*s with equal ease. But that is just not so. Certain stimuli "go with" certain others, so that, as one writer put it (Seligman, 1970), we are *prepared* to connect one with the other. Thus we are prepared to connect taste with nausea. As a result, we learn the taste-nausea connection very quickly. But we are not prepared to connect taste with pain—or, for that matter, bells with food in the mouth! These connections are "unprepared"—we learn them slowly if we learn them at all.

It used to be popular to distinguish "innate" and "acquired" responses to stimuli, or "instinctive" and "learned." These experiments, and many others, show that that division has to be reconsidered. *The ability to learn certain things can itself be instinctive.* What we have, in taste-aversion learning, is an *instinctive readiness to learn* certain sorts of things. If rats and humans are "prepared" to associate taste with illness, there must be a reason for this. The most likely reason is that both rats and humans are omnivores, capable of eating almost anything, and so they face the problem of distinguishing what is edible from what is dangerous. A mechanism for associating

Table 24.1
Design and results of the Garcia and Koelling experiment

Conditioned stimulus (CS)	Paired with (UCS)	Result
Sweet water	Illness	Conditioned aversion
Bright noisy water	Illness	No conditioning
Sweet water	Shock	No conditioning
Bright noisy water	Shock	Conditioned aversion

taste with illness, rapidly and with only one experience, would be very useful in our learning to avoid poisonous substances. And it would seem that we humans, along with rats and other species, evolved just such a mechanism.

But not all species have done this. If all this is so, it would follow that animals who do not identify food by taste, but in some other way, might be especially good at associating *different* sensations with nausea. This seems to be the case. For example, many birds—quail, for example—choose their foods on the basis of vision, not taste. And, sure enough, quail quickly learn to avoid a food with a characteristic *color* if it makes them sick after they eat it. They are not so good at avoiding foods that have a characteristic *taste* under such conditions.

In short, specific learning mechanisms, or "preparednesses," are themselves products of evolution. We can't draw a line and say, "This behavior is instinctive and that behavior is learned." Instead, we seem to have *instinctive* tendencies to *learn* some things, but not others.

How general is this conclusion? It may be very general indeed. To this point, we have been talking about the pairing of one event with another—that is, classical or Pavlovian conditioning. But once alerted to the importance of preparedness, researchers began looking for it in other contexts too, and found it. Take, for example, operant conditioning and the reinforcement principle (chapters 19 and 23). Stated abstractly: If a response (any response) is followed by a reinforcer (any reinforcer), the frequency of that response increases. Therefore, any reinforcer should strengthen any response. But this is not so. Some reinforcing events work very well with some responses, but not with others. Some responses are easily strengthened by one reinforcer, but not by another that may be very effective with a different response (Shettleworth, 1987). As with taste-aversion learning, some combinations work well, others poorly or not at all.

One further example. Something that human beings are surely prepared for is the learning of language (Rozin, 1976). Consider this apparent paradox: A child hears the spoken language of its community under what should be very poor conditions for learning—the child hears the grown-ups speak in fragmented sentences, interspersed with "uh" and "ah" and with parts inaudible, and all while a great deal else is going on. Yet virtually all children learn to speak, and they learn it rapidly,

151

effortlessly, and joyfully. But what happens when they must learn to read? Logically, this should be a far easier task. They should only have to memorize the sounds that letters represent, and presto! they should be fluent readers. But this is not what happens. This "unprepared" task is learned relatively slowly and, for many, with great difficulty—or not at all.

Aside from specific instances, these findings and ideas may lead us to rethink some fundamental issues about what the mind itself is like. John Locke (chapter 2) compared the mind to a blank tablet on which experience writes. This idea assumes that experience is free to write down a record of whatever "happens to happen." But this may not be true. Rather than Locke's blank tablet, we might think of the mind as something like a Swiss Army knife. It may be a set of tools, each one specialized for dealing with certain kinds of problems—problems like determining what events lead to pain, in one case, or what events lead to nausea, in another. These problems will be the sorts of problems that our remote ancestors encountered during prehistory, so that we may have evolved specialized cognitive tools designed specifically for each such set of problems.

At this point, it may seem that we've moved a long way away from rats and saccharin solutions! We have. But as is so often the case, little findings can bear on very large issues. Garcia's experiments are not "about" rats and saccharin solutions. They are "about" what learning is like, and whether the principles we once thought we had in hand are really as solid as we thought. And they are about what the *mind* is like, even for the lowly rat. Lockean blank slate, or Swiss Army knife (reminding us of the Kantian machine shop)? The pendulum is moving toward the latter. Garcia's experiments have given it a vigorous push in that direction.

BIBLIOGRAPHY

Bernstein, I. L. (1978). Learned taste aversions in children receiving chemotherapy. *Science, 200*, 1302–1303.

Bolles, R. C. (1993). *The story of psychology: A thematic history*. Belmont, CA: Brooks/Cole.

Garcia, J., Ervin, F. R., & Koelling, R. A. (1966). Learning with prolonged delay of reinforcement. *Psychonomic Science, 5*, 121–122.

Garcia, J., & Koelling, R. A. (1966). The relation of cue to consequence in avoidance learning. *Psychonomic Science, 4*, 123–124.

Pinker, S. (2002). *The blank slate*. New York: Penguin.

Rozin, P. (1976). The evolution of intelligence and access to the cognitive unconscious. *Progress in Psychobiology and Physiological Psychology, 6*, 245–289.

Seligman, M. E. P. (1970). On the generality of the laws of learning. *Psychological Review, 77*, 406–418.

Shettleworth, S. (1987). Foraging, memory, and constraints on learning. In N. S. Braveman & P. Bronstein (Eds.), *Experimental assessments and clinical applications of conditioned food aversions* (Vol. 443, pp. 216–226). New York: New York Academy of Sciences.

Shettleworth, S. J. (1998). *Cognition, evolution, and behavior*. New York: Oxford University Press.

25 ALBERT BANDURA: IMITATION AND SOCIAL LEARNING

Social learning theory can be seen as a fusion of the later, "neobehavioristic" approaches to behavior (chapter 10) with the more recent cognitive concepts. Social learning theory recognizes the contributions to knowledge made by the objective study of learning, as pioneered by writers such as Pavlov, Thorndike, and Skinner. However, it emphasizes a cognitive interpretation of these processes, as emphasized by Köhler and especially by Tolman (chapters 21 and 22). It also emphasizes the social context in which stimuli, responses, and reinforcements occur, and the role of other people in providing stimuli, making responses available, and following these up with reinforcements. Hence the term *social learning theory*. Other people have influence in other ways too, in particular the possibility of promoting learning through *imitation*. The importance of this latter process was explored in a classic series of experiments by Albert Bandura.

Albert Bandura (1925–) was born in Mundare, Alberta, in Canada. He earned his B.A. at the University of British Columbia in 1949 and his M.A. and Ph.D. at the University of Iowa in 1951 and 1952, respectively. He moved to Stanford in 1953, and is now a professor of psychology there.

In classic experiments that are cited in every textbook, Bandura showed that a child's aggressive behavior could be increased by letting the child watch another person behave aggressively. In an early experiment (Bandura, Ross, & Ross, 1961), small children watched a film showing two men, Rocky and Johnny, playing with toys. Johnny refused to share his toys, so Rocky took them away by force and marched off with a sackful of toys and a hobbyhorse under his arm, while Johnny sat dejectedly in a corner. Then, each child was left alone for 20 minutes, but watched through a one-way mirror. Children who had watched the film were much more aggressive in their play than children in the control condition who had not watched the film. After the session, one little girl even asked the experimenter for a sack!

In other experiments, the situation was simplified further (Bandura, Ross, & Ross, 1963). Nursery school children were allowed to watch an adult punch, kick, pummel, and otherwise mistreat a Bobo doll—the kind of inflated, child-sized doll that is weighted at the bottom so that when it is knocked down it bounces back up to the vertical position to be knocked down again. After watching the violent mistreatment of the Bobo doll, the children were taken into another room that contained a few toys, including a Bobo doll.

Compared with children who had not seen this aggressive behavior modeled, the children who had were enthusiastic in doing their own punching, kicking, pummeling, and otherwise mistreating the doll when allowed to do so. This was not just because the child's inhibitions had been lowered, or because they felt that they had permission to beat up the doll. The children imitated the very acts that they had observed, and used the very words that they had heard the adult "model" use.

The imitation was not automatic. Further experiments showed that children are selective about which behaviors they imitate; they do not imitate just anything they see. Other things equal, imitation is more likely if the model is rewarded for the behavior rather than punished; more likely if the model has high status; and more likely if the model is similar to the child. One can also investigate the trade-offs among various influences. For example, in one experiment, after the observation, participants were offered attractive rewards if they would do what they had seen the model do. This not only made such imitation more likely, it also quite erased the difference between the effects of reward and punishment for the model. That tells us that the children who had watched the "punished" model had learned just as much about how to beat up Bobo dolls as the children who had watched the "rewarded" model, though they did not imitate those actions until offered incentives for doing so.

Bandura (1973) sees four related processes operating in observational learning, each of which makes contact with a whole research literature in cognitive psychology. First, there are *attentional processes*: the model must be attended to. Second, there are *retention process*: what the model did, and the consequences of this, must be remembered. Third, the child must have the necessary *skills*, and so be able to reproduce the activities in question. Fourth, there are the conditions of *reinforcement*, or, more precisely, the conditions that the subject believes are in effect. People may perform a response that they have seen someone else perform, to the extent that they will be rewarded and not punished for performing the act.

Each of these processes is supported by direct experimental evidence. Take the second process, for example—retention. In one experiment, for example, children watched a model under three different conditions. In the first, the children described aloud the actions that were performed by the model. In the second, the children were instructed simply to observe carefully. In the third, the children were required to count rapidly while watching what the model did; this was designed to interfere with the children's "processing" of the information the model's actions provided (compare chapter 32). A later test showed that the children who had described the model's actions in words learned best, followed by those who simply watched. Those who watched under the "interference" condition learned least well.

These findings, establishing and investigating imitative learning, may bear on troublesome social issues. Many commentators have expressed concern, over the years, at the steady stream of violence and mayhem presented by the media—films and television. At a congressional hearing in the summer of 1993, it was estimated that the *average* 12-year-old has witnessed more than 100,000 acts of violence on television. Does a steady diet of violence encourage imitation? Experiments have shown directly that watching a violent TV episode, as compared to (for example) a nonviolent but exciting track meet, produces at least a *short-term* increase in children's tendencies to behave aggressively. In adults the picture is more complex and cannot be dealt with here, but there is some evidence for an imitative component there too (for discussion, see Aronson, Wilson, & Akert, 1994).

Certainly the media can encourage imitation of a less destructive kind:

> Matt Groening, the creator of the TV cartoon show *The Simpsons*, decided it would be funny if the Simpsons' 8-year-old daughter Lisa played the baritone sax. Sure enough, across the country, little girls began imitating her. Cynthia Sikes, a saxophone teacher in New York, told the *New York Times* (January 14, 1996) that "When the show started, I got an influx of girls coming up to me saying, 'I want to play the saxophone because Lisa Simpson plays the saxophone." (Wade & Tavris, 2000)

In his later work, Bandura has applied his ideas in clinical settings, in attempting to help people solve problems of living. For example, irrational fears, or *phobias*, may be treated by modeling procedures. A person who has a severe fear of (say) snakes or spiders may watch another person carry out increasingly bold approaches to the feared object. The model may encourage the client to follow along with the modeled responses, step by step, so that the imitation of the model's actions occurs in small steps. Thus the patient or client is reassured by the model's example that snakes (or whatever the object of the fear is) cannot be all that dangerous, and in addition is reinforced, by a series of small successes, for dealing with the feared object in a less fearful way. This has proved an effective way of treating specific phobias like fear of snakes or of heights. According to one team of reviewers (Seligman, Walker, & Rosenhan, 2001), it is as effective as systematic desensitization therapy (chapter 26).

An important component of the therapeutic process may be the development of what Bandura calls *self-efficacy* (Bandura, 1977a). The idea that it is not so hard to approach a snake, or even (later) to touch one, comes about first from watching someone else do it and mimicking those steps, and also from the cognition—the belief—that it is possible for the participant as well: "If he can do it, so can I." The importance of this, too, can be checked against data. It turns out that once patients have observed a model, the best predictor of how well they can perform a similar task is the extent to which they now *expect* that they will be able to do it themselves (Bandura, Adams, & Beyer, 1977).

Thus we see how behavioristic concepts (conditioning, reinforcement, and extinction) can be combined with concepts from cognitive psychology (attention, memory, beliefs about others, and beliefs about ourselves) into a single theoretical structure. Its various components can be investigated experimentally, and so can the effectiveness of treatment procedures derived from a provocative, carefully supported, and useful theory.

BIBLIOGRAPHY

Aronson, E., Wilson, T. D., & Akert, R. M. (1994). *Social psychology: The heart and the mind.* New York: Harper Collins College Publishers.

Bandura, A. (1973). *Aggression: A social learning analysis.* Englewood Cliffs, NJ: Prentice-Hall.

Bandura, A. (1977a). Self-efficacy: Toward a unifying theory of behavioral change. *Psychological Review, 84*, 191–215.

Bandura, A. (1977b). *Social learning theory.* Englewood Cliffs, NJ: Prentice-Hall.

Bandura, A., Adams, N. E., & Beyer, J. (1977). Cognitive processes mediating behavioral change. *Journal of Personality and Social Psychology, 35*, 125–139.

Bandura, A., Ross, D., & Ross, S. (1961). Imitation of film-mediated aggressive models. *Journal of Abnormal and Social Psychology, 66*, 3–11.

Bandura, A., Ross, D., & Ross, S. (1963). Transmission of aggression through imitation of aggressive models. *Journal of Abnormal and Social Psychology, 63*, 575–582.

Seligman, M. E. P., Walker, E. F., & Rosenhan, D. L. (2001). *Abnormal psychology.* New York: Norton.

Wade, C., & Tavris, C. (2000). *Psychology* (6th ed.). Upper Saddle River, NJ: Prentice Hall.

26 GORDON PAUL: LEARNING THEORY IN THE CLINIC

Pavlov's discovery (chapter 20), now known as classical or Pavlovian conditioning, was of historic importance on several counts. Pavlov himself saw it as a way of investigating how the brain works. Others saw it too as a new, objective way of studying the old and important notion of *association*, so fundamental to the Lockean theory of mind and the behaviorist emphasis on *responses to stimuli* (chapter 2).

Still others saw it as a method that could be applied to the study, and perhaps solution, of some human problems. This last emphasis led to the classic research of Gordon Paul (1966, 1967) on the therapeutic technique known as *systematic desensitization therapy*, first explored by Joseph Wolpe (1958), as a treatment for *phobia*.

Gordon L. Paul (1935–) was born in Iowa. He took his B.A. at the University of Iowa in 1960 and his M.A. and Ph.D. at the University of Illinois in 1962 and 1964, respectively. He was torn for a while between a career in psychology and one in music. Once settled on psychology, he held academic appointments as a clinical psychologist at the University of Illinois and the University of Houston, where he is now Distinguished Professor of Psychology and director of its clinical research program.

Like many investigators discussed here, Paul wanted his work to make a difference, to contribute to human betterment. However, his training had given him a strong background in scientific method, and he was concerned with the scientific status of psychotherapy. Can we psychologists be sure that our therapeutic procedures really do any good? Does our "helping" really help?

To understand what Paul accomplished, several items of background will be necessary. We need to understand what a phobia is, what systematic desensitization therapy is, and the technical problems one faces in evaluating a therapeutic procedure.

A *phobia* is an irrational, troublesome fear. One speaks, for instance, of *claustrophobia* (fear of being enclosed), or *agoraphobia* (fear of open and exposed situations). Some people are violently afraid of harmless snakes or spiders. Some are so afraid of germs that they literally cannot leave home. Even relatively mild phobias can be truly debilitating, as when one is so afraid of examinations, or of speaking in public (the example Paul focused on), that one is unable to do oneself justice in such situations.

Now, a behaviorist would at once point out that what we are dealing with in all these cases is a *response* (fear or anxiety, equivalent to salivation in Pavlov's experiments) to a *stimulus situation* (the exam setting, or the situation of getting up in front of an audience, equivalent to the bell in Pavlov's situation).

We need not commit ourselves to the idea that the fear itself is a conditioned response to that situation. Perhaps it is, or perhaps it is acquired in some other way. In either case, a way of combating it is suggested by Pavlov's work: we can try to *condition a different response* to that situation, a response that is incompatible with the fear and therefore makes it go away.

Systematic desensitization therapy is an attempt to do exactly that. Pavlov conditioned a salivary response to the bell as a stimulus. The therapist attempts to combat the irrational fear by *conditioning the response of relaxation* to the feared object (for example, snakes) or the feared situation (for example, giving a speech).

Pavlov conditioned the salivary response by pairing (say) a bell with food in the mouth, many times. The equivalent procedure would be to pair (say) the public-speaking situation with deep-muscle relaxation. Two problems arise, however. First, actually placing the person in a speaking situation might arouse so much anxiety that relaxation would be impossible. Second, one cannot realistically create a public-speaking situation the large numbers of times that conditioning would require. Because of this, the practice of systematic desensitization therapy (SDT) typically proceeds by a more indirect route. Briefly, one conditions the relaxation response to *imagined* situations, on the assumption that the conditioning will transfer to real ones.

First, clients are given training at total, deep-muscle relaxation, until they can relax completely when told to do so. This may take several sessions, for total relaxation on command is not easy to achieve.

After that, there will be a series of conditioning trials in which the patients imagine the feared situation—while remaining relaxed. Very often, this is done in stages: The clients first imagine the situation, say, the *morning of the day* when they are scheduled to give a speech in a public-speaking class. When they can do that while remaining relaxed, they then practice imagining the *beginning of the class* period— again, while remaining relaxed. Then they will imagine *approaching the front of the room* to begin the speech . . . and so on, until as a result of these stages they are able to imagine actually beginning the speech itself—while still remaining relaxed. Many trials are given at each of these stages, in an attempt to make the relaxation response a *conditioned response* to the image of the upcoming, then the imminent, then the actual public-speaking situation.

Notice that while this is a conditioning procedure, it is also a cognitive one—the "conditioned stimulus" is an imagined situation in the person's head, not a real one in the environment. The whole procedure is therefore a fusion of cognitive and behavioristic concepts. Images are real, and can be important influences on behavior, as a cognitive psychologist would insist. As internal stimuli, they can enter into conditioned associations, and in doing so they follow the laws of conditioning, as a behaviorist would insist. Thus SDT and related techniques are instances of *cognitive-behavioral therapy*, drawing ideas from both cognitive psychology and behaviorism.

To summarize thus far: the intent of SDT is to establish relaxation, in stages, as a *conditioned response* to a feared situation—for example, getting up before a class to give a speech. Once it is established, the person (assuming that the speech is well prepared) should be able to get up and give a good, relaxed, effective speech instead of being paralyzed by fear.

Now, all this makes good theoretical sense. But is the method really effective as a treatment for phobia? Does it *work?* Here we confront the problems of evaluating a therapeutic technique. Research on such questions, which seems so straightforward, is in fact enormously difficult to do well. It is instructive to see why.

Suppose one treats a series of patients with some method, and finds that some—or many—improve. Does this show that the method is effective? No.

First, *spontaneous improvement*—which means "improvement for unknown reasons"—is not at all rare. Many people improve even without treatment—because of life circumstances, maturation, changes in season, or whatever. Some may improve because, when they come to us for help, they are feeling especially bad. They may then improve because they have nowhere to go but up!

An early reviewer of the literature on psychotherapy, comparing treated with untreated clients, reached the pessimistic conclusion that about a third of our clients are going to improve no matter what we do (Eysenck, 1952). About a third of the treated clients will improve. About a third of the untreated ones will improve. We cannot show that our "treatments" are having any beneficial effects. His conclusion was overly pessimistic (Smith, Glass, & Miller, 1980), but it does underscore the point that we cannot ignore spontaneous recoveries.

So we need, at minimum, a comparison or control group of clients who do not receive treatment. Then, if the treated clients improve on average more than the untreated clients do, we can say that the treatment had an effect *over and above* spontaneous improvement.

(Does it raise ethical problems to withhold treatment for some of those who come to us for help? Remember that at this point, we do not know whether our therapeutic technique helps or not. For all we know, it might tend to make clients worse, in which case those assigned to the control group would be better off! Of course, if the data show that the technique does help, it can be offered to all participants; but at that point the experiment is over.)

That is not the end of our problems. Suppose we do divide our clients (at random) into treated and untreated groups. What happens to the untreated group? These participants might be put on a waiting list, let us say. But then the two groups differ in the following ways at least:

1. One group gets treatment, the other does not.

2. For one group, but not the other, someone is listening and attending to their problems, caring for them. Might this not be of benefit even if the specific treatment technique does not do any good in itself?

3. One group expects to get better, the other does not. Might the clients "see" what they expect to see, and perceive more improvement than there really is?

4. For the one group, but not the other, the *therapists* expect improvement. Might the *therapists* "see" what they expect to see, and perceive more improvement than there really is?

Figure 26.1
Systematic desensitization therapy as a classical-conditioning procedure

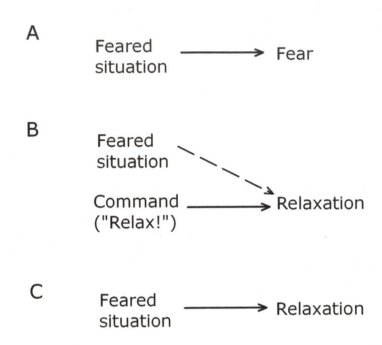

It is for reasons like these that competent researchers use *double-blind* controls wherever possible. In testing a new drug, for example, medical researchers will compare the drug with a dummy drug, or *placebo*. And—if possible—they will take steps to ensure (1) that the patients do not know whether they are receiving drug or placebo (*single-blind*), and (2) that neither do the physicians or staff who are interacting with them and evaluating them (*double-blind*). That way, not only is spontaneous improvement controlled for, but also the effects of expectations and biases are ruled out.

Paul, in his experimental evaluation of SDT, did use double-blind control procedures in *evaluating* his methods of treatment, though not in imposing them. It is time to look at what he did, and the decisions he had to face in setting up his experiment—for there were many decisions to be made.

Students at the University of Illinois were required to take a course in public speaking, and some of them found the prospect (or the reality) quite scary. Paul took advantage of this situation, which provided him with a sizeable pool of potential participants who all had the same problem. A substantial number of students volunteered for an experimental program designed to reduce speech anxiety. Based on a battery of personality and anxiety scales, Paul selected 74 severely fearful students to be participants. Five treatment groups were then formed, of which only three will be considered here: SDT, *insight-oriented psychotherapy*, and *attention-placebo*.

All participants underwent a five-week, one-session-a-week period of treatment. For one group, this consisted of SDT as described earlier.

The *insight* condition was the kind of therapy that the participants would have received had they come for help outside the experiment. The therapists in the study were all accustomed to using this kind of therapy, which attempted to help the client to gain "insight" into her or his irrational fear. This is closest of the three to traditional psychotherapy. The therapists all agreed that such insight is a valuable therapeutic goal, and all expressed high confidence (4 or 5 on a 5-point scale) in its effectiveness in producing therapeutic change.

The third group, *attention-placebo*, was an attempt to approximate a placebo control for psychotherapy. It included a literal placebo pill and practice at various tasks ostensibly designed to help the participant cope with stress. But no "insight" into the phobic symptoms was promised or sought, and no conditioning procedures were employed.

These differences in treatment were the independent variable in this experiment. What about the dependent variable? Paul's intent was to reduce the anxiety associated with public speaking. But to know whether speech anxiety is reduced, one must measure it. How could he measure the amount of speech anxiety a person had?

1. He could just ask the participants, as by asking them to rate their anxiety on a scale (for example, 0 for "not at all anxious" to 7 for "terrified"). But do these numbers or descriptive words mean different things to different people?

2. He could take physiological measures: how much the person is sweating, how fast the heart is beating, and the like. But how valid are such physiological measures as an indication of a person's anxiety level?

3. He could take behavioral measures. Assistants could be in the audience, simply checking off various behavioral indicators of speech anxiety: did the person grip the lectern with a death grip, was the throat tight so that his or her voice was hard to hear, and so on. This had the advantage that different observers could act as cross-checks on each other; if they did so without communicating with each other during the speech, then the records could be checked against each other to see how reliable their judgments were. (But how valid were they as indicators of how the person felt?)

In the event, Paul used all of these measures. All of them could be, and were, taken blind by assistants who did not know what group a participant was in. They were all flawed, but they were flawed in different ways. So, if these different measures all told the same story—and they did—then the *convergence among different measures* supports the conclusion far more strongly than any single method could do. The different methods cross-check each other, and fill in each other's gaps.

It may seem a little strange that Paul did not ask the course instructors whether the students actually gave better speeches than before. He did do this, but he realized that conversations between students and instructors could indicate to the instructors what treatment a given student had received. That would take away the blind control over instructors' expectations. Paul decided it was better not to use those data at all than to risk their being biased by preconceptions.

Having decided on his measures, Paul than faced a further and very difficult question. Who should give the treatments? Who should be the therapists?

As a practical matter, Paul had to work with therapists who were practicing in his area and willing to work with him. These therapists were paid for their extensive time commitment, from grant funds, so the experiment could be done without cost to the participants. As it happened, all of the therapists were trained in one or another form of insight therapy—so the new, behavioral therapy was new to them as well. This could have acted against the effectiveness of SDT as a method, but there was really no alternative. So Paul said to the therapists, in effect, "Would you be willing to try a different kind of therapeutic procedure with some of your clients? I'll teach you how to use it." He explained the logic of desensitization therapy and gave detailed instructions as to how to apply it. The therapists who were willing to do this then became the therapists who participated in the experiment, treating some of their clients with the old methods, some with the new. They tried SDT with strong reservations. Most of them began the experiment with the belief that this new method of therapy was not going to do much good, but they agreed to give it a try anyway. As Paul notes in appreciation, these were therapists who "possessed sufficient flexibility and open-mindedness to learn to use different, often conflicting, therapeutic theories and procedures" (1966, p. 15).

This method also opens the door to a problem that might have been serious, but in fact was not. This problem is discussed later.

After this planning, the experiment was run; and the most important results can be stated very simply. Comparing pre- and post-treatment measures, Paul found that by every measure—behavioral, self-reported, and physiological—SDT produced greater anxiety reduction than either insight-oriented psychotherapy or attention-placebo. Of the latter two, sometimes the one and sometimes the other took second place. But for *all* of the measures, the average anxiety reduction achieved by SDT participants was greater than for those who received insight-oriented psychotherapy or who received attention-placebo treatment. (Recall that insight-oriented psychotherapy had been the standard treatment before.)

These are averages, but the percentages of cases significantly improved told the same story. For different measures, the percentages ranged from 87 to 100 percent for the SDT participants, 53 to 60 percent for insight-treated ones, and 47 to 73 percent for the placebo controls. These effects were maintained on follow-up measures taken after six weeks. The therapists, initially skeptical, "began recommending systematic desensitization treatment, using the procedure with their own clients, and demonstrating it in conjunction with their training or consulting work" (Paul, 1966, p. 71).

This result was a fortunate one, for there was a problem with the experiment (as noted earlier) that the alert reader may have seen. Paul was comparing SDT with insight therapy, yes. But he was also comparing a treatment method in which the therapists had both experience and confidence with a new method in which they had neither. If insight therapy had led to a better outcome, would it have been *(a)* because it was a better therapy, or *(b)* because the therapists had more skill and confidence in its use? We would not know.

But in this case, *the data tell us* that we need not worry about this unavoidable confounding problem—not this time. The SDT procedure worked better *even though* the therapists expected the opposite result. The differences in experience and expectations actually worked *against* the results that were obtained, and that actually makes our confidence in those results all the stronger. In a sense, adopting this procedure was a gamble, but the gamble paid off—this time.

Now, one experiment is only one experiment: true. However, other investigators have followed Paul's lead, asking, in some cases, *how* well SDT works and, in others, *why* it works (e.g., Davison, 1968). A substantial literature now supports the effectiveness of SDT as a treatment *for phobia* specifically (other disorders may respond better to quite different treatments). One contemporary text sums it up: "Eighty to 90 percent of specific phobias improve greatly with such treatment. These gains are usually maintained over follow-ups of a year or two without new symptoms being substituted for those that have been eliminated" (Seligman, Walker, & Rosenhan, 2001, p. 177; see also Kazdin & Wilcoxon, 1976).

Clearly the psychological clinic owes much to Pavlov and his dogs, and to theorists who extended his ideas. And it owes much to researchers like Gordon Paul, who were willing to face the problems of a difficult research area.

BIBLIOGRAPHY

Davison, G. C. (1968). Systematic desensitization as a counterconditioning process. *Journal of Abnormal Psychology, 73*, 91–99.

Eysenck, H. J. (1952). The effects of psychotherapy: An evaluation. *Journal of Consulting Psychology, 16*, 319–324.

Kazdin, A. E., & Wilcoxon, L. A. (1976). Systematic desensitization and nonspecific treatment effects: A methodological evaluation. *Psychological Bulletin, 83*, 729–758.

Paul, G. L. (1966). *Effects of insight, desensitization, and attention placebo treatment of anxiety.* Stanford, CA: Stanford University Press.

Paul, G. L. (1967). Insight vs. desensitization in psychotherapy two years after termination. *Journal of Consulting Psychology, 31*, 333–348.

Seligman, M. E. P., Walker, E. F., & Rosenhan, D. L. (2001). *Abnormal psychology.* New York: Norton.

Smith, M. L., Glass, G. V., & Miller, T. I. (1980). *The benefits of psychotherapy.* Baltimore: Johns Hopkins University Press.

Wolpe, J. (1958). *Psychotherapy by reciprocal inhibition.* Stanford, CA: Stanford University Press.

27 | MARTIN SELIGMAN: LEARNED HELPLESSNESS

One of the most exciting things that can happen in science is that a discovery made in one research area can turn out to have implications for another, seemingly very different research area. Ideas that come from one set of findings can reach out across the arbitrary boundaries that separate one research area from another, to illuminate and be illuminated by both. The extension of Pavlov's work to the treatment of phobia is one example (chapter 26). The concept of *learned helplessness*, investigated and extended by Martin Seligman, is another.

Martin E. P. Seligman (1942–) was born in Albany, New York. He earned his A.B. at Princeton in philosophy in 1964 and his Ph.D. in psychology at the University of Pennsylvania in 1967. He taught at Cornell University 1967–70, then returned to the University of Pennsylvania, where he is now Leadership Professor of Psychology.

Seligman now teaches a course on what he calls *Positive Psychology*—the study of positive emotions, character traits, and institutions—and directs a research group devoted to its scientific exploration. He is now turning his attention to training Positive Psychologists, professional individuals whose practice, he believes, could make the world a happier place, as those who treat disorders can make the world a less unhappy place. Just as McClelland suggests that people can be trained to think like achievers, and that actual achievement will follow (chapter 12), so Seligman believes that positive habits of thought can be trained, to everyone's benefit (see Mook, 1996, for discussion).

And yet all this developed, in an unbroken series of steps, from—of all things—the study of learning in animals! As a graduate student, Seligman worked with Richard L. Solomon, a prominent experimenter and learning theorist at Penn. Learning was Seligman's initial interest, and he made important contributions to its literature. It was he, in response to findings such as Garcia's on conditioned taste aversion, who advanced the notion of *preparedness*—that animals of a given species are "prepared" to learn certain things, but not others that would seem just as easy (Seligman, 1970; see chapter 24).

The present story begins with the accidental discovery of learned helplessness in Solomon's laboratory, where a series of studies on negative reinforcement was in progress (Maier, Seligman, & Solomon, 1969; Overmeir & Seligman, 1967).

Negative reinforcement does not mean punishment. It means that a response is reinforced by the termination of some unpleasant event, like painful shock. If a shock comes on, and the animal must make some "correct" response to turn it off, then the shock is the negative reinforcer.

These studies in Solomon's laboratory were conducted in dogs, which were placed in an enclosed box divided in half by a chest-high barrier. The shock would come on, and the dog's task was to jump over the barrier, from whichever side of the box it was in to the other side; then the shock would end. After a timed interval, the shock would come on again, and again the dog had to jump over the barrier back to the original side. Thus, over a series of learning trials, the dog "shuttles" back and forth between the two sides of the box.

This is an easy task. Most dogs learn with no difficulty to jump over the barrier to safety when the shock comes on. But the experimenters included in their study a group of dogs that had *first* been exposed, in another experiment in a different apparatus, to brief shocks that they *could not control*. The shock came on, then quickly went off again, irrespective of anything the animal did.

When these dogs were moved to the shuttle-box task, they never did learn it. If they had been helpless in the first experiment, they were likely to act helplessly in the second one as well; they would stand there or lie there until the experimenters turned the shock off. All they had to do was jump to the other compartment! But they discovered this very slowly or not at all.

Seligman and his colleagues went on to show that the important thing about uncontrollable shock was not the shocks themselves; it was their uncontrollability. This is the classic experiment we shall focus on here (Maier et al., 1969).

There were three groups, and two phases to the experiment. The different conditions were imposed during the first phase. In that first phase, one group of dogs (Group 1) received shocks that they *could* turn off.

Another group of dogs (Group 2) received shocks that they could *not* turn off, but the shocks were delivered at the same intensity and pattern in time as for the first group. This was accomplished by matching each dog in the first group with a dog in the second group; recording how long each dog in the first group left the shock on, on each trial; and leaving it on for just that long, on each trial, for its pairmate in the second group.

Group 3 was a control. It received no shocks at all during Phase I.

After this, Phase II was conducted. This was the same for all groups: a series of trials in the shuttle-box, in which the shock, when it came on, could be turned off by the dog. The animal had only to learn to jump the barrier. (The design of the experiment, and its outcome, are summarized in table 27.1).

The animals in Groups 1 and 3, which had had controllable shocks or no shocks at all, quickly learned the task in Phase II. But the Group 2 animals never did. Each time the shock came on, they waited passively until the experimenter turned it off.

The experimenters concluded that the uncontrollable shocks had produced *learned helplessness* in the dogs that received it. It is a cognitive interpretation: the dogs came

Table 27.1
Design and results of the learned-helplessness experiment

Group	Phase I	Phase II	Results
1	Controllable shock	Shuttlebox task	Rapid learning
2	Uncontrollable shock	Shuttlebox task	No learning
3	No shock	Shuttlebox task	Rapid learning

to believe that nothing they did had any effect on what happened to them, so why do anything? A dog that believes that may simply give up and lie passive in the new situation. It *could* control the shocks now, but it may never discover that.

Further work showed that learned helplessness could be produced in rats, monkeys, cats—and humans. Moreover, Seligman was struck by some parallels between the helplessness in dogs and some characteristics of severe depression in humans: the failure to solve problems that are solvable and, related to this, a lack of initiation of action. And, like chronic depression, helplessness, once established, can be difficult to break up. Seligman writes,

> My colleagues and I worked for a long time without success on this problem: first, we took the barrier out of the shuttle box . . . but [the dog] just lay there. Then I got into the other side of the shuttle box and called to the dog, but he just lay there. We made the dogs hungry and dropped Hebrew National Salami onto the safe side, but still the dog just lay there. (1975, p. 56)

Finally, and again as in depression, dogs may lose interest in sex, food, and play:

> When an experimenter goes to the home cage and attempts to remove a nonhelpless dog, it does not comply eagerly; it barks, runs to the back of the cage, and resists handling. In contrast, helpless dogs seem to wilt; they passively sink to the bottom of the cage, occasionally even rolling over and adopting a submissive posture; they do not resist. (Seligman, 1975, p. 25)

Compare the self-description of a clinically depressed human being:

> I was seized with an unspeakable physical weariness. There was a tired feeling in the muscles unlike anything I had ever experienced . . . My nights were sleepless. I lay with dry, staring eyes gazing into space. I had a feeling that some terrible calamity was about to happen. I grew afraid to be left alone. The most trivial duty became a formidable task. Finally mental and physical exercises became impossible; the tired muscles refused to respond, my "thinking apparatus" refused to work, ambition was gone. My general feeling might be summed up in the familiar saying "What's the use" . . . Life seemed utterly futile. (Reid, 1910, pp. 612–613)

This sad description shows the characteristic symptoms of depression. First, there is *emotional disturbance*. The state of depression is characterized by sadness, lassitude, and a hopeless outlook on life. Second, a *reluctance to initiate action* is characteristic of severe depression: Third, there is a *cognitive* deficit, difficulty in solving solvable problems or learning learnable things. One study found that even mildly depressed college students did very badly at solving anagram problems, much worse than nondepressed college students. And the more depressed they were, the worse they did.

Seligman (1975), in an influential and controversial analysis, proposed *(a)* that at least some characteristics of depression are expressions of learned helplessness, and *(b)* that in depressed persons, as in helpless dogs, it is the *belief* in one's own helplessness that is the problem.

He and his colleagues went on to explore what they call the depressive *explanatory style*. If something bad happens, how do people explain this to themselves? Here his thinking makes contact with a whole literature, much of it from social psychologists, on *causal attribution* (for discussion, see Aronson, 1999; Mook, 1996). Once again, the critical issue is not so much what happens to a person as how he or she interprets it.

Seligman suggests that certain persons have adopted a set of beliefs—a depressive *explanatory style*—about the causes of misfortunes. It consists of cheerful beliefs like "It's my incompetence that caused the problem; I'll never be competent; I'm not competent at anything." These add up to a *belief* in one's own helplessness, and make a depressive reaction likely.

There is evidence to support these ideas (Peterson & Seligman, 1984). For example:

1. Hospitalized patients were asked what sorts of explanations they would give for hypothetical events (e.g., a broken romance). In depressed patients, a depressive explanatory style was more frequent than in schizophrenics or medical-student controls.

2. In college students, depressive explanatory style, as measured earlier by a questionnaire, was related to depressive reactions to grades that were lower than the students wanted them to be. This was just as true for a student who wanted an A and got a B as for a student who wanted a C and got a D. Students who did not show a depressive explanatory style were not depressed, but only disappointed, in such cases.

As a theory of depression, learned helplessness is unlikely to tell the whole story, but it may pinpoint a set of cognitive habits of thought that play a role in at least some cases. Perhaps this is one reason that *cognitive-behavioral therapy* is one of the more effective ways of treating depression. It will attempt to break up the habits of thought—the *beliefs* in one's own global and permanent incompetence—that can so easily become self-fulfilling prophecies (for discussion and references see Wade & Tavris, 2000).

Moreover, all this leads us to wonder, If habits of thought can lead to depression and giving up, can other habits of thought be substituted? If there is *learned helplessness*, can there be *learned optimism*? Seligman has written a book with that title (1990), and that insight has led to his present work in Positive Psychology.

We cannot follow this line of thought here. However, we should note once again that it all began with a "simple" conditioning experiment, and progressed step by step from there. As someone has said: a journey of a thousand miles begins with a single step. And taking one step after another can lead us to places where there are whole new vistas to explore.

BIBLIOGRAPHY

Aronson, E. (1999). *The social animal* (8th ed.). New York: Worth Publishers.

Maier, S. F., Seligman, M. E. P., & Solomon, R. L. (1969). Pavlovian fear conditioning and learned helplessness. In B. A. Campbell & R. M. Church (Eds.), *Punishment* (pp. 299–343). New York: Appleton-Century-Crofts.

Mook, D. G. (1996). *Motivation: The organization of action* (2nd ed.). New York: Norton.

Overmeir, J. B., & Seligman, M. E. P. (1967). Effects of inescapable shock on subsequent escape and avoidance responding. *Journal of Comparative and Physiological Psychology, 63*, 28–33.

Peterson, C. C., & Seligman, M. E. P. (1984). Causal explanations as a risk factor for depression: Theory and evidence. *Psychological Review, 91*, 347–374.

Reid, E. C. (1910). Autopsychology of the manic-depressive. *Journal of Nervous and Mental Disease, 37*, 606–620.

Seligman, M. E. P. (1970). On the generality of the laws of learning. *Psychological Review, 77*, 406–418.

Seligman, M. E. P. (1975). *Helplessness: On depression, development, and death.* San Francisco: Freeman.

Seligman, M. E. P. (1990). *Learned optimism: How to change your mind and your life.* New York: Simon & Schuster.

Wade, C., & Tavris, C. (2000). *Psychology* (6th ed.). Upper Saddle River, NJ: Prentice-Hall.

28 | LEPPER ET AL. ON THE COSTS OF REWARD

> Work consists of what a body is *obliged* to do, whereas play consists of what a body is not obliged to do.
>
> Mark Twain

To increase the probability or frequency of a response, follow it up with a reinforcing event. Thorndike stated this idea with his *law of effect* (chapter 19). Skinner made it the cornerstone of his system, and the idea has found applications in schools, workplaces, hospitals, and elsewhere (chapter 23).

The experiment to which we now turn does not challenge the principle, but it does ask, Given that reinforcement can have this effect, what other effects does it have? A drug may be very effective in curing a disease, but it may also have troublesome side effects that make the cure worse than the disease itself. The same may be true of reinforcement procedures, at least under some conditions.

Specifically: If reinforcement is contingent upon some action, then the person or animal is *obliged* to perform that action if he, she, or it wants the reinforcement. Something that is done as play is something that the "body" is not obliged to do. By introducing reinforcers, can we turn play into work? Apparently so. Mark Lepper, David Greene, and Richard Nisbett explored this question.

Mark Roger Lepper (1944–) was born in Washington, D.C. He earned his B.A. at Stanford University in 1966 and his Ph.D. at Yale University in 1970. He returned to Stanford in 1971 and has been a professor of psychology there since 1982.

David Greene (1945–) was born in Brooklyn. He took a B.A. at Amherst College in 1967, and a Ph.D. at Stanford in 1974. He has taught at Stanford and Carnegie-Mellon University and has held a variety of corporate and educational research positions. He is now a senior associate with the Bay Area Research Group in Palo Alto, California.

Richard E. Nisbett (1941–) was born in Littlefield, Texas. He earned an A.B. at Tufts University and a Ph.D. at Columbia with Stanley Schachter (chapter 16) in

1966. He taught at Yale University, then moved to the University of Michigan in 1971, where he remained, becoming a professor in 1976.

The experiment (Lepper, Greene, & Nisbett, 1973) was an elegantly simple between-groups comparison. Sets of felt-tip markers were placed in school classrooms, and the children (preschoolers) were allowed to play with them—something they seemed to enjoy doing. Some children were told they would receive a reward—a "good player" certificate with gold stars—for drawing with the markers. A second group of children was not given the rewards, or any other external incentive, for using the markers. A third group was not told in advance that they would receive rewards, but they received them anyway after the session was over. All children were then thanked for drawing so nicely and were dismissed.

Two weeks later, the drawing materials were again made available to the children among other things that they could play with. Two measures were taken—how much time children spent drawing, and how good the drawings were—by observers who did not know what group the child had been assigned to (i.e., *blind* observers). And it turned out that by both measures, the children who had expected to be (and had been) rewarded for drawing seemed much less interested in drawing now. Thus the children who had expected and received rewards for their drawings earlier spent only about eight percent of their time playing with the drawing tools now. The other two groups spent about twice that much time doing so—16 and 17 percent—and their drawings were rated as better drawings by the blind judges.

So it appears that rewarding children for their drawings, in the first session, decreased their interest in drawing later on, in the second session. This does not mean that the reinforcement was not effective. It was. Children worked hard at their drawings when they were rewarded for doing so. The downside of this, however, became apparent when the rewards were no longer given. Then the children who had been rewarded for drawing before now drew less, and less well, than those who had not.

It seems that for the children who had been rewarded for their play, drawing with magic markers was not play anymore. It had become work—and who wants to work if he or she is not obliged to do so? Everyone knows that work is no fun.

Finally, the performance of the children who received rewards they had not expected was about the same as those who received no rewards at all. Therefore, what mattered was not the rewards themselves, but the fact that the children in the first group had "contracted" for those rewards during the period when they were first drawing. They were drawing, in other words, *in order to* obtain the rewards. They were working for "pay," and not really playing at all. That is why this effect is often called the *overjustification effect*. If the person can say, "I'm doing this for a reward," then the further justification "I'm doing it because it's fun" is an unnecessary "overjustification" for doing it, and may not come to mind at all.

The finding has been replicated a number of times (see, e.g., Lepper & Greene, 1978; Greene, Sternberg, & Lepper, 1976). Notice two things about it. First, as noted earlier, the reinforcers did increase the amount of drawing that occurred, just as the theory says they should have done—for as long as they were delivered. The problem was that they also weakened what we call the *intrinsic* reward of playing and creating with the markers—the fun of drawing for its own sake.

Second, in offering this explanation for their findings, the authors appeal to cognitive processes—how the children *interpreted* the situation. The children may have said to themselves, "I'm drawing to get tokens" during the reinforcement phase. Then, after the tokens were withdrawn, they would quite reasonably ask, "If I was drawing for the tokens, why draw now when there are no more tokens?" If this is so, it means that we must consider not only the effects of reinforcement on behavior, but also how the person *interprets* the reinforcements and the behavior itself.

This is a troublesome finding. One can strengthen some desired behavior by supporting it with a powerful rewards, yes. But suppose that the rewards cannot be maintained indefinitely? Suppose that one must eventually turn the behavior over to other, more natural but less powerful, reinforcing consequences? The danger is that we may then leave the behavior weaker than it would have been if the powerful reinforcers had never been applied.

Consider one obvious and worrisome example. What happens to a child's love of learning for its own sake if such actions are supported by extrinsic rewards, such as grades or gold stars, for a number of years?

A second example. In trying to get a child to try an unfamiliar food, parents sometimes make the grave mistake of offering a child a reward for eating it. It turns out, as experiments have shown, that this is an excellent way to get a child to *dislike* the food in question. It is as if the child said, "If they have to reward me for eating this stuff, it must be pretty awful!"

Yet another example: What about the intrinsic reward of simply *doing the right thing?* A commentator—not a scientist this time, but a mother—expresses this concern:

> I recently read a newspaper article about an eight-year-old boy who found an envelope containing more than $600 and returned it at the bank whose name appeared on the envelope. The bank traced the money to its rightful owner and returned it to him . . . As a reward, the man . . . gave the boy 3 dollars . . . A simple "thank you" [would have been] adequate.
>
> But some of the teachers at the boy's school . . . took up a collection for the boy [and] presented the good Samaritan with a $150 savings bond.
>
> What does this episode say about our society? . . . A young boy . . . did the right thing. Yet doing the right thing seems to be insufficient motivation for action . . . we rely on external "stuff" as a measure of our worth. (Arguelles, 1991, p. 15)

Such concerns have led to a surge of interest in *intrinsic* motivation. This is the motivation provided by the action itself—the pleasure one gets from such activities as drawing, or singing, or doing an honest thing, or perhaps just doing our work if we are fortunate enough to find it rewarding. It is contrasted with *extrinsic* motivation—motivation that is provided not by the act itself, but by something external to it such as the promise of reward or the threat of punishment.

It hardly needs saying that the findings were controversial. Reinforcement theorists criticized the evidence, and cognitive theorists replied. We cannot review the controversy here (see, e.g., Deci, Koestner, & Ryan, 1999; Reiss & Sushinsky, 1975; Tang & Hall, 1995), but the evidence for the effect is now very strong. It is true that the developing literature paints a more optimistic picture than the one we have drawn to this point. Extrinsic rewards do not *necessarily* subvert intrinsic motivation: the professional singer can still enjoy singing, and the scientist who gets paid for making discoveries may still enjoy the process for its own sake. Again, it depends on how the rewards are interpreted. If a reward provides information about how well the task was done, rather than providing a reason for doing it, then intrinsic motivation may not suffer. Finally, if intrinsic motivation is not strong to begin with, so that there is nothing to undermine, reinforcement procedures may carry less risk.

We cannot survey this literature here. What it tells us is that the danger of undermining intrinsic motivation with rewards *can* be averted under some conditions. That danger is still there, however, and needs to be considered when we consider the use of reinforcement procedures.

BIBLIOGRAPHY

Arguelles, M. (1991, October 28). Money for morality. *Newsweek*, 15.

Deci, E. L., Koestner, R., & Ryan, R. M. (1999). A meta-analytic review of experiments examining the effects of extrinsic rewards on intrinsic motivation. *Psychological Bulletin, 125,* 627–668.

Greene, D., Sternberg, B., & Lepper, M. R. (1976). Overjustification in a token economy. *Journal of Personality and Social Psychology, 34,* 1219–1234.

Kohn, A. (1993). *Punished by rewards.* New York: Houghton Mifflin.

Lepper, M., Greene, D., & Nisbett, R. E. (1973). Undermining children's intrinsic interest with extrinsic rewards. *Journal of Personality and Social Psychology, 28,* 129–137.

Lepper, M. R., & Greene, D. (1978). *The hidden costs of rewards.* Hillsdale, NJ: Erlbaum.

Reiss, S., & Sushinsky, L. W. (1975). Overjustification, competing responses, and the acquisition of intrinsic interest. *Journal of Personality and Social Psychology, 31,* 116–125.

Schwartz, B. (1990). The creation and destruction of value. *American Psychologist, 45,* 7–15.

Tang, S. H., & Hall, V. C. (1995). The overjustification effect: A meta-analysis. *Applied Cognitive Psychology, 9,* 365–404.

5 MEMORY

29 | HERMANN EBBINGHAUS ON MEMORY

Hermann Ebbinghaus, along with Helmholtz, Fechner, and Wundt, can be considered one of the founders of modern experimental psychology. It was he who explored the experimental study of memory.

Hermann Ebbinghaus (1850–1909) was born near Bonn in Germany, and he studied history and philology there, receiving his Ph.D. in 1873. He spent some years in England and France, where he found a copy of Fechner's book on psychophysics (chapter 45) in a used-book store in Paris. Intrigued, he saw that Fechner's methods could be adapted to the study of higher mental processes, like memory. So, "without the stimulus of a university environment, without personal acquaintance with Fechner or Wundt . . . [he] set about adapting Fechner's method to the problem of the measurement of memory" (Boring, 1950, pp. 386–387). In 1880 he went to Berlin to teach, and published his experiments in 1885 (Ebbinghaus, 1913). He later founded a psychological journal, with Helmholtz among others as cooperating editor. After moving to Breslau, Ebbinghaus established another laboratory and published a new method for testing mental ability in schoolchildren, the *Ebbinghaus completion test*. In 1897, he published a highly successful textbook of psychology.

To understand what Ebbinghaus did, one must understand his assumptions. He began with a theory of mind that dates back at least to John Locke in the 1600s: the mind is a network of associations among elements. Thus, if two events occur together, the one is associated with the one with the other in the mind. Forming such associations is what learning is all about. Then, having formed such an association, one has it available thereafter, and that is what is called memory.

What is known about such associations? For one thing, an association is strengthened by repetition. That, he saw, allows one to measure the strength of an association! One can ask, how much must it be strengthened, by repetition, in order to bring it to some "standard" strength?

For example, suppose one learns that a person he has just met is named Alicia; the sight of Alicia is associated with the sound of her name. Later he encounters her again. Now there are several possibilities: *(a)* He may remember her name at once. His memory for her name is strong. Or *(b)* he may have to say, "Sorry, what is your name again?" If he remembers the name thereafter, then it only required one repetition to bring the memory back to full strength Or *(c)* if the memory is weaker still, he may have to be told the name again, and then later, still again—the original memory was so weak that it required several repetitions to make it usable. So the memory of the name is strong in the first case, not so strong in the second, and even less strong in the third. One determines this by asking, in effect, how much reminding it takes to bring the memory back to its full strength.

Ebbinghaus's method used a more precise form of that logic. But before embarking on it, he had to face another problem. If one is going to study someone's memory, what shall he or she be asked to remember? What materials shall be used? Our hypothetical person who learns to associate Alicia's name with her face is not using only memories for that name and that face: he will get some help from what he already knows beforehand. Until he meets her, it is true, he does not know whether her name will be Alicia or Abigail or Zelda, but he knows that it probably won't be Aardvark. So he already has *some* information about what her name is likely to be, even before he hears it.

Ebbinghaus wanted to study memories that are truly built up from zero strength. That way, he could study their formation and decay uncontaminated by a person's prior knowledge. In a word, Ebbinghaus wanted materials, to be learned and remembered, that were *totally new*, so that they had no associations with anything before the experiment began. This meant that the items to be remembered had to be literally meaningless—not associated with anything, until associations among them were formed in the course of the experiment.

So Ebbinghaus invented his famous *nonsense syllables*. He would take any two consonants and put any vowel between them. By doing that over and over, he produced a large number of one-syllable "words." Then he would go through these and discard any syllables that happened to be real words—like MOB, for example, in English. The syllables that were left were ones that did not form meaningful words—like MEB, for example. There are a surprisingly large number of such meaningless syllables, both in English and in German—Ebbinghaus's language.

So the materials to be associated were ones that had no, or at least very little, association with each other beforehand. In a sense, Ebbinghaus was doing what Pavlov later did (chapter 20). Like an association between MEB and FOT for a human, an association between a bell and food is purely arbitrary—nonsensical!—for a dog. But for that very reason, such an association exists at zero strength when the experiment begins, and so we can watch the formation (and decay) of that association from zero or close to it.

With lists of syllables in hand, the experiment could begin. Ebbinghaus would select a number of his nonsense syllables and arrange them in a list. He would then go over and over the list he had made, until he could recite the whole list from memory without making any mistakes. He would record how many repetitions, or "trials," it took him to do this. Then at some later time (which varied from one experiment to another), he would go over and over the list again, and note how many trials it took for him to rememorize it—again, until he could run it off from memory with-

Figure 29.1
Ebbinghaus's "forgetting curve"

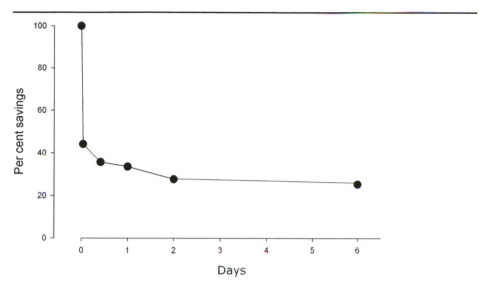

Source: From Ebbinghaus (1913).

out error. Now, if it took him only a few trials to do this, then the original memory must still have been quite strong. If it took many trials, the memory must have been weaker. And if it took him as many trials to rememorize the list as it had taken him to memorize it in the first place, then he might as well not have memorized it earlier at all—so, in that case, the memory must have decayed to zero strength.

This, the so-called method of *savings*, gave Ebbinghaus a measure of the strength of memory for the list after varying delays. If it took him only half as long to rememorize the list as it had taken him to memorize it in the first place, that was 50 percent savings. If it took him only a quarter as long, that would be 75 percent savings, and the memory must have decayed less. Finally, if it took him as long to rememorize the list as it had taken him to memorize it, then there would be no savings at all. The original memorization might as well not have occurred, and the memory must have decayed to zero strength.

Ebbinghaus went through many sessions, varying the delay between the original memorization and the later rememorization. With all the resulting data in his hand, Ebbinghaus then could show how the strength of memory decayed with time after learning—the famous *forgetting curve* (figure 29.1), which is still reprinted in all introductory psychology texts. Memory for a list of nonsense syllables falls off quite rapidly immediately after learning, and then decays more slowly after that. Careful experimentation, combined with an ingenious measurement procedure, has shown a clear and precise picture of the time course of memory—at least for lists of nonsense syllables.

All this was only the beginning, however, for the exact shape of the curve and its rate of decay vary with many other factors. Ebbinghaus went on to explore some of those as well. For example, what if he *overlearned* the material during the original

Figure 29.2
Remote associations between nonadjacent items in Ebbinghaus's experiments

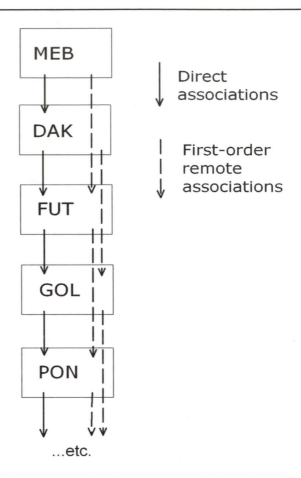

session? If he memorized a list to the point where he could recite it without any mistakes, and then went over it again many times more, would this slow down the later forgetting of the list? Yes, it did.

Or consider another question. We can think of the memorization process as a matter of forming associations between each word on the list and the next one. Consider the sequence MEB, DAK, FUT, GOL, PON, LIG. MEB is associated with DAK, DAK with FUT, and so on. But do associations also form between the nonadjacent items? Does some association form between, say, MEB and FUT—the next syllable but one—even though it does not have to be formed? This too can be tested. After the original list was learned, Ebbinghaus would make up another list consisting of items that had been separated by one syllable before. Thus we would have MEB, FUT, and PON, and then DAK, GOL, and LIG (figure 29.2). If this new list can be memorized faster than the original one, then one must be getting some help from associations formed between each item and the nonadjacent ones on the original list. And this is so. The amount of help decreases as the separation between syllables is increased, so it is not just that the syllables themselves are becoming more familiar. Rather, *remote associations* are forming between each item and the next item but one, weaker remote associations between each item and the next item but two, and so on. And all of these remote associations are formed even if one did not intend to form them. They are examples of what we would now call *incidental learning:* learning that occurs without our intending it.

It took a tremendous amount of effort to perform such experiments as the ones we have described. One has to memorize a list, wait awhile, and rememorize the list. At least one whole such experiment, with learning and then relearning later, would be required for *each one* of the data points graphed in figure 29.1. Then one must do it all again with a different interval between learning and relearning; and so on for many different intervals, just to get a single forgetting curve.

Then one might do the whole thing all over again, but this time overlearning each list when it is first memorized, to see if such overlearning would affect the shape of the forgetting curve—as it does. Ebbinghaus spent evening after evening at his experiments, literally for years, using himself as subject. He would try to perform all his experiments at about the same time, holding constant the interval between syllables by timing himself with a metronome. Not only that, but later in the project he repeated some of his earlier experiments, to see if the data were reliable. The whole project was a monument to perseverance, and it shows just how strong scientific curiosity can be.

The research resulted in a whole bookful of findings—about how memory weakens with the passage of time, and how the degree of overlearning, or the separation of items to be associated with each other, affects this weakening under various conditions, and much besides.

What is the scientific status of these findings? It is true that Ebbinghaus used only a single subject—himself—and one might reasonably wonder whether his conclusions would apply to other people. They do. More recent experiments, using groups of subjects rather than only one, have confirmed every one of Ebbinghaus's major conclusions about nonsense materials (Roediger, 1985).

But are those conclusions only about nonsense material? If one chooses to study meaningful material—a whole story, for instance, rather than a list of unconnected syllables—then there are complications, to be sure. Bartlett showed that stories undergo not just weakening, but also distortions, as time goes on (chapter 30). Distortions can also be produced by leading questions, as shown by Loftus and her colleagues (chapter 33). Finally, it has now become clear that there are different kinds of memory, not just one process of association formation (e.g., chapter 31).

Ebbinghaus, using the methods he used, could never have discovered these complications. He was concerned with the strength of memory for materials of just *this* kind (nonsense syllables), learned under just *these* conditions, and measured in just *this* way. His use of nonsense material ruled out prior experience, knowledge, and the like—as it was intended to do.

However, that also means that nonarbitrary, meaningful material may be different, and must be studied in other ways. If we want to study memory for meaningful material, we will have to present meaningful material to our participants—as Bartlett did, for example (chapter 30).

Does all this mean that Ebbinghaus's experiments were useless? No. Many modern theories of memory still incorporate the notion of association between one thing and another—we call these *retrieval cues* nowadays (see Reisberg, 1997)—and we may still think of memory as composed, in part, of networks of such associations. This gives only a partial picture of what memory is and does, but even a partial picture provides partial understanding.

Moreover, the fact that humans—and dogs, and rabbits, and even simpler creatures—can form such arbitrary associations leads to further questions. For instance, what is going on in the brain as this happens? This question remains a focus of active experimentation in our own time (see, e.g., Thompson, 1986).

Finally, the very limitations of Ebbinghaus's findings are valuable because they illustrate a fundamentally important point. What scientists learn will depend on what they do; what they discover about a problem will depend on how they go about investigating it. Ebbinghaus's methods could not have led to Bartlett's discoveries, but then Bartlett's methods could not have led to Ebbinghaus's discoveries either. This is not because either investigator was wrong, but because the differences in their methods meant that they were studying different things—the formation of brand-new associations in the one case, and the role of prior schematic knowledge in the other. Both of these are important. But they are different questions.

BIBLIOGRAPHY

Boring, E. G. (1950). *A history of experimental psychology*. New York: Appleton-Century-Crofts.

Ebbinghaus, H. (1913). *Memory: A contribution to experimental psychology*. New York: Columbia University Press. (First published 1885)

Postman, L. (1968). Hermann Ebbinghaus. *American Psychologist, 23*, 149–157.

Reisberg, D. (1997). *Cognition: Exploring the science of the mind*. New York: Norton.

Roediger, H. L. (1985). Remembering Ebbinghaus. *Contemporary Psychology, 30*, 519–523.

Thompson, R. F. (1986). The neurobiology of learning and memory. *Science, 233*, 941–947.

30 FREDERIC BARTLETT: MEANING AND MEMORY

Like Ebbinghaus (chapter 29), Sir Frederic Bartlett saw how memory could be studied objectively, without depending on introspection. Unlike Ebbinghaus, he argued that arbitrary, artificial material was not the best material to use. It permits control over conditions, yes, and it rules out the contaminating effect of previous memory and knowledge. But that also means that the *interesting* effects of previous memory and knowledge cannot be shown by such experiments. To study those, we need natural, meaningful materials, and Bartlett showed us how to use these in experiments.

Frederic C. Bartlett (1886–1969) was born in Stow-on-the-Wold, England. He received a B.A. in philosophy from the University of London, then an M.A. in moral sciences at Cambridge. He became director of the psychological laboratory at Cambridge University in 1922, and in 1931 he became the first professor of experimental psychology at Cambridge, where he remained until 1952. By 1948, he held honorary doctorates from seven universities.

In 1932, Bartlett published a book called *Remembering*, which reported a whole series of experiments dealing with memory, but also with what would usually be called *perception*. In his time, most research in cognition dealt with starkly simplified material—lights, tones, or the nonsense syllables of Ebbinghaus (chapter 29). Bartlett's approach was different. He studied perceptions and memories for organized, structured events—pictures, stories, and the like.

He describes, for example, experiments in which subjects were shown, very briefly, various drawings. These showed geometric shapes, like a rectangle with a corner missing, but also everyday objects: a wooden gate, a hand pointing a finger at an airplane in the sky. The participants would then be asked immediately to describe or draw what they had seen. Was this memory or perception? Where is the dividing line between reporting what we have *just seen*, and reporting what happened *a little while ago?* Bartlett argued that there is none. The processes involved, especially the use of *schemata* (singular *schema*) are common to both.

What he meant by a *schema* can perhaps be made clear by examples. His subjects' reconstructions of what they had seen were not always accurate, but they were not chaotic either. Thus, for the rectangle with one corner missing, some participants put the missing corner in the wrong place; but they all put it *somewhere*. They remembered, that is, that it was a rectangle (a familiar figure) with a gap—somewhere. Instead of the finger pointing at an airplane, one subject saw an antiaircraft gun pointing at it—again, wrong but not meaningless. In each case, the object was seen as *something familiar*. This "something" was the schema.

Schemata are preexisting knowledge structures, in terms of which we interpret what we see or remember. The idea is captured by the familiar phrase "hooks to hang things on." When we perceive an event, we find something familiar to which to relate it. This is the schema. We might think of it as the *meaning* the material has for us.

Bartlett's conclusion is clearly related to that of the Gestalt psychologists (chapter 2). Bartlett's idea is that we *relate* the input to concepts or images that we already have available. Our mind does not just passively register inputs. It goes forth to meet the inputs as they come in, organizing and transforming them.

The best known of Bartlett's experiments was a study of memory, among subjects of European ancestry, for a Native American folk legend called "The War of the Ghosts." Here is the story. The reader might want to let some friends read it, and test them later; perhaps the reader will confirm Bartlett's findings.

The War of the Ghosts

Two young men from Egulac went down to the river to hunt seals, and while they were there it became foggy and calm. Then they heard war-cries, and they thought: "Maybe this is a war-party". They escaped to the shore, and hid behind a log. Now canoes came up, and they heard the noise of paddles, and saw one canoe coming up to them. There were five men in the canoe, and they said:

"What do you think? We wish to take you along. We are going up the river to make war on the people".

One of the young men said: "I have no arrows".

"Arrows are in the canoe", they said.

"I will not go along. I might be killed. My relatives do not know where I have gone. But you", he said, turning to the other, "may go with them".

So one of the young men went, but the other returned home.

And the warriors went on up the river to a town on the other side of Kalama. The people came down to the water, and they began to fight, and many were killed. But presently the young man heard one of the warriors say, "Quick, let us go home: that Indian has been hit". Now he thought: "Oh, they are ghosts". He did not feel sick, but they said he had been shot.

So the canoes went back to Egulac, and the young man went ashore to his house, and made a fire. And he told everybody and said: "Behold I accompanied the ghosts, and we went to fight. Many of our fellows were killed, and many of those who attacked us were killed. They said I was hit, and I did not feel sick".

He told it all, and then he became quiet. When the sun rose he fell down. Something black came out of his mouth. His face became contorted. The people jumped up and cried.

He was dead. (Bartlett, 1932, p. 57)

Bartlett's participants read the story through to themselves twice, then tried to reproduce the story 15 minutes later. After that, subjects were asked to reproduce the story again "as opportunity offered"—that is, whenever it could conveniently be done. In one case, Bartlett happened to meet one of his participants six years after the original session, and tested him then.

These recollections of the story showed consistent changes. First, the remembered stories were shorter, so some details were lost; but also, details were added or altered. Words were replaced by more common words. The story line might be changed so as to resemble the format of a European folk tale. Some leaps of logic, or some bits of the story that sounded strange and foreign, were omitted or explained. As with the pictures, the memories drifted toward what was familiar—they were hung on whatever hooks were already available to the participants.

In fact, many participants reported that their memories were not for the words of story as they had read it. Rather, they remembered their visual images of the story's events, and *reconstructed* the story from those. To Bartlett, this notion of *reconstruction* is the key. When remembering, the participant says, in effect, "If *these* are the images I have of the story, then *this* must have been what the story said." Remembering is not "running off" a record of the past, as if with a mental tape recorder. It is more like a process of inference or deduction. Based on bits and pieces we remember now, the participants must have *deduced* what they must have read when the story was first presented. And the deduction drew on their ideas of what stories and events were like—their schemata.

The notions of schemata and reconstruction in memory fit in with a lot of other data gathered since Bartlett's time. They can serve a vital function in allowing us to remember well at all. Here is a contemporary example (not one of Bartlett's). The reader is invited to repeat this experiment and see if he or she can confirm the finding.

To half the participants, read, or have them read, this little passage:

The procedure is actually quite simple. First you arrange items into different groups. Of course one pile may be sufficient depending on how much there is to do. If you have to go somewhere else due to lack of facilities that is the next step; otherwise you are pretty well set. It is important not to overdo things. That is, it is better to do few things at once than too many. In the short run this may not seem important but complications can easily arise. A mistake can be expensive as well. At first, the whole procedure will seem complicated. Soon, however, it will become just another facet of life. It is difficult to foresee any end to the necessity for this task in the immediate future, but then, one can never tell. After the procedure is completed one arranges the material in different groups again. Then they can be put into their appropriate places. Eventually they will be used once more and the whole cycle will then have to be repeated. However, that is part of life. (Bransford & Johnson, 1972, p. 725)

Now, every sentence in that passage is intelligible. But what does it *mean?* Having read it once, could the reader repeat it back? How will the participants do? Both understanding in the first place, and recalling the passage later, will be extremely difficult.

For another group of participants, do the same thing, but begin by giving the paragraph a title: "Washing Clothes." Do the participants report less bewilderment if they have this schema as a hook to hang things on? Do they do better at recalling the passage? And do they report the use of *visual imagery*, forming mental pictures of the sequence of events described, as Bartlett's participants did?

The reader is invited to play with this instructive little experiment. For example, does it help to give the title *after* the passage rather than before? If so, what is the effect of delaying that added help? Many questions will surely come to mind.

This little experiment shows how vital a schema can be for retrieving material from memory, or even for "encoding" material into memory in the first place. Clearly, perception/memory for everyday events is not just the passive registration of these by the senses. As they come in, the mind goes forth to meet them, so to speak, classifying and interpreting them. This is sometimes referred to as *top-down* processing in perception and memory, as contrasted with the *bottom-up* linking together of elements by association, as in Ebbinghaus.

However, if schemata are essential to memory, they can also lead memory astray. If the person is inferring *now* what must have happened *then*, then these inferences may be influenced—and distorted—by what is going on *now*. And they are. The research on leading questions and "implanted memories" is a case in point (chapter 33), as is the literature on eyewitness testimony generally (Loftus, 1980).

For example, people may be picked out of a police lineup not because they are guilty, but simply because they are *familiar*. It is as if the witness said, "Hm, that person looks *familiar*—I've seen that person before, so that must be the person we're looking for." Here we see the process of *inference*, or *reconstruction* in memory, leading us astray—because our inferences and reconstructions may be wrong. In the courtroom, real injustices have been done, or narrowly averted, because of mistakes of just that kind (Loftus & Ketcham, 1991).

People can and do rewrite their memories—because memory involves inference, and inferences can be wrong. The discoveries of Frederic Bartlett, and the further discoveries that followed, have shown just how inventive, and how fallible, our memories can be.

BIBLIOGRAPHY

Bartlett, F. (1927). The relevance of visual imagery to the process of thinking. *British Journal of Psychology, 18*, 23–29.

Bartlett, F. (1930). Experimental method in psychology. *Journal of General Psychology, 4*, 49–66.

Bartlett, F. (1932). *Remembering.* Cambridge: Cambridge University Press.

Bransford, J. D., & Johnson, M. K. (1972). Contextual prerequisites for understanding: Some investigations of comprehension and recall. *Journal of Verbal Learning & Verbal Behavior, 11*, 712–726.

Loftus, E. F. (1979). *Eyewitness testimony.* Cambridge, MA: Harvard University Press.

Loftus, E. F., & Ketcham, K. E. (1991). *Witness for the defense.* New York: St. Martin's Press.

Reisberg, D. (1997). *Cognition: Exploring the science of the mind.* New York: Norton.

31 | BRENDA MILNER AND THE CASE OF H. M.

In the 1950s, brain surgery was performed on a patient who is known, to protect his privacy, as H. M. This man suffered from severe and uncontrollable epileptic seizures. When less radical tactics led to little improvement, it was decided as a desperate measure to remove the part of the brain from which the seizures appeared to originate. This involved removing the temporal lobe of the cerebral cortex (see figure 4.1, chapter 4), and also certain structures underlying it. These structures in turn form part of a complex interacting system deep within the brain.

Following surgery, H. M. did experience some relief from his epilepsy—but at a terrible cost. He experienced what is known as an *anterograde amnesia*: amnesia for events following damage to the brain. However, the deficit was more specific than that: H. M. seemed to be unable to form new, permanent memories. The neuropsychologist Brenda Milner and her colleagues studied H. M. for many years, commuting between Hartford and Montreal, for H. M. was quite unable to travel.

Brenda Langford Milner (1918–)was born in Manchester, England. At the University of Cambridge she took her B.A. in experimental psychology, then came to University of Montreal and then to McGill University. She completed a Ph.D. in physiological psychology there, and also studied clinical patients with Wilder Penfield at the Montreal Neurological Institute.

Penfield was treating patients who had epilepsy by removing a part of the brain called the *hippocampus*. But in two cases, the patients seemed to lose their memories after the surgery. The report of these cases was read by another neurologist, Dr. William Scoville, one of whose patients was H. M. (Milner, 1958; Penfield & Milner, 1958; Scoville & Milner, 1957)

As did Broca with the aphasic patient Tan (chapter 4), Milner devised probing tests—mini-experiments—in an attempt to pinpoint just what the deficits were: just what H. M. could and could not do.

H. M.'s intelligence appeared normal; he was able to speak fluently, so he remembered words and grammar; and he could read and write, so he remembered how to do those things. He was able to remember the events of his life that had taken place prior to surgery—but not after.

After the surgery, H. M. could not learn his way to the hospital bathroom. He could read a story, but he was unable to describe what happened in it, and he might read it again later with as much interest as the first time. Even after eight years, he could not find his way home from a distance of more than about two blocks. In 1980, he moved to a nursing home, and even after four years, he could not say where he lived or who cared for him. For several years after the operation, if he was asked his age or what year it was, he would answer "27" and "1953," but after a few years the numbers became more variable, as if he were guessing. He underestimated his age by 10 years or more and missed the date by as much as 40 years. A visitor might be introduced to H. M. and have a brief conversation with him, but if the visitor than left and returned 15 minutes later, H. M. would have no memory of having met him or her before and no memory of the conversation they had had.

What exactly was wrong? H. M. could hold a conversation, so his immediate memory was intact: He was able to remember what a visitor had said long enough to answer appropriately, and he could remember the beginning of a sentence long enough to complete it. He also remembered events that happened earlier in his life, and on these tests he did about as well as normal controls would do. Apparently, what is missing is an ability to take immediate memories and transfer them to long-term storage so that they can be remembered after that. This suggests right away that rather than having a single function or faculty called "memory," we have at least two forms of memory, or at least two processes that contribute to our forming memories and hanging onto them. There is immediate memory, and there is long-term, or permanent, memory. Besides these two, there must be a separate, identifiable process of *transferring* memories from one to the other. It is this process, it would seem, that H. M. lacked.

Some other experiments led to the same conclusion. For example, H. M. was shown a number of photographs of famous people—but they were of people who had *become* famous at different times. People who had become famous before H. M.'s operation were recognized without difficulty; indeed, for these faces, again H. M. did about as well as people with no brain damage. But those who had become famous later than the surgery were not recognized at all.

This loss of ability to form permanent memories was, as we would expect, highly distressing to H. M. At one point, he commented,

> Right now, I'm wondering. Have I done or said anything amiss? You see, at this moment everything looks clear to me, but what happened just before? That's what worries me. It's like waking from a dream; I just don't remember. (Milner, 1970, p. 37)

And on another occasion:

> Every day is alone in itself, whatever enjoyment I've had, and whatever sorrow I've had. (Milner, Corkin, & Teuber, 1968, p. 217)

To summarize thus far: We have dramatic evidence here that there is not one kind of memory, but at least two, *and* that there is a stage of transition between the two that can be disrupted even if the two are intact in themselves. But H. M. taught us more than that.

Still further experiments explored H. M.'s memories for acquired skills and found them to be surprisingly normal. In a particularly dramatic instance, H. M. was confronted with the "Tower of Hanoi" problem (see figure 31.1). This problem is an extremely difficult one, and normal participants can take a long time to solve it the first time; but, once having solved it, they can remember how to do it and solve the problem very quickly the second time. The same is true of H. M.: it took him about as long as intact subjects to solve the problem the first time. Confronted with it again later on, he ran through the procedure quickly and easily. Had he seen the problem before? No. Then how was he able to solve it so quickly? Because, he said, it was an easy problem. But it is not.

Findings like this, in other amnesic patients as well as H. M., have led most neuroscientists to distinguish (at least) two memory systems rather than one, even within long-term memory (Kalat, 2001). There is *declarative memory*, the kind that permits us to say, "Yes, I remember, that is what happened then." We are *declaring* what took place "then." But there is also *procedural memory*, the kind we use when we remember how to ride a bicycle, or how to solve a puzzle, or how to hit a baseball with a bat—in short, where we need to follow a *procedure* in order to accomplish something. If we think about it, we see that those two are separable in daily life, even in people with intact brains. Skilled batters can swing a bat so as to hit the ball, but it is unlikely that they can tell you exactly how they did it. Conversely, we can *tell* someone how to hit a baseball in one lesson, but it is unlikely that that in itself can make him or her a skilled batter. If it could, there would be many more skilled batters than there are.

Here, then, is another division between kinds of memory: procedural and declarative. The former can remain intact after damage to the brain that severely disrupts the latter.

There is yet more. Some contemporary neuroscientists believe that we will also have to distinguish *implicit* and *explicit* memories. Explicit memories are often declarative as well, so that amnesic patients have trouble declaring, explicitly, the answers to questions like "Do you remember this event . . . ?" or "What happened when . . . ?" Implicit memory, on the other hand, indicates that a person may be influenced by memory even without being aware of it; this is frequently shown with a word-fragment completion task. For example, a person might be shown the fragment

_L_P_A_T

and asked to complete the word. The task is quite difficult, unless the person has been *primed* by a conversation about elephants, or by having been shown a list containing the word *elephant*. If the person has been given such exposure to the correct word, he or she is likely to do much better, as if the memory for the word has been primed, and so made readily available.

As it turns out, amnesic patients also show the effect of priming. If they are first primed with the word *elephant*, and then given the problem to solve a few minutes later, they will solve it very quickly. "How were you able to solve the problem so fast?" "It was easy." "Had we been talking about elephants?" "No." The word *elephant* has been effectively primed, even though the patient has no memory for the priming event.

Figure 31.1
The Tower of Hanoi problem. The task is to move all the disks from the left peg to the right one, while only moving one disk at a time and never at any point placing a larger disk on top of a smaller one.

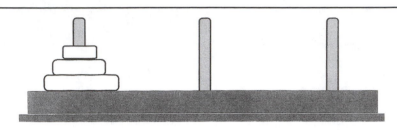

The distinction between implicit and explicit is not the same as the distinction between declarative and procedural. However, they do overlap. If study participants are able to tell us that they had just seen the word *elephant*, then the memory of having seen it is both explicit and declarative; they can declare, explicitly, that this is the case. However, if they do *not* remember having seen the word but are affected by it anyway, than the memory for having seen it is implicit, but not explicit. Nor is it procedural: the participants are not remembering *how* to do something. Rather, they have forgotten an event whose occurrence they would declare if they remembered it.

Since these observations were made, experiments like these have been repeated in patients with a similar memory disorder. In *Korsakoff's syndrome*, which may accompany chronic alcoholism, there is a similar inability to form new permanent memories. Patients may be able to recall details of early life, but almost no recent events. As with H. M., they may have a conversation with an interviewer, but a few minutes after the interviewer leaves, they will have forgotten the entire episode. One such patient read the same newspaper repeatedly, showing surprise all over again each time. Like H. M., Korsakoff patients may do much better at procedural than declarative memory tasks. Implicit memory too can sometimes be shown to be intact, as by priming, where explicit memory is gone. The brains of Korsakoff patients show damage to a system not identical with, but closely interconnected with, some cortical systems that were damaged in the case of H. M.

Korsakoff patients do often show a symptom that H. M. apparently does not show. Unable to remember events, they *confabulate:* that is, they fill in the blanks with false memories. Apparently this is not just an attempt to escape the embarrassment of not being able to remember, for the false memories may be ones that have very little chance of being believed. One hospitalized patient was asked, "Where have you been?" and replied that he had just returned from Paris by airplane—where this was definitely not so. It is tempting to see in this syndrome the role of *reconstruction* in memory running out of control (see chapter 30).

All of these findings are further evidence, if further evidence were needed, that a "tape-recorder" conception of memory, making a recording of events and playing them back on demand, will not do. We have not one memory system, but several. They have different properties, and they involve brain mechanisms that are distinct enough from each other to permit severe disruption of one or more of them where others survive intact. That is the important lesson that H. M., and many amnesic patients since, have taught us.

BIBLIOGRAPHY

Gazzaniga, M. S., Ivry, R. B., & Mangun, G. R. (1998). *Cognitive neuroscience: The biology of the mind.* New York: Norton.

Kalat, J. W. (2001). *Biological psychology* (7th ed.). Belmont, CA: Wadsworth.

Milner, B. (1958). Psychological defects produced by temporal lobe excision. *The Brain and Human Behavior, 36,* 244–257.

Milner, B. (1970). Memory and the temporal regions of the brain. In K. H. Pribram & D. E. Broadbent (Eds.), *Biology of memory.* New York: Academic Press, 35–57.

Milner, B., Corkin, S., & Teuber, H. L. (1968). Further analysis of the hippocampal amnesic syndrome: A 14-year follow-up study of H. M. *Neuropsychologia, 6,* 215–234.

Penfield, W., & Milner, B. (1958). Memory deficits produced by bilateral lesions in the hippocampal zone. *Archives of Neurology and Psychiatry, 79,* 475–497.

Scoville, W. B., & Milner, B. (1957). Loss of recent memory after bilateral hippocampal lesions. *Journal of Neurology, Neurosurgery, and Psychiatry, 20,* 11–21.

32 | LLOYD AND MARGARET PETERSON: SHORT-TERM FORGETTING

Surely we have all had experiences of this kind: We look up a telephone number. We walk to the telephone, repeating the number over and over to ourselves—a process known as *rehearsal*. An interruption distracts us for a few seconds. Then we can go back to the phone . . . to discover that we must go back and look up the number all over again.

We are talking about what has variously been called short-term memory, or working memory, or the "mental scratch pad." It is distinguishable from permanent or long-term memory in a number of ways.

First, it has limited capacity: the famous "magical number seven, plus or minus two" is about all it can handle (chapter 39). In contrast, our long-term memories—everything we know!—are for practical purposes unlimited. Second, it *is* short-term—even shorter than we might have thought. This was shown in a series of experiments by Lloyd and Margaret Peterson and their collaborators.

Lloyd Richard Peterson (1922–) was born in Minneapolis and earned his Ph.D. at the University of Minnesota. He joined the faculty of Indiana University in 1954, becoming a professor in 1964. Margaret Jean Peterson (now Intons-Peterson; 1930–) was also born in Minneapolis. She earned her B.A. at the University of Minnesota in 1951, her M.A. at the University of Denver in 1953, and her Ph.D. at Minnesota in 1955. The Petersons married in 1953. Lloyd Peterson and Margaret Intons-Peterson are now professors emeriti at Indiana.

The Petersons' research on short-term memory began with the realization that most experiments on memory involve several memory processes all going at once. One may memorize a list of items now, and then test for "memory" after a matter of hours or days. But after all, memory is going on even during the period of memorizing. If an item appearing on one learning trial is recognized on the next one, then that is also memory, showing its effects *during* the learning period, not just *after* it.

The Petersons asked, in effect, What would happen if we miniaturized the nonsense-syllable experiment, and looked at how well a very small item (say, one syllable) was remembered over a very brief time (seconds rather than minutes or hours)?

The Petersons, like Ebbinghaus, used nonsense material, and for the same reason—a participant would have nothing with which to associate such items, and so could not use prior knowledge to supplement memory. But rather than making lists of these syllables, which would have taken too long even to read through, they let every trial begin with the presentation of a single three-consonant "syllable," or *trigram*, like BRX.

Then they had to find a way to prevent a participant from "renewing" the material by rehearsing it—by saying it to him or herself over and over. Of course, anyone could remember three letters that way indefinitely, whereas the Petersons' interest was in what happens over time to the memory of a *single* presentation. The solution they tried—a happy one—was to tie up the rehearsal system by requiring it to concentrate on something else. The "distractor" task they hit upon was mental arithmetic.

Lloyd Peterson began by using himself as subject—again, like Ebbinghaus—though he soon moved to more standard procedures. In his initial explorations conducted in his living room, Margaret would select three consonants. As Peterson lay on a couch with his eyes closed, she would read the three consonants to him at the rate of about two a second. Then she would call out a number, such as 375, and Peterson gave himself the task of counting backwards by threes from that number, aloud: "372, 369, 366 . . . " as rapidly as possible, until at the end of a timed interval, Margaret signaled him to stop. Then Peterson would recall the three consonants—if he could. He found the task surprisingly difficult, and had no confidence that his memory was accurate even on trials for which it did turn out to be.

After these preliminary studies, the Petersons tried their procedures in a laboratory, with college-student participants tested individually. Three-letter sequences were read, at a rate timed with a metronome—again, as in Ebbinghaus's experiments!—and then the participants were given a number and would start counting backwards by threes as fast as they could. After a timed interval—the *retention interval*—they would be signaled to stop counting and recall the three letters if they could. Then another three letters would be read and the process repeated, perhaps with a different retention interval. In all, each of the 24 participants was tested eight times at each of six retention intervals.

In Ebbinghaus's experiment (chapter 29), retention of a list of nonsense syllables decayed rapidly over the first few minutes, then progressively more slowly, becoming quite poor after one or two days. The Petersons' experiment showed a similar pattern: performance fell off rapidly, then more slowly, until it was quite poor after the longer intervals.

The difference was that in this experiment, the initial rapid drop in memory (to about 30 percent retention) occurred after the first nine *seconds*; and performance settled down to a poor 10 percent retention after only about 15 seconds. And this was for retention, not of a long list of nonsense syllables, but for a list of just three consonants.

The Petersons and their colleagues, and other research teams, went on to explore the properties of this rapid forgetting—for science is a cooperative enterprise (Peterson, 1976). For example, the material did not have to be consonant trigrams;

it could be groups of three unrelated words, and the results were similar (Murdock, 1961). (Compare *chunking*, chapter 39).

But *why* is forgetting so rapid? If the memory vanishes within seconds, where does it go? What happens to it?

There are two obvious possibilities. First, the memory may simply fade out over time—the *fading-trace* theory of short-term forgetting. Second, it may not so much fade out as get crowded out—the *interference* theory of short-term forgetting. If short-term memory has little capacity, then as further information comes in, it may displace information that is already there—*retroactive interference*. Or the information that one is trying to remember now may be confused with information that was given before—*proactive interference*.

Time, or amount of interfering material? How can one decide between these two possibilities? We must vary one of them without the other, and one way of doing this is to vary the *rate of presentation*. If lists of material were presented at different rates, that would mean that when the test for recall was made, items in the list would have had more time to fade away if presentation rate were slow than if it were fast. Therefore, if short-term forgetting is time-dependent, one should see poorer retention for words or syllables presented at a slower rate.

A number of experiments have used this logic. One of them, conducted by Bennett Murdock (1961), will be described here.

In Murdock's experiment, 19 participants listened to a list of 20 unrelated words, presented at the rate of either 1 per second or 2 per second. Then, at the end of the list, they were given 1.5 minutes to write down as many of the words as they could remember, in any order. Then, 5 to 10 seconds later, a new list was begun and the procedure was repeated. This procedure takes us back to earlier methods (like those of Ebbinghaus), in which whole lists are given to be remembered. Rehearsal was not prevented in these experiments.

Figure 32.1 shows some results. Retention scores are plotted for *each item* in the list, from left to right: for the first list item, then the second, then the third, and so on.

In these curves, reading from left to right, the percentage of items remembered is relatively high for the very beginning of the list, then it drops, and then it rises again for the last seven or eight items in the list (seven plus or minus two! See chapter 39). Retention is always near 100 percent for the very last item, roughly 90 percent for the next-to-last item, and so on back through the last seven or so items. Scores got progressively lower as one looks back from the end of each curve, and the slopes tell us that they got lower at the same rate under both conditions.

Why does this happen? It seems that when they are asked to recall the words, participants adopt the strategy of *emptying their short-term memories first*. Since these can hold only the last few items that were given, this leads to better recall for the *last few items only*. The participants, in other words, worked back from the end of the list for as far back as they could. This idea could be tested, for the data contained a record of the *order* in which participants recalled the words that they could remember (Remember that they were allowed to write the words down in any order.) Sure enough, the first words written down did tend to be the words that were at the end of the list.

In short, the data suggest that the rise at the end of each curve reflects short-term memory specifically. Can that idea be tested? Yes. In other experiments the

Figure 32.1
Short-term forgetting. The most recent items of a list are best remembered (right-hand parts of the curve), and performance rapidly drops as items get less recent (reading right to left). However, the rate of forgetting for those recent items is the same whether the items are presented at fast or slow rates. Therefore, short-term forgetting is not time-dependent.

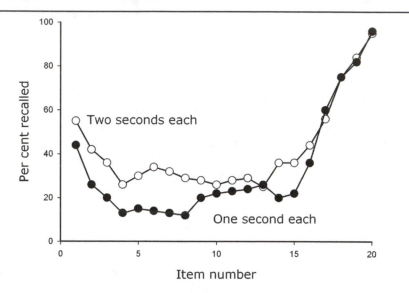

Source: From Murdock (1962).

participants were allowed to write down the words they could remember right after the list was finished. Suppose instead of testing recall right away, the experimenter imposes a delay of 20 seconds after the list is finished and prevents rehearsal of the last few items. This can be done just as the Petersons did it: Right after the list is finished, the participants are given a number (say, 841) and told to count backward by threes, as rapidly as they can, for (say) 20 seconds. If that procedure wipes short-term memory clean, and if short-term memory is responsible for the final rise in each curve, that final rise should now be abolished.

And that is exactly what happens, though this is not shown in the figure. When that extra step is added, the rise at the right-hand end of the curve disappears. The rise at the left end, reflecting longer-term memory for the earliest items on the list, is not affected at all.

What then of the two possible explanations of short-term forgetting? Is it a fading process dependent on time, or an interference process depending on number of items? The variation in *rate of presentation* allows us to answer that question.

Suppose short-term forgetting depends on *time*—the fading-trace theory. If 20 items are presented at 1 per second, then after the whole list has been presented, one second has gone by for the last item, two seconds for the next-to-last item, and so on. But if they are presented every two seconds, then all those times double: The last item will be two seconds old, the next-to-last item four seconds old, and so on, when recall is tested. In short, at the slower presentation rate, there will have been *twice as much time* for each item to be forgotten, by the time retention is measured. So, if forgetting is time-dependent, performance should be poorer with the slower retention rate.

As we see, nothing of the sort happened. For items late in the list, where short-term memory is the predominant factor, there was no difference at all between the two presentation rates.

There are other experiments too that have addressed the question that way (e.g., Waugh & Norman, 1965), and they have reached the same conclusion: the primary factor in short-term forgetting is interference by other information, not the fading of new information. It seems to reflect a limit on *how much* information we can hold onto, not on *how long* we can do so.

And that is why, after the conversation with a friend, we had to look up the telephone number all over again. It was not that the memory for the number faded away. Rather, the conversation erased it—retroactively this time.

Finally, figure 32.1 shows that retention for the *early* items in the list was actually better at the slower presentation rate. The simplest explanation is that the slower rate gave more time for rehearsal of the earlier items, before later ones began to crowd them out or interfere with them.

All this from the simple question "I wonder what would happen if we had to remember only a little information for a little while?" Let Lloyd Peterson have the last word on this line of investigation: "Thus, measurement of the effect of one kind of interval has led to experiments which in turn led to other experiments in which other intervals were measured [as in figure 32.1]. Thus research is a never-ending process, since each new finding leads to new questions, which in turn lead to new experiments" (1976, p. 226).

BIBLIOGRAPHY

Keppel, G. K., & Underwood, B. J. (1962). Proactive intereference in short-term retention of single items. *Journal of Verbal Learning and Verbal Behavior, 2*, 102–106.

Lindsay, P. H., & Norman, D. A. (1972). *Human information processing: An introduction to psychology.* New York: Academic Press.

Murdock, B. B., Jr. (1961). The retention of individual items. *Journal of Experimental Psychology, 62*, 618–625.

Murdock, B. B., Jr. (1962). The serial effect of free recall. *Journal of Experimental Psychology, 64*, 482–488.

Osgood, C. E. (1953). *Method and theory in experimental psychology.* New York: Oxford University Press.

Peterson, L. (1976). Memories of research on memory. In M. H. Siegel & H. P. Zeigler (Eds.), *Psychological research: The inside story* (pp. 213–226). New York: Harper & Row.

Sternberg, R. J. (1999). *Cognitive psychology* (2nd ed.). New York: Harcourt Brace.

Waugh, N. C., & Norman, D. A. (1965). Primary memory. *Psychological Review, 72*, 89–104.

33 ELIZABETH LOFTUS: LEADING QUESTIONS AND FALSE MEMORIES

> The most horrifying idea is that what we believe with all out hearts is not necessarily the truth.
>
> Elizabeth F. Loftus

When Elizabeth Loftus was 14 years old, a tragic event took place: her mother drowned in a swimming pool. Thirty years later, her uncle told her that she herself had been the one to find her mother. She had no memory of this, but the memories and images came back quickly, and Loftus soon remembered the event in full, horrifying vividness. But later, her uncle called to tell her he had made a mistake: it was her aunt who had found her mother, not she. Loftus's memories, clear and vivid as they were, were *false memories*. Later, she became a public and controversial figure through her studies of just such false memories.

Elizabeth Fishman Loftus (1944–) was born in Los Angeles. She originally planned to teach mathematics, but discovered psychology while at UCLA. She took her undergraduate degree in mathematics and psychology in 1966 at UCLA, then went on to Stanford, taking her Ph.D. in 1970. In 1973, she accepted a position at the University of Washington, where she remained until 2002, when she became a distinguished professor at the University of California at Irvine.

She began her career with questions about how the mind classifies and remembers information. But, like Gordon Paul (chapter 26), she wanted her work to make a difference; and, having been led by her work to the study of memory distortions and errors, she became an expert on eyewitness testimony and the dangers of relying too much on its accuracy, as juries often do. She has published a cautionary book on eyewitness testimony (Loftus, 1979).

In her early book on memory, Loftus pointed out that one can identify various stages in memory—any kind of memory. The event must be encoded into memory, held or "stored" there, and then retrieved from memory. But we need to remember that when the brain retrieves a memory of some past event, the brain is doing something *now*. That means that its actions can be affected by things that are happening *now*—leading questions, for example. These can have profound effects on what people remember—or think they remember.

In one classic experiment conducted with John Palmer (Loftus & Palmer, 1974), participants watched a videotape of an auto collision—the same videotape for all. Later, they were divided into groups. The members of one group were asked, "How fast were the cars going when they hit each other?" For others, "hit" was replaced with "smashed into," "collided," "bumped," or "contacted." That's all it took! Subjects who heard the words *smashed into* gave an average speed estimate of 40.8 mph; the other averages were 39.3 for *collided*, 38.1 for *bumped*, 34.0 for *hit*, and 31.8 for *contacted*.

Not only that: memories for the earlier event could literally be invented, later, in response to questioning. Asked, "Did another car pass the red Datsun while it was stopped at the stop sign?" many subjects "remembered" a stop sign that simply had not been there. Asked "Was there broken glass?" more subjects in the *smashed* than in the *hit* group "remembered" seeing broken glass. There hadn't been any. Even one word could make a difference: In a similar study, if participants were asked, "Did you see *the* broken headlight?" far more responded "Yes" than if they were asked, "Did you see *a* broken headlight?"—which does not presuppose that there had been one. (There had not.)

A difference in estimated speed of some eight mph may not seem like much. Then again, it did not take much to produce it! The point is that the questions we ask can affect the replies we get, and therefore give us a distorted picture of what is actually going on. Witnesses, clients in therapy, and respondents to a poll might give us misleading answers because of the way we question them.

All this reminds us of Bartlett's work (chapter 30) on the role of *reconstruction* in memory. Memory is not reading from a record of what happened "back then," but involves a reconstruction of, or inference about, what *must have happened*. The inference can be quite distorted or even dead wrong, and yet be reported in all sincerity. Incidentally, there is yet another disturbing finding that recurs throughout this literature: people's confidence in the accuracies of their own memories tends to bear surprisingly little relation to how accurate they really are.

Thus began Elizabeth Loftus's research on memory and eyewitness accounts. Later, however, she found herself in the midst of violent controversy—the "recovered memories" controversy.

In the 1970s, there was a virtual epidemic in the United States of cases in which adults who were in therapy found themselves, at the therapists' insistence, "remembering" episodes of shocking abuse, by their parents or others, that had occurred when they were little. They might "remember" that the parents had abused them sexually or had forced them to participate in horrendous Satanic rituals. The "memories" had been quite forgotten until they were "recovered" with the help of a therapist.

These episodes the parents vigorously denied, and they were devastated at what they insisted were utterly false accusations. But some parents were arrested and imprisoned for long-ago crimes recently recovered from their children's memories. Families were destroyed.

In any given case, it was of course possible that the parents were lying to escape punishment. But the other possibility was that false memories were being implanted by the insistent questioning and probing of therapists, helped out by a growing atmosphere of public hysteria. Certainly some of the "memories" could never have been believed except in an atmosphere of hysteria. One adult remembered, as a child, parachuting from a plane with her father, who molested her on the way down! And there were cases in which actual medical examination proved that the alleged abuses, remembered in all sincerity, could not have occurred. (Strange as it seems, many recovered-memory therapists did not take even the elementary precaution of checking the allegations by medical examination, when it could easily have been done.)

The theory underlying the practice of "recovering memories" in therapy was that such horrendous events had occurred, but had been pushed out of memory—*repressed*—as a way of escaping the pain of the memories, and that such repressed memories, denied expression, were toxic and produced symptoms until they were brought into the light of consciousness. The fact is, however, that the evidence for such a theory is much weaker than is often believed. For most children who are known to have undergone traumatic experiences—concentration-camp survivors, for example—the problem is likely to be quite the opposite: not an inability to remember but an inability to forget, with obsessive reliving of the traumas. In fact, of a sample of women who were known to have been sexually abused in childhood, most remembered the abuse all too clearly.

But a therapist committed to the theory, and believing that repressed memories of abuse are common, may use insistent suggestion—"This must have happened, you must remember, you must allow yourself to remember!" In group therapy, the pressure of the group may be brought to bear to the same end. But these are the very tactics that are likely to produce "memories"—quite sincere, but quite false—of things that never happened.

There is more. Not only may accusers accept false memories as real—so may those who are accused! Here is such a case:

> In the fall of 1988, Mr. Paul Ingram was accused by his two daughters, now young adults, of having abused them sexually when they were little. Mr. Ingram first denied the charges, but later, at the urging of detectives and his pastor, began to produce memories that supported them . . .
>
> As time went on, the daughters' accusations spread to the mother and to two male friends of the family, and were elaborated into "memories" of ghastly Satanic rituals involving torture and the sacrifice of animals and human babies. Eventually, the stories became too bizarre and contradictory for even the prosecution to believe; but by that time, Mr. Ingram had already pleaded guilty to the original charges of abuse and had been imprisoned . . .
>
> [If the alleged abuses had never happened], why had Mr. Ingram confessed?
>
> A psychologist, Richard Ofshe, tried an experiment: Could he actually implant in Mr. Ingram a memory for something that had never occurred, by insisting that it had occurred, and that Mr. Ingram would remember it if he allowed himself to do so? Yes, he could, and did. The experimental implantation of such false memories has been demonstrated by others too. (Mook, 1996, pp. 418–419)

Therefore, even a confession is not proof positive of guilt, and requires corroboration by other evidence.

Loftus was called to the courtroom to testify in over 200 trials as an expert witness on the unreliability of eyewitness testimony, and the possibility that memories of abuse, reported by victims, were actually based on false memories, implanted by well-meaning but incompetent therapists or overzealous law-enforcement officers. She also went on to demonstrate, by direct experiment, just how easily one can be led to "remember" what never took place (see Loftus & Ketcham, 1994). In one such study, children and teenagers were told of a time when they were lost in a shopping mall as a child. It had never happened; but just being questioned about it led the little participants to report increasingly clear memories. False events can become memories, indistinguishable to the person from the real thing.

One might object that perhaps the event had really happened after all—though it would be quite remarkable if an event had been invented that just happened to correspond to a real but forgotten one. In any case, there are experiments in which even that remote possibility can be ruled out. In another experiment, children were led to "remember" a conversation with a Bugs Bunny character at Disneyland. That "memory" we can be sure was false. Bugs Bunny is not a Disney character!

It need hardly be said that Loftus's doubts were not well received by recovered-memory practitioners. Some asked, "Why would children lie about such things?" Let us be clear: No one is accusing the children of lying. False memories do not come with labels. They may be quite indistinguishable from real ones, and reported sincerely.

Others accused Loftus of siding with child abusers. Let us again be clear: No one, least of all Loftus, condones abuse of children. Child abuse, sexual and otherwise, does occur, and when it does, it is imperative that it be stopped and the perpetrator held to account. But the false-memory syndrome can and does occur too, and surely it is also imperative that we take every precaution—difficult though it may be—to avoid destroying the lives of the innocent.

In 1992, a number of accused parents created the False Memory Foundation to aid and support parents falsely accused by their children. Over 3,700 people so accused came forward in the first year alone. More recently, courts have begun insisting upon corroboration of "recovered memories," and therapists have been successfully sued for malpractice as adult children have retracted their accusations, recognizing the sources of these in unsupported theory and irresponsible practice. The episode is a case study in what can happen when well-meaning "helpers" fail to look at the scientific literature, and so are unfamiliar with what scientists—Elizabeth Loftus among many others—have learned about human memory.

BIBLIOGRAPHY

Loftus, E. F. (1979). *Eyewitness testimony*. Cambridge, MA: Harvard University Press.

Loftus, E. F., & Ketcham, K. E. (1991). *Witness for the defense*. New York: St. Martin's Press.

Loftus, E. F., & Ketcham, K. (1994). *The myth of repressed memory: False memories and allegation of sexual abuse*. New York: St. Martin's Press.

Loftus, E. F., & Palmer, J. C. (1974). Reconstruction of automobile destruction: An example of the interaction between language and memory. *Journal of Verbal Learning and Verbal Behavior, 13*, 585–589.

Mook, D. G. (1996). *Motivation: The organization of action* (2nd ed.). New York: Norton.

Ofshe, R., & Watters, E. (1994). *Making monsters*. New York: Scribner.

34 | GORDON BOWER ON STATE-DEPENDENT MEMORY

Consider what happens when experimental participants learn a list of familiar words. They may be handed the list of words to memorize, or see them on a computer screen, or have them read to them, or whatever. Then, some time later, they will be asked to recall the words.

In such an experiment, what the participants are learning is not the words themselves. The words, we have assumed, are familiar. What they are really learning is that *these particular words* go with *this particular experiment*. We might say that they are forming *associations* between each word and the context of the experiment: "These are the words that were presented on this list, in this place at this time. They are the words that go with this experiment."

But if that is so, then they are actually forming associations between the words and the whole situation in which the experiment is conducted. The "situation" includes the room and whatever is in it, and it also includes the cues that arise from their own internal state. If the words are associated with all of these cues, then participants should best be able to remember them if they are tested for recall in the same situation—internal and external—as the one in which they learned them. That way, they have the greatest number of cues that are already associated with the material to be recalled. Gordon H. Bower set out to test this idea (1981).

Gordon Howard Bower (1932–) was born in Ohio. He took a B.A. from Western Reserve University (now Case Western Reserve University) in 1954, then went for graduate study to the University of Minnesota and Yale University, where he earned his M.S. and Ph.D. in 1956 and 1959. In 1959 he accepted a faculty position at Stanford University, where he is today.

Bower chose to manipulate his participants' *mood*—an internal state. He did this by the use of hypnosis, placing half his participants in happy moods, the other half in sad moods, at the time they learned their lists of words. Then, later, half the participants in *each* group were placed in happy mood, the other half in sad moods, and they were asked to recall the words that they had learned earlier. Thus we have what is called a

Table 34.1
Design of Bower's state-dependent-memory experiment

| | Mood when tested for retention | |
	Happy	Sad
Mood while memorizing		
Happy	Memorized happy, tested happy	Memorized happy, tested sad
Sad	Memorized sad, tested happy	Memorized sad, tested sad

factorial design. There were two independent variables—mood at learning, happy or sad; and mood at testing, happy or sad; each possible combination was presented to an independent group of participants. The design is shown in table 34.1.

Figure 34.1 summarizes the results, and it shows a beautiful "crossover" effect. If the subjects were sad when they learned the material, they remembered it better if they were tested while sad. If they had learned it happy, they did better if tested while happy. In other words, how well they remembered the material depended on whether there were in the *same* state when tested as they had been in while learning the material originally. Same state, good performance; different state, poorer performance. Therefore, we refer to this phenomenon as *state-dependent memory*.

There have been many variations on the theme, and the findings tell a consistent story. Participants' internal state can be varied in other ways. For example, it has been shown that if some participants learn the material while slightly intoxicated, whereas others learn it while sober, retention is better if it is tested under the same conditions as the ones in which the original learning occurred. (It is best of all, however, if both learning and retention are done while sober.)

These have to do with the participants' *internal* states. What about the *external* situation? In one heroic experiment (a classic in its own right), the participants were scuba divers. In the experiment, some of these participants learned a list of words while they were 10 feet underwater; others learned it on dry land (Godden & Baddeley, 1975). All subjects wore scuba gear and were read the words through headphones, so that these aspects of the situation could be constant for all. But half the participants were read the words while underwater, whereas the others were read them while on dry land. Then half of each group was tested dry and the other half was tested wet, so we have the same design as in Bowers's experiment. Sure enough, retention was better if the conditions at testing were the same as those at learning. Those who learned wet, remembered better wet. Those who learned dry remembered better dry.

These findings could shed light on many puzzling things, and might be very useful to know—for, as figure 34.1 shows, the effect is a very strong one. Where the

Figure 34.1
The effect of mood on memory. Memory is better if it is tested under the same mood condition (whether happy or sad) as when the material was learned initially.

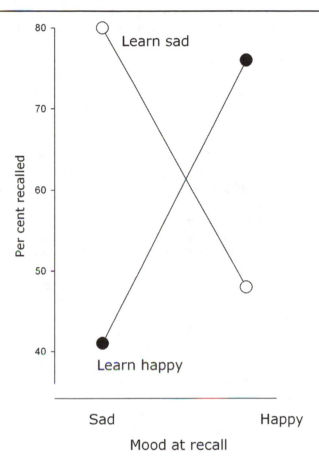

Source: From Bower (1981, p. 132). Copyright © 1981 by the American Psychological Association. Adapted with permission of the author and the American Psychological Association.

choice exists, one might do well to take examinations in the same room as the one in which classes were held, so that the external cues at recall are similar to the external cues that were present when the material was first presented. Similarly, many students—and others—find it helpful to have a particular place in their home, perhaps even a particular chair, in which to do their serious reading and studying. That place then comes to "mean" serious reading and studying, and this again sounds like a matter of association between the act of studying on the one hand and the setting on the other.

The concept also may apply more widely than in rote memory only. In chapter 38, we describe Luchins's "mindlessness" results. We may settle on a way of solving a problem that does not work, or works less well than an alternative might—and yet we "blindly" stay fixed on that same set of ideas or procedures. Now, we noted in that context that many people find it helpful to take a break—and to make a complete break, as by going for a walk in the woods in the case of Helmholtz, whose advice is always worth heeding. Perhaps the effect of such a change in setting is to break up unproductive lines of thought that have come to be strongly *associated with* the particular setting in which we were having such difficulty. Moving to a setting with which they are not strongly associated might weaken the associations enough to allow more productive ideas to come to the front of our minds instead.

State-dependent memory could also color our remembrances of things past, perhaps more often than we realize. A team of investigators (Lewinsohn & Rosenbaum, 1987) studied a large sample of people over a 15-month period. Of these, some became clinically depressed over the course of the study, and of these, some recovered while the study was still in progress. Among the questions they were asked was what their relations with their parents had been like when they were young. Depressed subjects, more than nondepressed ones, tended to report that their parents had been cold and rejecting and their childhoods unhappy. This, on its face, might tempt us to think of parental coldness and indifference as factors that might lead to depression.

The trouble was, these reports were characteristic of participants *while they were depressed.* When interviewed in a *nondepressed* state, the *same* participants described their childhoods and relations with their parents in ways that were indistinguishable from the participants who were never depressed.

We have to wonder, were these people's memories of their childhood influenced by state-dependent memory? Perhaps people who are depressed are more likely to remember depressed and depressing events, about their childhoods or anything else, than people who are not depressed. If so, then even if the depressed people's childhoods were really no more unhappy than anyone else's, they might, *because* they are now depressed, remember the unhappy side of it more readily. We could then get a very misleading picture of the relation between childhood events and depression. We do not know that this is so, but the possibility is worth bearing in mind.

One final example—or speculation—comes from Bower himself.

In 1968, presidential candidate Robert Kennedy was shot to death by a man named Sirhan Sirhan. After that,

> Sirhan had absolutely no recollection of the actual murder . . . Sirhan carried out the deed in a greatly agitated state and was completely amnesic with regard to the event . . . Under hypnosis, as Sirhan became progressively more worked up and excited, he recalled progressively more, the memories tumbling out while his excitement built to a crescendo leading up to the shooting. (Bower, 1981, p. 129)

Psychoanalytic theory might suggest that Sirhan had *repressed* the stressful events of the shooting, as a way of defending against the high anxiety that they aroused. But in this case, that does not seem very likely. The murder was political, and was planned in advance; it is unlikely that the memory of the murder caused intolerable anxiety or guilt in Sirhan. Instead, in light of what we know now, it seems quite possible that the episode is an instance of state-dependent memory. The events that happened during a state of high arousal are best remembered when one returns to the same state, as Sirhan did when hypnotized.

Of course, we do not know for a fact that this is what is going on, but it does seem more plausible than an account in terms of repression, which would depend on a state of high anxiety or guilt for which there is no evidence. In addition, state-dependent memory has been demonstrated by direct experiment. In contrast—and this may come as a surprise—the Freudian notion of repression has never been demonstrated under controlled conditions (which simply means conditions under which we know what is going on). If nothing else, it as an alternative possibility, and an instance of the sort of consideration that has led modern investigators to look beyond Freud.

BIBLIOGRAPHY

Bower, G. H. (1981). Mood and memory. *American Psychologist, 36,* 129–148.

Bower, G. H., & Cohen, P. R. (1982). Emotional influences on memory and thinking: Data and theory. In S. Fiske & M. Clark (Eds.), *Affect and cognition* (pp. 291–331). Hillsdale, NJ: Erlbaum.

Godden, D. R., & Baddeley, A. D. (1975). Context-dependent memory in two natural environments: On land and under water. *British Journal of Psychology, 66,* 325–332.

Lewinsohn, P.M., & Rosenbaum, M. (1987). Recall of parental behavior by acute depressives, remitted depressives, and nondepressives. *Journal of Personality and Social Psychology, 52,* 611–619.

Reisberg, D. (1997). *Cognition: Exploring the science of the mind.* New York: Norton.

35 COLLINS AND QUILLIAN: THE STRUCTURE OF SEMANTIC MEMORY

"Does a canary sing?" "Yes, a canary sings."

"Does a canary breathe?" "Um, well, yes, a canary breathes."

The imaginary participant hesitated a bit on the second question; later we will see just why that might be so. What is most remarkable, however, is that she was able to answer the question so rapidly at all. She was drawing on information stored in what is sometimes called "semantic memory." Semantic memory is distinguished from other kinds of long-term memory such as, for example, procedural memory (or memory for how do things) and episodic memory (or memory for specific events, such as a high school graduation). Semantic memory has to do with words and their meanings, and with our general knowledge about the objects to which words refer—like the facts that canaries are animals, can sing, and breathe.

In contrast with short-term or working memory, the amount of information stored in semantic memory is enormous. It includes the facts that Rome is the capital of Italy, that Madrid is the capital of Spain, that Columbus crossed the ocean in 1492, that zebras do not wear overcoats . . . and clearly we could go on expanding the list for a lifetime. The problem is, how do we get to the information that we need? If we had to search through *all* our semantic memory in order to say whether canaries breathe or not, we would still be pondering the question weeks from today.

Clearly, we cannot search at random; it simply would take too long. What do we do instead? Allan M. Collins and Ross M. Quillian (1969; Collins & Loftus, 1975) proposed, and tested, one way in which memory might be organized for efficient search.

Allan M. Collins (1937–) was born in Orange, New Jersey. He took a B.B.A. in accounting in 1959, an M.A. in communication sciences in 1962, and a Ph.D. in psychology in 1970, all at the University of Michigan. Since then he has been associated with the Office of Naval Research, Northwestern University, and Harvard

Graduate School, and is currently Research Professor at the School of Education at Boston College.

Ross M. Quillian (1931–) was born in Los Angeles. He studied at UCLA, then, after a stint in the army, went to the University of Chicago to study mass communications and sociology, taking an M.A. He earned his Ph.D. at Carnegie-Mellon in 1968, and in 1969 moved to the University of California at Irvine, where he is now a professor emeritus.

Let us return to the problem of how to find what we need in the vast library of semantic memory. One way around the problem is to do what libraries do: set up a systematic cataloging system. Then, if the catalog is well organized, we can find what we need with minimal time and effort.

In a library, entries will be classified in a hierarchical system or network, such that books about (say) animals will be in a place reserved for them. Then books about birds will likely be found within that section, and books about canaries will have a special place within *that* section, and so on. There may be a number of different routes, in other words, by which we can get to the information that we need, but the point is that from a given starting place, we only have to search among a limited number of entries that are *connected to* that starting place, rather than plodding through the entire library.

Is human semantic memory organized in such a way? How can we find out? An ingenious experiment (Collins and Quillian, 1969) showed one way in which it can be done. It made use of a familiar idea: we can learn something about a process by measuring how long it takes.

Figure 35.1 shows a very small part of the cataloging system to which we might refer in answering the kinds of questions with which we began. There is a "place" within the network of semantic memory that has information about animals, and within that place we can find information about birds, and then down to canaries. Now, under *canaries*, will we find the information that canaries sing? Yes, we probably will. That is because canaries sing and not all birds do, let alone other animals; so we cannot tag *birds* or *animals* as "can sing."

Will we find there the information that canaries breathe? That would be a very inefficient way to organize a library. There would then have to be a note that canaries breathe, another note that ravens breathe, another one that lions breathe, and so on for all the species there are. That makes no sense, when we can simply note in *one* place that animals—all animals—breathe. The breathing note, in other words, can most efficiently be assigned to the highest category to which it applies. It then goes without saying (or noting) that the note applies to all creatures within the category *animal*.

Notice, however, that if the system is organized that way, one may have to make a quick jump from level to level in order answer certain questions. If asked, "Does a canary sing?" one goes to the canary place on the shelf and can read off immediately, from that place, the fact that canaries sing. But if asked, "Does a canary breathe?" we must start with *canary*, then go up one level to *birds*, and then one more level after that to *animals*—and sure enough, animals breathe.

And that may be why our imaginary participant hesitated just a bit when asked whether canaries breathe. Going from place to place within the network to find the information that one needs takes a bit of time. In effect, the person had to say to herself, "Well, canaries are birds, and birds are animals, and animals breathe; so,

Figure 35.1
Part of the organization of long-term or semantic memory

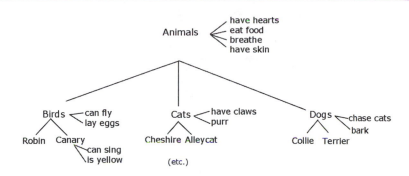

Source: From *Cognition: Exploring the Human Mind*, second edition by Daniel Reisberg. Copyright © 2001, 1997 by W. W. Norton & Company, Inc. Used by permission of W. W. Norton & Company.

yes, canaries must breathe." Thus we see again the close link between *remembering* and *inferring* (chapter 30).

If the system in fact is organized this way, then we can make a testable prediction. If a participant is asked a question that can be answered at the lowest level ("Do canaries sing?"), her answer should come quickly. If she has to move up one level to answer it ("Can canaries fly?"), it should take her just a bit longer to do so: canaries are birds, and (most) birds can fly, so yes. And if she must move two levels ("Do canaries breathe?"), it should take longer still: canaries are birds, and birds are animals, and animals breathe. The important thing is not how high or low in the hierarchy the search begins, but only how many steps up or down it requires. Thus "Do animals eat?" should be answered as quickly as the question about canaries' song. Since all animals eat, that fact should be noted in the *animals* place, and not separately for each species of animal.

Collins and Quillian tested this prediction in the following way. Participants (college students) were seated in front of a computer screen on which a series of sentences was flashed. The sentences included such items as "A robin is a bird" or "Cats have claws," but also ones that required a jump of one level ("A canary can fly" [because a canary is a bird and birds can fly]) or of two levels ("A canary has skin" [because a canary is a bird and birds are animals and animals have skin]).

Interspersed among these true sentences were a number of false ones: "A cat is a bird." The reason for that will be apparent shortly.

The participants had their index fingers of each hand on a keyboard key, and were instructed to press one key as quickly as possible if the sentence on the screen were true, and the other key if it were false, again as quickly as they could. The various sentences were presented in different orders for different subjects, so that on average the effects of practice and fatigue should be about the same for all conditions. The latency of response—time between presentation of the sentence and the yes-or-no key press—was recorded.

The data bore out the predictions nicely. Responses to sentences like "A canary can sing" took, on average, approximately one second. But responding to "A canary is a bird" took about a fifth of a second longer, and responding to "A canary is an animal" took even longer. The differences were small, as we would expect, but the important point is that they were there.

Similar results were found for questions about properties. "A canary can sing" was accepted after about 1.3 seconds on average. "A canary can fly" took a bit longer, for one must jump from *canary* to *bird* to find "can fly." And "A canary has skin" took longer still, reflecting the jump to *bird* and then another jump to *animal* before "has skin" is found.

It is worth pausing to note the precise experimental control that these investigators had over their situation. All the sentences were short and punchy, and all were approximately the same length. The experiment was conducted in a room free from distractions. Each participant was exposed to all the sentences, true and false and requiring all three levels, so participants could be compared with themselves, and so individual differences in reaction speed were controlled for.

Why were some sentences true and others false? This too was a control, designed to keep each participant's attention on the task. If the answer to each question had been yes, the bright college student would surely catch on quickly to that fact, and might begin simply responding with the "yes" key as fast as possible, perhaps not even paying attention to what the question asked. Instead, the participants were set a task in which it was possible to make a mistake on each trial, and so were forced to keep their minds on what the question asked.

Collins and Quillian's data make a compelling case that hierarchical organization, with entries and subentries like a library's indexing system, is *part* of the organization of semantic memory. However, other considerations make it clear that this cannot be the whole story.

First, most things can be classified in various ways, not just one. Thus, for example, a turkey is a bird, yes, and so it is cataloged under *bird* along with robins and ducks. But *turkey* is also a member of the class *edible things*, along with cheese sandwiches and pizzas. It is a member of the class *things that make noise* (because it goes gobble-gobble), which classes it with radios, jet airplanes, and ravens that say, "Nevermore." Again, the concept *personal computer* could be represented within the category of *electronic devices* (along with radar, cell phones, and stereo systems), but could also be a member of the category *office equipment* (along with staplers, pencils, and file cabinets). An item, in other words, may be represented within a variety of higher-order categories. This is not a fatal criticism, however; after all, books in a library may be cross-referenced, too. Clearly, however, the system envisioned here would entail a cross-referencing system of mind-numbing complexity. (For further discussion, see Reisberg, 1997.)

A more serious difficulty is that in experiments similar to this one, participants are much quicker to agree that a *robin* is a bird than they are to agree that a *turkey* is a bird, though all know that both of these are true. This idea has been cross-checked with other methods, too: asked just to list the birds that come to mind, most participants will list *robin* long before they list *turkey*. It appears that some birds are more, well, "birdy" than others—we think of them as more *typical* birds. We might say that the lines in figure 35.1 can vary in their strength: some connections are stronger than others (Rosch, 1975).

Nevertheless, the data do strongly suggest that a hierarchical organization of the kind proposed is *part* of the story of the organization of knowledge, just as Ebbinghaus's study of the formation of associations is (chapter 29). Indeed, a network conception of memory draws on Ebbinghaus's ideas; each of the pathways shown in figure 35.1 can be considered an *association* between an idea and the superordinate category into which it fits. And after all, in dealing with the phenomenon as complex as human knowledge, "part of the story" is all we can expect any single experiment to tell us.

BIBLIOGRAPHY

Collins, A. M., & Loftus, E. F. (1975). A spreading-activation theory of semantic processing. *Psychological Review, 82*, 407–429.

Collins, A. M., & Quillian, M. R. (1969). Retrieval time from semantic memory. *Journal of Verbal Learning and Verbal Behavior, 8*, 240–247.

Reisberg, D. (1997). *Cognition: Exploring the science of the mind.* New York: Norton.

Rosch, E. (1975). Cognitive representation of semantic categories. *Journal of Experimental Psychology: General, 104*, 192–233.

6 COGNITION

36 F. C. DONDERS AND REACTION TIME

Even classic investigations do not just happen. Most often they will build on experiments performed, and questions asked, by earlier investigators, and those earlier experiments will be part of the background even for classic experiments. Moreover, they may spring from a line of research that began with a different problem altogether. The investigation of *reaction time* by F. C. Donders, leading to classic early investigations but to many modern ones as well, is a case in point.

Franciscus Cornelius Donders (1818–89) was born in Tilburg, the Netherlands. He went to medical school in Utrecht, and for the rest of his academic career he was a professor of physiology at the University of Utrecht. Donders was one of the pioneers of ophthalmology, but he also was interested in the physiology of the brain. He investigated cerebral circulation and measured the metabolic activity of the brain. Comparing blood flowing into a brain area with blood flowing out, he showed that oxygen is consumed by the brain as it does its work. This insight became the basis of the two most widely used modern neuroimaging techniques, positive electron tomography (PET) and functional magnetic resonance imagery (fMRI; see Kalat, 2001). Today, there is the new F. C. Donders Centre for Cognitive Neuroimaging in the Netherlands, named in his honor.

Of present concern is Donders's work on reaction time. That story began with a field far removed from psychology—astronomy. It began with a rather sad historical event. In 1796, the astronomer royal of the Greenwich Observatory in England, Nevil Maskelyne, fired his assistant, David Kinnebrook, because the two differed in their judgments of the precise times at which stellar events occurred. The difference was almost a full second, which represented a very substantial error. Kinnebrook was warned repeatedly that he must observe more carefully, but the difference persisted until the astronomer royal dismissed him.

In 1816, another astronomer, Friedrich Bessel, the astronomer at Königsberg in Germany, heard about this episode. It seemed to him curious that a capable young astronomer would persist in blatant carelessness—for the error was large—even after repeated warnings. He wondered whether perhaps there were differences from one observer to another in the time it took them to make perceptual judgments—for example, about the precise time at which a star crossed a line in the reticle of a telescope.

Bessel checked his own observations against those of another experienced astronomer, and sure enough, they were different—by over a second! It occurred to him that if he could measure consistent differences between one astronomer and another, he could compute a "personal equation"—a constant that could be subtracted from the measurements of the slower observer—and thus bring the observations into agreement with each other. The trouble was that the differences between one astronomer and another were not only considerable, but variable from time to time even in the same pair of observers. Even so, an average correction was better than no correction at all, and if Bessel's method had been in use at the time, it could have saved Kinnebrook's job.

Astronomers lost interest in the personal equation in years following because better instrumentation did much to reduce the contribution of individual observers to the measurements. In the meantime, however, physiologists had become interested in it. (There were no psychologists at the time.) Why should the difference be there? Was it in the nerves that led from the eyes to the brain? That seemed unlikely, because nerve conduction was thought to be instantaneous. Then came Helmholtz's experiment that showed that it was not (chapter 3). In any case, there had to be more to it than that, for the time it took to react to an event depended on such things as whether one was expecting the event at a precise time. If one were, one might react to the time at which the event was expected rather than to the event itself. It was even possible to begin reaction before the signal for that reaction had occurred. Clearly, therefore, reaction time was affected by complicated mental states of attention and expectation that must involve the brain.

By the 1860s, a number of investigators had interested themselves in this seemingly simple problem—Wilhelm Wundt, the founder of the first psychological laboratory, among them (chapter 2). But here we will focus on the work of Donders, who used the reaction-time method to ask questions about the mental processes involved in perceiving, judging, discriminating, and reacting.

The basic idea was that if one were to elaborate the "simple" reaction-time experiment by adding psychological operations to it, one could measure how long such psychological operations took. Suppose one starts with a simple reaction-time experiment: call it Experiment 1. A light comes on, and that also starts a timing device that stops timing when the reaction is made—for instance, pressing a button. Then one knows the total time it takes to sense the event and react to it.

Then one can add a complication; call this Experiment 2. Now either of two stimuli might come on, on a given trial. The participant's task is to make one response if stimulus A comes on and a different response if stimulus B comes on. On successive trials, sometimes A will come on, sometimes B, and reaction time is measured for each trial. Reaction times are longer under this condition than when only one stimulus is used.

That may seem like an obvious finding, but actually it is quite puzzling. Experiment 1 uses only one stimulus, A. In Experiment 2, the same stimulus A might be used, associated with the same response as before; but there will also be trials with stimulus B instead, calling for a different response. Now, even on trials where stimulus A is presented, the reaction time is longer than it was in Experiment 1—even though both the stimulus and the response on that trial are the same as in Experiment 1. The only difference is that there was another event, B, which might have occurred on that trial but did not. Clearly, then, what Donders called the act of *choice* took a measurable amount of time.

Donders pushed it further. It occurred to him that these "choice" reaction times must really include two steps: *discrimination* between the two stimuli, and *choosing* one response over another. Could one measure discrimination separately? Donders would present at random each of a number of stimuli—A, B, C, D, and so on—on different trials, but a response was to be made only to (say) stimulus A and not to the others. So the participants had to *discriminate* stimulus A from all the others before they could choose whether or not to react, but no *choice* among different reactions was involved. Again, by appropriate subtractions, Donders could get estimates of the time required for choice, discrimination, and reaction.

Others picked up the method, including Wundt, who made a number of other comparisons among experimental conditions. His research found, for example, that even in a "simple" reaction experiment, it made a difference whether one focused one's attention on the *stimulus* that was about to come on, or on the *response* that was to be made when it did come on. Reactions took measurably less time in the latter case. A pretty convincing answer to those who still doubted that mental events could be measured!

This "subtraction procedure," as used by Donders and Wundt, has not stood the test of time very well. However, the reaction-time experiment certainly has. It has been a staple of the psychological laboratory ever since (see, e.g., Kantowitz, Roediger, & Elmes, 1994; Sternberg, 1999; Titchener, 1902; Woodworth & Schlosberg, 1954). The finding that, for example, reaction times are longer if there are more possible events is a very solid finding—and a puzzling one, as noted earlier.

More generally, the simple measurement of *how long a process takes* has been used to investigate how we search through memory (chapter 35), how we manipulate mental images in our minds (chapter 41), and much besides. Even the study of animal learning uses it. Thorndike's studies of animal learning (chapter 19) were reaction-time experiments of a sort: if an animal is shut up in a confining box, *how long does it take* before it makes the correct response and frees itself? That is what Thorndike measured.

The use of time as a measure has given psychological research an invaluable tool. Donders first showed us some ways in which it could be used.

BIBLIOGRAPHY

Boring, E. G. (1950). *A history of experimental psychology* (2nd ed.). New York: Appleton-Century-Crofts.

Kalat, J. W. (2001). *Biological psychology* (7th ed.). Belmont, CA: Wadsworth.

Kantowitz, B. H., Roediger, H. L., & Elmes, D. G. (1994). *Experimental psychology: Understanding psychological research*. St. Paul, MN: West Publishing Company.

Sternberg, R. J. (1999). *Cognitive psychology* (2nd ed.). New York: Harcourt Brace.

Titchener, E. B. (1902). *Experimental psychology: A manual of laboratory practice*. New York: Macmillan.

Woodworth, R. S., & Schlosberg, H. (1954). *Experimental psychology*. New York: Holt.

37 | THE CAUTIONARY TALE OF CLEVER HANS

This case is different from most of those considered in this book in two ways. First, rather than focusing on the *results* of research, it focuses on a *problem* of research. But that too is within the topic, for part of the history of any science is learning how research can go wrong, and how researchers can avoid doing so. The process of anticipating and avoiding mistakes in research is called *experimental control* (chapter 1), and this topic too has a history (Boring, 1954). Briefly, one can easily mistake one effect for another. And experimental control is simply a set of techniques for making that mistake less likely.

Experimental control plays a role in the physical sciences, too, and there too its neglect can lead to big mistakes. Thus the great Greek scientist Aristotle laid it down that heavy objects fall faster than light ones. He was wrong. A stone does indeed fall faster than a feather; but this is because it is less affected by air resistance, not because it is heavier. If there is no air (because the experiment is done in a vacuum—*experimental control!*), then the feather and the stone will fall at exactly the same rate.

Second, in the history of science, not all famous names are the names of scientists. The amnesic patient, code-named H. M., has a place of his own in the annals of memory research (chapter 31). And not all the famous names are even of human beings! A story known to every researcher—as it should be, for it is a classic cautionary tale—is the story of Clever Hans, the Wonder Horse (Miller, 1962; Pfungst, 1998).

The story takes place in Germany in 1904. A schoolteacher, Wilhelm von Osten, had discovered that a horse he owned, named Hans, had remarkable capabilities. Hans the horse could do arithmetic! If asked to add (say) 7 and 4, he would tap 11 times with his hoof, and then stop. He was just as gifted at subtraction, and even multiplication and division. Nor did his talents stop at math. He understood German! If asked a question, he would give the answer in a tapping code.

Hans's owner was not a fraud. To anyone who doubted what he said about Hans's achievements, he would give the scientist's reply: See for yourself! Scientists observed Clever Hans, and came away convinced that von Osten was not giving Hans surreptitious cues. Indeed, he did not even have to be there. He could be out of sight altogether, and still Clever Hans could perform his feats.

But an experimental psychologist, Oskar Pfungst (1874–1932), was still not quite satisfied. He arranged a series of classic experiments.

He set up a large canvas tent in the courtyard so that the experiments could be carried out without distractions. He tried different questions and different questioners. On some trials, Hans was fitted with large blinders.

The most important control, however, was this: *On some trials, none of the observers knew what the correct answer was.* This was arranged as follows: One onlookers might whisper into Hans's ear, for example, "Seven." Then another, different observer might whisper into the horse's ear, "Plus four." That way, since neither of the whisperers could hear the other, *none of the observers knew the correct answer,* until Hans told them—if he could.

He could not. Under these conditions, Hans could answer no questions and solve no problems. Asked a question, he would go on tapping and tapping, indefinitely.

It seems that what had been happening was a case of unconscious cuing. As long as the audience knew what the correct answer was—7 + 4 = 11—they would wait until Hans had tapped 11 times, and then lean forward alertly or make some similar movement: "That's the right answer. Is he going to stop now?" Hans would detect those signals as his cue to stop tapping. To show Hans's true capabilities (or their absence), the observers had to be kept from knowing what the correct answer was until *after* Hans had answered—or failed to do so.

This finding in itself would have been convincing enough, but Pfungst checked further. In effect, he brought the Clever Hans effect into his own laboratory. He brought in human participants, and connected them to apparatuses for measuring head movements and respiration. He then told them to ask him questions, to which he would respond by tapping and to which he did not know the answers. Sure enough, over 90 percent of the participants provided him with cues to stop tapping, cues of which they were quite unaware.

So it seems that Hans was a clever horse indeed—but he was not clever at arithmetic. Instead, he was clever at reading humans and the unconscious signals they gave. Herr von Osten too must have been giving him such unconscious cues all along, quite without realizing or intending it.

Since this episode, the term *Clever Hans effect* has been a standard phrase, used to remind researchers—and the rest of us—of the danger: an observer can give unintended cues that can affect what his subjects do. And if that happens, very misleading data can result. It may appear that a horse can do sums, when a horse—or at least *this* horse—cannot.

Aware of this danger, what do modern scientists do about it? If one wants to know whether an animal can solve this or that problem, how can one be sure that the animal does not cheat by reading our unintended cues? How, in a word, can we *control for* the Clever Hans effect?

In some cases, scientists may do what Pfungst did. They may simply keep the observers from knowing what the answer to the problem is until *after* the data are in. That way, an observer cannot unconsciously give cues to the right answer, for that observer does not know what the right answer is.

Alternatively, one may turn the experiment over to automatic apparatus, which presents the problem and records the animal's reply to it. Then one needs to be sure that the apparatus itself provides no cue as to what the correct answer is! But if that can be done, then we can rule out the Clever Hans effect as an explanation for accurate performance. This was done in the ingenious experiments on concepts in the pigeon (chapter 42).

In short, modern students of animal cognition are very conscious of the Clever Hans effect and are careful to control for it in their experiments. Some animals are very clever—make no mistake. But to see how clever they are, one must make sure that no cues are given that could make them look more clever than they are.

Finally, it is not only in animal research that the problem of unconscious cuing arises. Here is a modern-day repeat of the Clever Hans story. It shows that in human clinical research, too, we cannot afford to neglect experimental control (see Stanovich, 2001, for details of this sad story).

Autism is a severe developmental disorder, apparent in early childhood and characterized by (among other symptoms) an extreme difficulty—or better, an extreme *lack of interest*—in communicating with other human beings. An exciting development was reported in the 1970s, when it was announced that a technique called Facilitated Communication (FC) could unlock such children's ability to communicate. The claim was that these children could type highly literate messages on a keyboard if their hands and arms were supported over a keyboard by a trained and sympathetic "facilitator."

Reports of success with this technique were widely publicized, and led to a great surge of optimism among therapists and, of course, parents too. There was also a downside. Some children would "report" sexual abuse or incest occurring in the home. In some cases, children were actually removed from their homes on the basis of such "uncovered" abuses.

More careful experiments made it clear that FC is simply the Clever Hans effect all over again. Facilitators were unconsciously cuing the children as to what keys to press. And this was shown by the same sorts of controls as were used to expose Clever Hans (Stanovich, 2001). In one such experiment, questions were read to the patient and to her "facilitator" through headphones. When the questions were the same for both, the patient would type correct answers every time. But when the questions were different, the patient would type answers to the questions that the *facilitator*, not she herself, had received.

Many such experiments made it clear that the clinicians were, like Clever Hans's observers, unconsciously cuing the children as to what keys to press (Green, 1994). If this is so, then it is also likely that the stories of abuse, incest, and the like were not really reports by the children but unconscious inventions of the therapists.

At this writing, the useless and dangerous FC fad is mercifully fading away. But in the meantime, it has led to false accusation of parental abuse and destroyed homes. And it has prevented autistic children from getting the kind of treatment that might have been helpful.

Why did this happen? The therapists who developed FC were, like Herr von Osten, quite sincere. But, untrained in research, they were unaware of how subtly and unintentionally one can influence what horses, or fellow humans, do. Professionals trained in research would have known about the Clever Hans effect and how it might be controlled. Tragedies and disappointments would have been averted.

Experimental control—which really just means "Let us be sure we know what is going on"—is a cornerstone of science. It is also a cornerstone of the applications of science to human problems. It can help us avoid doing harm as we try to do good.

BIBLIOGRAPHY

Boring, E. G. (1954). The nature and history of experimental control. *American Journal of Psychology, 67,* 573–589.

Green, G. (1994). Facilitated communication: Mental miracle or sleight of hand? *Skeptic, 2,* 68–76.

Miller, G. A. (1962). *Psychology: The science of mental life.* New York: Harper & Row.

Mook, D. G. (2002). Observer effects and observer bias. In M. Shermer (Ed.), *The skeptic encyclopedia of pseudoscience* (Vol. 1, pp. 158–163). Santa Barbara, CA: ABC-CLIO.

Pfungst, O. (1911). *Clever Hans (The horse of Mr. Von Osten). A contribution to experimental animal and human psychology.* New York: Henry Holt.

Stanovich, K. E. (2001). *How to think straight about psychology* (6th ed.). Boston: Allyn & Bacon.

38 A. S. LUCHINS ON NOT BEING MINDLESS

It seems that the physicist Robert Oppenheimer was so engrossed in his newspaper one morning at breakfast that when he got up, he left a tip on the table. His wife, we are told, was not amused.

Many problems are more difficult to solve than they have to be. This may be because we look at the problem in the wrong way, and we may do that because we bring to the problem a particular *mental set*—sometimes referred to in psychology by the German word *Einstellung*. One brings to a problem a set of attitudes, beliefs, or procedures that look as if they ought to be applicable, and may indeed be applicable in a variety of instances. However, they may not be well suited to the particular problem at hand. In such cases, another word for *mental set* might be *preconception*, or perhaps *force of habit*. (What does one do at the end of a meal? Leave a tip—unless one is at home, but that qualifier may come to mind too late.)

A set of experiments by A. S. Luchins showed the powerful effect of mental set very clearly.

Abraham Samuel Luchins (1914–) was born in Brooklyn. He graduated from Brooklyn College in 1935, then took an M.A. at Columbia in 1936 and a Ph.D. from New York University in 1939. He taught at Yeshiva College till 1949, during which time he was research assistant to Max Wertheimer, the Gestalt psychologist (chapter 46). With his wife, Edith Hirsch Luchins, he edited and published a multivolume collection of notes and records from Wertheimer's seminars. He is now a professor at the State University of New York at Albany.

In his most famous experiments, Luchins (1942) gave his experimental participants a series of problems—the "water-jar problems" associated with his name. In all of them, there are three jars, A, B, and C. The participant is told how much water each jar will hold. The problem is to get a specified amount of water in one of the jars.

Here is one such problem. Jar A holds 21 cups of water; B, 127 cups; and C, 3 cups. How do you get exactly 100 cups?

The procedure is as follows: Fill up Jar B with 127 cups. Pour 21 cups into Jar A, leaving you with 106 cups in Jar B. Then fill Jar C from Jar B, dump out Jar C and fill it again, and 100 cups are left in Jar B.

Participants who worked along at a series of such problems quickly found a formula—a rule for proceeding—that would work for all the problems. For each problem, the procedure was the same. From B, fill A, and then fill C twice: B-A-2C.

There were six such problems, and for all of them that formula worked. But then, without telling the participants anything about it, Luchins changed things. Another set of five problems was given. For these, the same strategy as before would work. But now, in each case, there was a much simpler way of solving the problem.

For example, if A holds 14 cups, B holds 36 cups, and C holds 8 cups, how would you get just 6 cups?

One could proceed as before. To get 6 cups, one can fill Jar A from Jar B, leaving 22 cups in B; then fill Jar C twice from B. The result will indeed be six cups.

But now there is a much easier way. One could just fill Jar C from Jar A—14 cups minus 8 cups leaves 6 cups, the desired amount. What could be simpler?

Yet this elegantly simple strategy was seldom used, if the *mental set* had been formed that identified the long way around as the "correct" procedure to follow. In Luchins's experiments, between 64 and 83 percent of the participants continued to use the old, cumbersome method when confronted with the new, much simpler problems. They showed what Luchins called *mechanization*—one follows a procedure mechanically, without thinking. The findings were replicated with participants of varying ages, from children to graduate students.

Control participants were given the last, easy set of problems without encountering the hard ones first. Of these, only one to five percent failed to apply the simpler solution.

By varying the procedure, Luchins was able to learn more about mechanization and what affected it (Luchins & Luchins, 1950, 1959). Time pressure, as we would expect, made matters worse. Giving the participants some easier problems first, before they encountered the long-way-around problems, brought little improvement. Finally, in some experiments using the original procedures, participants were taken aside before the easy problems were presented, and told to write the words "Don't be blind!" on their papers. This did increase the number of insightful solutions to the simpler problems, *except* in younger schoolchildren. Perhaps typical school procedures had produced a set for following rules mechanically. When they were asked, "What does 'Don't be blind' mean?" the younger children gave such answers as "Just do what you did before" or "Don't be blind to the rule that solves all the problems"!

Looking over these experiments, we may be reminded of the cognitive-map experiments (chapter 22). When rats were offered a new, quicker way to reach the goal box from the start box, they would take the new route *unless* they had received too much training in the old, long-way-around route to the goal. But if they had received a great deal of training, their cognitive maps seemed to have narrowed. They mindlessly followed the old way when they did not have to.

One tactic that sometimes helps to break up mechanization is what has been called *incubation*—laying aside the problem for awhile. The great Hermann von Helmholtz noticed this; so did the mathematician Henri Poincaré. It seems to happen after prolonged and intensive work on a problem (this is essential) is followed by rest *and* a change of scene (Helmholtz recommended a walk in the woods).

Poincaré had noticed it as well: after laying aside a problem on which he had been working intensely, he might, on returning to it, find that a solution had emerged. He too, however, noticed that this did not happen unless there had first been a period of serious effort.

Even if incubation "works," how it does so is still not clear (Sternberg, 1999). Helmholtz attributes it to dissipation of fatigue, but it may also involve relaxing the focus of our attention so that more peripheral ideas—including alternative approaches to our problem—may come to mind. Or a change in situation (a walk in the woods, or even going to bed) may, just because it is a change, break the hold of the repetitive and unproductive approaches that have stayed in the front of our minds before, holding us up (compare *state-dependent memory*, chapter 34).

Since the time of these classic experiments, the phenomenon of mechanization has been extended into social and workplace contexts. Examples are the experiments of Ellen Langer (2000), who uses the unkind term *mindlessness* for Luchins's mechanization.

In one of her experiments, Langer and her colleagues sent a brief memo to 40 secretaries at a university. The memo read, "This paper is to be returned immediately to room 238 by messenger mail." The memo was unsigned. This is obviously a nonsensical request: if the person who sent the memo wanted it back, why did he or she send it in the first place? Yet 90 percent of the secretaries did what Luchins's participants did: they mindlessly followed the rule "Do what memos tell you to do."

The researchers also reasoned that this mindless conformity should be broken up if the secretaries were induced to stop and think. They sent other secretaries the same memo, except that it was signed—a highly unusual thing. This caused at least some of the secretaries to turn off their automatic pilots and think about what they were doing. In this condition, compliance dropped to 60 percent. (One wonders what the effect would have been of writing "Don't be blind!" on the memo.)

Finally, we should note that mechanization is not a bad thing in itself. Of course we go through many, perhaps most, of our daily activities on autopilot. We could not function if we did not. Imagine what life would be like if at every turn we had to stop and say to ourselves, "Careful now. Don't be blind! Is this really the best way to tie my shoes?" We would never get anything done if we had to stop and think at every step. Perhaps the real path of wisdom is to come to recognize *when* we need to stop and think, and not be blind.

BIBLIOGRAPHY

Langer, E. J. (2000). *Mindfulness*. Boston: Addison-Wesley Longman.

Luchins, A. S. (1942). Mechanization in problem solving: The effect of Einstellung. *Psychological Monographs, 54*, 1.

Luchins, A. S., & Luchins, E. H. (1950). New experimental attempts at preventing mechanization in problem solving. *Journal of General Psychology, 42*, 279–297.

Luchins, A. S., & Luchins, E. H. (1959). *Rigidity of behavior—A variational approach to the effect of Einstellung*. Eugene: University of Oregon Books.

Sternberg, R. J. (1999). *Cognitive psychology* (2nd ed.). New York: Harcourt Brace.

39 | GEORGE MILLER ON THE MAGIC NUMBER SEVEN

My problem is that I have been persecuted by an integer. For seven years this number has followed me around, has intruded in my most private data, and has assaulted me from the pages of our most public journals . . . Either there really is something unusual about the number or else I am suffering from delusions of persecution.

George A. Miller

Thus George A. Miller begins his discussion of the "magical number seven, plus or minus two" (Miller, 1956). Miller does not present a single classic experiment, but a discussion of many experiments, his own and those of others. His synthesis is so important to the field that it is presented here anyway.

George Armitage Miller (1920–) was born in Charleston, West Virginia. He received a B.A. from the University of Alabama in 1940 and Ph.D. from Harvard in 1946. At Harvard, during and after World War II, he studied speech production and comprehension. Impressed by C. E. Shannon's mathematical theory of communication (Shannon & Weaver, 1949), he extended it to his research on speech perception and later to memory; the parallels between these inspired the ideas summarized here.

Miller moved to the Rockefeller University in New York in 1968 and to Princeton in 1979. There he is now James S. McDonnell Distinguished University Professor of Psychology Emeritus.

To understand the research that Miller brings together in this paper, it will be helpful to take a brief look at *information theory*. The advantage of this mathematical technique is that it can bring together data that are quite different—taking different forms, with different materials—and summarize them all with a single measure.

The idea can be illustrated by the following example. Suppose someone says to you,

I am thinking of a number between one and eight. Your task is to determine what that number is. You may ask questions, but they have to be yes-or-no questions.

You could, of course, just guess one number at a time. Then it could take you up to eight guesses, if you were unlucky, to get the right number. A different strategy would guarantee the correct answer in exactly three guesses, no more. You should ask: "Is it between one and four? No? Then is it either five or six? No? Then is it seven? No? Then it must be eight." Of course, if the answer to the first question were yes (it is between one and four), then again two more questions, each cutting the alternatives in half, would specify what it is: "Is it either one or two? Yes? Then is it two?" If no, then the number has to be one.

We could say, then, that the original problem required three *bits of information* for its solution. A bit, when the term is used this way, does not mean an *item* of information, a statement like "It is raining outside." It stands for *binary digit*, and what it means is a single yes-or-no question where "yes" and "no" are equally likely. So we can also say that the original problem has in it *three bits' worth of uncertainty*; we have to ask three binary (yes or no) questions to answer it. We can also say that after we have answered the question, we have reduced our *uncertainty* about what the number is, from three bits to zero bits; and, therefore, a total of three *bits of information* has been transmitted.

Where there are more alternatives, and especially when they are not all equally probable, the mathematics gets more difficult, but the underlying idea remains the same. If one person transmits a message to another, we can ask how much uncertainty the receiver had, before the message came, as to what it would be. When the message comes, *if* it is received with complete accuracy, then it has reduced uncertainty by just that much, and just that much information has been transmitted. But if there are errors—if the messages is garbled—then there has been less information transmitted than there might have been. And we can use the mathematics of information theory to specify how much information has in fact been transmitted and, therefore, how much has been lost.

Miller then summarizes a number of experiments, published and unpublished, to which the information measure can be applied. When that is done, something surprising happens.

Suppose an observer is presented with a series of tones, varying in pitch. His task is to keep straight which tone is which, perhaps by giving each one a number. Then the tones are presented one by one, and the observer tries to call out the corresponding number for each. If there were eight tones, and if they were all equally likely, *and* if the observer made no mistakes, he or she would be transmitting three bits of information. If the observer made mistakes, he or she would transmits less.

Such an experiment was done. (References to these many experiments are in Miller, 1956.) It was found that when there were only two or three tones, the participants never confused them. With four, confusions were rare, but they occurred. With more than about six or so, the participants made many mistakes. In information terms, information transmission leveled off at about 2.5 bits, showing that the number of tones that could be identified without error was somewhat less than eight (3 bits). It was around six. "Stated slightly differently, no matter how many alternative tones we ask [the participants] to judge, the best we can expect him to do is to assign them to about six different classes without error" (Miller, 1956, p. 85).

(Miller adds, "Of course, there is evidence that a musically sophisticated person with absolute pitch can identify accurately any one of 50 or 60 different pitches. Fortunately, I do not have time to discuss these remarkable exceptions." Fortunately, neither do we—fortunately, because neither Miller nor the present author has any idea why this is so.)

The finding held up under a surprisingly wide range of conditions.

> The range of frequencies can be changed by a factor of about 20 without changing the amount of information transmitted more than a small percentage . . . if you can discriminate five high-pitched tones in one series and five low-pitched tones in another series, it is reasonable to expect that you could combine all ten into a single series and still tell them all apart without error. When you try it, however, it does not work [because the tones within each group, which had been discriminated perfectly before, now began to be confused with each other]. The channel capacity for pitch [that is, the maximum amount of information that can be transmitted in an experiment like this] seems to be about six and that is the best you can do. (Miller, 1956, p. 86)

So we have seen data for tones of different pitch. What if they differed in loudness? Again, there is a limit. The channel capacity for loudness is 2.3 bits; about five tones of different loudness can be identified without error.

Similar results apply for the intensities of tastes, where the observers identified salt solutions of different concentrations. The channel capacity was 1.9 bits; that is, about four different concentrations could be distinguished from each other. With visual position, channel capacity seems to be somewhat larger—channel capacity of 3.2 to 3.9 bits. It is about 2.8 bits for different sizes of objects seen, 3.1 bits for different colors, and 2.3 bits for brightness—between four and eight in each case. For vibrations on the skin, a good observer can identify about four intensities, about five durations, and about seven locations without error—from two bits to just under three.

Therefore, there seems to be some built-in limitation that keeps our channel capacities in this general range, for many—perhaps all—sensory attributes.

Now, all of these tasks required participants to make judgments along one sensory dimension only—pitch or size or saltiness. If we ask for judgments along two dimensions at once—if, for example, we ask participants to keep straight what number or name goes with what sound where the sounds vary in both pitch *and* loudness—participants do somewhat better. The amount of information transmitted increases, but it does not increase to the sum of the two dimensions separately. There are diminishing returns in accuracy as the number of dimensions increases.

Let us now look at another kind of perceptual judgment—the judgment of *numerosity*, or "how-many-ness." On a screen, slides are flashed briefly that show varying numbers of dots. The observer is asked simply to say how many dots there are.

With up to about five dots, *(a)* errors are extremely rare, and *(b)* the time it takes participants to make their judgment does not vary with the number of dots. It appears that one can see at a glance how many there are. With six or more dots, however, participants begin to make mistakes, they make more mistakes as the number increases, and their judgments take longer the more dots there are. It

Table 39.1
List of random numbers

8	9	5							
1	7	6	2						
6	9	0	9	8					
1	4	3	5	0	1				
5	0	3	8	9	3	7			
8	2	3	7	8	6	1	6		
9	6	7	6	5	8	9	4	2	
3	8	0	7	3	5	8	0	6	4

appears that a separate process comes in when the number of dots goes beyond six or so: one does not see at a glance how many dots there are, but has to count, and counting takes time. Here it is again: seven, plus or minus two.

Let us look again.

What is sometimes called *memory span*, sometimes called *digit span*, and sometimes called *attention span* can be measured in the following way (which, by the way, dates back to Wundt's laboratory). The participants may be read a series of letters (or see them on a screen; it doesn't much matter which). Or they may be read a series of digits, or shown those on the screen; again, it doesn't much matter. There will be few or no errors up to about five items; with more than that, errors will begin to creep in, and performance will be very poor if the number of items is greater than about nine. The magical number seven, plus or minus two!

This is so reliable that it can easily be used as an in-class demonstration. The reader can verify it. Make up lists of random numbers, varying in length from 3 to 10 digits. Table 39.1 gives a list of lists to get you started.

Read each list, then at the end of each list ask participants to write down the numbers they remember. Then read the next list, and so on. You will find that about four to five numbers can be recalled without mistake. Beyond that, errors get more and more frequent as the length of the list increases; with lists longer than eight or nine, hardly anyone will be perfectly accurate.

It does not have to be numbers. It can be lists of one-syllable words, and the same results will be obtained.

Or it can be (say) three-syllable words, and now a real mystery emerges. A three-syllable word is only one word, yes. But it is three syllables long. So the limit on the immediate memory—about seven—seems to apply to the words, not the syllables. In other words, one can remember almost three times as many *syllables* if the syllables are organized into three-syllable words. It seems that the multiple syllables

Figure 39.1
A partial "wiring diagram" of the mind

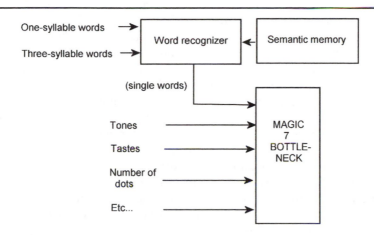

are given a certain unity by the perceptual apparatus *before* they meet the bottleneck at roughly seven items. Miller speaks of these unities as *chunks* of information. The bottleneck seems to apply to the chunks, not to the elements within them. The limit for three-syllable words is not very different from the limit for one-syllable words. Some part of the system, therefore, must "code" three-syllable words into single chunks of information *before* they reach the bottleneck of seven or so items.

The drama of this demonstration should not be overlooked. The bottleneck at roughly seven items applies to stimuli in a variety of sensory modalities, so they may in some sense "converge" at or before the bottleneck itself. Moreover, there must be a pattern-recognizing device that can chunk three-syllable sequences into single words, drawing on semantic memory, by which we recognize words. And that pattern-recognizing device must also come into play *before* the bottleneck is reached. This much can be summarized as in figure 39.1—a kind of provisional wiring diagram of the mind!

The chunking process can greatly increase the amount of information we can handle all at once. We probably cannot hold in our memories a string of 21 numbers: 101001000100001000100. But if we group them into fewer, larger numbers— 10, 100, 1000, 10000, 1000, 100—we can probably hold onto them (Sternberg, 1999). The larger numbers are chunks. Long strings of words may also be remembered if they can be chunked into familiar phrases remembered as single units: "Fourscore and seven years ago . . . "

For most psychologists, however, what is most impressive about Miller's conclusions is not that we can escape the "seven plus or minus" limit by chunking. information. It is that the limit is so stringent to begin with.

As an analogy, consider a computer with an enormous hard drive, on which an enormous amount of information—everything we know!—is stored. But now suppose that the monitor screen is so small that there is room for only about seven icons. That would be all the information we could work with *at any one time*. The data Miller summarizes suggests that our minds are very much like that. It is true that the icons may be file folders—chunks—in which larger quantities of information can be stored. But to look at the contents of any folder, we must open it, and this may preclude our looking inside the other folders. The fact seems to be that in the normal course of events, the number of items that we can consider all at one time is far more sharply limited than we would have supposed.

This fact has many ramifications. Our store of memories and knowledge is enormous, yes. But we can *search* our memories only within the limits of the tiny monitor screen. How can we search that enormous memory effectively, given the very limited amount of space we have on our cognitive "monitor screen"? To pull out the information we need in any reasonable amount of time requires an efficient filing system (chapter 35). We also resort, of necessity, to rules of thumb, or *heuristics* (Tversky & Kahneman, 1974), to guide our search through memory. We may deal only with information that is readily available in memory, or information that we have used before in similar situations, or information that fits our preconceptions. Such information is not always the *best* information we could use, and so these rules of thumb can lead us to make mistakes (for discussion, see Nisbett & Ross, 1980). But if we did not make use of them, we might not be able to remember effectively at all, given our limited capacity.

Miller concludes,

> Finally, what about the magical number seven? What about the seven wonders of the world, the seven seas, the seven deadly sins, the seven daughters of Atlas in the Pleiades, the seven ages of man, the seven levels of hell . . . , and the seven digits in the span of immediate memory? For the present I propose to withhold judgment. Perhaps there is something deep and profound behind all these sevens, something just calling out for us to discover it. But I suspect that it is only a pernicious, Pythagorean coincidence.

Perhaps.

BIBLIOGRAPHY

Attneave, F. (1959). *Applications of information theory to psychology: A summary of basic concepts, methods, and results.* New York: Holt.

Miller, G. A. (1956). The magical number seven, plus or minus two: Some limits on our capacity for processing information. *Psychological Review, 63,* 81–97.

Miller, G. A. (1962). *Psychology: The science of mental life.* New York: Harper & Row.

Nisbett, R. E., & Ross, L. (1980). *Human inference: Strategies and shortcomings of social judgment.* Englewood Cliffs, NJ: Prentice-Hall.

Shannon, C. E., & Weaver, W. (1949). *The mathematical theory of communication.* Urbana: University of Illinois.

Sternberg, R. J. (1999). *Cognitive psychology* (2nd ed.). New York: Harcourt Brace.

Tversky, A., & Kahneman, D. (1974). Judgment under uncertainty: Heuristics and biases. *Science, 185,* 1124–1131.

40 | FESTINGER AND CARLSMITH: COGNITIVE DISSONANCE

The theory of *cognitive dissonance* originated with Leon Festinger, a student of Kurt Lewin (chapter 55). A highly influential theory, it reverses the relation between cognition and action that is most familiar. The familiar theory says, On the basis of what we think and feel, we decide what to do. But also—and this was Festinger's insight—there can be effects in the other direction. What we do may affect what we think and feel (Festinger, 1957). The present experiment, by Leon Festinger and J. Merrill Carlsmith (1959), was a test of that idea.

Leon Festinger (1919–89) was born in New York City. He earned a B.A. from the City College of New York, then his Ph.D. at the State University of Iowa in 1942; here he studied with Lewin. In 1968 he went to the New School for Social Research in New York City, where he remained until his death.

James Merrill Carlsmith (1936–85) was born in New Orleans. He received his A.B. from Stanford in 1958 and his Ph.D. from Harvard in 1963. He taught at Yale from 1962 to 1964, then returned to Stanford, where he remained until his untimely death.

Cognitive dissonance does not refer just to an inner conflict, as when we have difficulty deciding whether to study or go to a party, or whether to accept—or offer—a proposal of marriage. It refers to a specific conflict between something that we believe and some action that we have taken. If we believe X, but have done something that is incompatible with X, we feel an uncomfortable tension because of the inconsistency itself. The dissonance—a kind of mental clash—is between two contradictory ideas: "I believe X," and "I have done this thing that is incompatible with X." The simultaneous presence of these two ideas makes us uncomfortable. We don't like to be inconsistent. That discomfort is the result of cognitive dissonance.

That was Festinger's original idea. More recently, some writers have suggested that dissonance requires a more specific conflict: the action we have taken must clash with our self-esteem. The dissonance, in other words, is between the idea "I am an honest, sensible, kind person—in other words, I'm OK" on the one hand,

and "I have just done this dishonest, foolish, or cruel thing" on the other. (For discussion see Aronson, 1999).

Either way, the theory says that feeling that uncomfortable dissonance, we attempt to reduce it. How can we do that? We could act differently, perhaps, in a way that fits our attitudes and values better. But what if the action has already taken place? We cannot change it now. What we can change, however, is our *attitude toward* that action. If we can manage to convince ourselves that the action really was not dishonest, foolish, or cruel, then the dissonance will be reduced. The thought "This action was really a reasonable one after all" is compatible with the thought "I'm a reasonable, sensible, good person, and I performed that action." If we can believe both these things, dissonance is removed, or at least made less.

Thus far, the theory is only a theory. However, in science, theories must be tested to see if they are valid. Predictions based on *this* theory have been tested, by experiment, many times—and confirmed. The present experiment was one of the earliest of these.

The experiment was done in three phases. First, the investigators asked their participants (college students) to perform a boring and repetitive series of tasks. These tasks included things like putting spools into a tray, then dumping them out, then putting them in again—over and over—a pointless, dull task, and intended to be so. The students engaged in activities like this one for a full hour. The procedure, in a word, was specifically designed to induce stupefying boredom.

Then came the second phase, when the participants thought the experiment was over—but it was not. A young woman was waiting to participate in the experiment, or so the participants thought; what they did not know was that she was an assistant to the experimenter.

The experimenter said, in effect, "Look, someone else is waiting to do the same things you did, and it's important that she think the task she's about to perform is interesting and enjoyable. Please tell her it was. I will pay you . . . " And then some participants were offered a dollar, but others were offered 20 dollars, to tell the lie.

In short, the participants were asked to lie to the woman, telling her that the task she would be performing was interesting and enjoyable when it was not. They were asked, that is, to be dishonest. The independent variable was how much the participant was rewarded for telling the lie: some were offered 20 dollars to tell the lie; others were offered only 1 dollar for doing so. (An ingenious cover story made all this sound quite plausible.)

Finally, as the third phase, an interviewer asked these participants—the ones who had told the lie—how they themselves felt about the tasks they had performed earlier in the experiment. Were the tasks enjoyable, or not, and how enjoyable? The results were clear. Those students who had been paid $20 for lying—that is, for saying the spool packing and the like had been enjoyable when they had not—rated the activity as dull (which of course it was). But the students who had been paid only a small amount to tell the lie actually rated the task as more enjoyable. In other words, people who received an abundant reward for lying did not change their attitudes about the tasks. But those who received little reward changed their attitudes in the direction of *believing that what they had said was true*. After having said it, they came to believe it. Saying was believing.

Why would that happen? Cognitive-dissonance theory supposes that under each condition, participants will engage in an internal dialogue with themselves, something like the following.

For the $20 condition, they can say, "I just told a lie. That is not consistent with [it is dissonant with] my image of myself as a truthful, honest person." Those two items do not fit together. Then again, perhaps they do—for they can also say, "Well, for 20 dollars, who wouldn't tell a harmless lie? I did it, but anyone would. I'm still OK." In other words, the large external reward makes the two items of knowledge ("I told a lie," and "I'm OK") compatible with each other: "I told a lie, but anyone would do so in these circumstances, so I'm OK anyway."

But what if there were no large external reward? A mere dollar doesn't justify a barefaced lie. A participant in that condition should feel the discomfort of the two dissonant cognitions: "I'm OK," but also "I lied."

Then, says the theory, some cognitive work must be done. They could reconcile their actions with their self-esteem if they could change one of the two cognitions so that they no longer clashed. Well, the lie is told, and the participants cannot change that. However, what they can change is their *attitude about the boring task itself.* If they can persuade themselves that it really wasn't so boring—that packing spools is a relaxing thing to do, actually—then they *would not have lied.* And they could then have two quite compatible cognitions: "I'm OK" and "I told the truth about the task."

Therefore, the subjects who had told a lie for only a little money should later rate the task itself as *more interesting and enjoyable* than did the subjects who were paid well for their lie. And that is exactly what happened.

Before leaving this experiment, we should address an issue that often troubles readers on their first contact with this theory. Participants, we have said, change their minds about what they're feeling, in order to reduce dissonance. But do we not know directly what we are feeling? Cannot participants just look inside themselves, see how they feel about (say) a boring task, and report it?

It would seem that the answer has to be no. If it were that simple, then the experimental manipulation should have had no effect. The small reward, for the participants who received it, could not have acted backward in time to make the task actually less boring. So if it seems less boring to participants now, this can only be because the experimental manipulation affects our present judgment about how boring it must have been. But if that is so, then our report of its "boringness" does depend on our later judgment about what "must have been the case" back then. And this judgment can be affected by such factors as cognitive dissonance as well as by what we actually felt at the time.

The concept of cognitive distance has been applied to a wide variety of cases, and the student of cognitive psychology, social psychology, or the psychology of motivation will encounter it often. We cannot begin to survey these investigations here (see Aronson, 1999), but a small sample may help to convey just what a widely applicable idea it is.

Here are a few.

1. Consider this case of dissonance: "I have hurt this person. That means that I, a kind and humane person, have done a cruel thing." Can we reconcile these conflicting ideas? Perhaps, if we can say, "I hurt this person, but he deserved it! In which case my hurting him was not such a bad thing after all. Maybe I ought to hurt him some more!" This process, which has been shown by direct experiment, may shed some light on the atrocities that occurred during World War II—and elsewhere.

2. "I have sold my house, given away my possessions, stripped away my entire life, in anticipation of a prophecy—but then it did not come true! How could a sensible person like me have done such a thing?" One can escape such a clash of cognitions if one can say, "Well, maybe it was sensible after all—maybe the prophecy will still come true. In fact, I'm sure it will!" (see chapter 57).

3. Cognitive dissonance may play a role in the notorious *sunk-cost* effect, which can be illustrated as follows.

First, which would we rather do, spent $100 and be in a place we want to be, or spend $100 and be in a place we don't want to be? Not a hard decision. Of course we'd choose the first of these options!

But now consider a specific instance. Suppose a couple are driving from their home in the city to a beach, where they plan to spend the day and night. They have made a nonrefundable deposit of $100 for a hotel room. As they drive along, they see that there are thunderclouds in the sky, which seem to be getting more and more threatening as time goes by; and suppose that they are not feeling very well anyway. Our couple might agree with each other that, all things considered, time at the beach will not be much fun. Perhaps they really would prefer to spend the day and the evening together at home, in comfort and without the stress of a long drive. Will they then turn around and head for home? That is exactly the kind of problem that was posed earlier: be $100 poorer and in a pleasant place, or be $100 poorer and be in a less pleasant place. Since $100 is spent either way, better to be comfortable than not to be.

However, cognitive dissonance may come into play. One or both of our couple might say, "If we go back, we won't get our deposit back and the money will have been wasted. It's foolish to waste money, and we are not foolish people. So we should go ahead and use the hotel room that we have already paid for."

In strict rationality, this argument makes no sense at all. The $100 has already been spent and is irrevocably lost—it is a *sunk cost*. Nothing the couple can do will bring it back. So the only decision that confronts the couple now is, having already spent the $100, should we now go to a place where we would rather be, or to a place where we would rather not be?

The $100 deposit is what decision theorists refer to as a *sunk cost*—sunk because it is irretrievable, as if it had sunk to the bottom of the sea. That money has already been spent, so it ought to drop out of the equation for a decision that we go on to make *now*.

But our tendency is not to think of it that way. Instead, cognitive dissonance is likely to kick in. We think of the decision to go back home as spending $100 for nothing, which seems foolish; and we don't like to seem foolish. We are likely to go on, even though we only add a miserable weekend to the cost we have already incurred. At least we have reduced our cognitive dissonance!

The sunk-cost effect is what we refer to as "throwing good money [or time or energy] after bad." It can come about when we say to ourselves, "We—who are rational, sensible people—have invested all this time, money, or other resources into trying to bring about such-and-such an outcome by this or that method. It hasn't worked. Maybe we should try something different." But then cognitive dissonance says, "How could rational, sensible people like us have invested so much in an ineffective program?" And we can reduce the dissonance by saying, "Well, maybe it isn't so ineffective after all. Surely if we invest even more resources or try harder, it will work—next time." So we try the old way—once again.

The consequences of this can go far beyond laboratory experiments and whether packing spools is fun. Historian Barbara Tuchman tells us, "No matter how often a campaign that depended on living off a hostile country ran into want and even starvation, as in the English invasion of France in the Hundred Years' War, campaigns for which this fate was inevitable were regularly undertaken" (1984, p. 8). Festinger's theory may help us understand why we so often do not learn from our mistakes.

Again, these are only samples of an idea that has many ramifications. For more, the reader is referred to Aronson's excellent review (1999).

BIBLIOGRAPHY

Aronson, E. (1999). *The social animal* (8th ed.). New York: Worth Publishers.

Festinger, L. (1957). *A theory of cognitive dissonance*. Evanston, IL: Row, Peterson.

Festinger, L., & Carlsmith, J. M. (1959). Cognitive consequences of forced compliance. *Journal of Abnormal and Social Psychology, 58*, 203–210.

Hastie, R., & Dawes, R. M. (2001). *Rational choice in an uncertain world*. Thousand Oaks, CA: Sage.

Tuchman, B. W. (1984). *The march of folly*. New York: Knopf.

41 | ROGER SHEPARD AND MENTAL ROTATION

The rise of behaviorism began with a controversy: Can one study mental events scientifically at all? In this debate, the topic of *mental imagery* was one of the major battlegrounds.

Imagery—the thoughts of goals not yet attained, of times gone by, of imaginary persons, places, and events—is an important part of our mental life. But how can we study it? A person's images are locked up inside his or her own head; no one else can observe them. Scientific data, on the other hand, should be accessible to everyone, so that scientists can check and verify each other's conclusions, or resolve any differences that might arise. This did not seem possible with such "private" events as images. Indeed, the study of images by introspection did bog down in unresolvable disagreements (Humphrey, 1951). The failure of these early attempts to study imagery was one of the factors that drove the behaviorist revolution early in the twentieth century.

Yet there proved to be ways, and, ironically, the successful study of imagery was one of the factors that drove the *cognitive* revolution of the 1960s! Among these success stories, the experiments of Roger Shepard and his colleagues were landmarks.

Roger Newland Shepard (1929–) was born in Palo Alto, California. He graduated from Stanford in 1951, and in 1955 received his Ph.D. from Yale University. Following this he was a postdoctoral associate at Washington's Naval Research Laboratory and then at Harvard University. In 1968 he returned to Stanford, where the present experiments were performed and where he has remained. He retired from teaching in 1996, but continues his theoretical research and writing.

The experiment now discussed (Cooper & Shepard, 1973; see also Shepard & Cooper, 1982; Shepard & Metzler, 1971) asked this question: Does the manipulation of mental images, like the manipulation of physical objects, *take time?* We shall examine the experiment itself first, and then look more closely at the careful thinking that went into it.

Figure 41.1
Stimuli of the kind used by Cooper and Shepard in their mental-rotation experiments

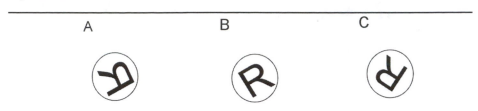

Each participant was seated in front of a screen, on which an image would appear. On each trial, the image consisted of a letter, like the letter *R*, either facing correctly (on some trials) or facing the wrong way (on others). And for both correct and backward letters, the letter was rotated to some degree or another (including zero). Figure 41.1 shows some of the stimuli that were presented.

Suppose, on a given trial, a stimulus like figure 41.1 A appears. The participant's task is to judge whether the *R* is facing the right way or backwards. The participant presses one of two keyboard keys to record his or her judgment, one if he or she thinks it's right, the other if he or she thinks it's backwards. In this case, the participant should judge that it is backwards. But the crucial point is this: to see whether it is backwards or not, the participant has to rotate the figure mentally, "in the mind's eye," to the upright position, and then decide.

Each participant was shown a series of *R* and reverse-*R* figures like these, some right, some reversed. For each one, the participant was asked to judge whether it was facing the right way or not. The various figures, both correct and reversed, were shown at different orientations on different trials. Sometimes they were rotated only a little (figure 41.1 B); sometimes they were rotated much more (figure 41.1 C), so that they had to be rotated mentally sometimes a little, sometimes a lot, to be imagined in the upright position. On each trial, the subject recorded his or her judgments as quickly as possible by pressing one key or the other.

Now, if the mental rotation of an object takes time, then it should take longer to make such a judgment if a great deal of rotation is required than if only a little is required. And that is exactly what was found (figure 41.2). The differences were small, but they were very consistent and formed a clear pattern. The line running through the points is a straight line, and that means that each degree of rotation added a constant amount to the total time required to make the decision. In other words, the mental rotation of these figures proceeded at a constant rate.

So two things about mental rotation have been discovered: mental rotation does take time, and it occurs at a constant speed. Other experiments showed that the speed of mental rotation was about the same whether the stimulus had to be rotated mentally in two dimensions (as here), or in three dimensions (Shepard & Metzler, 1971); and in three dimensions too, it occurred at about the same constant rate as for two.

This experiment may seem a simple one, but in fact a great deal of thought went into it. Besides its surface conclusions—mental rotation takes time, and proceeds

Figure 41.2
Results of Cooper and Shepard's mental-rotation experiment. The more mental rotation was required, the longer participants took to make their judgments, showing that mental rotation takes time.

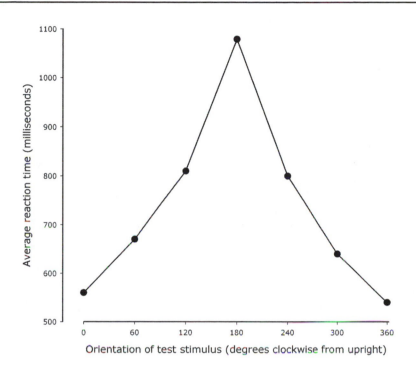

Source: Reprinted from Cooper & Shepard (1973, pp. 75–176). © 1973, with permission from Elsevier.

at a constant rate—the experiment is a case study in *how mental events can be studied objectively.*

In early studies of mental imagery, participants were asked to *describe* their mental images (Humphrey, 1951). It was found that different people describe their images very differently: some describe them as sharp and clear, others as blurred and fuzzy. The trouble is that we do not know that the different people are using words in the same way. For all we know, an image that one person describes as blurred and fuzzy, another might describe as sharp and clear. All this makes it very difficult to compare one introspective report with another.

In the Cooper and Shepard experiment, the problem does not arise. Nowhere in the experiment were the participants asked to *describe* their imagery. Instead, they were required to *use* mental imagery to solve a problem: Is the letter reversed, or not? And the time required to solve the problem varied with how much manipulation of the mental image was required—an *objective* fact that anyone could verify.

In short, these experiments show that "private events" like mental images can in fact be studied experimentally. It is true that no one can see anyone else's images—

just as no one can see an electron. However, images—like electrons—can be made to have *consequences* that we can observe; and by observing them, we can learn things about invisible entities like electrons—or mental images. The early behaviorists were overly pessimistic.

Besides showing us one way in which mental imagery can be studied objectively, this experiment is instructive as an excellent example of *control procedures* in experimentation. It is worth looking at the experiment again, to understand just why it was done the way it was.

Over a series of trials, the orientation of the letter was varied. Sometimes it was upright, sometimes it was rotated a little bit, sometimes it was rotated a lot. Suppose instead that the experiment had used a single orientation throughout, and that the experimenters had measured the time from presentation of the figure to the button press itself. The trouble is that that total reaction time would have been composed of the time required to (1) register the stimulus; (2) rotate it mentally; (3) decide whether it was correct or reversed; (4) on the basis of this, decide which button to press; and (5) send out the command from the brain to the finger-moving muscles. Then there is (6) the time required by the mechanical events at the muscle itself. We would not know how much of this total time was attributable to step 2, the mental rotation, which is the step that is of interest.

Varying the degree of rotation, however, isolates step 2. All of the other events in the chain should take the *same* amount of time, whatever the degree of rotation might be. But if mental rotation itself takes time, then the *total* time should be longer if a lot of rotation is required than if only a little rotation is. And that is exactly what was found. (It is worth noting that the logic of this was exactly the same as in Helmholtz's experiment, in which the position of the stimulus was varied so that only *one* step in the chain of events—how far the message had to travel—could affect the differences in total reaction time [chapter 3].)

Why were some of the letters backwards and others not? This too was a control procedure, designed to keep the participants' attention on the task and to ensure that they were actually performing the mental rotation. Suppose instead that the letter had always been backwards. Then alert participants would very quickly have caught on to that fact. They might then simply have responded with the "reversed" button on every trial, either out of boredom or out of the desire to look like a good, fast-responding participant. They might have responded that way on every trial without even looking at the screen!

As it was, the participants had a decision to make on each trial, and it was possible to make a mistake. Therefore, the participants *had* to attend to what was on the screen in order to avoid such mistakes. And it seems that the participants did do that, for, as it turned out, the number of incorrect responses was very low at all degrees of rotation.

Finally, like most good experiments, this one raises questions. Mental rotation, we saw, proceeds at a constant speed. But surely this is not true of all "mental movement." Consider: A reader sitting in a chair in New York City can imagine being in Philadelphia some 90 miles away, or being in London several thousand miles away. It does not seem as if the second of these requires any more time than the first. If it does not, why not? Why should such "mental translation" halfway around the earth be different from mental rotation in these experiments? The reader is invited to think of some possible reasons, and then—the real challenge—think of some ways of testing the various possibilities.

BIBLIOGRAPHY

Cooper, L. A., & Shepard, R. M. (1973). Chronometric studies of the rotation of mental images. In W. G. Chase (Ed.), *Visual information processing.* New York: Academic Press.

Humphrey, G. (1951). *Thinking.* London: Methuen.

Reisberg, D. (1997). *Cognition: Exploring the science of the mind.* New York: Norton.

Shepard, R. N. (1978). The mental image. *American Psychologist, 33,* 125–137.

Shepard, R. N. (1990). *Mind sights.* New York: Freeman.

Shepard, R. N., & Cooper, L. A. (1982). *Mental images and their transformations.* Cambridge, MA: MIT Press.

Shepard, R. N., & Metzler, J. (1971). Mental rotation of three-dimensional objects. *Science, 171,* 701–703.

42 | RICHARD HERRNSTEIN: CONCEPTS IN PIGEONS

How smart are animals? The question intrigued many of us when we were small, and continues to intrigue some of us now that we are large. The difficult question is, How do we find out?

The story of Clever Hans (chapter 37) is a cautionary tale, showing how easily we may be misled without proper controls. This chapter is a success story, which shows (with proper controls) just how impressive are the cognitive capacities of one animal species—the lowly pigeon. The experiments were conducted by Richard Herrnstein and his colleagues.

Richard J. Herrnstein (1930–94) was born in New York City. He graduated from New York's High School of Music and Art as a violinist. He completed his undergraduate studies at the College of the City of New York, then earned his Ph.D. from Harvard in 1955, working with B. F. Skinner. After stints in the army and at the University of Maryland, he returned to Harvard in 1958 and remained there until his death.

His experimental work focused on the study of choice in operant behavior, experiments in which a pigeon might have two responses available, each reinforced on a different schedule (chapter 23). What rules govern their choices, and how were these related to the "rational" choices made, purportedly, by humans? He was one of those who looked both at economic theories of choice and the findings of behavioral psychology, and so helped found the emerging field of *behavioral economics* (compare chapter 43). This line of thought also brought the study of *discrimination* in nonhuman animals into contact with the study of concept formation, and led him to the study of how pigeons form and use complex, open-ended concepts. Those are the experiments this chapter will discuss.

The techniques of operant conditioning, developed by Skinner and his associates (chapter 23), permit astonishingly powerful control over behavior in experimental situations. The effects of schedules of reinforcement, for instance, can be seen reliably in the behavior of individual animals and humans.

These effects are of interest in their own right. But they can also be used as a tool with which to study other things. Operant conditioning can give our animal a kind of language, with which it can tell us something about what it perceives, or knows, or understands (compare the work of Tolman, chapter 22).

A simple example is the following. Suppose a pigeon is in a box, with a key mounted on the wall at which it can peck, and that pecking is reinforced with food. In the box, a light is sometimes on, sometimes off. Suppose too that the experimenters set this rule: When the light is on, pecking the key will *occasionally* be reinforced; that is, it will lead to food. When the light is off, the response will never be reinforced. Thus, the presence of the light is a cue that food is available; absence of the light is a cue that it is not. The use of *occasional* (e.g., variable-interval) reinforcement means, first, that a great deal of behavior can be observed without the bird's becoming satiated, and, second, that the bird cannot use the absence of reinforcement for any *single* peck as a cue that reinforcement is unavailable.

When well trained at this *discrimination learning*, the pigeon will respond only when the light is on, and not respond, or respond at a much lower rate, when the light is off. If this happens, it tells the experimenters (a) that the bird can master that rule, and (b) that it can see the light. In other words, we can use this technique to learn something about the bird's perceptual capabilities. We can even determine how sensitive its visual system is, by measuring thresholds (Blough, 1956).

The same logic can be extended. One can ask whether an animal is capable of more complex and subtle perceptual and conceptual feats.

A dramatic example is the demonstration by Herrnstein and his coworkers that pigeons are capable of forming and using highly abstract concepts. For example, consider the concept *human being*. That is an extraordinarily complex concept. Human beings come in a wide variety of sizes, shapes, colors, and so on. And it is not clear that we can even list the features that define *human being*. We can see, for example, that a person lacking all four limbs is still a human being; so is a person wearing a mask so we cannot see his or her face. We can come across a person who looks quite different from any person we have ever seen before and still recognize him or her as a human being. We must have very abstract and open-ended rules for deciding whether this or that figure that we are now seeing is or is not a human being.

Can a pigeon learn such a complex concept? The ingenious series of experiments by Herrnstein and his colleagues (Herrnstein & Loveland, 1964; Herrnstein, Loveland, & Cable, 1976) showed how that question can be investigated, and showed that the answer is yes.

Return to the idea of a pigeon in a box, with a pecking key mounted on the wall. But now, there is also a translucent screen mounted on the wall. Slides can be projected from outside the box onto the screen so that the bird can see them. In these experiments, a large number of such slides were presented. They were presented one at a time, each for a few minutes; then the slide projector would advance, and the next slide would appear. The slides were photographs, and they showed various scenes from natural settings.

Now, in some of these slides, there was a person, or people, in the scene. In others, there was not. Then the experimenters set this rule: If a person or people appeared in the picture, pecking at the key would occasionally be reinforced with food. If there was no person, pecking was never reinforced. This is analogous to the light on/light off experiment described earlier: A person in the picture is a cue that food is (occasionally) available. No person in the picture is a cue that it is not available.

If the pigeon could master the concept *human being*, then eventually the pigeon ought to stop pecking when shown a picture with no people in it. But the pigeon should peck away at a high rate when the picture did show people.

And that is what the pigeons did. After extensive training, every bird came to respond at a high rates to pictures with people, but at a lower rate when nonpeople pictures were shown. The birds made mistakes, of course (it is a difficult concept), so that they sometimes pecked at pictures with no people. However the *rate* of response came to be reliably higher if there were people in the picture than if there were not. The pigeons had grasped the concept *human being*. They were able to recognize any instance or instances of that concept, and to use that instance as a cue to peck away at a high rate.

All the slides were presented, and responses were recorded and reinforced (when they were reinforced) by automated equipment. The experimenters were removed from the situation altogether. They could not see the pigeon, and the pigeon could not see them. So they could not have fed the pigeon unconscious cues as to when to peck, even if they had wanted to. Thus the Clever Hans effect (chapter 37) was controlled for.

However, there is perhaps another difficulty here. It is possible that the birds had simply memorized all the pictures there were and memorized for each picture whether or not it signaled that food was available. That would still be an extraordinary feat of memory, but it would be a matter of memory rather than of understanding a concept. To check this possibility, well-trained birds were tested with new slides that they had never seen before. Once again, some slides showed a person or people; some did not. The birds continued to respond appropriately: people in the picture, high response rate; no people in the picture, low response rate.

Other experiments extended these findings to other abstract and open-ended concepts, such as *tree*, or *body of water*. Indeed, one of these extraordinary experiments (Herrnstein et al., 1976) showed, with different animals, that pigeons could come to recognize a *particular* human being, a certain Ms. X. The procedure was the same as before, but now the rule was, If a picture shows Ms. X—alone or with others, full-face or side view or partially blocked by something else—then food is available. If Ms X is not in the picture, regardless of who or what *is* there—then food is not available.

The birds came to respond appropriately, pecking at a high rate when, and only when, Ms. X was somewhere in the picture. Again, once they had mastered it, they maintained this discrimination with new slides shown for the first time. The experimenters even tried to fool the pigeons, showing pictures of Ms. X in someone else's apartment, or someone else in hers, or Ms. X wearing her boyfriend's coat and hat. They could not fool the pigeons! If a slide showed Ms. X, response rate was high; if not, it was low. The pigeons could recognize Ms. X on sight—even in new settings, and even though they never saw her in the flesh, but only her pictures on a screen.

What does it matter that a pigeon can do this? Consider that a pigeon's whole brain is comfortably smaller than a human being's thumb. Yet the cells of a pigeon brain are about the same size as those of a human brain, so the pigeon must have vastly fewer of them. Thus, this complex cognitive operation can be performed by a system that is much simpler than we might have supposed. By studying the process in a simpler system, we can gain insights into how a more complex system might work. In addition, we can perform experiments with pigeons that would be quite impossible with human beings.

The findings, in other words, give us a whole new way of studying how *a* brain—even if it is not *our* brain—can form and use complex concepts. And they certainly put the expression "bird brain" in a new light.

BIBLIOGRAPHY

Blough, D. S. (1956). Dark adaptation in the pigeon. *Journal of Comparative and Physiological Psychology, 49*, 425–430.

Ferster, C. B., & Skinner, B. F. (1957). *Schedules of reinforcement*. New York: Appleton-Century-Crofts.

Herrnstein, R. J. (1985). Riddles of natural categorization. In L. Weiskrantz (Ed.), *Animal intelligence* (Vol. 7, pp. 129–144). Oxford, UK: Clarendon Press.

Herrnstein, R. J., & Loveland, D. H. (1964). Complex visual concept in the pigeon. *Science, 146*, 549–551.

Herrnstein, R. J., Loveland, D. H., & Cable, C. (1976). Natural concepts in pigeons. *Journal of Experimental Psychology: Animal Behavior Processes, 2*, 285–301.

Pearce, J. M. (1997). *Animal learning and cognition: An introduction*. Hove, UK: Psychology Press.

43 TVERSKY AND KAHNEMAN: THE FRAMING OF DECISIONS

Our cognitive apparatus would be of little use if it were not able to guide our actions. But of course it is: it allows us to make *decisions*, and life is one decision after another. Shall one have scrambled eggs for breakfast this morning, or cereal, or no breakfast at all? Sign up for this course or for that course? Accept this person's proposal of marriage, or reject it? Decisions everywhere. How do we make decisions? How ought we to do so?

Interest in the problem is centuries old. Mathematical theories of the process began with gamblers and their mathematician colleagues and consultants, and since then have also recruited the efforts of economists, computer scientists, and, of course, behavioral and cognitive scientists.

We cannot survey this literature here, but we can say this much: a fundamental assumption is that our decisions are *rational*, at least to the extent that they are consistent with each other. If we prefer A to B and B to C, then we ought to prefer A to C. Or, if we like A better than B, we ought to like B less than A. Surely our decisions and choices are rational to that simple extent!

They are not—at least, not always.

Now, we hardly need to be told that behavior is not always rational. But the experiments on this problem are so simple, yet the results are so irrational, that they can serve as simplified models of human irrationality that perhaps will allow us to understand it better. They also suggest that perhaps our concept of what rationality *means* is less clear than we have supposed. Among the classic experiments on this point are the elegantly simple experiments on the "framing" of decisions, conducted by Amos Tversky and Daniel Kahneman.

Amos Tversky (1937–96) was born in Haifa, Israel. He received his B.A. degree from Hebrew University in Jerusalem in 1961, majoring in philosophy and psychology. He received his Ph.D. from the University of Michigan in 1965. Tversky taught for many years at Hebrew University (1966–78) and at Stanford University (1978–96). From 1992, he held an appointment as senior visiting professor of economics and psychology and permanent fellow of the Sackler Institute of Advanced Studies at Tel Aviv University. He also taught at the University of Göteborg (Sweden), the State University of New York at Buffalo, the University of Chicago, and Yale University.

Daniel Kahneman (1934–) was born in Tel Aviv. He studied psychology and mathematics at Hebrew University in Jerusalem, and received his Ph.D. in psychology at the University of California in 1961. He taught at Hebrew University from 1961 to 1978, becoming a professor in 1973, and at the University of British Columbia from 1978 to 1986. From 1986 to 1994, he was a professor of psychology at the University of California at Berkeley, and in 1993 became a professor of public affairs at the Woodrow Wilson School of Public and International Affairs at Princeton University.

The two scientists together developed an approach to the study of judgment and decision making that influenced both psychology and economics, by introducing psychological concepts and methods into the study of economic decisions. The approach is now known as *behavioral economics.*

In one of their experiments (Tversky & Kahneman, 1981), the procedure was as follows: Participants were divided into two groups. Then two forms of a decision problem were presented, one to each group. They both began with the following "stem":

> Imagine that the U.S. is preparing for the outbreak of an unusual Asian disease which is expected to kill 600 people. Two alternative programs to combat the disease have been proposed. Assume that the exact scientific estimate of the consequences of the programs are as follows.

Then, for half the participants, the scenario continued as follows:

> If program A is adopted, 200 people will be saved. If program B is adopted, there is a 1/3 probability that 600 people will be saved, and a 2/3 probability that no people will be saved. Which of the two programs would you favor?

But for the other half, the continuation was,

> If program C is adopted, 400 people will die. If program D is adopted, there is a 1/3 probability that nobody will die, and a 2/3 probability that 600 people will die. Which of the two programs would you favor?

If we look over the two scenarios, which the participants were not able to do, we see that the two decision problems are exactly the same. Programs A and C describe the same outcome: 200 people will be saved, but 400 people will die. Programs B and D also describe the same outcome: a 1/3 probability that all will be saved (no one will die), and a 2/3 probability that no one will be saved (600 people will die). If outcome A is preferred to B by most people, then outcome C should be preferred to D, for they represent the same pair of consequences.

But in fact, the reactions of the two groups of participants were very different. Of those who received the first alternative programs A and B, which stated the decision in terms of *lives saved*, 72 percent of the participants preferred A. But in the second case, where the problem was stated in terms of *lives lost*, the preference was reversed: 78 percent preferred D!

This inconsistency simply cannot be reconciled with our minimal requirement of consistency. The choices change, not because the actual outcome of lives saved or lives lost do, but because of the way we look at the problem.

We can see why the notion of *framing* is appropriate. It is as if some participants were looking at the problem through a window that showed lives lost, and others were looking at the same problem through a different window that showed lives saved. Different window, different decisions—even for what was actually the same decision problem.

Why does this happen? These and other findings point to what seems to be a consistent pattern in our decision making. We are *risk seeking* in cases where we are contemplating *losses*. Thus, when the disease problem is framed in terms of deaths, we choose the risky alternative, where at least there is *some* prospect of saving everyone. But when we are contemplating *gains*, then we are *risk averse*; we would rather hold onto a sure thing. (As to why this should be so, see Kahneman & Tversky, 1979.) The results follow immediately from these two tendencies.

This simple, classic experiment is only one of many that have since been done, with similar findings: decisions may be affected by the way the alternatives are presented. (For review and discussion, see Reisberg, 1997; Mook, 1996.) In one experiment, participants were to evaluate two medical procedures—surgery and radiation—as treatments for cancer. But the question could be framed in different ways. Some participants were given *survival rates;* these tended to favor surgery. But when the same data were presented in terms of *mortality rates* instead, the picture was quite different: a much higher percentage of the participants chose radiation. The same effect was observed in college students, medical students, and physicians.

In another, simulated juries were asked to make decisions in a child-custody case following a divorce. The participants were given descriptions of each parent, each presenting some positive and some negative features. Then they were asked either "Which parent would you *award* custody to?" or "Which parent would you *deny* custody to?" The decision problem was the same for both: one parent awarded custody, the other denied it. However, participants' responses were markedly different, depending on which way the question was posed to them.

Finally, we see framing effects very often in everyday life. One merchant offers a *discount for cash*. Another imposes a *surcharge for using a credit card*. The numbers resulting may be exactly the same in the two cases, but the one sounds like a bargain and the other like gouging Or, a very real-world example: the United States Internal Revenue Service may be wise to deduct taxes from citizens' paychecks, rather than letting them keep the money and pay some of it to the IRS at the end of the tax year. Might one be more likely to cheat on income taxes—taking a risk in order to avoid the certainty of a loss—than one would be if one were not contemplating a loss, but only foregoing a gain? We accept risks if threatened with a loss!

There is yet another, even more worrisome problem posed by data such as these.

Consider again the disease problem that we began with. Different frames led to different outcomes for the same set of alternatives. It is natural to wonder which of the two frames is the *right* one—which way of looking at the problem is most rational.

The trouble is, *there is no theory that tells us how we ought to look at the problem.* Either solution is as rational as the other. But the two are contradictory, leading to opposite decisions. If we can look at the same problem in either of these two ways, with two opposite decisions each being a *rational* one, then the most fundamental criterion of rationality—consistency—is violated.

This is catastrophic for our concept of rationality. If it can permit directly contradictory conclusions like this, then maybe our notion of rationality is not as clear as we have supposed. Certainly we must wonder what role strictly rational processes play—or *can* play—in the decisions we make.

In 2002, Kahneman was awarded the Nobel Prize in Economic Sciences, along with Vernon Smith, a professor of economics and law at George Mason University.

BIBLIOGRAPHY

Hastie, R., & Dawes, R. M. (2001). *Rational choice in an uncertain world.* Thousand Oaks, CA: Sage.

Kahneman, D. (2002). Maps of bounded rationality: A perspective on intuitive judgment and choice [Nobel lecture, December 8, 2002]. Retrieved October 17, 2004, from http://www.nobelprize.org/economics/laureates/2002/kahnemann-lecture.pdf.

Kahneman, D., & Tversky, A. (1979). Prospect theory: An analysis of decision under risk. *Econometrica, 47,* 268–291.

Kahneman, D., & Tversky, A. (1984). Choices, values, and frames. *American Psychologist, 39,* 341–350.

Mook, D. G. (1996). *Motivation: The organization of action* (2nd ed.). New York: Norton.

Reisberg, D. (1997). *Cognition: Exploring the science of the mind.* New York: Norton.

Tversky, A., & Fox, C. R. (1995). Weighing risk and uncertainty. *Psychological Review, 102*(2), 269–283.

Tversky, A., & Kahneman, D. (1981). The framing of decisions and the psychology of choice. *Science, 221,* 453–458.

7 PERCEPTION

44 ERNST WEBER: THE MUSCLE SENSE AND WEBER'S LAW

In the contest for the title of First Experimental Psychologist, it is Wilhelm Wundt (chapter 2) who has received the most votes. There are other contenders too, however: for example, Gustav Fechner (chapter 45), Hermann von Helmholtz (chapter 3)—and the very earliest figure who could reasonably claim the title, Ernst H. Weber (*vay*-bear).

If we do not consider Weber the founder of experimental psychology, we must certainly consider him the founder of that branch of psychology known as *psychophysics*. This, as its name implies, is the study of the relation of psychological events (*psycho*) to physical events (*physics*). In simple cases like the ones Weber studied, it asks such questions as, What is the dimmest light (physical) that we can just barely see (psychological)? Or, what is the smallest difference between two lights (physical) that we can just barely detect (psychological)? And in each case, how do the answers depend on other variables, like the brightness of the two lights? Weber showed us how to answer such questions as these.

Ernst Heinrich Weber (1795–1878) was born in Wittenberg, Germany. He studied medicine at Wittenberg University, where in 1815 he wrote his M.D. thesis. He then went to Leipzig and in 1821 was appointed Fellow Professor of anatomy and physiology. He remained at Leipzig, publishing voluminously on sensory systems, with particular reference to the sense of touch.

What we call *touch* is actually a collection of senses, not just one, and Weber's research did much to demonstrate this. He noted, for example, a clinical case in which the person remained sensitive to the touch of an object on the skin, but could not tell whether the object was warm or cold. Therefore, the temperature sense must be separate from the sense of touch. Yet these channels are not wholly independent of each other. One of Weber's simple but convincing demonstrations of this was that a coin (a German *taler*), placed on the forehead, actually felt heavier— much heavier—if it was cold than if it was warm. Again: the sensitivity to differences in weight depends not only on the weights, but also on the areas of objects placed on the skin. To Weber, all this was evidence that the perception of warmth, cold, pressure, and the like were not dependent only on what took place at the skin. The brain must be involved as well.

Beyond these discoveries (and many more), Weber can be credited with the very first success at actually relating psychological events to physical events—mind to body—quantitatively, in a single equation. This is *Weber's Law* (though it was not he, but later writers, who named it that). To understand it, we must first consider Weber's work on difference thresholds.

A *difference threshold* is a measure of the resolving power of a sensory system— that is, how sensitive it is to small differences. If it is very sensitive, the difference threshold will be small; the person can detect small differences. If insensitive, then a difference will have to be larger to be detected.

Consider an example from vision. A participant might be presented with two straight lines. One of these is of fixed length; we will call it the *standard stimulus*. The other has (for example) a slider that can be moved, so that the length of the line can be varied. Now, we might ask, What is the minimal *difference in length* of the two lines that the participant can just detect? That difference is the difference threshold. The idea is that at some point, the difference between the two lines becomes great enough to cross a "threshold" that divides differences large enough to be perceived from differences that are too small to be perceived. Therefore, the difference threshold is also called the "just noticeable difference," or *jnd*.

So Weber would permit the participant to adjust the length of the slider line until it was just perceptibly longer than the fixed line. He would do that a number of times, take the average setting for the variable-length line, and that would be the line that, *on average*, was just noticeably longer than the standard line. The difference between that line and the standard line would be the just noticeable difference, or difference threshold.

(Of course, we could determine in the same way what length of the variable line is just noticeably *shorter* than the standard line. In actual research it is best to do both, though the reasons are complex [see Woodworth and Schlosberg, 1954].)

Clearly, this method can be applied to any sense modality. We can ask what sound intensity is just noticeably louder than a standard one, or what light intensity is just noticeably brighter than a standard one, or what weight is just noticeably heavier than a standard one.

Now let us look at some of the ways in which Weber applied that method. First, he used it to demonstrate the *muscle sense*.

Consider what happens when a person picks up a weight, hefts it, and feels how heavy it is. Now, there are two kinds of information that the participant might be receiving that allow him or her to form that impression. First, of course, the object will be exerting pressure down on the skin. The heavier the object, the more pressure, so that is one way to tell how heavy the object is.

But there is another source of information that might be available as well. In hefting the object, the person is raising his or her hand, which means that the muscle that flexes the arm is doing some work. So there might be further information available, based on the amount of work the muscle has to do in order to lift the object; the heavier the object, the more vigorously the muscle must contract. Question: Is the participant using information from the muscle, as well as pressure information from the skin?

Before going on, consider how very difficult it would be to answer the question by simple introspection or "looking within." Heft an object, feel its weight, and ask yourself if you are you using your pressure sensations only, or if you are receiving and using information from the contraction of your muscles as well. It is an enormously difficult question to answer. Worse still, there is no way that anyone else could check what you say. Perhaps if you *think* you are using information from your muscles, you are deceiving yourself. We would have no way of telling.

Weber did something else instead. He measured the difference threshold for weights placed on the hand when the participants had their hands extended on a tabletop, and the weights were simply placed on the palm without movement of the hand or arm. The various weights were placed in little boxes of constant size, so that all that varied was the object's weight, and not its size—experimental control! Weber then measured how different in weight the two objects had to be before the participants were able to detect that difference (to some criterion—say, 75 percent of the time). That was the difference threshold for weight under that condition.

Weber would then repeat the experiment, with this difference: now, instead of having the weights placed in the hand, the participants would heft the weights, lifting them slightly and lowering them again.

Under these new conditions, the threshold was measured again. And it was smaller—much smaller. The participants, in other words, were more sensitive to small differences in weight when they used their muscles than when they did not. There is a clear and *objective* answer to our question. If the participants are more sensitive when they use their muscles, then the muscles must be providing information to permit the greater sensitivity. There *is* a muscle sense. And so, to the classic five senses—vision, hearing, taste, smell, and touch—we must add a sixth: the muscle sense.

We turn now to another of Weber's major contributions, one which bears his name: *Weber's Law*. It is psychology's first quantitative law.

Roughly, Weber's Law says that we find it harder to detect a change in anything the more of it there is to begin with. But the law is more precise than that: it says that the size of the difference threshold, for a given sensory channel, is a *constant fraction* of the standard stimulus. In other words, the *jnd* is a constant proportion of whatever it is a difference *from*.

Imagine a darkened room, and suppose that in it a single candle is lit. The illumination level in the room increases noticeably. But now suppose that there already 100 candles burning, and now one more is lit. The increase in the level of illumination is the same, but the psychological experience is not: in the first case, the change in illumination is noticed very clearly; in the second, it is not noticed at all.

Other sensory channels behave similarly. If we are lifting a light weight, we only have to add a little bit to that weight in order for the difference to be felt. If we begin with a very heavy weight, we will have to add much more weight in order for the difference to be detected. Weber was able to show that this effect can be stated as a direct proportionality: the magnitude of the difference threshold is a *constant fraction* of the magnitude of the standard stimulus.

The length-of-lines experiment could be modified to demonstrate this. Suppose the standard line is three inches long. If we measure the difference threshold, we will find it to be about 1/40 of that length, or 0.075 inches. But now suppose we change the standard stimulus to six inches—twice as long as it was before. The difference threshold now will be about 1/40 of that, or 0.15 inches. It too has doubled. If we went to 12 inches, the difference threshold would still be 1/40 of that, or 0.30 inches, and so on. As the standard gets longer, the difference threshold gets bigger—and in direct proportion.

Weber showed that this relation holds for a variety of sensory channels. In all of them, he found that the ratio of the difference threshold to the standard stimulus remained constant across a wide range of intensities.

All this can be stated as an equation:

$$jnd / I = K$$

I is the magnitude of the standard stimulus, jnd is the difference threshold or "just noticeable difference," and K is a constant that depends on which sensory channel one is concerned with. The ratio, jnd / I, is known as the *Weber fraction*. And *Weber's Law* is what is stated by the whole equation: that fraction remains constant as we go from short lines to longer lines to even longer lines.

The equation also applies for other sensory channels. The Weber fraction itself will be different for different sensory channels. For example, for lengths of line, the Weber fraction is about 1/40. That is, a line must be changed by about 1/40th of its length—whatever that length may be—in order for the difference to be perceived. The taste of salt is much less sensitive to differences: the concentration of salt in water applied to the tongue—whatever that concentration may be—must be changed by about 1/5 in order for the difference to be detected. Notice that the Weber fraction permits us to compare the sensitivity to change—the resolving power—of two quite different sensory channels in this way.

Other sensory channels will each have its own Weber fraction (Woodworth & Schlosberg, 1954). But Weber's Law says that whatever that fraction is, it will remain constant across the whole range of stimulus magnitudes within each channel.

What makes this finding so exciting is this: It is the first instance in the history of psychology in which a mental quantity (the difference threshold) was related quantitatively to a physical quantity (the magnitude of the standard stimulus) in a single equation. We actually have here a law relating mental events to physical events—mind to body.

Think again about our length-of-line experiments. When we measure the standard line, we have a measure in physical units—say, inches—of a physical variable, length. Then the difference threshold—how much the length must change before the subject can detect the change—will also be measured in inches. But the fact that that *is* the difference threshold—that *that much* difference is what is just noticeable to a human observer—is something that no physical measurements can tell us. It takes a human observer, reporting on his or her *conscious experience*, to give us the value for the *jnd* that we need to complete the equation.

How well does Weber's Law hold up? How can we test it? We test it by the same procedures that led to it. Within a given sensory channel, we measure the difference threshold for a weak standard stimulus (for example, a faint tone). Then we measure it again using a stronger standard (a somewhat stronger tone), and so on for a range of intensities. Or we can do the same thing with lights of varying brightness, weights with standard stimuli that are light and ones that are heavier, and so on. If Weber's Law holds, the ratio of the difference threshold to the standard stimulus *(jnd / I)* should remain the same *(K)* within each sensory channel.

What we find it is that for many sensory channels, and within a wide range of stimulus intensities, Weber's Law holds quite well. It breaks down at the extremes: if the standard stimulus is very faint, the difference threshold will be higher than Weber's Law says it will be. It is also higher than it should be if the standard stimulus is very intense. But that leaves a very large middle ground, within which the experimental data fit the predictions made by Weber's Law quite closely.

Finally, later researchers realized that the logic of Weber's procedures goes far beyond simple sensory magnitudes. For one thing, it leads us to wonder whether more complex psychological variables could be measured in a similar way.

Here is just one example, an experiment that the reader is invited to try. Let there be an observer, standing by him or herself. Let another person—the *variable person*—gradually, step by step, approach him or her more and more closely. Let the observer call out the point at which he or she becomes *uncomfortable*. That distance gives the *threshold of discomfort*. Or, saying it another way, it gives the boundary—in feet, or inches, or centimeters—of what has been called the *personal space*, that "bubble" around each of us whose boundaries we do not like to have crossed. The boundaries of that personal space are defined by the *threshold* of discomfort as another person moves closer and closer.

The reader is invited to play with these threshold measurements. Does "personal space" extend farther in front of the observer than at the sides? To find out, let the variable person approach from different directions. Again: there are cases in which the "personal space" collapses like a punctured soap bubble. Otherwise, two people could never hug each other—and, for that matter, there could never be any little people around!

Why and how does personal space collapse like that? There are real mysteries here, and threshold measurements give us a way of investigating them.

Also, in everyday life, examples of Weber's Law abound. Suppose a dollar were added to the price of a 60-cent candy bar. Customers would surely notice the difference and might well be upset. But suppose a dollar were added to the price of a new car. Would that raise any eyebrows? There we have Weber's Law: how sensitive we are to a change is proportional to what it is a change *from*.

The idea that we are sensitive to *proportional* rather than *absolute* changes may go far beyond "simple" sensory magnitudes. Weber's Law is a lasting and widely applicable contribution to a science of mind.

BIBLIOGRAPHY

Boring, E. G. (1942). *Sensation and perception in the history of experimental psychology*. New York: Appleton-Century-Crofts.

Sekuler, R., & Blake, R. (2002). *Perception* (4th ed.). New York: McGraw-Hill.

Weber, E. H. (1996). *E. H. Weber on the tactile senses* (H. Ross & D. J. Murray, Trans.). Philadelphia: Psychology Press.

Woodworth, R. S., & Schlosberg, H. (1954). *Experimental psychology*. New York: Holt.

45 | GUSTAV FECHNER AND THE MEASUREMENT OF MIND

Gustav Theodor Fechner (1801–87), like Helmholtz, was a generalist if there ever was one. He was trained initially as a physician and took his degree in medicine in 1822; but then his interests shifted to physics and mathematics, and he became professor of physics at Leipzig in 1834. There he made important contributions in his new field.

However, after a few years there his health collapsed catastrophically. He had not only overworked himself, but because of an interest in sunspots, he had injured his eyes by staring at the sun through colored lenses for long periods. He resigned his professorship in physics in 1839, and for the next several years he cut all social contacts and all professional work. He was bedridden and in a great deal of pain.

But all this did not keep his active mind from working. The problem that he was now concerned with was, What are the mathematical relations among various parts of nature? He was convinced that nature was all one system: physical events and mental events were all aspects of one reality, all were parts of one whole. (Fechner had written a book on the mental life of plants.) In other words, Fechner was one of many who rejected the Cartesian division between mind and body (chapter 2).

But if mind and matter were one, there ought to be a way to relate physical events to mental events mathematically. Ernst Weber had shown the way (chapter 44), and Fechner knew his work well, but Weber had stopped short of actually relating physical variables to mental ones over the whole range of magnitudes of physical and psychological variables.

The two variables, physical and psychological or subjective, are not the same. The observations that led to Weber's Law (chapter 44) are enough to tell us that. Suppose a candle is lit in a dark room. The increase in illumination is clearly visible. Light a candle when 100 candles are already burning, and the difference will not be noticed at all. The same *physical* difference makes a *psychological* difference—that is, it is perceived—in one case but not in the other. So physical and psychological differences are not the same.

The problem, however, goes beyond what is or is not perceived. Suppose you were listening to a tone, and someone turned up the volume control so that the *physical* amplitude of the tone was doubled. Then it would indeed sound louder to you, but it would not sound anything like twice as loud. To double the *heard*, or *subjective*, loudness of the tone, we would have to much more than double its physical intensity. This doesn't mean that you're making a mistake. It only means that the magnitude of the sensation does not bear a one-to-one relation to the magnitude of the physical stimulus.

But then, if the relation is not one to one, what is it? And how do we find out? To find out, we must be able to measure both variables—the *physical intensity* of (say) tones, but also, and separately, the *mental intensities* of the experiences they produce. If we can do that, then we can plot the one against the other and see how they are related. In a word, we must measure subjective, experienced magnitudes. We must measure the mind! How can we do that?

What we need is a *unit of measurement* for the subjective, or psychological, magnitude of the tone. And on the morning of October 22, 1850—which some consider the precise date of the founding of experimental psychology—Gustav Fechner leaped out of bed with the solution in his mind.

The solution is based on Weber's Law (chapter 44). Weber's Law says that the just noticeable *change* in magnitude of a stimulus—the "just noticeable difference," or *jnd*—is proportional to the magnitude of the stimulus itself. In other words, a stimulus has to increase by a constant *proportion* of its value in order for the change to be just noticeable to a human participant. This means that as the stimulus gets more and more intense, the amount of change that is required to be just noticeable also increases, as a constant proportion of the stimulus itself. That is Weber's Law.

Now, the *jnd* is itself a psychological quantity. It is measured in physical units, yes; but the fact that a change *is* "just noticeable" is not something that physical measurements can reveal. It is a statement about the observer's mind: change the stimulus just *this* much, and the change is just noticeable to him or her. That is what the *jnd* is.

Fechner asked himself that October morning, what if we take the *jnd* itself as our unit of sensory magnitude?

Suppose we want to measure the subjective magnitude or loudness of a tone, in units of the *jnd*. We could do an experiment like the following. We need a sound source to generate the tone, and a volume control to vary its physical intensity. We present our participant with a tone whose subjective magnitude we want to measure.

Then, using our volume control, we lower the intensity of the tone until the participant can just detect the difference. The resulting tone will be one *jnd* below the original tone, in subjective loudness. Then we do it again, reducing the tone a second time until, again, he or she can just detect the difference. The resulting tone will be two *jnd*s below the original tone in subjective loudness. And so on. We continue this stepwise lowering of the tone until finally it disappears altogether—until its subjective magnitude is zero. Then the number of such steps—the number of times we had to lower it just noticeably before it disappeared—is the magnitude of the original sensation, in units of the *jnd*. If we had to reduce the tone's loudness 10 times to make it disappear, then it was 10 *jnd*s above subjective zero to begin with.

Notice that we don't have to keep track of the tone's physical magnitude at all in order to do this, as long as we can control that magnitude. All we need to do is count the *number* of just noticeable reductions that we had to make in order to make the tone disappear. That is our measure of its original subjective magnitude, in units of the *jnd*. We can say that it is so many *jnd*s above zero in subjective magnitude.

Clearly we could do this for any sensory dimension that we can vary. The procedures for measuring the brightness of a light in *jnd*s, or the saltiness of a solution applied to the tongue, would be exactly analogous.

All this is much oversimplified. If the experiment strikes the reader as already a rather tedious one, be assured that the reality would be much worse. Every single determination of each *jnd* would have to be repeated a number of times, because the size of the *jnd* will fluctuate from one trial to another. The data would therefore have to be treated statistically, and Fechner worked out ways of doing that too.

But Fechner also saw that such a horrendous task might be unnecessary. It would be possible to derive, mathematically, what the relation between physical and psychological magnitudes *had* to be. It would, that is, if two assumptions could be made.

The first assumption is that Weber's Law is true. The second assumption is this: that the *subjective magnitude of the* jnd *itself* is constant throughout the range of intensities. If we take a faint tone and decrease it until the decrease is just noticeable, we have the *jnd* for loudness for that tone. Now if we start over, using a tone of higher intensity, we will find that the *jnd* is physically larger than it was before. But subjectively, Fechner is assuming, the *perceived change is the same* for both cases. One just noticeable difference should seem the same as any other just noticeable difference, independently of what these are differences *from*. In other words, the subjective experience of *just barely noticing a difference* should be a constant experience, irrespective of the amount of physical change required to produce it.

If those two assumptions hold, then, Fechner argued, we do not have to go through the very laborious procedure of actually measuring sensory magnitudes in *jnd*s. If Weber's Law is true, and if all *jnd*s are subjectively equal, we can calculate what the relation between the physical and the psychological magnitude of the tone has to be. For readers who have had calculus, this amounts to integrating Weber's Law, and doing some arithmetic to get rid of the constant of integration.

If we do that, the relationship turns out to be a logarithmic one:

$$S = K \log I$$

S is subjective magnitude measured in *jnd*s, I is physical intensity measured in physical units, and K depends on several things, including what sensory channel we are dealing with (length of a line, intensity of a tone, intensity of a light, and so on) and what units we use for our physical measurement (line length in inches or in millimeters, for example).

Fechner named this logarithmic relation *Weber's Law*. History, however, has decided that he was being too generous here; it should be called *Fechner's Law*, giving Weber credit for the earlier law: *jnd* / I = K. That remains the terminology most writers use today, though some compromise and call the logarithmic law the Weber-Fechner law.

But was Fechner right? Does his law—the subjective magnitude of a stimulus is a logarithmic function of its physical magnitude—hold true? The very great strength of his method is just this: One can find out:

We test the law just as we would test any other purported generalization in science: we make predictions based upon it, and see whether the predictions are confirmed by experiment.

For example, consider a variation of the original experiment. A participant listens to a tone and notes how loud it sounds to him. He listens to a second, more intense tone, and notes the loudness of that. He is then given the volume control, and asked to adjust the tone until it sounds *midway between the two* in loudness. Now, from Fechner's Law, we can calculate what that setting ought to be, if the law is correct. Similar experiments could be performed for other sensory modalities: We could ask the person to adjust a length of a line so that it looks midway between two "standard" lines in length, and again compare the setting he gives us with the setting Fechner's Law predicts.

In each case, then, we calculate what the subject's judgments ought to be if Fechner's Law is true, and then do the experiment and see if the prediction holds. Do the results of such experiments confirm Fechner's Law?

The results, it must be said, are mixed at best. Many experiments have found such settings *not* to vary with the physical magnitudes in the way that Fechner's Law predicts that they should.

And at this point, the reader may understandably ask, Why, then, spend so much time on Fechner's Law?

For two reasons. First, whether Fechner was right or wrong is less important than the fact that the *test can be made*. The controversy showed that one can do experiments to test the law, and, if it fails, look for a better one. That is why a prominent later investigator titled a paper "To Honor Fechner and Repeal His Law" (Stevens, 1961).

Second, we can expand Fechner's idea into something much more general, as follows. Fechner's unit, the difference threshold or *jnd*, is really a measure of how well two stimuli are distinguished from each other by an observer—or, conversely, how often they are confused with each other. The observer's judgments fluctuate over repeated trials. Therefore, to say that two stimuli are one *jnd* apart is really to say that the two are distinguished from each other *some fixed proportion of the time*—say, on 75 percent of the trials on which they are presented. That also means that on 25 percent of those trials they are not distinguished, but are confused with each other. Then Fechner's idea can be turned around and restated this way: *The more often two stimuli are confused with each other, the more* subjectively *similar they must be.*

The use of *confusion* as a way of measuring mental events may seem strange at first, but it has been enormously fruitful (see Lindsay & Norman, 1972; Torgerson, 1958). It was used to calibrate items for the first attitude scales. It has been used to measure the subjective value, to us, of gains and losses of money or goods or, indeed, of anything. It paved the way for the very useful theory of *signal detection*. We lack space to consider this theory here (see Sekuler & Blake, 1994), but it is yet another way of measuring the subjective difference between two stimuli (among other things). And it again depends on how often, and in what ways, two states of affairs are confused with each other. A versatile approach to mental measurement indeed!

Fechner himself turned his mind later to the study of aesthetics, developing ways of measuring the "pleasingness" of objects or geometric figures—another kind of mental measurement. Today, the International Association of Empirical Aesthetics, whose founders include the psychologist Daniel Berlyne, gives a biennial award in Fechner's name.

Right or wrong, we can say that Fechner started something in psychology, and it is far from having stopped.

BIBLIOGRAPHY

Boring, E. G. (1950). *A history of experimental psychology* (2nd ed.). New York: Appleton-Century-Crofts.

Fechner, G. T. (1966). *Elements of psychophysics* (H. E. Adler, Trans.). New York: Holt.

Gescheider, G. A. (1997). *Psychophysics: method, theory, and application* (3rd ed.). Mahwah, NJ: Erlbaum.

Lindsay, P. H., & Norman, D. A. (1972). *Human information processing: An introduction to psychology.* New York: Academic Press.

Sekuler, R., & Blake, R. (1994). *Perception* (3rd ed.). New York: McGraw-Hill.

Stevens, S. S. (1961). To honor Fechner and repeal his law. *Science, 133,* 80–86.

Torgerson, W. S. (1958). *Theory and methods of scaling.* New York: John Wiley & Sons.

46 MAX WERTHEIMER ON APPARENT MOVEMENT

If we take behaviorism to be the modern incarnation of John Locke's philosophy, Gestalt psychology could be treated as an incarnation of Kant's. Though there were many differences in detail, the Gestalt psychologists argued forcefully for his fundamental principle: There is more in the mind than there is, or ever was, in the senses.

Their method, too, was recognizably Kantian: look at what experience is like, see what it would be like if it consisted only of sensory elements produced by the physical stimulus, and the difference is the perceiver's own contribution. This argument runs through Wertheimer's studies of apparent movement and productive thinking to Köhler's experiments on problem solving in apes (chapter 21).

Though there were forerunners within psychology too, we will consider the founder of Gestalt psychology to be Max Wertheimer (1880–1943). Born in Prague, he studied law there before moving to Berlin to study psychology; then he took his doctorate at Würzburg in 1904.

Wertheimer was on a train passing through Frankfurt when he was struck by an idea about how to investigate the perception of movement—or *apparent movement*, which means the appearance of movement in the absence of anything moving. He got off the train, found a toy stroboscope in a store, and began setting up experimental apparatuses in his hotel room. When a professor at Frankfurt heard of this work, he offered Wertheimer space for research and the use of his own, better, timing apparatus. It happened that Köhler was already at Frankfurt, and Kurt Koffka joined the pair a little later. These three were the founding fathers of Gestalt psychology.

In 1933, Wertheimer fled from Europe in the face of the Nazi menace and took a position in the New School for Social Research in New York. His classic volume on productive thinking (1959) was published posthumously in 1945.

This chapter will focus on his earlier work on apparent movement, which can be demonstrated in the following way. One arranges two light sources a short distance apart and turns them off and on in alternation: left, then right, then left, then right, and so on. If the spatial separation between the lights, the interval between them, and their brightness are just right, what one will see is a *single* light, moving back and forth between the two positions.

Here we have it: what is physically present is a pair of lights blinking in alternation. What the observer sees is a single light, moving—when in fact nothing is moving. Hence the term *apparent movement*. The observer adds something to what the actual stimulus provides: the fusion of two stimuli into one, and the appearance of movement where there is no movement.

This "contribution" of our perceptual system, by the way, is the basis for motion pictures: a series of still photographs is each presented very briefly by stroboscopic illumination, so that the picture is not blurred as the film moves. If the photographs show, say, a person moving, a series of still photographs, each slightly different from the previous one, will fuse together in the observer's perception to produce the very strong *appearance* of movement—that is, apparent movement.

But why should this happen? One idea comes immediately to mind. Perhaps the light produces an afterimage on the retina, so that as one light goes off and the other comes on, and we shift our eyes from one to the other, we "see" the afterimage moving as well. A good idea, but Wertheimer showed that it was wrong. If one does the experiment exactly right (and has very precise timing apparatus), one *can* get apparent movement with *two* pairs of lights, where the apparent movement goes in opposite directions for the two pairs. Since the eyes cannot move in two directions at once, the afterimage hypothesis can safely be discounted.

Here is another possibility. Perhaps the movement is not really a perception, but an inference based on experience. This is the kind of explanation Locke might have advanced, and Helmholtz did advance it, speaking of "unconscious inference." If we see what appears to be the same thing first here and then there, we *infer* that it must have moved across. But there are some serious difficulties with that possibility too.

First, it does not account for the quantitative properties of apparent movement. Wertheimer and his associates went on to show that the conditions for apparent movement depended on a number of variables. These dependencies were summarized in *Korte's laws*, as they have come to be called (Osgood, 1953). For example, as the spatial separation between the two lights increases, the optimal time interval between them for apparent movement also increases. For another, the optimal separation increases as the brightness of the lights increases. It is not clear why an unconscious inference should be so strongly dependent on the precise values of all of these variables considered together.

Second, it does not account for some further discoveries. A particularly striking example is this: Suppose that the two lights are of different colors. Once apparent movement is set in motion, so to speak, the observer will see the light begin its excursion at one point, and change color in the *middle* of the apparent movement before getting to the other point. This can happen even at the beginning of a sequence, the very first time that the one light goes off and the other comes on. It would seem that either (*a*) a sequence of events is rearranged in the observer's perceptual apparatus before it is actually seen, or (*b*) the sequence is rearranged in the observer's short-term memory, and the report is based on that. Or it may be that these two possibilities amount to the same thing. (For a contemporary discussion, see Dennett, 1991.)

However it works, the important point is simply this: We cannot think of what happens as a series of distinct events—light here, then light there—laid end to end to form a sequence. It is the other way around. The whole sequence determines what the properties are of the perceptual events that are embedded in it. In no other way could a light at the midpoint, which isn't there, change the color that it doesn't have.

The notion of *embedding* may help us understand where Gestalt psychology got its name. The word *Gestalt* does not translate easily; it means something like "whole," as in "the whole thing." It is the *whole sequence* that gives the parts their properties, not the other way around. Further examples abound; indeed, Gestalt writers give us whole bookfuls of them. For example, consider the Necker cube again (figure 2.1, chapter 2). It is the configuration of the *whole thing* that causes us to see the lines and angles arranged so as to form a three-dimensional cube—which is not there. And yet it is virtually impossible for us to see the "whole thing" as a two-dimensional array of lines, which is what it is.

For that matter, the idea had been anticipated by some earlier writers even before Wertheimer's work began. A melody is made up of a sequence of notes, yes. But we can transpose the whole melody into another key, changing all of its elements—and yet it will be recognized as the same melody, and an observer may even be unaware of the change. Clearly, the experience of the whole melody does not depend on the properties of any—or all—of its parts. The "whole thing" has properties in its own right.

As the Gestalt psychologists saw it, these demonstrations do require us to change our thinking, but they need not be mysterious, and they certainly do not imply anything mystical or commit us to mind-body dualism. In fact, shortly before these developments, physicists had begun thinking along similar lines, and the Gestalt psychologists—especially Köhler, who had trained as a physicist—saw some parallels between these perceptual phenomena and *field theory* in physics. The two poles of a magnet generate a magnetic field, capable of moving (say) iron filings into various configurations. But these iron filings, their positions and movements, do not generate the field. It is the other way around: the movements and positions of the filings depend on the properties of the field in which they are embedded.

Now, the brain consists of conducting fluid, in which charged particles are dissolved. Perhaps sensory input, affecting the cells of the brain, causes currents to flow inside the brain, and the resulting distribution of charged particles in space may be the immediate cause of the perception that results. Thus, as one light goes off and the other goes on, the distribution of excitation in the brain may move from one location *through the intervening points* to the other. And if what is perceived is the entire sequence—the whole thing—there is no reason why the apparent color might not change in the middle as easily as anywhere else.

The pattern of electrical charges will tend toward simple, stable ones—what Wertheimer called "good figures." Finally, the brain is three-dimensional, though the paper on which the Necker cube is drawn is not. In the brain, therefore, the representation of the figure is free to snap into a simple, coherent three-dimensional pattern, and that is what we see.

As to apparent movement, Wertheimer's own explanation was very much in this spirit. As a light comes on, a focus of excitation builds up in a corresponding area of the visual cortex of the brain. The light goes off and another comes on, so the one focus dies away as another, nearby one builds up. Current then should flow between them. Thus the single light appearing to move could be a direct reflection of physical events—not movement of the light, but the flow of currents in the brain produced by the sequence of lights.

We have moved very quickly through the brain-currents theory of visual perception, because subsequent experimentation gave it little support. As just one example, the lights can be placed so that excitation from one light is relayed to one cerebral hemisphere of the brain, the other to the other (for explanation, see chapter 9). Here, then, there is excitation in two brain areas that, while connected to each other, are not physically *adjacent* to each other. Still, apparent movement is seen (Osgood, 1953).

Even so, if psychologists did not accept the Gestalt explanations for these perceptual effects, they had to accept the effects themselves. Gestalt demonstrations today continue to appear in every introductory textbook, showing us just how much the observer contributes to a perceptual event. We understand some of these effects better now. Some we still do not understand. In this sense if no other, the Gestalt psychologists—Wertheimer and his colleagues and subsequent generations—have done valuable service by showing us how far we have still to go.

BIBLIOGRAPHY

Boring, E. G. (1942). *Sensation and perception in the history of experimental psychology*. New York: Appleton-Century-Crofts.

Dennett, D.C. (1991). *Consciousness explained*. Boston: Little, Brown.

Ellis, W. D. (1938). *A source book of Gestalt psychology*. New York: Harcourt, Brace & World.

Osgood, C. E. (1953). *Method and theory in experimental psychology*. New York: Oxford University Press.

Wertheimer, M. (1959). *Productive thinking*. New York: Harper & Row.

Wertheimer, M. (1965). Max Wertheimer (1880–1943) on the phi phenomenon as an example of nativism in perception, 1912 (D. Cantor, Trans.). In R. J. Herrnstein & E. G. Boring (Eds.), *A source book in the history of psychology* (pp. 163–168). Cambridge, MA: Harvard University Press.

47 SELIG HECHT AND ADAPTATION TO THE DARK

The subdivisions among the fields of psychology are loose and arbitrary—as, indeed, are the divisions between disciplines. A number of classic contributions to psychology have been made by physiologists (Helmholtz, Pavlov, Weber) or by philosophers (Fechner).

A model case of such investigation is the work of Selig Hecht on the mechanism of dark adaptation in the visual system. As with Weber, Hecht's training and academic identity were in physiology, not psychology; but among the experiments he is best remembered for are ones that depended on psychological methods and could as well have been done by a psychologist.

Selig Hecht (1892–1947) came to the United States from Austria in 1898, graduated with a B.S. from the College of the City of New York in 1913, and took his Ph.D. at Harvard in 1917. After working and teaching in several countries, he came to Columbia University in 1926, where he organized a laboratory in biophysics. He remained at Columbia until his death. Another prominent vision researcher, George Wald, says of Hecht,

> Never ceasing to test the validity of his ideas . . . he made the most comprehensive contribution to the field since Helmholtz. He explored adaptation to the dark in molluscs (*Mya* and *Pholas*), tunicates (*Ciona*), and primates (man); visual acuity in insects with compound eyes (the bee and fruitfly) and in man; intensity discrimination in . . . the fruitfly, and man; and flicker in the clam and in man. (Wald, 1991, p. 81)

Here, we consider Hecht's experiments on dark adaptation in humans.

Dark adaptation—that is, adaptation, or adjustment, to the dark—is a familiar phenomenon to all of us. Suppose one walks into a dark movie theater from a well-lighted street, in the daytime. At first, one sees very poorly and has to grope. After a few minutes, however, the eyes will have adjusted (*adapted*) to the dim illumination,

273

and one can see quite well. Since the theater is no brighter, this must mean that the person's eyes have grown more sensitive.

How does this happen? The first step in examining this process is to describe it carefully.

One way of doing this is the measure the visual *absolute threshold*—to determine, in other words, what is the dimmest light a human participant can see under a given set of conditions. Weber had shown how to do this (chapter 44) with his measurements of *difference thresholds*—what is the smallest difference between two stimuli one can just distinguish? The absolute threshold is just a special case of this: what is the smallest difference one can just distinguish between a faint stimulus and no stimulus at all?

The experiment is done this way: The participant looks into a microscope eyepiece, in a dark room. One may begin with the eyepiece dark. Then a very dim light is presented through the eyepiece and the participant is asked, "Can you see that?" If he or she says, "No," gradually increase the intensity of the light until he or she says, "Yes." The intensity of the light that can just barely be seen is then taken to be his or her visual threshold on that trial.

Several measurements will be taken, to minimize the effects of lapses of attention, or "noise" in the apparatus or in the visual system itself, and there are some procedural subtleties (Woodworth & Schlosberg, 1954). But the logic is straightforward.

These methods can be extended to explore the process of dark-adaptation. To repeat: As dark adaptation occurs, the eye becomes more sensitive. That means that the visual threshold is lower now than it was at first. (Remember that a *lower threshold* means *greater sensitivity*: the visual system is more sensitive if it takes less light to activate it.) And we can describe that change in more detail if we *measure* the change in visual threshold.

In figure 47.1, look first at the open circles. These are data from a single participant (though of course they were confirmed in others as well). In this experiment, the participant came into the dark room where the experiment was conducted. Then his visual threshold was measured, repeatedly, for about 40 minutes as he sat in the dark. The figure shows the successive measurements, left to right. A diffuse white light, illuminating the whole retina, was used as the stimulus. So Hecht at this point was asking specifically: What is the dimmest *white light* the participant can just manage to see, and how does this change as he spends more and more time in the dark?

First, as we would expect, the threshold went down—the eyes grew more sensitive—with time in the dark. That is dark adaptation. But in addition, there was a distinct break in the curve. The threshold got lower over the first 4 or 5 minutes; then it leveled off; but then, at about the 7-minute mark, the threshold suddenly began to drop again, and continued to drop over the next 20 minutes or so. By the 30-minute mark, sensitivity has increased about 10,000-fold (four log units, where each such unit is a 10-fold change) from its original value.

This complex curve suggests that there may be *two* processes operating in dark adaptation. The first of these causes a rapid, but relatively small, drop in threshold; that is, sensitivity increases only moderately before the process is complete and the threshold levels off. The second process is slower, but much bigger. It begins to operate only after a delay of about 7 minutes, but then it continues for another 20

Figure 47.1
The two-phase dark-adaptation curve. Hecht's experiments showed the two-phase dark-adaptation curve to result from an early cone component (dark circles) and a later but much larger rod component (open circles). The vertical axis is logarithmic, which means that a change of one unit on that axis actually represents a 10-fold change in sensitivity. After about 30 minutes in the dark, this participant's eye had become more than 10,000 times more sensitive than it was at the beginning!

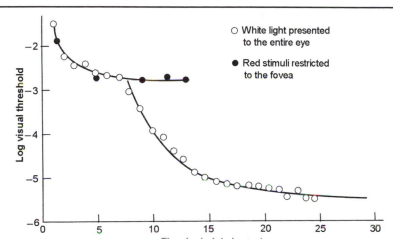

Source: From Hecht (1934, p. 727). Reprinted by permission of Clark University Press.

minutes or more, making the eye very much more sensitive at the end than it was at the beginning (Hecht, 1934).

Why should that be so? Why is there that "break" in the curve? We can understand this if we look at some facts about the human *retina*—the layer of light-sensitive cells at the back of the eye.

First, microscopic inspection of the retina reveals that there are two kinds of cells there, differing from each other anatomically. These two kinds of cells are called the *rods* and the *cones*. Many other species also have both these kinds of cells, though some have only one. In species with both (including humans), we find that the cones tend to be clustered in the center of the retina, whereas the rods cluster *around* the center rather than in it. So the two kinds of cells differ both as to what they look like and where in the retina they are located.

Are these cells sensitive to light? They are. Biochemists can extract certain chemicals (called *pigments*) from rods or cones, put them in test tubes, and see how the chemicals respond to light. It turns out that these pigments undergo chemical changes when they are exposed to light—literally, they bleach. Then, if they are allowed to sit in the dark, the chemical process is reversed and the original pigments are regenerated. Perhaps the gradual increase in sensitivity in the dark occurs because, in the dark, these pigments are restored after having been bleached by light.

Many other findings support this idea. First, the regeneration process takes longer for pigments extracted from rods than from cones. Second, once regeneration is complete, the rod pigments are much more sensitive to light than the cone pigments are; that is, it takes much less light to get the bleaching reaction going again. Finally, the *wavelength* of the light can be varied, and the threshold can be measured at each of several wavelengths of light. It turns out that sensitivity of the rod pigment is greatest—that is, it takes least light to cause it to bleach—in the blue-green portion of the spectrum, at wavelengths of light around 500 nanometers. That is also where sensitivity to light is greatest (the threshold is lowest) for the dark-adapted human eye. On the other hand, if we measure sensitivity before dark adaptation has had a chance to occur, we find it greatest at roughly 550 nanometers; and it is light in that band of wavelengths to which the cone pigments are most sensitive on average. (Things are more complicated for the cones, for we now know that there are three cone types in the human retina, having greatest sensitivity at three different bands of wavelength. All three, however, are much less sensitive than are the rods.)

Combining all these data reveals a point-for-point parallel between the behavior of pigments in a test tube and the thresholds measured for the human participant who is describing what he sees. When the eye has not dark-adapted—it is "adapted" to daylight or artificial room illumination—sensitivity is low at all wavelengths. That is why we cannot see very well when we move into the darkened movie theater: the rods have bleached as much as they can and are no longer responding. However, what sensitivity there is, is greater at about 550 nanometers than at other wavelengths. The same is true for the cone pigments.

When the eye *has* become dark-adapted, the sensitivity is much greater. We can see in the darkened theater now, because the rods have had a chance to regenerate their pigments. And sensitivity is greatest at wavelengths around 500 nanometers. The same is true of the rod pigments. Finally, returning to the anatomy of the eye, we find yet another parallel. Cones are densest near the center of the retina, whereas rods are most dense around the center, but not in it. Sure enough, in the light-adapted eye, the threshold for small points of light is lowest—sensitivity is greatest—in that portion of the eye where the cones are most dense. In the dark-adapted eye, sensitivity is greatest in that portion of the eye where the rods are most dense.

Putting all these findings together, we get this suggestion: *The cones are specialized for day vision in relatively bright light. The rods are specialized for night vision in relatively dim light.*

With just that much, we can understand quite a bit about how the eye responds at different illumination levels:

1. As darkness falls at the end of the day, we notice that colors become less vivid. That is because at low illumination, the cones are too insensitive to contribute much to what we see. We now see primarily with our rods. But the rods are not very sensitive to differences in color, so in what we see, the colors become muted as the rods take over.

2. If, on a dark night, we are trying to see a very faint object (such as the planet Uranus, which can barely be seen with the naked eye under optimal viewing conditions), we do best not to look straight at where the object should be. It is better to look a little bit to one side. That shifts its light away from the center of the retina, where the less sensitive cones are densely packed, to off-center, where the more sensitive rods are to be found.

3. Finally, does all this help us understand the complex dark-adaptation curve we saw earlier in figure 47.1? It might. Maybe the rapid, but small, increase in visual sensitivity that we see in the figure represents cone function; the cones become only

slightly more sensitive in the dark, but they do so quickly. The slower, but bigger, increase in sensitivity may reflect the contribution of the rods; they become very much more sensitive in the dark, but it takes them awhile to do it.

Can we test that idea? Again, using psychophysical experiments in human participants, Hecht did test it. He did so by taking advantage of the things we have just learned about rods and cones.

He repeated his threshold measurements, but with two changes, both designed to stimulate *the cones and not the rods*. First, rather than presenting light to the whole eye, he presented a small dot of light. That allowed him to confine the stimulus to the center of the retina, where there are many cones but relatively few rods. Second, he made the dot of light red rather than white. Red light is a relatively weak stimulus for the rods, which are much more sensitive in the blue-green part of the spectrum. So, by presenting what was only a weak stimulus for rods, he could reduce their contribution to the dark-adaptation process.

In short, by using small dots of light and turning them red, Hecht was now stimulating the *cones* selectively The rods were receiving minimal stimulation. If it is true that the early, fast-but-small component of the complex curve reflects cone function, then *only* that component should be seen now. And as the dark circles in figure 47.1 show, that is exactly what happened. The delayed, but much greater, increase in sensitivity now did not occur. So, in the earlier experiments in which it did occur, it must have been produced by the rods. The two-phase dark-adaptation curve is explained (Hecht & Hsia, 1945).

These experiments are excellent examples of how different findings, even from different kinds of experiments, converge to support a conclusion. We have drawn some conclusions about the contributions of rods and cones to vision. Our conclusion draws on information from psychophysics: This is what humans see, and this is how what they see is affected by illumination level, time, and the wavelength of what is shown. But it also draws on information from histology (there are these two kinds of cells, and they look different, and *here* is how they are distributed spatially in the retina), comparative anatomy (not all animals have both rods and cones), and biochemistry (the "bleaching" of pigments with exposure to light, and the effects of time and wavelength on this bleaching). All this and much more has contributed to our present understanding of what the receptors in the eye—the rods and the cones—tell the brain.

Second, they are good examples of how experiments can shed light on occurrences in everyday life, even if the experiments themselves are far removed from everyday settings. The following is just one example of how the understanding of a process—night vision in this case—can be brought from the laboratory into the everyday world.

Some people suffer from a condition known as *night blindness*, in which they have trouble seeing clearly in dim illumination, though in bright light they see normally. The usual big increase in visual sensitivity in the dark does not occur, or is less than it should be. It was discovered that the condition is especially prevalent in certain parts of the world, and that its incidence increases in periods of famine. These data suggest a possibility that was further supported by an unintended "experiment of nature." During World War I, Denmark began exporting butter in large quantities. Shortly thereafter, many Danes, especially children, developed night blindness. Later, when the Danes stopped exporting butter and returned to eating it themselves, the incidence of night blindness went down again.

Could night blindness result from a dietary deficiency?

Experiments showed that it can. Volunteers who ate only a vitamin-A-deficient diet for a while developed night blindness. Restoring vitamin A to their diets restored normal vision very rapidly (Hecht & Mandelbaum, 1938). Physicians were able to treat night blindness by adding butter or cod liver oil to their patients' diet. Something in these additives, then, contributes to normal visual sensitivity in dim light.

To make the story short, it turned out to be a vitamin—vitamin A. By methods very much like the ones we have seen, Hecht and other investigators (Hecht & Mandelbaum, 1938; Wald & Steven, 1939) showed the following: (a) a diet deficient in vitamin A could cause a 100-fold loss in sensitivity in the dark (note that we can specify that because we can measure sensitivity as described earlier); (b) it is the second, larger phase of the dark-adaptation curve that is affected; and (c) visual sensitivity could be restored to normal, sometimes within minutes, by feeding vitamin A to a deficient person. (Notice again: we can speak of a "return to normal" only after we have specified quantitatively—that is, in meaningful numbers—what the normal range is.)

Finally, the story was completed when Hubbard and Wald (1951) synthesized the rod pigment—that is, they literally made their own—in a test tube. Vitamin A was one of the necessary components. Therefore, people lacking in vitamin A are unable to produce this pigment in sufficient quantities. That is why their sensitivity in the dark is impaired.

This story has taken quite a path—from the psychophysics laboratory, to the anatomist's microscope, to the biochemist's test tube, and back to psychophysical experiments—and then to the physician's office besides. And there is more: our understanding of the contribution of rods and cones to vision has informed the design of highway signs, the best procedures for reading X-rays in dim illumination or for flying airplanes at night, and much besides. A dramatic case study in how simple experiments, each putting a simple question to nature, can support and explain each other, and lead to understanding.

BIBLIOGRAPHY

Hecht, S. (1934). Vision II: The nature of the photoreceptor process. In C. Murchison (Ed.), *Handbook of general experimental psychology* (pp. 704–828). Worcester, MA: Clark University Press.

Hecht, S., & Hsia, Y. (1945). Dark adaptation following light adaptation to red and white lights. *Journal of the Optical Society of America, 35,* 261–267.

Hecht, S., & Mandelbaum, J. (1938). Rod-cone dark adaptation and vitamin A. *Science, 88,* 219–221.

Hubbard, R., & Wald, G. (1951). The mechanism of rhodopsin synthesis. *Proceedings of the National Academy of Sciences, 37,* 69–79.

Wald, G. (1991). Selig Hecht. In *Biographical memoirs: Vol. 60* (pp. 80–101). National Academies Press.

Wald, G., & Steven, D. (1939). An experiment in human vitamin A deficiency. *Proceedings of the National Academy of Sciences, 25,* 344–349.

Woodworth, R. S., & Schlosberg, H. (1954). *Experimental psychology.* New York: Holt.

48 H. K. HARTLINE: LATERAL INHIBITION IN THE RETINA

Vision begins with light striking the light-sensitive cells, or *visual receptors,* which form a layer of cells in the *retina* at the back of the eye. In humans and many other species, these sensitive cells activate further layers of cells, which in turn affect the *ganglion cells.* These are large retinal cells whose *axons*—the long, threadlike parts of nerve cells—gather together to form the a cable of axons. This cable is the *optic nerve.* It is this cable of axons that runs up into the brain, carrying visual information. This is how the eye tells the brain what it sees.

However, information processing begins immediately, at the very start of this sequence, in the retina itself. A striking example of this processing is the phenomenon of *lateral inhibition,* discovered by H. K. Hartline and his associates.

Haldan Keffer Hartline (1903–83) was born in Pennsylvania. He graduated from Lafayette College in 1923, then entered Johns Hopkins, where he was encouraged to continue his research interest in vision in the Department of Physiology. In 1931 he took a position at the University of Pennsylvania, where he began his studies on the activity of single optic-nerve fibers in the eye of the horseshoe crab, *Limulus.*

By the 1930s, neuroscientists had learned how to detect and record the electrical activity from individual nerve cells, or *neurons,* in sensory or motor channels. A nerve cell conducts a message as a series of *action potentials*—changes in the electrical charge across the membrane of the cell. The action potential then moves along the axon from (in this case) the eye up into the brain. It proved possible to use a *very* thin wire, or an even thinner glass tube filled with conducting fluid, and mount this *electrode* in a device that permits it to be moved very slight distances at a time. One can then bring it up close to a nerve cell, or even penetrate a cell with it. The electrical signals generated by the cell can then be amplified and fed into an oscilloscope so that the scientists can see them. These tiny electrical signals can also be fed into a loudspeaker so that one hears them as they occur; one is then literally listening in on the cell's message. And the signals can be recorded on magnetic tape and fed into a tape recorder (or, nowadays, a computer) to be examined later.

Figure 48.1
A recording of nerve impulses from a single cell in the optic nerve of the horseshoe crab. Each vertical "spike" is produced by a nerve impulse passing under the recording electrode.

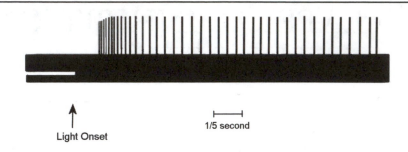

Light Onset

1/5 second

Source: From Hartline (1967). © The Nobel Foundation 1967.

An example of what the data look like is shown in figure 48.1, which shows what happens in an optic nerve fiber when a beam of light is directed onto a *photorecep-tor*—a cell that is sensitive to light—in the eye of the horseshoe crab. Very shortly after that, nerve impulses are generated. These are the upward spikelike blips that we see in the record; indeed, they are often called *spikes* for short. These are the messages that are sent from the eye to the brain.

Not shown in this single record is the *frequency code:* the more intense the light is, the more action potentials are generated per unit of time. In other words, nerve impulses follow each other more closely in time as the light reaching the sensitive cell is made more intense. One can see this in a visual record like figure 48.1, and one can also arrange to hear it as noted above. Each spike is heard as a popping sound. Then a high intensity of light will yield a rapid burst of impulses: *pop-pop-pop*. Whereas if the light is less intense, the train of impulses will be less rapid: *pop . . . pop . . . pop*. There will also be a hissing background "noise" produced by other cells and by electrical noise in the room, with the action potentials superimposed on it. Thus one hears the song of the nervous system as it processes information.

Why a horseshoe crab? In that species, the long nerve fibers that make up the optic nerve can easily be teased apart from each other, until only one fiber remains. Then one can explore the eye of the crab with a thin pencil of light until there is a response in the single fiber from which one is recording. Then one knows that that receptor cell, on which the light is impinging, is the cell that is driving the activity of that nerve fiber.

Such experiments show that a number of visual phenomena, familiar to us from psychological experiments, can be seen in the eye of the crab. More intense light yields more rapid firing of the nerve fiber, yes; but not proportionally more. An extremely wide range of light intensity is translated into a much narrower range of nerve-cell output. In other words, the very wide range of physical intensities is "compressed" into a much narrower, and thus more manageable, range of nerve-cell outputs (compare Fechner's Law, chapter 45). In addition, the initial burst of nerve impulses is not maintained. If the light continues to illuminate the receptor cell, the neuron quickly reduces its rate of firing. This process is known as *adaptation*. Because of this, the cell is better able to report *changes* in the intensity of light. If it is responding now at a modest rate, the cell has more room to increase its rate of firing if illumination level should increase. The system, in other words, is highly sensitive to "news"—that is, to *changes* in the amount of light input.

But then Hartline made an important discovery by accident. He noticed that if the amount of stray light in the laboratory increased, then, rather than increasing, the cell's activity would often *decrease*.

Now that is strange! If the neuron fires at a higher rate when the light that it "sees" is made more intense, why should it not fire at a higher rate when background illumination increases? Should that not *add* to the total amount of light the sensitive cell is receiving, and so increase its output? But output decreases instead. Why should that be?

It would make sense if neighboring cells in the crab retina have *inhibitory* effects on each other. One cell, in other words, might actually *suppress* the activity of its neighbors. The possibility is there: along with the connection of receptor cells to the brain via the optic nerve, there is a layer of cells running laterally, connecting receptor cells not with the brain, but with each other. Perhaps this network of cells allows one receptor cell, when it is activated, to suppress the activity of neighboring cells.

To see whether this was so, Hartline and his associate, Floyd Ratliff, began stimulating two retinal cells concurrently, while recording from one of them. It turned out that, indeed, a cell might respond vigorously if it were stimulated all by itself, but less vigorously if a neighboring cell was stimulated concurrently. This is known as *lateral inhibition*—inhibition because it suppresses, lateral because it acts "sideways" on neighboring cells. The more intense the light, the greater the output from the cell being stimulated, but also the greater the inhibitory effect that it had on its neighbors. The effect also varied with distance, active cells having greater inhibitory effect on cells close to them than on cells farther away The effect was reciprocal: if cell A inhibited cell B, then B would also inhibit A. Finally, if the lateral interconnecting cells between A and B were severed, the inhibitory cross-effects disappeared.

Further investigation, by these scientists and many others, established this lateral inhibition phenomenon in a number of species. But why is it there? What is it *for*? What is the advantage that lateral inhibition confers? Hartline and Ratliff turned to a more complicated stimulus to clarify what lateral inhibition is for.

In these follow-up experiments, the eye of the crab was exposed, not to single pencils of light directed at single receptors, but to a pattern of light that affected a large number of them. This consisted of an *edge*—a bright part, a boundary, and a dark part. Then the entire pattern was moved back and forth, so that the edge moved back and forth over the retinal cell whose activity was being recorded—the "target cell," for short. This is easier and simpler than moving the recording electrode from cell to cell.

The resulting situation is shown schematically in figure 48.2, which shows what happens in a single row of cells (actually there would be a whole checkerboard of them, some on the bright side of an edge, some on the dark side); it shows the edge in one particular location. On the left part of the figure, each cell *and its neighbors*

Figure 48.2
How lateral inhibition enhances edges in the crab visual system

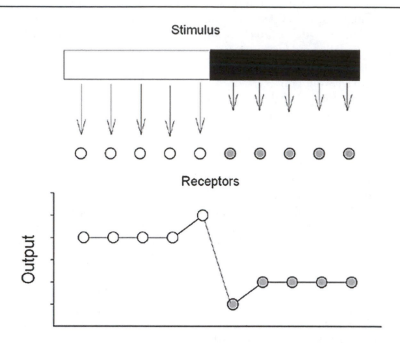

are all "looking at" the bright part of the stimulus. Activity in each cell is high. But close to the edge, it rises even higher, producing the upward "bump" in the figure.

Why? In the left part of the figure, all the cells are receiving a great deal of light, and so each cell's output is high. But each cell is also receiving inhibitory input from its neighbors, which are also "seeing" bright light. So its output, though high, is not as high as it might be. However, right at the bright side of the edge, cells are receiving less inhibitory input from the neighboring cells that are in darkness. Since inhibition is less, their output increases. Hence the "bump."

At the dark side of the figure, the cells are receiving less light, so their output is low. But right at the dark side of the edge, the cells are receiving little light, *and* they are receiving strong inhibitory input from those neighboring cells that are "seeing" brightness. As a result, their output is reduced even further, to produce the "dip" in the figure.

Both the bump and the dip, then, are caused by the effects of cells neighboring the target cell from which one is recording. This was shown directly when the edge was covered over by placing a mask over the eye, with a tiny opening in it so that only one retinal cell was exposed to light or dark. No lateral inhibition can occur here, because only one cell, and none of its neighbors, is being stimulated. Sure enough, both the bump and the dip disappeared when this was done.

In short, the activity of each retinal cell is affected by the amount of light it is receiving, which causes it to be excited; but also by how much light its neighbors are receiving, which causes it to be inhibited. Therefore, as the figure shows, the

Figure 48.3
Lateral inhibition in the human eye

difference between bright and dim illumination is greatest at the boundary between light and dark—in other words, at the edge.

And now we begin to see what is the use of all this. We have a system that *enhances the edges or contours* within whatever pattern of input the eye is seeing. And edges or contours are where most of the information is. A line drawing or cartoon, all by itself, can give us all the information we need to identify the objects and even the people in the picture. Perhaps the horseshoe crab sees the world as a cartoon, with only the outlines of the objects in it.

The real point, however, is not how the horseshoe crab perceives the world. It is that by the time we get to the optic nerve, even before the input gets to the brain, it has already been organized and transformed. Certain important features—like edges or contours—are enhanced. Even in the crab, therefore, what reaches the brain is not a photographic picture of the world, but an enhanced representation of its important features—boundaries and contours.

Before leaving this topic, we noted earlier that the human eye, too, shows lateral inhibition. It is easy to demonstrate this, and figure 48.3 shows it.

As you inspect the figure, look particularly at the places where the white bands, between the black squares, intersect. Those "junctures" look darker than the rest of the white bands. In fact they are not, as can be seen if we inspect the figure through a piece of paper with a tiny hole cut in it, so only a little bit of the figure can be seen at a time. (This is the equivalent of the mask that was used in the crab experiment.) Why then do the junctures look as if they were darker? Because of lateral inhibition.

Consider a retinal receptor that is "seeing" a place along one of the vertical white bands, between two black blocks. It is receiving strong light input from the white paper. But so are its neighbors both above and below. Their activity will have an *inhibitory* effect on our receptor cell's output. That output might be high, but not as high as if the receptor were being stimulated by itself. Lateral inhibition is reducing it.

But what about a receptor that is "seeing" an *intersection* of the white lines? It is receiving the same white light as in the previous case. However, this time the cell is receiving inhibitory input from *all four* sides, from the left and from the right, as well as from above and from below. So those cells are subject to more inhibition. Therefore, the brain "sees" these points of intersection as dimmer than the rest of the white lines in the figure. All because of lateral inhibition: suppression of cells' activity by the activity of their neighbors.

In both horseshoe crabs and humans, then, the visual system transforms and organizes the information it receives. The eye, in reporting to the brain, tells the brain about the most important features of the visible world.

In 1967, Hartline shared the Nobel Prize in physiology and medicine with two other students of vision, Ragnar Granit and George Wald.

BIBLIOGRAPHY

Hartline, H. K. (1941). The neural mechanisms of vision. *Harvey Lectures, 37,* 39–141.

Hartline, H. K. (1967). Visual receptors and retinal interaction [Nobel lecture, December 12, 1967]. Retrieved October 17, 2004, from http:// nobelprize.org/medicine/ laureates/1967/hartline-lecture.pdf.

Lindsay, P. H., & Norman, D. A. (1972). *Human information processing: An introduction to psychology.* New York: Academic Press.

Ratliff, F., & Hartline, H. K. (1959). The response of Limulus optic nerve fibers to patterns of illumination on the receptor mosaic. *Journal of General Physiology, 42,* 1241–1255.

49 | GEORG VON BÉKÉSY: THE MECHANICS OF HEARING

We humans are visual animals, and it is not surprising that vision is the sensory modality that is of the greatest interest to us. Let there be no doubt, however, that classic experiments have been done in all sense modalities. There is not space to consider them all here, but one such research program—the elegant and ingenious experiments of Georg von Békésy on the workings of the ear—must surely be included.

Georg von Békésy (1899–72) was born in Budapest, Hungary, and studied chemistry at the University of Berne in Switzerland. He received his Ph.D. from the University of Budapest in 1926, for development of a fast method for determining molecular weight. Then for a while he worked at the Hungarian Telephone and Post Office Laboratory in Budapest, where his interests moved towards problems of telecommunications and how best to design a telephone earphone.

In 1947 he came to the United States and Harvard University; it was here that he developed his mechanical model of the inner ear (described later). He moved to the University of Hawaii in 1966, attracted by construction of a special laboratory that was built for him, the prospect of closer contact with Asian culture, and the fact that he could avoid forced retirement with the move.

But back in 1928, Békésy was a communications engineer, studying how telephone equipment could be best adapted to the human hearing mechanism. One day, an acquaintance asked him whether any major improvements in the quality of telephone systems could be expected. This set Békésy thinking: How much better is the human ear than any telephone system? And why? How, after all, does the human ear work?

To understand his work, we need a brief introduction to the physics of sound, and to the ear.

Sound waves are rhythmic waves of pressure created when an object vibrates. As a sound wave reaches the ear, the air pressure on the eardrum increases, decreases, increases again, and so on. Even very complex sounds can be shown to be combinations of these simple rhythmic waves of pressure—*sine waves*, as they are called.

Simple sound waves vary along two dimensions. One is the *amplitude*, or intensity, of the sound. The greater the changes in pressure, the greater is the amplitude of the sound, and, other things equal, the louder it will sound to a listener.

The other is the *frequency* of the sound: how many are there, per unit of time, of these rhythmic waxings and wanings in pressure? The frequency of the sound determines the *pitch* that a hearer will hear: the higher the frequency, the higher the pitch. Thus, a pure tone whose frequency is 256 Hz (*hertz*, or cycles per second) gives us middle C. A tone of higher frequency—say, 440 Hz—will have a higher pitch, in this case the A above middle C. It is this that we will be focusing on in this chapter: How does the brain know what frequency of sound is reaching the ear? How, in other words, does *pitch perception* work?

One answer might seem obvious: greater frequency of the sound wave might translate into greater frequency of bursts of nerve impulses running up into the brain. This will not work, however, simply because we can distinguish frequencies that are far higher than the highest frequencies with which nerve impulses can follow each other. Direct "following" of sound frequency by nerve-impulse frequency cannot account for pitch perception, at least at the higher frequencies (it may play a role at lower ones, a complication not considered here).

Let us now look at the receiving mechanism—the ear. What we call the *ear* is actually the *outer ear*, which collects the sound and leads it to the eardrum. Past the eardrum we encounter the *inner ear*, where the real work of hearing begins (figure 49.1). The inner ear is not visible from outside, but is enclosed in a tiny cavity within the skull, where it connects with the auditory nerve (not shown) that runs from the cochlea up into the brain.

The eardrum vibrates with the incoming sound waves, and as it does so it vibrates a chain of tiny bones, which transmits the vibration to another membrane at the entrance to the snail-shaped structure, the *cochlea* (*cock*-lee-ah). This causes fluid to move within the cochlea.

Running down the length of the cochlea, following its spiral-shaped curvature and dividing it, is another membrane, the *basilar membrane*. Closely associated with the basilar membrane, all along its length, are the *hair cells*, and these in turn make contact with nerve cells. The axons of these cells collect to form a cable of axons, the *auditory nerve*. These cells convey information from the inner ear up into the brain, just as another cable of fibers, the optic nerve, conveys information from the eye to the brain (chapter 48).

It is at the basilar membrane that the properties of the incoming sound waves are translated into the language of the nervous system. And the question is, How does this translation, or "encoding," take place? How, specifically, is *frequency of the sound wave* encoded by the nervous system?

Hermann von Helmholtz (chapter 3) had already made a suggestion about this, with his "resonance" theory of pitch perception. If the cochlea itself suggests a snail shell, the basilar membrane, coiled within it and varying in width (as it does), might be like a harp. It might consist of a set of strings. Then the longer strings, in the wide part of the membrane, might be "tuned" to resonate to low frequencies, so that they would be set in motion by low-frequency sounds. The strings in the narrower part of the membrane, being shorter, would vibrate in response to higher

Figure 49.1
The inner ear. Vibrations of the eardrum produced by sound waves are conveyed to the basilar membrane, which is supplied with nerve cells that translate its movements into nerve impulses relayed to the brain.

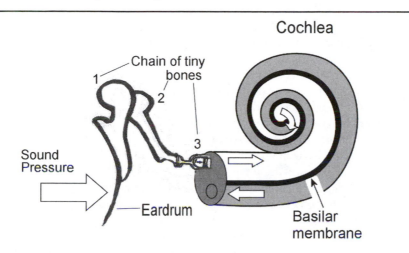

Source: Adapted from Lindsay & Norman (1972). © 1972 with permission from Elsevier.

frequencies. Finally, since different nerve cells would be excited in the two cases, the cochlea could "encode" pitch information in terms of which nerve cells were being excited. *Which pitch* is perceived would depend on *which nerve cells* were being stimulated—hence the handy mnemonic "pitch is which."

There were difficulties with this theory. The strings of a harp vary in length over a much wider range than the variation in the width of the basilar membrane, and yet the range of frequencies that humans can hear is wider even than that. That would be all right if the shorter "strings" were also under greater tension; but unfortunately the basilar membrane is not under side-to-side tension. Something else is going on.

Békésy decided that he needed a closer look at what the basilar membrane was actually doing when vibrations were applied to it. What he did was to remove the entire inner ear from the bodies of people who had recently died. In these fresh cadavers, he was then able to drill a small hole through the surrounding bone and expose the cochlea itself. Then, with the equivalent of a miniature dentist's drill, he would grind away one outer surface of the cochlea to expose the basilar membrane hidden within it. To appreciate the meticulous precision that this required, consider that the whole snail-shaped cochlea is only about three millimeters across—roughly an eighth of an inch! Békésy had to design his own surgical instruments; one pair of scissors had blades only a few thousandths of an inch long.

Even then the difficulties were only beginning. The basilar membrane, housed inside the cochlea, is transparent. To see it, Békésy sprinkled tiny quantities of a silver powder over it. The powder reflected the light of the strong surgical lamp under which all this was being done, and so Békésy could see the membrane shining up at him.

Then came yet another ingenious twist. He intended to vibrate the membrane, mimicking the way it is naturally vibrated, using a tiny piston, electrically driven and attached to the entrance to the cochlea. To mimic the effects of sound, he had to drive the piston hundreds of times per second—making it go back and forth far faster than any human eye could follow. He could see what it was doing only if it moved much more slowly—or if it appeared to do so. So, in order to make the membrane *seem* to move more slowly, he used stroboscopic illumination—brief flashes of light at very short intervals, the kind sometimes used in discos, where it "freezes" the movements of the dancers and makes the movements appear jerky. By appropriate adjustments of the flashes, he could slow down the apparent movement of the basilar membrane, so that he could actually watch it as it moved.

Thus Békésy could see directly what the basilar membrane was doing. The vibration of the piston would set a wave of movement—a bulge in the membrane—traveling down the basilar membrane. As the piston moved in and out, these traveling waves would run down the membrane from their source at the piston. Imagine a rug held out flat in space by two people, each holding the rug at two corners. One person shakes her end of the rug, up and down and up and down, while the other person holds her end steady. It is easy to see that waves will run from the shaker's end toward the other end of the rug. So it was with the basilar membrane.

It developed further that, just because of the mechanical properties of the membrane and its surroundings, there would be a point of *maximal displacement* along the membrane—a place where the bulge was biggest. And sure enough, the place where the wave was biggest depended on the frequency with which the membrane was driven. If it was driven at very high frequency (say, around 1200 Hz), the vibration would be greatest close to the piston. As frequency was made lower, the point of greatest vibration would move progressively away from the piston, toward the far end of the snail shell.

So Helmholtz was right and wrong. He was right that different frequencies of sound have their greatest effect at different portions of the basilar membrane, and, therefore, on different nerve cells. So pitch perception probably does depend on *which* cells in the auditory nerve are stimulated—pitch *is* which! However, resonance has nothing to do with it: the fact that different frequencies stimulate different parts of the basilar membrane results from the mechanics of the inner ear, and not from anything that is tuned to the frequency of the sound itself.

But there was something else that was puzzling. Except at very high frequencies, very large portions of the basilar membrane were set in vibration by the piston. This was true at both high frequencies and low. Yet human beings are capable of making very fine discriminations between one frequency and another. How are they able to make such fine distinctions, if most tones wiggled most of the membrane?

Békésy knew about Hartline's work, and the role of *lateral inhibition* in sharpening the perception of edges and contours in the visual system (chapter 48). Perhaps something like that occurs in the auditory system too. Maybe the nerve cells that were being affected most by the movements of the membrane were *inhibiting* the activity of their neighboring cells. That would sharpen the perception of pitch, because at each frequency, only the input from the small group of *maximally stimulated* cells would be passed on to the brain.

But to demonstrate this, Békésy would have had to record the electrical activity of the nerve cells with which the basilar membrane was in contact. This simply was

Figure 49.2
von Békésy's mechanical ear. The arm resting on the apparatus feels the vibrations of the fluid produced by the piston. The frequency of vibration (its "pitch") determines where on the arm it will be felt. That is because the *pitch* of the vibratory stimulus determines *which* location on the arm will be maximally stimulated, and that determines which location will be felt as the source of the vibration.

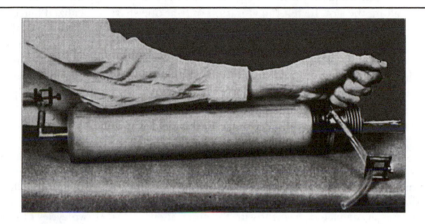

Source: From Békésy (1961). Reprinted courtesy of The Nobel Foundation, © The Nobel Foundation 1961.

not possible. The basilar membrane retains its elasticity for some time after the person has died, but nerve cells die very quickly. If only there were some way he could get to the nerve cells supplying that tiny strip of skin in a *living* human being . . .

Wait a minute.

The basilar membrane is a tiny strip of skin! It comes from the same embryological layer as the skin that covers our bodies. Can we arrange for a person to *hear with his skin?*

Békésy built a mechanical ear (figure 49.2). This was a scaled-up model of the cochlea, a metal tube filled with water, with a rubber membrane at one end that could be vibrated by a piston. Along the length of the tube, at its upper surface, ran a narrow slot covered by a membrane stretched across it—the basilar membrane of the model. When the fluid was set in motion by the piston moving at one end, again there was a bulge that swept like a wave along the membrane. By adjusting the tension of the membrane along the slot, he was able to confine the biggest part of the bulge to a particular region on the membrane. What region? It depended on the frequency of vibration—the equivalent of sound frequency. As in the ear, frequency of the vibratory input determined *which* portion of the membrane vibrated most strongly.

Using this mechanical ear, could a person actually hear with his skin? Yes. If a person simply laid his arm lengthwise along the rubber membrane covering the slot, vibration of the fluid in the mechanical ear would be sensed by the person; and, sure enough, vibrations at different frequencies were felt in different places along the arm. The skin was on the arm rather than in the ear, but pitch was still which.

But there was more. Just as with the basilar membrane, the vibrations set up in the membrane involved very large segments of that membrane and, therefore, a long strip of the skin on the participant's arm. It would seem that it should be very hard to tell one frequency from a neighboring one. But when a human observer laid his arm along the slot, he felt the vibration only at one sharply localized place—the place where the vibration of the membrane was maximal. So there *was* lateral inhibition going on. The areas of skin that were *close to* the point of maximal vibration, though they too were being vibrated, produced no sensation of vibration. Only the area that was at the point of maximal vibration produced a sensation. Obviously, input from the neighboring portions was being *inhibited* by the closely adjacent, and greater, activity at the maximally affected point.

His excitement at this discovery comes through clearly:

> The model had all the properties of a neuromechanical frequency-analyzing system, in support of our earlier view of the frequency analysis of the ear. My surprise was even greater when it turned out that two cycles of . . . vibration are enough to produce a sharply localized sensation on the skin, just as sharp as for continuous stimulation. This was in complete agreement with the observations . . . that two cycles of tone provide enough cue to determine the pitch of the tone. Thus the century-old problem of how the ear performs a frequency analysis—whether mechanically or neurally— could be solved; from these experiments it was evident that the ear contains a neuro-mechanical frequency analyzer, which combines a preliminary mechanical frequency analysis with a subsequent sharpening of the sensation area.
>
> I think the happiest period of my research was when I started to repeat all the great experiments that have been done on the ear in the past—but now on the model ear with nerve supply. All the small details could be duplicated on the skin. Nothing has been more rewarding than to concentrate on the little discrepancies that I love to investigate and see them slowly disappear. This always gives me the feeling of being on the right track, a new track. (Békésy, 1961, pp. 744–745)

Békésy went on to study the role of inhibition in various sensory systems. This project occupied him over the rest of his career.

Any ear was of interest to Békésy. While still in Europe, he learned that an elephant had died in the Budapest zoo, so he went to the zoo to ask for the ears. But the body had been sent to Budapest University, whose authorities had already shipped the carcass to a glue factory. So Békésy went to the factory—and found the head still intact. After some further vicissitudes (including an assistant who underestimated the size of an elephant's inner ear and sawed part of it away), Békésy was able to see that traveling waves occurred in the elephant cochlea too.

In 1961, Georg von Békésy received the Nobel Prize in physiology and medicine for his research on the mechanics of the ear.

BIBLIOGRAPHY

Békésy, G. (1967). *Sensory inhibition*. Princeton, NJ: Princeton University Press.

Békésy, G. von. (1960). *Experiments in hearing* (E. G. Wever, Trans.). New York: McGraw-Hill.

Békésy, G. von. (1961). Concerning the pleasures of observing, and the mechanics of the inner ear [Nobel lecture, December 11, 1961]. Retrieved October 17, 2004, from http://nobelprize.org/medicine/laureates/1961/bekesy-lecture.html.

Lindsay, P. H., & Norman, D. A. (1972). *Human information processing: An introduction to psychology*. New York: Academic Press.

Yost, W. A. (2000). *Fundamentals of hearing: An introduction* (4th ed.). London: Academic Press.

50 | JEROME BRUNER: MOTIVATION AND PERCEPTION

> An office that I pass each day is numbered 400 D; inevitably, when the hour is near mealtime, I perceive this as FOOD. The car I used to drive had the euphemistic label SILVER STREAK on its dashboard; inevitably, when the hour was near mealtime, I would read this as SILVER STEAK.
>
> C. E. Osgood

Do our motives influence our perceptions? In a particularly memorable experiment, briefly describable but a classic in its own right, Hastorf and Cantril (1954) had participants watch a movie—the same movie for all—of a football game between Dartmouth and Princeton. It was a rough game, with many penalties, a broken nose on one side, and a broken leg on the other. The participants were students from Dartmouth and Princeton, and their task was to tabulate infractions that occurred on both sides. Princeton students "saw" the Dartmouth team make over twice as many rule infractions as the Dartmouth students "saw."

Jerome Bruner brought the question into the laboratory. He and his collaborators presented experimental evidence that even simpler perceptual processes can be affected—and distorted—by our motives and values.

Jerome S. Bruner (1915–) was born in New York City. He completed his undergraduate education at Duke University, then took his Ph.D. at Harvard in 1941. During World Was II he worked with the United States Army's Intelligence Corps, where his work focused upon propaganda (the subject of his doctoral thesis) as well as public opinion in the United States. He was editor of *Public Opinion Quarterly* in 1943–44. Bruner returned to teach at Harvard in 1945 and was instrumental in establishing the pathbreaking Center for Cognitive Studies, where he served as director from 1961 through 1972. He came to New York University in 1991, and is now Research Professor of Psychology there.

Bruner was a founder of the "New Look" in perception: the study of perceptual processes as subject to nonperceptual influences—for example, motivational ones (Bruner, 1992). The experiment described here was an early landmark in that research tradition.

The idea was that the *value* of objects should influence how they are perceived. Our perceptual apparatus should emphasize the perception of *important* things. Might this even affect how prominent we perceive them to be—perhaps even how large? Bruner and his colleagues explored this possibility.

In the first experiment (Bruner & Goodman, 1947), the participants were 10-year-old schoolchildren. Of these children, some were drawn from an affluent community in the Boston area, others from a settlement house in a more deprived area of Boston; for these latter children, presumably, coins would have more value.

Each participant saw a circular spot of light on a screen just in front of him. A knob was available that controlled the size of the light, and each child was given some practice in the use of this before the experiment began. Their task was to estimate the size of various coins by adjusting the circle of light to the appropriate size. Each child held a coin in his or her hand as he or she manipulated the knob. Control participants were tested in the same way, but with gray cardboard disks instead of coins. This was done several times for each of several coins of different value.

What happened? When the coins were present, all children overestimated their sizes relative to their actual size. Moreover, the degree of overestimation depended on the value of the coin, not on its size. Thus a U.S. dime, which is smaller than a penny but is worth more, was overestimated more. Finally, the estimates were much greater for the nonaffluent children than for the affluent ones. If the coin was a quarter (this produced the greatest overestimates), the average overestimate was about 20 percent for the affluent children, but a full 50 percent for the less affluent ones. Errors with the cardboard disks were much smaller.

Bruner and Postman (1948), in a similar experiment, looked at the effect of both positive and negative symbols on perception of size. The apparatus was the same as before, but in this case plastic disks with signs drawn on them were the items to be matched. On some trials the sign was an abstract geometrical figure (neutral), on others a dollar sign (positive), and on yet others a swastika (negative). (This was shortly after World War II had ended.) In this case, both the positive and negative signs led to overestimation of size as compared with the neutral control.

Why should the swastika, a negative symbol, be perceived as larger? Bruner and Postmen suggest that dangerous or threatening stimuli, as well as positively valued ones, may be enhanced by the perceptual system—perhaps it exaggerates dangers as well as positive things. But there are other possibilities. The critical factor may simply be enhanced distinctiveness—though that would still imply that such factors as distinctiveness, as well as value, may distort our estimates of size.

These effects have not turned out to be very reliable ones; a number of attempts to replicate the findings have not succeeded. However, experiments of other kinds strongly suggest that our perceptions can be distorted by a "better is bigger" mechanism. (For discussion, see Matlin & Stang, 1978.) As Christmas approaches, children have been observed to draw larger pictures of Santa Claus, though not of more neutral objects. Before the election of 1960 between John F. Kennedy and Richard Nixon, participants were asked which of the two they thought was taller. As it turned out, more Kennedy supporters then Nixon supporters thought Kennedy was the taller of the two—which he was, by half an inch. In another experiment, groups of American college students were introduced to a man identified for some as "Mr. England, a student from Cambridge" and for others as "Professor England from Cambridge." When the students were later asked to estimate the man's height, "Professor England" was judged on average to be taller than "Mr. England"!

That the effects are small is not surprising; after all, we can see how large the true coins, or persons, actually are. If we look at cases that are not so constrained by what is right before our eyes, we find even stronger support for the idea that our motives—our preferences, values, and desires—can and do influence the judgments we make and the impressions we form about what is "out there" in the world.

As just one example, our wishes can influence our judgments of the *probabilities* of various events. In one experiment with schoolchildren, for example, the experimenter used a card-drawing game in which some of the cards were worth points and others were not. The children knew how many point cards were in each deck. Even so, when asked before each draw how likely they were to draw a point card, the children consistently overestimated the likelihood of that favorable outcome. Indeed, a positive outcome that had a probability of only 10 percent was predicted almost as often as a negative outcome that had a probability of 90 percent. This was with schoolchildren, it is true, but the results were similar with college students. The value of outcomes affects, not perception of *size* this time, but judgment of *likelihood* (for discussion, see Mook, 1996).

Also related is the *illusion of control* (Langer, 1975)—unjustified beliefs that one can control the outcome of events. Participants tend to believe that they can make good things happen and bad things not happen, even in situations where events are objectively quite out of their control.

In all these cases, what we are seeing is that our desires can produce a distorted perception not of objects visible before us, but of the likelihoods of future events. We can still speak of perception here, because those likelihoods are being perceived, and courses of action are being decided upon, *now*.

These processes appear to lead to a pervasive optimism, at least in this society. The average person believes that he or she will live longer than average, is less likely than average to have an accident, and is better off than the average person who is in circumstances similar to his or her own (Nisbett & Ross, 1980). Of course, if the *average* person believes that he or she is above average in any or all of these ways, then it is just a cold fact of arithmetic that the average person is mistaken.

These distortions have their advantages. As Nisbett and Ross (1980) point out, if a couple is about to marry, it may be just as well if they do not have it clearly in mind that their chances of divorce are about even. And in dangerously ill patients, the belief that they have some control over their illness, even if the belief is false, may actually make for better outcomes (Taylor, 1989). Optimism, even if unjustified, may keep us going in the face of disappointments and may make us more effective in dealing with challenges (Seligman, 1990).

On the other hand, it can also be extremely dangerous. For example, consider how a person may drive a car even *knowing* he or she has had too much to drink. Obviously the person risks terrible consequences in doing so—a fatal collision, or hitting a child. We are led to wonder, do we sometimes do these things, not in spite of the risks, but *because* of them? Motivational effects on judgment of probability may come into play directly: "That would be so terrible that it must be very unlikely." Unfortunately, that may not be true.

Something to think about.

BIBLIOGRAPHY

Bruner, J. S. (1984). *In search of mind: Essays in autobiography*. New York: Harper Colophon.

Bruner, J. S. (1992). *Acts of meaning*. Cambridge, MA: Harvard University Press.

Bruner, J. S., & Goodman, C. C. (1947). Value and need as organizing factors in perception. *Journal of Abnormal and Social Psychology, 42*, 33–44.

Bruner, J. S., & Postman, L. (1948). Symbolic value as an organizing factor in perception. *Journal of Social Psychology, 27*, 203–208.

Hastorf, A., & Cantril, H. (1954). They saw a game: A case study. *Journal of Abnormal and Social Psychology, 49*, 129–134.

Langer, E. J. (1975). The illusion of control. *Journal of Personality and Social Psychology, 32*, 311–328.

Matlin, M., & Stang, D. (1978). *The Pollyanna principle*. Cambridge, MA: Schenkman.

Mook, D. G. (1996). *Motivation: The organization of action* (2nd ed.). New York: Norton.

Nisbett, R. E., & Ross, L. (1980). *Human inference: Strategies and shortcomings of social judgment*. Englewood Cliffs, NJ: Prentice-Hall.

Osgood, C. E. (1953). *Method and theory in experimental psychology*. New York: Oxford University Press.

Seligman, M. E. P. (1990). *Learned optimism: How to change your mind and your life*. New York: Simon & Schuster.

Taylor, S. E. (1989). *Positive illusions: Creative self-deception and the healthy mind*. New York: Basic Books.

51 GIBSON AND WALK: THE VISUAL CLIFF

A long-standing problem in the study of mind is that we perceive things and know things that the sensory information simply does not provide. This was a cornerstone of Kant's objection to Locke's dictum that there is nothing in the mind that was not first in the senses (chapter 1). A striking example of this is the perception of distance and depth.

The receptive surfaces of the eyes—the retinas—are two-dimensional. The image of one object on the retina may be above or below the image of another, or to the left or to the right of it—but not nearer or farther. Thus, for example, as we see a person walk away from us, the person's image on the retina gets smaller. It has to; that is just geometry. But we do not see the person getting smaller; rather, we see him or her as the same size but getting farther away. How does this happen?

One answer, implicit in Locke and held by many writers such as Helmholtz, is that this is something we learn. We do perceive the person getting smaller, but when we do, knowing that people do not grow or shrink like that, we *infer* that the person must be remaining the same size but getting farther away. This *unconscious inference*, as Helmholtz called it, is based on long experience with objects and with the cues, such as perspective and our knowledge of the size of objects, that allow us to make such inferences. In short, strictly speaking the "perception" of distance and depth is not really a perception at all; it is a perception of the retinal image, *plus* an inference or judgment based on experience. It is a matter not of what we see but of what we know.

The other possibility, held by other writers such as the Gestalt psychologists, is that the brain is wired up in such a way that the various cues to distance and depth result in the perception of distance and depth—directly. We do not need to make inferences, and prolonged experience is not required.

Comparing these two ideas suggests a way to distinguish them. If experience is required for judgments of distance and depth, then a human or animal that lacks such experience should not be able to perceive distance and depth very well. A number of experiments have used this logic in different ways, and this includes the classic experiments with human babies by Eleanor Gibson and her colleague, Richard Walk.

Eleanor Jack Gibson (1910–2002) was born in Peoria, Illinois. She received her bachelor's and master's degrees from Smith College, and her doctorate at Yale in 1938. She married James J. Gibson, also a prominent researcher in perception. When he joined the faculty of Cornell University in 1949, she was ineligible for a faculty position because of antinepotism rules, so she stayed on as research associate. But in 1965, after the rules changed, she was appointed to an endowed chair as a professor of psychology at Cornell. A student of perceptual development, Gibson also did research on perception and reading.

Richard David Walk (1920–99) was born in Camp Dix, New Jersey. His A.B. was earned at Princeton in 1942, his M.A. at the University of Iowa in 1947, and his Ph.D. at Harvard in 1951. He taught at Cornell from 1953 to 1959, then at George Washington University until 1991, when he returned to Cornell as a professor emeritus.

The *visual cliff* experiment occurred to Gibson as she was eating a picnic lunch on the rim of the Grand Canyon. Would a toddler perceive the edge of the canyon as a dangerous place, threatening a nasty fall? If so, then the toddler must be able to perceive depth. Back at Cornell, she and Walk set up an experiment—with smaller and more portable apparatuses than the Grand Canyon—to find out.

In the first visual-cliff experiments (Gibson & Walk, 1960), human babies were observed. These babies were between 6 and 14 months old, which means they had had some visual experience, but far less than an adult; and it is likely that they had never had the experience of falling off a cliff! And a cliff was exactly what they were presented with—what Gibson and Walk called a *visual cliff*.

The apparatus is shown in figure 51.1. Two checkerboard patterns were arranged so that one was mounted 40 inches above the other, seeming to form a cliff that a careless baby, crawling around on the upper side, could fall over. In fact, the cliff was perfectly safe. The entire upper surface was covered by a sheet of nonreflecting glass, so that it could not be seen but would prevent the babies from falling if they ventured across the apparent cliff. The question was, Would the babies avoid crawling over that apparent cliff? Would it *be* an apparent cliff to them? If so, then they could perceive the different distances of the upper and lower surfaces.

In the initial experiment, 36 infants were tested. Each baby was placed at the center of the visual cliff. The infant's mother, who had also been recruited for the experiment, called to the baby first from the deep side and then from the shallow side. Nine of the children refused to move at all, but all of the remaining 27 approached their mothers *if* they were called from the shallow side. But when called from the deep side, all but three of the children either crawled away from the mother toward the shallow side or stayed where they were, often appearing distressed; and those who did crawl toward their mothers seemed very hesitant in doing so. "Often they would peer down through the glass of the deep side and then back away. Others would pat the glass with their hands, yet despite this tactile assurance of solidity would refuse to cross" (Gibson & Walk, 1960, p. 64). Apparently, even the mothers' reassurance was insufficient to overcome the babies' reluctance to "risk" a fall.

Figure 51.1
The visual cliff. The top pane of nonreflecting glass makes the apparatus perfectly safe. However, it *looks as if* the child could receive a painful fall if it ventures over the edge. So the child should avoid doing so—if, that is, the child can perceive distance and depth.

Source: Drawing by Marcie Ewasko. Copyright © 2004 by Marcie Ewasko. All rights reserved. Used by permission.

Now this experiment does not, it is true, rule out all visual experience. The babies had to be old enough to crawl, and so they had had a few months of visual experience—though most of them, chances are, had never had the experience of falling from a height. Nevertheless, now that the preliminary data with babies were in, it was worth exploring what animals would be like who had had even less visual experience. Some animals are able to move around from birth—chicks, lambs, and kids (baby goats), for example. So, chicks, lambs, and kids were duly brought into the laboratory and tested with appropriately sized variations of the visual cliff. All of them passed the test.

On the other hand, rats failed the test, and so did some turtles. These exceptions are instructive. Rats are not visual animals; they are most active in the dark, and they get around by smell and the cues from the whiskers on their faces, by which they feel their way around. They do not need to use visual cues to avoid cliffs, and sure enough, it seems that they do not use them.

As for turtles, whereas the majority of them chose the shallow side, a sizable minority did not. This might mean that the turtle has poorer depth perception than the other species tested. Or it might mean that turtles in their natural environment (underwater) have little reason to fear a fall, and so little reason to evolve the sensorimotor apparatuses for avoiding falls.

These animal experiments avoid the problem that arose with babies: the participants in these experiments all had virtually no visual experience prior to testing. It raises the other problem, of course, that these are nonhuman species, and we cannot assume that baby humans are wired to perceive depth just because baby chickens are. Even so, the findings do tell us that a species *can* be wired to avoid falls based on visual input, without having to learn the cues that signal the danger of a fall. This includes even some mammals, such as kids and lambs.

All told, these experiments (and many subsequent ones) are clear evidence that an organized three-dimensional world is perceived by at least some animals, and by children who are just old enough to crawl, in the absence of the prolonged experience that might support inferences, unconscious or otherwise, about the nearness and distance of objects in that world.

In fact, later observations with the visual cliff showed that some recognition of distance and depth is likely in babies even younger than those Gibson and Walk studied. At only two months of age, babies show a drop in heart rate when they are placed on the deep side, but not the shallow side, of a visual cliff. A drop in heart rate may be a sign of increased attention, rather than fear; but the difference still means that the babies could perceive the difference between shallow and deep.

More impressive still: Babies can use not only depth cues, but also social cues, in deciding what to do about a visual cliff. In one experiment, a modified cliff was used in which the drop was a less sharp one—really a ramp, not a drop—and so evoked fewer signs of fear. One-year-old babies were placed (individually) on the "upper" side in this apparatus. Then, when the mother put on a happy, reassuring expression as the baby approached the ramp, over two-thirds of the babies crossed over to the "deep" side. If instead the mother put on a fearful, worried expression, every single baby pulled up short and did not cross. Thus the method can be used to study not only depth perception, but what is called *social referencing* as well (Sorce, Emde, Campos, & Klinnert, 1985).

The fact is that until rather recent times, babies' capabilities have not been appreciated. William James assumed that their world was a "blooming, buzzing confusion," until prolonged learning had taught them that there were three dimensions out there, and objects and people as well. These experiments and, in the past few years, many others as well have come down on the Gestalt side of things. The perceptual system does pick up distance and depth with at most minimal experience in humans and virtually none in some other species. Babies have much to learn, but it is surprising how much they already know.

BIBLIOGRAPHY

Gibson, E. J. (1991). *An odyssey in learning and perception.* Cambridge, MA: MIT Press.

Gibson, E. J. (2002). *Perceiving the affordances: A portrait of two psychologists.* Mahwah, NJ: Erlbaum.

Gibson, E. J., & Walk, R. (1960). The "visual cliff." *Scientific American, 202,* 80–92.

Sorce, J. F., Emde, R. N., Campos, J., & Klinnert, M. D. (1985). Maternal emotional signaling: Its effect on the visual cliff behavior of 1-year-olds. *Developmental Psychology, 21,* 195–200.

52 LETTVIN ET AL.: WHAT THE FROG'S EYE TELLS THE FROG'S BRAIN

"Why do we see things and not the holes between them?" Kurt Koffka (1935), one of the founders of Gestalt psychology, begins his discussion of vision with this artless question.

For a long time, it was assumed that the sensitive cells in the retina respond to light, and that they transmit the resultant excitation back to the brain, preserving spatial relations. It is as if the retina consisted of little pixels, like those of a computer monitor, and as if these pixels were joined one-to-one with another two-dimensional sheet of pixels, in the visual area of the brain. Thus a picture of the world would appear first on the retina, and then in the brain. This is the "picture in the head" theory of visual perception.

Clearly, matters are not so simple. In discussing Gestalt psychology (chapter 2), we saw how information is transformed so that two dimensions look like three, or how a figure, once seen, becomes impossible to "unsee." Clearly the visual system is doing something—transforming the input and organizing it. We may say that the brain is performing *computations* on the input. That is why the work of the visual system is of such great interest to engineers and computer scientists as well as to psychologists and physiologists. The work of Lettvin, Maturana, McCulloch, and Pitts (1959)—first published in an engineering journal—is an early, excellent, and enormously influential example of this convergence of ideas.

Jerome Y. Lettvin (1920–) graduated from the University of Illinois Medical School in 1943. After World War II he worked at the University of Rochester and at Mantego State Hospital near Chicago, where he began "building [his] own amplifiers, remaking old oscilloscopes, and so forth" (Lettvin, 2000, p. 8) so as to set up a laboratory for research in neurophysiology. By then he had become close friends with Walter Pitts and Warren McCulloch. After World War II, when Pitts was homeless and Lettvin didn't want to live with his parents, the two moved in with McCulloch and his wife for a while. The three, along with Patrick Wall, another young neurophysiologist, arranged to move together to the MIT laboratory in 1951.

Humberto Maturana (1928–) is an experimental biologist and philosopher in Santiago, Chile. He was visiting at Harvard when these experiments were done.

Warren S. McCulloch (1898–1972) was born in Orange, New Jersey. He received his M.D. from Columbia University. He worked at Yale University from 1934 to 1941, before moving to the University of Illinois at Chicago, then to the Research Laboratory for Electronics at MIT. He is perhaps best known for "A Logical Calculus Immanent in Nervous Activity" (McCulloch & Pits, 1943), a contribution to the theory of neural networks and related ideas in the neurophysiology of mind and behavior, which he coauthored with Walter Pitts.

Walter Pitts (1924–67?) apparently never took a degree. Beginning at age 17, he was making mathematical contributions to the theory of neural networks, including a paper on neural networks that he coauthored with McCulloch. In 1947, Pitts moved to MIT with McCulloch and Lettvin. Lettvin tells us, "He died alone in a boarding house in Cambridge after doing his best for close to a decade to avoid being found by his friends. Nothing of his work was left" (Lettvin, 2000, p. 10). No more can be said of this matter here.

Meanwhile, this group of friends had performed a definitive series of experiments on the workings of the visual system in the frog.

In an experiment on vision, what should an experimenter present for the eye to see? If the picture-in-the-head theory were true, then it would make sense to explore the visual system with spots of light, for these are what it responds to. On the other hand, if we wish to know how the frog's visual system handles *things* (and not the holes between them), we must show it *things*—things that the frog should care about.

So Lettvin and his colleagues presented various stimuli—changes in illumination level, but also various objects and edges, moving or stationary. As Hartline and his colleagues had done (chapter 48), they recorded the electrical activity of single nerve cells, this time at the place where the optic nerve terminates in the brain.

Why frogs? Because the frog seems to use relatively little information from the visible world, and so the code by which it communicates with that world should not be too difficult to break. The frog does not seem to be concerned with stationary objects in the world. Its food, for example, consists of flying insects; in other words, small dots that move. A frog will starve if surrounded by dead flies, because they do not move. The frog escapes from enemies simply by leaping toward a darker place. Capturing bugs and escaping from enemies—these are what vision in the frog is for. (Its sex life is conducted by sounds and touch, and so was not intruded upon here.) So Lettvin et al. published their findings under the engaging title "What the Frog's Eye Tells the Frog's Brain" (1959/1968).

The frog's retina, like the human's, communicates with the brain by way of the optic nerve, a cable of axons coming from retinal ganglion cells. Between these two layers of cells is a dense network of interconnecting cells. Indeed, most of the frog's retinal cells are interconnecting ones: there are 2.5 to 3.5 million of these, as compared to only about 1 million receptor cells, and half a million ganglion cells whose axons form the optic nerve. By way of these interconnectors, one tiny part of the retina can be kept informed about what is going on in other parts, which may be some little distance away. This at once suggests that a great deal of information processing, involving the interaction of cells in the retina with each other, is going on, in the frog as in the crab (chapter 48). Information is passed on to the brain only after it has already gone through several stages of information processing. This allows it to report to the brain, in code, a simplified description of those aspects of the world that its visual system detects.

For the experiment, the frog was placed so that its eyes were looking at the inside of a gray hemisphere that covered its entire visible field. Various objects—the "things"—were metal cutouts, held on the inside of the hemisphere where the frog could see them by magnets on the outer surface of the hemisphere. This also permitted the experimenters to move the objects simply by moving the magnets, without breaking into the gray "visible world" of their participant. In this way, they could present a wide variety of things for the frog's eye to look at.

To repeat: The pixel-to-pixel or picture-in-the-head theory of vision implies that a given optic-nerve cell should respond to the amount of light that impinges on the receptors. The more light, the more response there should be, and so the array of light and darkness in the outside world should be transformed into an array of activity in the cells at the termination of the optic nerve.

Not one of the cells the experimenters found behaved in this way. Instead, the experimenters found four kinds of cells in the frog eye, each kind telling the brain some specific thing about the world it was seeing.

First, some cells were *net dimming detectors*. These cells responded to a decrease in illumination with an increase in their own activity. And that increase was nearly independent of the absolute illumination level; a decrease from bright to less bright produced the same response as a decrease from dim to dimmer.

Second, some cells were *moving-edge detectors*. This kind of cell would respond to any edge that moved through its receptive field—that is, the part of the visible world that that cell responded to. The size of the edge made little difference, but its movement did: the cell responded to an edge only if the edge was moving, and the faster the movement, the greater the response. Varying the overall illumination level affected these cells only slightly, in marked contrast to the first group.

Third, there were *sustained contrast detectors*. If a sharp-edged object either lighter or darker than the background moved into the receptive field and stopped there, the cell would respond promptly and continue responding. Responding would stop if the lights were turned off, resuming if they were turned on again; but short of turning the lights off entirely, variation in illumination level had surprisingly little effect. In very dim light where the experimenters could barely see the stimulating object themselves, these cells still responded vigorously. The frog's eye could clearly see edges even where the human eye had trouble doing so.

Fourth, and most intriguing, were the *net convexity detectors*. Again, these cells were unaffected by changes in illumination level. They responded if a small object passed through the receptive field. The object had to be small, it had to be convex, and it had to move into the receptive field; jerky movement caused a greater response than smooth movement. Finally, if a whole pattern of little dots, or a checkerboard pattern, moved across the receptive field, there was little or no response. In other words, the small convex object had to *move relative to its background* to activate these detectors.

To further confirm this point and its implications, the experimenters replaced the gray hemisphere with a large color photograph of a natural frog habitat, with its flowers, grasses, and puddles. Then, if the whole photograph was moved through the receptive field of one of these cells, there was no response. But if a small complex object was moved *relative to* this background, then there was a strong response. If the small object was then fixed to the background and the whole assembly moved, there was no response. In other words, to "decide" whether to respond, these cells had to take account of what was happening all over the visible world at the moment! If something small was moving relative to the rest of that visible world, the cell responded. If the same object made the same movement *along with* the rest of the world, it did not.

A small, convex object moving against its background! Where would a frog encounter such an array in the course of an its daily life? Lettvin et al. happily named these cells *bug detectors*. They seemed to have just the properties required for identifying, and locating, a small flying insect—something for a frog to eat.

Since the time of this paper, much has been learned about systems within the visual system that detect particular *kinds* of things (e.g., moving objects) or *features* of things (e.g., lines and edges). With these findings and their follow-ups, we are moving closer to an answer to Koffka's question. Why do we see things and not the holes between them? Because our visual system is wired up so as to detect *things* (like bugs) or the features of things (like edges). We can even compute the movement of a whole complex background, and determine whether a dot is moving *against* the background or *with* it.

Certainly the picture-in-the-head theory of vision must give way. Vision does begin with elements—the retinal receptors. However, the interaction among elements extracts "thing" information and tells the brain about it. As to just how the wiring accomplishes this, the work of Hartline and Ratliff has pointed the way (chapter 48).

Nor does the perceptual apparatus look much like a Lockean blank slate (chapter 2), on which is written whatever is "out there" to be seen. It looks more like a Kantian machine shop, in which information is filtered and categorized so as to tell the frog's brain about things that matter to the frog—bugs to eat, obstacles to be avoided, or the sudden darkening that might signal the power dive of a hawk from above. Some very old issues are being clarified.

At least all this is true if we are frogs or crabs. But also in mammals, "feature detectors" in the retina and in the brain have been identified, as by the work of the physiologists David Hubel and Torsten Wiesel, which won them the Nobel Prize in 1981. In humans, too, feature detectors can be demonstrated (Reisberg, 1997; Weisstein, 1969). The methods must change—few humans are willing to have electrodes placed on their optic nerves—but the experiments can be done. A couple of examples will give the flavor.

Let the participant stare at a screen on which there is a series of vertical bars, black on white. After a few minutes, the bars will fade as fatigue occurs: they look less sharp and clear, and if we gradually reduce the contrast until the bars disappear, they will disappear much sooner if the eye has been gazing at them for a while than if it has not. That is how we can measure the amount of fatigue that has occurred.

But fatigue of what? Of the retinal light receptors themselves? No, for if we substitute a set of *horizontal* bars for the vertical ones, they appear with full intensity, and the eye must be fatigued, or adapted, all over again before they fade. Obviously, what has been fatigued is not the visual receptors, but a set of detectors that respond specifically to *vertical lines*. These *vertical-line detectors* were fatigued in the first phase of the experiment, but horizontal-line detectors were not. The latter, when activated by horizontal bars, respond with full vigor. In animals, physiological studies have shown directly that such detectors exist (Hubel and Wiesel, 1979).

Another dramatic instance is one that the reader can verify for him or herself: the *waterfall illusion*. Next time you are close to a waterfall, stare at the falling water for about two minutes. Watch the water as it falls and falls. Then switch your gaze to something that is standing still—the opposite bank, perhaps, with its trees and foliage. For a few seconds, there will be the definite impression that the stationary scene is moving *upward*. (If you do not have a waterfall handy, water falling from a tap in the kitchen will do.)

Notice that when this happens, there is no blurring or fading of vision. The trees and shrubs on the opposite bank, or the accouterments of the kitchen, are there, bright and clear. It is just that the whole perceptual pattern appears to be moving when it is not. Clearly, the perception of motion *as such* is separate from the perception of the details of the things moving. It further seems that the perception of standing still seems to be generated not by a visible scene that *is* standing still, but by a balance between two systems producing the perception of upward and downward movement, respectively. Staring at the waterfall produces fatigue in the downward-movement system, shifting the balance in favor of the perception of upward movement. A striking example of how the visual system tells us about *movement* independently of the rest of the message it conveys!

All told, our conception of what vision is all about has been revolutionized in the past few decades. For this, we remain indebted to the horseshoe crab (chapter 48)—and the frog.

BIBLIOGRAPHY

Hubel, D. H., & Wiesel, T. N. (1979). Brain mechanisms of vision. *Scientific American, 241*, 150–162.

Koffka, K. (1935). *Principles of Gestalt psychology.* New York: Harcourt, Brace & World.

Lettvin, J. Y. (2000). Jerome Y. Lettvin. In J. A. Anderson & E. Rosenfeld (Eds.), *Talking nets: An oral history of neural networks*, (pp. 1–21). Cambridge, MA: MIT Press.

Lettvin, J. Y., Maturana, H. R., McCulloch, W. S., & Pitts, W. H. (1959). What the frog's eye tells the frog's brain. *Proceedings of the IRE, 47*, 1940–1951. Reprinted in W. C. Corning and M. Balaban (Eds.). (1968). *The mind: Biological approaches to its functions*, (pp. 233–258). New York: Interscience Publishers.

McCulloch, W., & Pitts, W. (1943). A logical calculus of ideas immanent in nervous activity. *Bulletin of Mathematical Biophysics, 5*, 115–133.

Reisberg, D. (1997). *Cognition: Exploring the science of the mind.* New York: Norton.

Weisstein, N. (1969). What the frog's eye tells the human brain: Single cell analyzers in the human visual system. *Psychological Bulletin, 72*, 157–176.

8 SOCIAL PSYCHOLOGY

53 THEODORE NEWCOMB: ATTITUDE CHANGE AT COLLEGE

Not all classic studies are experimental. There are cases in which experiments cannot be performed—for example, in investigating the impact of the social situation that one is immersed in for long periods of time. Such matters must be studied in other ways; for example, by what is called a *quasi-experiment*. Rather than *making* something vary, one may observe what happens when it *does* vary naturally—for example, when it changes over time.

The inferences we make must be guarded here, for other things may be changing along with the variable of interest. Even so, especially if other plausible variables can be ruled out, ideas can be tested and much can be learned from quasi-experimental procedures. The study of the Seekers by Festinger et al. (chapter 57) is a classic example. Another is the research of Theodore Newcomb and his colleagues dealing with attitude changes over, and after, students' four-year experience at Bennington College. This research project began in the 1930s and has spanned over 50 years.

Theodore Mead Newcomb (1903–84) was born in Rock Creek, Ohio. He earned his A.B. at Oberlin College, and his Ph.D. at Columbia University in 1929. He taught at Lehigh, Western Reserve (now Case Western Reserve) University, and Bennington College before becoming professor at the University of Michigan in 1941. He founded Michigan's Department of Social Psychology in 1946 and served as its chairman until his retirement in 1972.

The study to be examined here was concerned with the impact of a group—one's fellow students and teachers in college—on the attitudes of the group members. Specifically, he wondered, What happens when people who hold one set of attitudes find themselves immersed in a larger group whose attitudes are very different?

An experiment might randomly assign some students to attend a college where different attitudes prevails from their own attitudes. Others would be assigned to attend one where their own attitudes prevail (or, perhaps, not to attend college at all). That way, only the first group would experience tension between their own attitudes and the surrounding ones. Such an experiment obviously could not be done. It would be both impractical and unethical to assign subjects at random to attend one or another college for four years of their lives. Again, however, even where we cannot *make* something occur, we can look carefully at what happens when it *does* occur, testing hypotheses about the process and ruling out alternatives.

Bennington College, in Bennington, Vermont, was established in 1932 as an experimental college for women. It was small—in 1936 it consisted of about 300 people, students and faculty—and a close-knit community. Most of its faculty lived on campus, many of them in student dorms.

Bennington had a reputation for political liberalism, both among its faculty and among the students who had been there a few years. Many incoming students, in contrast, were from affluent families that tended to have quite conservative attitudes. What happens when people with one set of attitudes—the relatively conservative entering students—are placed in close and long-term contact with a group whose attitudes are different—older students and faculty with relatively liberal views?

Newcomb (1943) and his coworkers interviewed students who had been at Bennington for varying periods of time. Where possible, they also repeated the interviews as students advanced from freshman to senior. What they found was that as students spent more time at Bennington, there was a consistent drift toward more liberal attitudes on political and social issues. It is not that all the older students became what would be called *liberal*—they did not—but most of them became *more* liberal than they had been before, as they spent time at Bennington.

This change was shown in many ways—pencil-and-paper attitude tests, which political candidates the students favored, and the opinions they expressed on various social issues of the day. As just one example: In the 1936 presidential election, about two-thirds of the incoming class preferred the Republican (and more conservative) candidate, Alfred Landon, to the Democratic (and more liberal) candidate, Franklin D. Roosevelt. Juniors and seniors, in contrast, preferred Roosevelt 3 to 1.

Other measures told the same story. Consistently and by many measures, students—not all, but most—tended to move away from their initial conservative attitudes and values and toward more liberal ones as they spent time at Bennington.

Was this just because the more conservative students tended to leave Bennington? No. That could be checked by the repeated interviews in the students who did remain there. Here, even in the *same* students, the drift toward more liberal attitudes was clear.

Why did it happen? For one thing, there was substantial social pressure toward such a change. Those students whose attitudes did not change tended to be, or to become, rather isolated. Other students named them less often as friends, as people who were admired, or as suitable to be leaders than those students whose attitudes did change. In short, there were social rewards for becoming less conservative in that community.

That raises a question. Did the students' attitudes really change? Or were the students only paying lip service to the prevailing attitudes at Bennington, while keeping their own, more conservative attitudes to themselves?

One way of addressing that question is to ask whether the changes in attitude were *lasting*. Once they had graduated and left Bennington, and so had left the social pressure behind, did these women maintain their more liberal views? Or did

Figure 53.1
Bennington College in 1933

Source: From the Bennington College Archives. Reprinted courtesy of Bennington College.

they move back toward the more conservative attitudes they had entered college with? They maintained their views, as a follow-up study showed.

Twenty-five years later, Newcomb and his coworkers were able to locate 94 percent of the women they had studied originally and study them again (Newcomb, Koenig, Flacks, & Warwick, 1967). Some were reinterviewed, and where this was not possible, they responded to mailed questionnaires. New questions had to be asked, of course, for the issues that separated liberals from conservatives in the 1960s were different from those that had distinguished them in the 1930s. Questions were asked about attitudes toward a variety of current social issues and toward public figures who were identified as conservative (e.g., Dwight Eisenhower, Joseph McCarthy) or as liberal (e.g., Adlai Stevenson) in the 1960s.

Would these Bennington alumnae remain more liberal years later? But wait a minute: More liberal than whom? Than they themselves had been when they entered college? Not good enough, for two reasons. First, the questions had changed, as we have just seen, making more recent scores hard to compare with earlier scores. Second, suppose these women are on average were more liberal now than they were then. That would mean little by itself. Perhaps the whole culture might have drifted in a liberal direction over the intervening years. Maybe *most* people were more liberal in the 1960s than they were in the 1930s, in which case the Bennington experience might have had nothing to do with the difference. This may or may not seem likely, but it is a possibility, and it had to be checked.

What is needed is a control, or comparison, group. Who should be in that group? Well, the real question is, are these Bennington alumnae more liberal (on average) than similar women who have *not* attended Bennington? But then, how are "similar women" to be located?

Newcomb and his colleagues solved this problem in an imaginative way. They interviewed the *sisters* of women who had gone to Bennington, where the sisters had gone to college elsewhere or not at all. This was a group closely matched to the Bennington graduates for family ethnicity, affluence, and parental attitudes, but without the experience of having gone to Bennington. The conclusions were checked with other comparison groups as well, again matched for age and social background with the Bennington alumnae.

It was found that Bennington alumnae in the 1960s did, on average, express more liberal attitudes and values than their non-Bennington sisters or peers—even a quarter of a century after graduation.

Apparently the change toward liberal attitudes *(a)* was greater in Bennington students than in their sisters or peers, and *(b)* was genuine and lasting, not just a matter of surface conformity. That finding, in view of the close matching between groups, suggests that it was in fact the presence or absence of the Bennington experience that produced the differences in attitudes and values.

This doesn't mean that the Bennington experience somehow stamped a liberal attitude on its graduates once and for all. Rather, having formed new attitudes, the Bennington graduates chose careers and lifestyles that were compatible with those new attitudes, and therefore supported and maintained them. For example, the data showed that Bennington women tended to select, or be selected by, husbands with more liberal attitudes than non-Bennington women. They were also more likely to describe their close friends as having such attitudes. In short, if it was *social pressure* that produced the attitude change in the first place, it was *social support* that maintained it over the following years.

Newcomb's study, we have said, was not an experimental one. We cannot assign some students, at random, to attend a college with a liberal atmosphere and others to attend a more conservative one. But that does not mean that researchers cannot ask about the impact that the college environment has. Newcomb's data—not arguments or impressions, but data—show the lasting changes in attitudes and values that characterized his Bennington sample.

Perhaps most impressive of all was the thoroughness with which Newcomb's group checked and cross-checked their findings with different questions and different measures. After all, any single measure of "liberalism" might be flawed, but when multiple measures are used, and when they all tell the same story, they cross-check each other and fill in each other's gaps. Then they converge to offer powerful support for a conclusion.

Thus: Did women who were relatively liberal when they graduated from Bennington tend to describe themselves as liberal 25 years later, as compared to ones more conservative? Yes. Did they more often describe their friends as liberal? Yes. Did they read more magazines with a liberal slant? Yes. Were they more likely to vote for the more liberal candidate (Kennedy) in the 1960 Kennedy-Nixon election? Yes. Were their attitudes and values less conservative than the control group of non-Bennington sisters? Again, yes. And so on—page after page of it. Measure after measure was taken, all converging on the same conclusions.

Many more findings came from the study, but this is enough to show what interview and questionnaire data can do by way of identifying a process of attitude change and investigating its causes and characteristics. Finally, the conclusions fit in with many other data, including experimental findings, on what happens to people who deviate from a group's prevailing attitude. There will be pressure on such a deviant to change his or her attitude; and if the pressure doesn't work, he or she will likely be rejected and isolated by the group (see, e.g., Schachter, 1951).

In short, the Bennington studies were not experiments, but they were rigorously scientific nonetheless. They show how observations can give rise to questions that can be answered with further observations that test various possibilities. And the answers can be checked with yet more observations that ask the questions in different ways and so act as cross-checks on each other.

The Bennington studies by Newcomb and his colleagues are monuments to careful investigation—and persistence. The group checked their findings yet a third time, *50 years* after the initial observations (Alwin, Cohen, & Newcomb, 1991). The major conclusions were unchanged.

BIBLIOGRAPHY

Alwin, D. F., Cohen, R. I., & Newcomb, T. L. (1991). *Political attitudes over the life span: The Bennington women after fifty years.* Madison: University of Wisconsin Press.

Newcomb, T. M. (1943). *Personality and social change.* New York: Dryden.

Newcomb, T. M. (1950). *Social psychology.* New York: Dryden.

Newcomb, T. M., Koenig, K. E., Flacks, R., & Warwick, D. P. (1967). *Persistence and change: Bennington College and its students after twenty-five years.* New York: John Wiley & Sons.

Schachter, S. (1951). Deviation, rejection, and communication. *Journal of Abnormal and Social Psychology, 46,* 190–207.

54 | MUZAFER SHERIF: PREJUDICE AND THE ROBBERS' CAVE

Of all the social behaviors we discuss in this book, prejudice is probably the most widespread and certainly among the most dangerous . . . Many of us are victims of stereotyping and even violence, all because of a particular group to which we belong—whether it is ethnic, religious, gender, national origin, sexual preference, or what have you. Those who hold the prejudiced beliefs are affected negatively as well; living a life punctuated by active dislike or hatred for other groups of people is surely not a life-affirming, positive experience.

E. Aronson, T. D. Wilson, and R. M. Akert

The point hardly needs elaboration in today's world.

What causes prejudice? How is it possible to hate an entire group of people, most of whom one has never met? No doubt there are many possible reasons (see Aronson, Wilson, & Akert, 1994, for discussion); it would be foolish to look for some one single cause of so complex a phenomenon. Yet science proceeds to untangle such a web by studying one process at a time—knowing that what one scientist does not study, another will (chapter 1).

One idea about the origins of prejudice is known as *realistic conflict theory*. It suggests that groups become hostile toward each other when they must compete with each other for scarce resources. Under conditions of scarcity, one's attitudes toward members of groups different from one's own—*out-groups*—become more rigid, stereotyped, and hostile. In Nazi Germany, attitudes toward Jews followed this pattern; Adolf Hitler rose to power in the catastrophic German economy of the 1930s. So, in California in the nineteenth century, did attitudes toward Chinese immigrants, who were competing with Caucasian workers for jobs. And in a classic correlational study, Hovland and Sears (1940) found that the number of lynchings of black people in the southern United States was inversely correlated with the price of cotton over the period from 1882 to 1930. As the price rose, the number of lynchings fell—and conversely. They suggested that in an economy heavily dependent on cotton, low prices meant economic hard times, generating hostility that in turn was murderously directed onto the black community.

But can competition, by itself, produce hostility between competing groups? This is the kind of question that requires an experiment. If the idea is correct, then *introducing* competition where it was not there before should lead to intergroup hostility. Just such an experiment was conducted by Muzafer Sherif and his colleagues in the famous Robbers' Cave experiment (Sherif, Harvey, White, Hood, & Sherif, 1961).

Muzafer Sherif (1906–88) was born in Izmir, Turkey. He attended the American International College in Izmir, earning his B.A. in 1927; he earned an M.A. at the University of Istanbul in 1929. After coming to the United States, he attended Harvard University, taking a second M.A. in 1932; he then went to Columbia University, where he took his Ph.D. in 1935. He then went back to Turkey to teach, but returned to the United States in 1945 to join the faculty at Princeton University. He later taught at Yale University and the University of Oklahoma before joining the University of Pennsylvania as a professor of sociology in 1966. He became a professor emeritus in 1972.

Sherif was no stranger to the laboratory. In chapter 56 we mention his laboratory work on the *autokinetic effect*—a laboratory study of conformity.

The present experiment, however, was taken out of the laboratory and into a natural setting, producing what we call a *field experiment*. It was an experiment because something was made to vary, and a field experiment because it was made to vary in a natural setting. Such experiments have the advantage that they occur in the "real world," so we know that the results apply there. The disadvantage is lack of precise control over the situation, but if the effects of the independent variable are clear—as they were in this case—then the data show that this drawback is not serious.

The experiment, which lasted about three weeks, was conducted in the natural setting of a summer camp in Robbers' Cave State Park, Oklahoma. The 20 participants—who did not know they were in an experiment—were 12-year-old boys. They had been screened by Sherif to be normal, unaggressive boys. Sherif did not want troublemakers in the situation, or boys who were "naturally" hostile and resentful. He wanted to leave plenty of latitude for his experimental manipulations to have their effects.

The resulting sample of boys was divided *at random* into two groups, which meant that the two groups were unlikely to differ much from each other on average. Each group gave itself a name, the Eagles and the Rattlers.

The procedure, in overview, was in three phases. First, within each group, a feeling of cooperation and cohesiveness was fostered within each group; the two groups were separated during this time. In the second phase, the two groups were set in competition with each other, to see if hostility between groups would result—as it did. In the third, various attempts were made to undo that hostility. This proved surprisingly difficult to do. Once established, the hostility between groups seemed to take on a life of its own! One tactic in particular, however, turned out to be highly successful.

How could the dependent variable be measured—feelings and acts of hostility on the one hand and cooperation and team spirit on the other? This was done in a variety of ways. Sherif's research team realized, as had Newcomb's (chapter 53), that any one measure could be misleading for any number of reasons. The most convincing findings are those that are supported by a number of different measures, which could thus cross-check each other.

The camp counselors, who were also Sherif's assistants, recorded episodes of cooperative or hostile actions and words. Where possible, episodes were recorded by two observers independently, so that they could compare notes later—much as in the study of the Seekers (chapter 57). The boys also were interviewed from time to time by the counselors and by Sherif himself, posing as a maintenance man. Here the boys responded to such questions as, Who are your friends? Whom do you like and whom do you dislike? How well do you think your campmates are described by these adjectives: brave, tough, friendly, sneaky, smart-alecky, and stinky? Do you think each of these traits describes all, most, a few, or none of the boys in your group? What about the other group? In addition to this, some ingenious little "probe" measures were introduced, as described later.

Now let us look more closely at what happened.

In the first phase, the two groups were kept separate from each other and were encouraged to cooperate within each group. They cooperated in such activities as preparing group meals and building a diving board and a rope bridge. Strong feelings of cohesiveness within each group developed.

In the second phase, competition between groups was introduced. The groups became teams who competed against each other in games like tug-of-war, football, and baseball, with prizes awarded to the winning team.

Going further, the experimenters arranged some truly diabolical situations in an effort to induce resentments. In one such case, a camp party was arranged, but it was also arranged so that (a) some of the food offered was very tasty, whereas some was rather uninteresting, and (b) that one group arrive well ahead of the other, so they were in a position to preempt all the best food. They did exactly that—whereas they could have cooperated instead, and shared all the goodies with each other.

When the latecomer group arrived, they were quite annoyed at being left with the remains. The earlier group felt entitled to the good food because they had come earlier, and were annoyed at the others' annoyance. Name-calling escalated into a full-blown food fight.

In this atmosphere, resentment and hostility were made apparent in a number of ways. A simple count of the name-calling overheard by the counselors showed escalating bad feelings between groups. The members of each group rated the other groups' members as sneaky, smart-alecky, and stinky, whereas the boys in their own group were brave, tough, and friendly. Conflict, in other words, led to polarization and stereotyping in the way each group saw the other.

The hostility was not purely verbal. Each group raided the other's site. They spoke of "raids" and "counter-raids." Each burned the other's flag.

More interesting still, the groups saw each other in negative ways that went beyond simple resentment. In one ingenious "probe" experiment, Sherif arranged a bean-hunt contest. Sherif had spread beans around the campground, and each boy would pick up as many as he could; the group with the highest total count would win a prize. The boys were told not to lose time counting beans, for they would all be counted in the end. Then, after the beans were collected but before they were counted, Sherif obtained from each boy an estimate of how many beans each of them had picked up.

The results were dramatic. On average, the Rattlers judged that they had picked up over four times as many beans as the Eagles. The Eagles judged that they had picked up nearly three times as many beans as the Rattlers! In other words, the tendency to judge the other group negatively went beyond judgments of personality traits (sneaky versus brave), to judgments of performance and competence—even at a silly task like bean collecting.

The third stage of the experiment was an attempt to undo the intergroup hostility produced during the second. This proved not an easy task.

Merely removing the forced competitions was not enough. Nor was forcing the two groups into contact. It is often assumed that simply bringing two groups together should have such an effect, for it allows each group to discover that people in the other group are not such bad fellows after all. This tactic was a resounding failure. Activities that simply brought the two groups together, even repeatedly, were likely to end up in food fights rather than harmony.

What did work, however, was a series of experiences in which the two groups had to work together to *achieve a common, superordinate goal*. This possibility is quite distinct from the first. It proposes that what matters is not that the two groups come together, but that they act together to achieve a goal that is shared by both groups and is therefore "outside" each of them. One comes to think of what *we* must do together, and that is not consistent with an *us*-versus-*them* perception. It is a recognizably Gestaltist idea; the separate groups become parts of a single "whole thing" defined by the higher-order goal, and come to perceive themselves that way.

Again some ingenious scenarios were staged in order to bring this about. In one, Sherif arranged for the camp's water supply to fail. To find out what was wrong and fix it, the groups went their separate ways, but then they converged on the water tank, which was where the problem was. They had to cooperate in fixing it. They did so, and got along together while working together.

In another case, a truck carrying the boys' food to a cookout got stuck in a rut (this too was arranged). The combined efforts of both groups were required to free it. Sure enough, the combined efforts of all the boys led to further reduction in the friction between the Rattler and Eagle parts of this new whole.

The reduction in hostility again was shown by a number of measures. Name-calling became less frequent. The boys began listing members of the other group as friends far more often than they had done before. The unfavorable character ratings of the out-group became less unfavorable now, and, interestingly, the favorable character ratings of those within the group also declined. There was, in other words, a reduction of both stereotypes—less feeling of "We're the good guys" as well as less feeling of "They're the bad guys."

The whole story has a happy ending. The groups had come to camp in separate buses, but they decided to go home together. The Rattlers still had the money they had won in the bean-hunt contest, but instead of keeping it among themselves, when they stopped for lunch they decided to treat everybody—Eagles and Rattlers alike—to malted milks. And they did.

Many implications have been drawn from the Robbers' Cave study (Aronson, 1999; Aronson et al., 1994; Sabini, 1992). As just one example, Elliott Aronson and his colleagues have used these ideas in a classroom situation—normally a rather competitive setting—creating *jigsaw classrooms*. Groups of schoolchildren are given a project, such as writing a biography; and each child is given *some* of the information required to do it. They must pool their information to get the job done; none of them can do it alone. As they work together toward a *superordinate goal* (recall the truck stuck in the mud), students in jigsaw classrooms have not only performed better on objective examinations, but also showed decreased prejudice and increased liking for their groupmates, both within ethnic groups and across them. And not only in the classroom: on the playground as well, there was more evidence of intergroup mingling among children in jigsaw classes than among those in more traditional ones. (For discussion, see Aronson et al., 1994).

Again, however, the important factor is not just contact between groups, but cooperation among them—working together toward a common goal. In this connection, Aronson recalls a remark made to him by a school principal in 1971: "Look, Professor, the government can force black kids and white kids to go to the same school, but no one can force them to enjoy hanging out with each other" (1999, p. 363). Perhaps Sherif's investigation has helped show a way in which contact *under certain conditions* can, indeed, lead people—not force them—to enjoy hanging out with each other.

BIBLIOGRAPHY

Aronson, E. (1999). *The social animal* (8th ed.). New York: Worth Publishers.

Aronson, E., Wilson, T. D., & Akert, R. M. (1994). *Social psychology: The heart and the mind.* New York: Harper Collins College Publishers.

Hovland, C. I., & Sears, R. R. (1940). Minor studies in aggression: VI. Correlation of lynching with economic indices. *Journal of Personality, 9,* 301–310.

Sabini, J. (1992). *Social psychology.* New York: Norton.

Sherif, M. (1970). On the relevance of social psychology. *American Psychologist, 25*(2), 144–156.

Sherif, M., Harvey, O., White, B. J., Hood, W. R., & Sherif, C. (1961). *Intergroup cooperation and conflict: The Robbers' Cave experiment.* Norman, OK: Oklahoma Book Exchange.

Sherif, M., & Sherif, C. W. (1969). *Social psychology.* New York: Harper & Row.

55 | KURT LEWIN: TENSIONS IN THE LIFE SPACE

Kurt Lewin was one of the founders of modern social psychology. (Lewin's name is properly pronounced le-*vin*, but most American psychologists have anglicized it to *loo*-in.) He showed how to use experimentation to test hypotheses, and how even complex social processes can be brought into the laboratory for experimental analysis. He had a profound influence on social psychology, not only through his own research, but through the influence of his provocative ideas and of the warmth of his personality on a whole generation of students.

Kurt Lewin (1890–1947) was born in Germany. He took his degree from the University of Berlin in 1916, just after Kurt Koffka and Wolfgang Köhler had taken their degrees there. He, with them, was among the early Gestalt psychologists, and, like them, he emphasized the importance of the *field* of influences within which a person is embedded. Köhler, Koffka, and Wertheimer had explored this approach in perception and learning. Lewin extended it to the study of motivation and social interaction.

Lewin emigrated to the United States in 1933, teaching at Stanford and Cornell and then at the University of Iowa. After World War II, the Massachusetts Institute of Technology brought him to Cambridge as chief of their new Research Center for Group Dynamics. Unfortunately, he died suddenly only two years later.

Lewin, like many other behavioral scientists, emphasized that behavior is subject to two sets of influences: internal and external, the person and the situation (1935). Again, like many others, he insisted that the situation has a more potent influence than we tend to believe. We are inclined (at least in this society) to emphasize the characteristics of the person—personality characteristics, personal preferences, and the like—and to downplay the importance of the situation. This may be a mistake (e.g., Nisbett & Ross, 1980).

More is involved, however, than a simple tradeoff between the external situation and the person. What matters is the situation *as the person perceives it*. To understand its effects, we must understand the person's subjective interpretations of stimuli and responses, as well as the stimuli and responses themselves.

The person perceives him or herself within an environment—what Lewin called the *life space*, by which he means the totality of things, goals, and persons that are affecting the person *right now*. The life space has parts—objects, other persons, and the like, but also memories of past events, and expectancies of events to come. Of these, many, and the most interesting ones, carry a motivational charge—they have what Lewin called *valences*, positive or negative. These are the things or states toward which one is drawn (positive valence), or from which one is repelled (negative valence). These attractions and repulsions are seen as operating like attractive or repelling forces in a *field*, like the field of forces that surrounds the poles of a magnet and can cause iron filings to move. The iron filings do not create the field; they are embedded within it, and their movements depend on its properties.

A writer, for example, wants to finish a chapter; that is a goal toward which he is drawn at the moment. If all his attention is on moving toward that goal, his life space may shrink down to the keyboard, monitor screen, and the things he wants to say. There may be little space left for anything else, and so he may resist being drawn into conversation or, if he is so drawn, may converse poorly and superficially—and impatiently! There is little of his life space left over to deal with the conversation, if it is dominated by the goal of finishing a project.

Many modern cognitive psychologists agree with Lewin, though they may use different imagery to express the ideas. They speak of *limited cognitive resources*, so that if a task ties up much of our resources, we may not have enough left to meet the demands of other tasks (like conversation). So, for example, if busy with a demanding task, we may blurt out a remark that we would suppress if we had enough resources left for its careful consideration. (For discussion, see Wilson, 2002.)

Returning to the writer: there is a tension within his life space. He wants the chapter finished, and it is not finished yet. Like a stretched rubber band, the difference between the present state and the desired state pulls the writer toward completion. The tension becomes stronger as nearness to the goal approaches, so an interruption will be much more annoying if it occurs when the chapter is nearly finished then if it occurs when he has only begun. (Compare Miller's analysis of conflict [chapter 11], which is often compared with Lewin's analysis. A rat runs faster or pulls harder as it comes closer to the goal of food.) But if an interruption does occur, the intention is maintained, and the uncompleted task may nag at the writer until the task gets done. That is why, at least under some conditions, one remembers interrupted tasks better than tasks that have been completed (the *Zeigarnik effect*; see Osgood, 1953). For completed tasks, the pull toward completion is dissipated; for uncompleted tasks, it is still there.

Then, too, there may be positive and negative valences associated with some one state of affairs, producing the further tension of *conflict*. One may be drawn toward an attractive person that one sees at a party (positive valence), but at the same time pushed away from that person by fear of rejection (negative valence). How this will play out depends on the relative strength of the two valences, and on what other options the situation affords.

Finally, the life space may contain *barriers* between the existing state of affairs and the desired one. These may be physical (there may be a wall between oneself and the desired object), or psychological (the desired object is forbidden). Consider how people may refrain from eating as much as they want to eat, in the interest of maintaining a diet. They have put a *psychological* barrier between themselves and that attractive piece of apple pie. We also know, however, that if they do violate the diet "just a little bit," that psychological barrier may collapse like a punctured soap bubble (a very Lewinian analogy), and they may simply give up the attempt to restrain their eating—at least "just for now" (chapter 17).

Of the many classic experiments conducted by Lewin and his colleagues, perhaps the best known is one he performed with Roger Barker and Tamara Dembo (Barker, Dembo, & Lewin, 1941). The procedure was as follows.

First, children of kindergarten age were allowed to play with a roomful of toys. The toys were rather strange and not really very good, including such things as ironing boards without irons or water toys without water. But that was all right with the children, who played imaginative games with what was available and seemed quite happy.

Then, however, they were allowed to *see* a collection of much more elaborate and interesting toys—but not to play with them. These toys were inaccessible behind a wire screen. After that, the children were no longer content to play with the original toys. They were more likely to throw the toys against the wall, step on them, or otherwise be destructive and aggressive. When they did play with the toys, their play was rated by observers as less complex and creative than it had been before.

Now, why? The toys had not changed. The authors argue that the change resulted in part from what Lewin called *dedifferentiation* of the life space. A life space has parts, and a complicated life space has many parts; this is *differentiation*. And inventing imaginative games with incomplete toys is a complicated activity, which itself has many parts and many possibilities. Registering all these parts and possibilities means that the life space is itself complex.

But if there is a barrier between the child and attractive things to play with, their attraction creates tension between them and the child—again, like a stretched rubber band. The pull of the attractive toys may so dominate the child's life space that there simply is little cognitive *room* remaining for thinking of complicated things to do with the toys he or she has—and so the remaining "room" has fewer parts. That is *dedifferentiation*. Children (or adults) preoccupied with inaccessible things may not see the possibilities of the accessible ones. Less creative play, and perhaps the discharge of tension via aggression, may follow.

As Barker, Dembo, and Lewin point out, there may have been dedifferentiation in time as well. The children now were vividly aware that their playtime was under the control of an experimenter's whim. Now, complicated play changes in complicated ways over time. But the children might have reasoned as follows: If play could be interrupted at any time, there was no guarantee that time would be available for anything complicated enough to be interesting. In short, planning over any considerable period was no longer possible, and so the children's life spaces shrank to the here and now.

There was much more to Lewin's active research program. Often his ideas led him to experiments in applied settings, directed toward practical problems; he himself said that there is nothing so practical as a good theory. As just one example (Lewin, 1952): During World War II, meat was in short supply in the United States, and nutritionists were trying to change the food-consumption habits of American families. They tried to persuade homemakers to use sweetbreads, kidneys, hearts, and other underutilized meat sources. How might homemakers best be persuaded to try these?

Posters, pamphlets, lectures about the nutritional value and low cost of these foods, appeals to patriotism—none of these had much success. What worked much better was the use of small discussion groups of homemakers, in which members talked about how people like themselves could be persuaded to try these new foods.

This approach was tested against the earlier ones by an actual experiment. The results were clear. In a control group that just received informative lectures, only three percent of the homemakers reported that they tried the new foods within their families. Of those assigned to discussion groups, a full 30 percent did so.

In short, if the dietary change was perceived as coming from *within the group itself*, the procedure was often effective. If the change was seen as imposed from outside, it was not—even though the change itself, with all its objective costs and benefits, was the same. Another striking example of the role of the social situation, *as perceived by its members*, in producing behavioral change!

These brief examples can hardly convey Lewin's great influence on social psychology, partly through the students he inspired with his imaginative ideas, the bold way in which he took hold of research problems and turned them into experiments, and his personal magnetism. He attempted a geometric approach to describing behavior and the forces acting upon it. This has not endured, though some spatial metaphors still ring true (for example, the collapsing soap bubble of the dieter's self-restraint). What has endured is Lewin's emphasis on *situations*, as perceived in the here and now, on the actions we take. As two contemporary writers put it, "People can be seen to act in ways that seem either cowardly or brave, honest or dishonest, prejudiced or unprejudiced, or apathetic or concerned, depending on the situational constraints and opportunities present at the time of action" (Nisbett & Ross, 1980, p. 32). Lewin not only called our attention to these influences, but also showed us how they can be studied.

BIBLIOGRAPHY

Barker, R., Dembo, T., & Lewin, K. (1941). Frustration and aggression: An experiment with young children. *University of Iowa Studies in Child Welfare, 18*, 1–314.

Lewin, K. (1935). *A dynamic theory of personality*. New York: McGraw-Hill.

Lewin, K. (1952). Group decision and social change. In G. E. Swanson, T. M. Newcomb & E. L. Hartley (Eds.), *Readings in social psychology*, (pp. 197–211). New York: Holt.

Nisbett, R. E., & Ross, L. (1980). *Human inference: Strategies and shortcomings of social judgment*. Englewood Cliffs, NJ: Prentice-Hall.

Osgood, C. E. (1953). *Method and theory in experimental psychology*. New York: Oxford University Press.

Wilson, T. (2002). *Strangers to ourselves: Discovering the adaptive unconscious*. Cambridge, MA: Harvard University Press.

56 | SOLOMON ASCH ON CONFORMITY

Solomon Asch was strongly influenced by the Gestalt psychologists, and he, like Kurt Lewin (chapter 55), extended his holistic emphasis to the study of social behavior. His career centered around the application of careful scientific experimentation to human social influence—the influence of one person (or group of persons) on another—while still capturing the richness and complexity of those influences. He did this by introducing experimental variations into controlled, but real, social settings. His experiments on conformity pitted physical reality against social influence, and the results showed just how powerful the latter could be.

Solomon E. Asch (1907–96) was born in Warsaw, Poland, and came to the United States in 1920. He received his B.S. from the College of the City of New York in 1928, and his M.A. and Ph.D. from Columbia University in 1930 and 1932, respectively. He taught at Brooklyn College, the New School for Social Research, Swarthmore College, and Rutgers University before joining the University of Pennsylvania, where he remained. During his 19 years at Swarthmore, he was part of a group of Gestalt psychologists that included Wolfgang Köhler (chapter 21).

Asch was familiar with previous experiments by Muzafer Sherif (chapter 54) on the *autokinetic effect*. This effect refers to the fact that a spot of light in an otherwise darkened room may after a while appear to move around. In Sherif's experiment, groups of participants made judgments of how much they thought the light was moving, and in which direction. He showed that the judgments tended to converge. Since the movements were wholly illusory, this can only mean that each participant's judgments of the movement were influenced by the judgments of others—social influence.

Asch wished to explore the limits of such conformity in judgment. After all, the autokinetic effect is illusory; one is making judgments about a movement that does not in fact occur. But can social pressure also affect one's judgment about a real situation that one perceives directly? It can.

Figure 56.1
Stimuli of the kind used in Asch's conformity experiments. Of the lines in the right-hand card, which one is the same length as the line on the left?

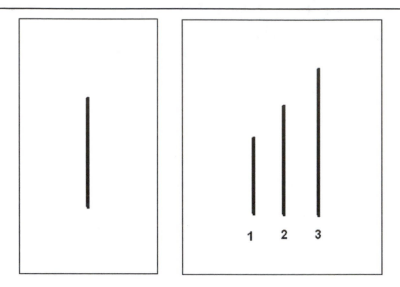

In Asch's original experiment (1951), a group of 9 or 10 "participants" were brought together around a table. They were shown pairs of cards placed a few feet in front of them (figure 56.1). On one card was a black vertical line; on the other card there were three black lines of varying lengths. The participants' task was very simple indeed: they were to decide, for each of several such pairs, which of the three lines was equal in length to the one line of the other card. Here, obviously, it is line 2. The task was so easy, the experimenter said, that he would save time by letting the participants simply call out their judgments one by one rather than writing them down.

Now in fact, there was only one real participant. All the other people seated around the table were assistants to the experimenter, and they all acted out a pre-arranged scenario. Seating was arranged so that the real participant came last; he called out his judgments only after all the others had called out theirs.

For the first few trials, all of the false participants gave the answer that was obviously correct—and, of course, the real participant did the same. But then, the confederates began giving unanimous, but wrong, answers. Confronted with an array like figure 56.1, they might all agree that line 1, rather than line 2, was the one that matched the single line. Around the table, the confederates called out the same wrong answer—until it was the real participant's turn. The participant had just heard person after person make the same judgment, when that judgment was obviously wrong. What would he himself do?

We can surely empathize with the real participant's intense discomfort here. The direct evidence of his senses shows the one answer is correct. But the group's unanimous opinion is that another answer is correct. Is there perhaps something wrong with his eyes? With his sanity? Can everyone else really be so wrong as it appears?

Figure 56.2
**A bewildered participant in Asch's conformity experiment. The participant (center)
is uncertain whether to doubt his eyes or his ears, as he hears everyone else in the
room give an answer that he sees is obviously wrong.**

Source: From Asch (1955). Photograph by William Vandivert.

He must now call out his own judgment. What shall he do? Shall he trust his senses,
or shall he defer to the group and give the same wrong judgment as they?

In fact, only about one in four participants (over several repetitions of this experiment) consistently gave the correct answer. All the others deferred to the group
on at least some trials, letting the judgments of the group override their own. On
average, such conformity occurred on about a third of the trials.

When they were interviewed after the experiment was over, only very few participants reported that the group's unanimous response has actually changed how
they saw the lines. It was clear to most of them that the group answer was simply
wrong. But they wondered whether they were right, they expressed concern for
their eyesight, and they found it extremely embarrassing to go against the judgment
of the group so directly and publicly. Asch went on to check this point directly: in a
repetition of the experiment, the real participant wrote down his answers privately
rather than calling them out publicly. Under these conditions, nearly everyone
wrote down the correct answers even after hearing the unanimous, incorrect judgments of other group members.

Apparently, then, the pressure to conform came from the fact that nonconfor-
mity was public, which meant that the participant would risk looking strange or
foolish to the other members of the group if he reported publicly what he actually
saw. If so, this itself is striking. Why should he care? The other, false participants
were complete strangers, and the real participant would probably never see them
again. Despite this, their good opinion of him was a powerful inducement for him
to deny the direct evidence of his senses.

Asch explored his finding further, and discovered more about it (1955). He asked,
for example, Does conformity increase with the size of the majority group? Up to
a point it does, but that point is reached quickly. When Asch repeated his experiment, varying the number of unanimous confederates from 1 to 14, he found that

the conformity increased up to a group size of 4, but showed little increase beyond that. It doesn't take many to form a commanding "majority."

In addition, it makes a difference whether the group is unanimous in its wrong judgments (Asch, 1956). Asch again repeated his original experiment, with seven confederates present in addition to the participant. But in this variation, only six of the seven gave the wrong answer; the remaining one gave the right answer on every trial (and, of course, it was arranged that he do so before it was the real participant's turn to speak). This was a great help in permitting the participant himself to disagree with the majority. On average, people conformed only six percent of the time when there was one other dissenter from the majority. If there were no other dissenter, 32 percent conformed in this experiment.

That raises another question. Why does having one "fellow dissenter" make it easier for a person not to conform? Is it because the dissenter agrees with him? Or is it because the dissenter breaks up the unanimity of the group? It turns out to be the latter. Asch separated the two possibilities with another elegantly simple twist to his original experiment. In this one, again all the confederates but one gave the same wrong answer. The remaining confederate also gave a wrong answer, but it was a *different* wrong answer from the majority one. This was enough! It greatly reduced the tendency of the participant himself to conform to the majority.

Apparently, someone does not have to agree with us, but only has to break up the *unanimity* of the group's opinion, in order to reduce the force of that opinion in producing compliance. Other investigations of conformity and compliance, such as Milgram's experiments on obedience to authority (chapter 58), found a similar effect: What matters is not that one have an ally, but only that one not be alone in dissenting.

Much further work has been done, using this procedure to explore not only the effect itself but also how it depends in turn on gender, personality variables, the cultural background of the participants, and much besides. We cannot explore this literature here (see Aronson, Wilson, & Akert, 1994, for discussion). But Asch's own series of experiments, considered by themselves, show how much—and how easily—what we say can be affected by even the most minimal social pressure.

Finally, it is worth recalling Asch's criteria for a good experiment: controlled enough to permit sound science, but asking questions of importance to human beings. Conformity to a group's opinion, despite one's own reservations, happens in the real world, not just in the laboratory:

> In 1961, President John F. Kennedy, after meeting with his advisors, approved a CIA plan to invade Cuba at the Bay of Pigs and overthrow Fidel Castro; the invasion was a humiliating disaster . . . Arthur Schlesinger, one of Kennedy's advisors, later reported that he had grave doubts about the Bay of Pigs invasion, but he did not express them out of fear that "Others would regard it as presumptuous of him, a college professor, to take issue with august heads of major government institutions." (Wade & Tavris, 2000, pp. 677–678)

Psychologist Irving Janis calls it *groupthink*, this tendency for dissenters from a unanimous opinion (or what they take to be one) to suppress their doubts and reservations rather than stand alone in opposition. Janis's book discusses many instances of groupthink—and its consequences, which can be severe.

One final point. Asch's series of experiments is a particularly good example of the *progressive* nature of a research project. His first experiment showed the conformity effect—the willingness to suspend one's own judgment in response to group pressure. Asch then went on to ask, How big does such a group have to be? (Not very.) Is it important that it be unanimous? (Yes.) Then is this because another dissenter supports the correct answer, or just because he *is* a dissenter? (The latter.) Each question leads to a further experiment, which leads to another in turn; and all the while, in small steps, our understanding advances.

BIBLIOGRAPHY

Aronson, E., Wilson, T. D., & Akert, R. M. (1994). *Social psychology: The heart and the mind.* New York: Harper Collins College Publishers.

Asch, S. (1951). Effects of group pressure upon the modification and distortion of judgments. In H. Guetzkow (Ed.), *Groups, leadership, and men,* (pp. 177–190). Pittsburgh, PA: Carnegie Press.

Asch, S. (1952). *Social psychology.* New York: Prentice-Hall.

Asch, S. (1959). A perspective on social psychology. In S. Koch (Ed.), *Psychology: A study of a science* (Vol. 3, pp. 363–383). New York: McGraw-Hill.

Asch, S. E. (1955). Opinions and social pressure. *Scientific American, 193,* 31–35.

Asch, S. E. (1956). Studies of independence and conformity: I. A minority of one against a unanimous majority. *Psychological Monographs, 70*(9), Whole No. 416.

Janis, I. (1982). *Groupthink: Psychological studies of policy decisions and fiascoes* (2nd ed.). Boston: Houghton Mifflin.

Rock, I. (Ed.). (1990). *The legacy of Solomon Asch: Essays in cognition and social psychology.* Potomac, MD: Erlbaum.

Wade, C., & Tavris, C. (2000). *Psychology* (6th ed.). Upper Saddle River, NJ: Prentice-Hall.

57 FESTINGER ET AL.: WHEN PROPHECY FAILS

The research project we now discuss is not, strictly speaking, an experiment. The researchers did not actually cause anything to happen. Rather, they observed carefully the response to something that did happen in the natural course of events. It can be thought of as a kind of "natural experiment." As accidental brain damage can be followed by an abrupt change in cognitive functioning, so an external event can be followed by an abrupt change in behavior. In such cases, it is at least a possibility worth following up that the change was *caused* by the event in question. Such a case was reported by Leon Festinger, Henry W. Riecken, and Stanley Schachter (1956).

Leon Festinger (1919–89) was born in New York City. He received a B.S. from the College of the City of New York in 1939, then went to the University of Iowa to do graduate work under Kurt Lewin. He received his Ph.D. in 1942, then followed Lewin to the Research Center for Group Dynamics at the Massachusetts Institute of Technology, where he became an assistant professor. In 1947, Festinger moved to the University of Michigan, then to Stanford University. In 1968 he returned to New York, where he remained until his death.

Henry W. Riecken (1917–) was born in Brooklyn. He took an A.B. at Harvard in 1939 and a Ph.D. in 1950. He has held a variety of research and advisory positions in academics and government and is now a professor emeritus in the School of Education, University of Pennsylvania.

Stanley S. Schachter (1922–97) was born in New York City. He received his B.S. and M.A. from Yale in 1942 and 1944, respectively. After working on vision in the Aero-Medical Laboratory of the Armed Services during World War II, Schachter went to MIT in 1946 to work with Kurt Lewin (chapter 55), who had just set up his Research Center for Group Dynamics. The young social psychologists attracted to the center included Leon Festinger, with whom Schachter did his dissertation research. He received his Ph.D. in social psychology from the University of Michigan in 1949. He later went to Columbia University, where he remained until his retirement.

Leon Festinger is best remembered for his theory of *cognitive dissonance* (1957). He suggested "that the 'psychological' opposition of irreconcilable ideas (cognitions), held simultaneously by one individual, create[s] a motivating force that would lead, under proper conditions, to the adjustment of one's beliefs to fit one's prior behavior—instead of changing one's behavior to express one's beliefs" (p. 18).

Notice that cognitive dissonance does not mean just a state of conflict, as between wanting two incompatible things at once. It is a state of discomfort (the "motivating force") produced by an inconsistency between our beliefs and our actions. As long as the inconsistency is there, we are troubled by the feeling that our actions do not or did not make sense. And Festinger proposes that if the action has already been taken and cannot be changed, we may change our beliefs to fit the action, and thus remove the inconsistency.

The case of the Seekers was one of the investigations from which this idea developed.

In the 1950s, Mrs. Marian Keech, a middle-aged woman in Michigan, became convinced that she was receiving messages from outer space, from a race of extraterrestrial "Guardians." One evening in September, she received such a message, informing her that in December most of the world would be destroyed by a catastrophic flood. However, she, and those close to her, would be rescued by flying saucers coming in from outer space.

Mrs. Keech attracted followers, a small but loyal group—the Seekers—who believed her messages and, along with her, prepared to meet the catastrophe. The degree of commitment to these ideas varied among group members, but in some of them it was quite striking: some quit their jobs and gave away their possessions, and some sold their homes. (Why not? They would not need them on another planet.) Some even left their spouses.

It is important to realize that the Seekers seemed perfectly normal people except for these bizarre beliefs There was a physician among them, and several college students. They were quiet and reclusive, making no attempt to publicize their beliefs; they discouraged converts and refused to grant interviews when these were requested by reporters who had heard about the group.

Festinger and his colleagues were told by students about this group, and they decided to watch from close at hand how the group members would prepare themselves for the coming catastrophe, and what would happen when (as seemed to them very likely) the catastrophe failed to arrive. They and their student observers joined the group, posing as believers themselves. They were able to sit in on the group's discussions and keep careful records of what was said and done. This method—observing the actions of the group from the inside, as a member of the group—is called *participant observation*.

The care with which the researchers kept these records is impressive in itself. Well aware that memory is fallible and that one may easily see what one expects to see, they checked the accuracy of their records in two ways. First, wherever possible, at least two members of the research team would be present at a meeting, so that after the meeting they could compare notes as to what had happened before the memories grew old. Second, when anything of particular interest occurred, a member of the group would duck into the bathroom to jot down an account of what had happened immediately after its occurrence.

In the event, there was no flood, and no space people came. After the predicted catastrophe failed to happen the first time, Mrs. Keech reestimated the date, but nothing happened on the revised date either. The group's prophecy failed not once but twice, and so Festinger et al. published their findings in a book titled *When Prophecy Fails* (1956).

What did the group do?

One might have expected a reaction of the form "Well, I guess we were mistaken." Some perhaps did conclude this; at least, they left the group. But in others, nothing of the sort happened.

The group of course offered reasons for the failure of the prophecy. Mrs. Keech herself reported that she had received messages assuring her that the "light" of the group's faith had itself averted disaster: the Seekers had saved the world!

Other actions by the remaining group suggested that their commitment to their beliefs not only had not weakened, but had actually *intensified*. They began making speeches to the public and handing out leaflets. Mrs. Keech herself made audiotapes for the media, explaining her beliefs and their bases in the messages she had received. All these were things that she and the group had never done before.

Was this because only the most devout and activist members remained with the group after the predicted doomsday had come and gone? Fortunately, because they had kept detailed notes, Festinger et al. were able to go back through these and check that possibility. They ruled it out. Those members who were now proselytizing and publicizing had, before the crisis of Doomsday, expressed no more commitment and activism than other group members had, who left.

The most important point is this: It would appear that even in perfectly sane people, a strong belief can survive even the clearest possible evidence that it is wrong. Indeed, a belief can not only survive such disconfirmation, but show every sign of becoming stronger following it.

How could that be? In explaining it, the authors appealed to the developing theory of *cognitive dissonance*.

The idea, again, is this: One is uncomfortable if one's actions conflict with one's beliefs and values. People do not like to be inconsistent. Suppose, then, that one is confronted with such an inconsistency, acting in accordance with one's belief, but now faced with evidence that the belief was false all along. Then, if the actions have already occurred and cannot be changed, one may modify the beliefs instead, to bring them into line with the actions one has taken.

Now, many of the Seekers had devoted a great deal of time and energy to promoting their liaison with the extraterrestrial beings; recall that some had even quit their jobs and sold their homes. Clearly their knowledge that they had done these things would be inconsistent with a belief of the form "Oh well, it was all a mistake; we've been wrong all along." One member of the group (the physician) said,

> I've had to go a long way. I've given up just about everything. I've cut every tie; I've burned every bridge. I've turned my back on the world. I can't afford to doubt. I have to believe. (Festinger et al., 1956, p. 168)

So the group members who stayed on felt strong pressures toward sticking to their beliefs and convincing themselves that they had done the right things after all. Maybe they had just got the details wrong, that was all, and the prophecy would still be confirmed—someday. Or perhaps the "light of their faith" had saved the world from disaster, as Mrs. Keech herself came to believe.

Then the group members cast around for support for their beliefs that they really had done the right thing after all. How might they strengthen that belief? One way to do that would be to convince other people that they had been right after all. Hence, perhaps, the new willingness to broadcast their beliefs and argue for them publicly, and to seek converts—again, things they had never done before the prophecy failed.

One other observation sheds light on this episode. Those who did begin to publicize the group's beliefs were those who *remained with the group* after the prophecies had failed. Those who drifted away, though they may have been just as committed earlier, did not participate in publicizing and proselytizing. It appears that just as *social pressure* can promote attitude change, as at Bennington (chapter 53), so *social support* can help a person maintain an opinion, even in the face of the clearest possible evidence that that opinion is wrong.

The concept of cognitive dissonance does not rest solely on this episode, however. Indeed, some experiments that can be considered classic in their own right were designed either to test the theory directly or to show its applicability to a very wide variety of topics involving attitude, attitude change, and the clashes that can occur between what we do and what we think. Some of these experiments are considered elsewhere in this book (chapter 40; see also Aronson, 1999).

But the present study alone shows how Festinger's cognitive-dissonance concept can offer an explanation for observations that would otherwise be extremely puzzling: the outright failure, indeed refusal, to modify an opinion, even in the face of direct evidence that the opinion is false.

BIBLIOGRAPHY

Aronson, E. (1999). *The social animal* (8th ed.). New York: Worth Publishers.

Aronson, E., Wilson, T. D., & Akert, R. M. (1994). *Social psychology: The heart and the mind*. New York: Harper Collins College Publishers.

Festinger, L. (1957). *A theory of cognitive dissonance*. Evanston, IL: Row, Peterson.

Festinger, L., Riecken, H. W., & Schachter, S. (1956). *When prophecy fails*. Minneapolis: University of Minnesota Press.

58 STANLEY MILGRAM ON OBEDIENCE TO AUTHORITY

In 1945, World War II ended. At and around the time of its ending, the world became aware of two terrifying realities. First were the atomic bombings of Hiroshima and Nagasaki. Humankind had the power of the sun in its hands. Second, the concentration camps were opened, and documents were captured; these showed firsthand, and in cold print, the inhumanity of which human beings were capable. Combine immense power with a capacity for unspeakable cruelty, and the fear that swept over the world is not hard to understand.

Perhaps we could console ourselves with the thought that the Nazi leaders, and the concentration camp guards and wardens, were unusually bad people. Some of them no doubt were. As far as could be seen, however, many others were simply normal human beings, carrying out orders. Well, then, perhaps certain societies are particularly at risk for this sort of barbarity. Perhaps there is an "authoritarian personality" that is particularly inclined to follow orders blindly, even inhumane ones, and perhaps certain societies foster the authoritarian outlook. Both of these possibilities offer comfort. Perhaps barbarities are perpetrated only by a pathological minority—pathological individuals, and perhaps pathological societies.

When Stanley Milgram began his studies of obedience, his intention was to compare different societies. He sought a way in which one's willingness to follow inhumane orders could be measured. Then, with that method in hand, he could compare people drawn from different societies—for example, Germany and the United States. Other studies have in fact compared people from different countries. But what Milgram found in the United States was revelation enough.

Stanley Milgram (1933–84) was born in New York City. He earned his bachelor's degree from Queens College in 1954 and his Ph.D. at Harvard in 1960; during his time there he was research assistant to Solomon Asch, another student of response to social pressure (chapter 56). Milgram then joined the faculty at Yale, where his classic experiments on obedience began. Later he returned to Harvard and then, in 1967, to the City University of New York, where he remained. Milgram's book on obedience (1974) was translated into seven languages and nominated for a National Book Award for what it showed us about ourselves.

In Milgram's initial experiments (1963), the participants were recruited from newspaper ads and posters placed around the city. These invited people to "learn about themselves" in a psychological experiment. That, plus how to reply, was all the information that they were given in advance. This is important, for it means that none of the participants had volunteered to be prison guards or concentration camp guards or to give punishment to anyone else for any reason. They simply had volunteered to participate in a psychological experiment, nothing more.

Then each of the resulting volunteers was put through a staged scenario, as follows. Upon entering the laboratory, they were introduced to another person who they were led to believe was another participant. Actually, this other person was an actor who was in the pay of the experimenter. But the participants did not know that.

The participants were told that they had been assigned the role of "teacher" in a learning experiment, whereas the actor had been assigned the role of "learner." As teacher, the participant's task was to punish the "learner" when he made mistakes in a learning task. The "learner" then went into a cubicle where the participant could not see him, but the two could communicate by voice, and the "learning session" began.

Now the "punishment"—so participants believed—consisted of electric shocks. The "learner"—the actor—had electrodes strapped to his wrist, connected by wires to a box identified as a shock generator. There was a control device that could be set at various levels. The purported intensities ranged from 15 V to 450 V (115 V is standard wall-socket voltage in the United States). Alongside these various settings were verbal descriptions ranging from "Slight shock" to "Danger: severe shock."

In short, the participants were told that their task in the experiment was to deliver electric shocks to the "learner" when the learner made a mistake. And the participants believed that they were in fact doing this.

The experiment began with the "shock" set at very low intensity. As the task went on, the participant was told to deliver the shocks at greater and greater intensity, as indicated on the shock generator. Remember that the "learner" was an assistant to the experimenter; he was playing a role, and in fact was receiving no shocks at all. But *the real participants did not know that*.

The test was to memorize a list of paired items, so that, seeing one member of each pair, the participants were to call out the other. The actor deliberately made mistakes and received a "shock" after each one. The participant was told to increase the level of the shock with each error, so the shock level kept rising.

The interest in the experiment was the real participants, who thought they were delivering these painful shocks. As the supposed level of shock went up and up, at what point would the participants simply say, "No. I'm not going to administer any more shocks"? They could, after all, have said that at any point. The experimenter had no power to prevent them from simply quitting and walking out the door.

But most did not. At about 120 V, the actor shouted that the shocks were becoming too painful. At 150 V, he demanded that the experiment end. So it went, until the actor was screaming with pain, and then, at higher levels still, there came only an ominous silence from the cubicle in which the actor sat. But the experimenter calmly told the participant that failure to respond was to be counted as an error, and that he was to continue delivering shocks of greater and greater intensity. And the fact is that a full 65 percent of Milgram's subjects—both men and women—continued to obey the experimenter to the very end. *Sixty-five percent.*

They did not do so blindly. Early on, they would look to the experimenter for guidance and say things like "Shouldn't we stop?" But the experimenter would reply calmly, "You have no choice. You must continue." Not surprisingly, many of the participants became seriously upset:

> I observed a mature and initially poised businessman enter the laboratory smiling and confident. Within 20 minutes he was reduced to a twitching, stuttering wreck, who was rapidly approaching a point of nervous collapse. He constantly pulled on his earlobe, and twisted his hands. At one point he pushed his fist into his forehead and muttered "Oh God, let's stop it." And yet he continued to respond to every word of the experimenter, and obeyed to the very end. (Milgram, 1963, p. 376)

Milgram went on to repeat the experiment under different conditions, and thus learn more about what he had discovered (1974). For instance, he showed that what he saw was a matter of *obedience to authority*, not of *conformity to a group* (though his work is often erroneously discussed under the latter heading).

One experiment that shows this began in the way described earlier. But then, shortly after the "learning session" began, the experimenter left the room to answer a bogus telephone call, leaving an assistant in charge. Here, where the person giving orders lacked the authority of a scientist, many fewer participants continued to follow orders.

At the same time, elements of the situation could also modulate the tendency to obey. One of these was the "psychological distance" between the participant and the apparent victim. In the original experiment, the actor was isolated in a booth. But in a variation, the actor was in the same room directly adjacent to the participant, who was told to administer the shock by pressing the victim's hand upon a shock electrode. Under these conditions, obedience dropped. It dropped all the way to 30 percent—which still means that about a third of the participants continued to obey even under these conditions.

This variation reduced the "psychological distance" between participant and victim; what if it is increased instead? Again there was a separate experiment, and this time there were two actors: one pretended to receive the shocks, and the other pretended to administer them. The real participants gave no shocks, but simply read the stimuli over a microphone and recorded the "learner's" responses. They did not have to administer shocks, but it was made clear to them that their presence was required to conduct the experiment. In other words, by quitting and walking out the door, they could prevent any further shocks to the learner. But in fact, under these conditions over 90 percent of the participants obeyed orders all the way to the end.

Finally, there does seem to be a parallel with the research on conformity in that it only takes one or a few dissenters to break up the influence of the authority figure (compare chapter 56). In these experiments, the single participants were in the company of two other people whom they thought were participants too, but who were actually assistants to the experimenter. Early on in the experiment, first one, then the second, refused to obey the experimenter's orders and "quit" the experiment. When they did so, all but 10 percent of the true participants also quit. Of course, all participants could have quit in all the other experiments as well, and surely at some level they "knew" that this was so. Apparently, though, this option had to be made a salient part of their life spaces (chapter 55). It rarely came to mind without the "prompting" of disobedience by another person.

Why were these perfectly ordinary people willing to go on complying with what they thought was a cruel and dangerous procedure? No doubt there were a number of reasons. One is dehumanization of the victim. The "teacher" may put on psychic blinders and concentrate on his task, learning to ignore the suffering victim. One of Milgram's participants said, "You really begin to forget that there's a guy out there, even though you can hear him. For a long time I just concentrated on pressing the switches and reading the words" (Milgram, 1974, p. 515).

Then there is what we might call *transfer of responsibility*, by analogy with *diffusion of responsibility* (chapter 59). If we are acting on someone else's orders, we may come to feel that it is the other person who is really performing the action, and not ourselves; some writers have compared this to a hypnotic state (Wegner, 2002). As we can dehumanize a victim, so it seems that we can also dehumanize ourselves, becoming instruments rather than agents in our own minds. Another of Milgram's participants, who had obeyed to the very end, said, "*I* stopped, but he [the experimenter] made me go on" (Aronson, 1999, p. 43).

Another factor promoting compliance may have been the *gradualness* of the sequence (the "slippery-slope" phenomenon). "Suppose the experimenter had explained, at the outset, that he would like people to deliver a possibly fatal shock to the other participant. How many people would have agreed? Very few, we suspect" (Aronson, Wilson, & Akert, 1994, p. 304). But Milgram's experiment set up a situation in which what was done changed gradually, from not at all dangerous to (apparently) very dangerous, with no prominent line of demarcation. At what point should the participants switch from one role (participants whose job is to follow the experimenter's instructions) to another role (people who can make their own decisions and decide not to hurt someone)? The gradualness of the dilemma might even mean that a shift of role would be accompanied by a certain *cognitive dissonance* (compare chapter 40). The participants might say to themselves, "I have obeyed orders thus far, and it is only a small increase in shock intensity that I am being asked to administer now; why refuse now if not before? It would be inconsistent of me."

Whatever the reasons, the willingness of Milgram's participants to comply with these abhorrent orders often comes as a surprise—as it did to Milgram himself. When people are asked, "How many people do you think would deliver the maximum amount of shock in such a situation?" a typical estimate is around one percent. These were the results with psychology majors at Yale University, a sample of middle-class adults, and a panel of psychiatrists. But the data are clear. This commonsense answer is simply wrong. We should remember once again that the participants in Milgram's experiments were ordinary people, presumably not much different from you and me. We may feel very strongly as individuals that we would refuse to comply with such abhorrent demands, and most of us will say so if asked. It is humbling to remember that when actually faced with the situation, roughly two-thirds of "people like us" do in fact comply. As noted in other chapters, we tend to minimize the important role of the *situation* in affecting our thoughts and actions.

Direct experience with situational constraints on behavior can be very revealing. Elliott Aronson tells this story:

> One year, when, as usual, I asked my social-psychology students whether they might continue delivering shocks until the end of the scale, only one hand slowly rose; everyone else in the class was confident that he/she would defy the experimenter's instructions. But the student who raised his hand was a Vietnam veteran who was in a position to know; he had experienced the impact of similar pressures, and he painfully and tragically came to recognize his own vulnerability in certain situations. (1999, p. 46)

Before leaving these experiments, a word should be said about the ethical issues that they raise. Milgram's participants were put through very stressful experiences, as indicated earlier, and they had not consented to this. Apart from issues of informed consent, we have to wonder whether the procedures of these experiments might have done damage to the participants' conception of themselves.

Of course, all of them had the procedure and the reasons for it carefully explained to them after the experiment was over. They were told that no one had in fact received any shocks or undergone any pain at all. Even so, they were also fully aware that they had not known this while the experiment was going on. Therefore, they left the experiment knowing that they had been willing to inflict pain (whether they had actually done so or not) just because someone in authority had told them to do so. How damaging might that knowledge be?

On the other hand, we could ask, if we refuse to learn unpleasant truths of ourselves, it is that not also damaging in the long run? Perhaps it is; but it is not clear that that is for us scientists to say. We do not have the right to put people in stressful situations without their consent just to "teach them a lesson."

Milgram discussed the matter with his participants, and he reports that most thought that it was a valuable experience, that they had learned something important about themselves. Even so, we cannot be sure of all participants will react that way. What about those who do not?

We find ourselves, in short, in a conflict for which there is no easy resolution. It seems very likely that an experiment like Milgram's would not be permitted today. Supervisory boards would forbid it, for the reasons we have just given. And yet the fact remains that Milgram's experiments are cited in every introductory psychology text, and are presented as having taught us something valuable about human beings—including ourselves.

BIBLIOGRAPHY

Aronson, E. (1999). *The social animal* (8th ed.). New York: Worth Publishers.

Aronson, E., Wilson, T. D., & Akert, R. M. (1994). *Social psychology: The heart and the mind.* New York: Harper Collins College Publishers.

Milgram, S. (1963). Behavioral study of obedience. *Journal of Abnormal and Social Psychology, 67,* 371–378.

Milgram, S. (1974). *Obedience to authority.* New York: Harper & Row (Colophon Books).

Wegner, D. M. (2002). *The illusion of conscious will.* Cambridge, MA: MIT Press.

59 | LATANÉ AND DARLEY: THE UNRESPONSIVE BYSTANDER

In 1964, an event happened that frightened the nation—both for what took place, and for what did not.

> Kitty Genovese is set upon by a maniac as she returns from work at 3 a.m. Thirty-eight of her neighbors in Kew Gardens [in New York City] come to their windows when she cries out in terror; none come to her assistance even though her stalker takes over half an hour to murder her. No one even so much as calls the police. She dies. (Latané & Darley, 1970, p. 2.)

Thirty-eight witnesses to this tragic event. And not one of them took action—not even the simple, safe action of phoning the police. How could this have happened? This was the topic of a series of experiments by Bibb Latané (rhymes with *matinee*) and John Darley.

Bibb Latané (1937–) was born in New York City. He earned his B.A. at Yale in culture and behavior in 1958, then a Ph.D. in psychology with a minor in journalism at the University of Minnesota in 1963. He taught at Columbia until 1968, then moved to Ohio State University, the University of North Carolina, and Florida Atlantic University, where he is now.

John M. Darley (1938–) was born in Minneapolis. He earned a B.A. from Swarthmore College in 1960, then an M.A. and Ph.D. from Harvard in 1962 and 1965, respectively. He taught at New York University from 1964 to 1968, then moved to Princeton, where he has remained.

After the murder of Kitty Genovese, many explanations for the "apathy" of the onlookers were put forward. It was suggested that large cities, and the anonymity that goes with them, had led to alienation—people no longer felt like part of a group, and hence responsible for each other. Or perhaps people were so fearful that they hid from disaster. Or perhaps the pace of modern city life so overwhelms us—"information overload"—that we simply tune out even the most acute emergencies.

Latané and Darley found these explanations unconvincing. In the first place, interviews with these eyewitnesses revealed that they had not felt at all apathetic, alienated, or tuned out. They were horrified at what they were witnessing—and *still* they took no action. Second, the fact is that we do sometimes help each other, even at great risk. We are not always apathetic or indifferent. Rather, it seems that we act that way under some conditions, but not under others.

So the question is, What are these conditions? What conditions promote helping in an emergency, and what conditions discourage it—and why?

Maybe the crucial difference between action and apathy is not within ourselves, but in the *situation*. And it might have to do, not with our feelings or motives, but with our thoughts—with how we *interpret* the situation. Thus:

> When only one bystander is present in an emergency situation, if help is to be given it must be he who gives it. The situation is not so clear when a crowd of bystanders are present. Then the responsibility for intervention is diffused among the bystanders and focuses on no single one. In these circumstances, each person may feel less responsibility to help the victim. "Why me?" he can say. (Latané & Darley, 1970, p. 157)

In other words, if there is a crowd of onlookers, maybe no one is likely to help— *because* there is a crowd of onlookers! Precisely because there are so many, no one of them may take responsibility for action. Each one may wait upon the others, with the result that no one offers help.

Latané and Darley tested that idea in a classic series of experiments. Their question was just this: If a person witnessed an emergency, would the presence of other onlookers make him or her less likely to offer help? The answer, time after time, was yes.

In one such experiment, a male college student was sitting in a waiting room. He was waiting to participate in an experiment, or so he thought; he did not know that he was already in one. Then an emergency was staged: from a vent in the wall, smoke began to pour into the room. Would the participant leave the waiting room to report the "emergency," or otherwise offer help?

In one experimental condition, each participant was in the room by himself when the smoke came. When the "emergency" occurred, only he could report it; if he did not, no one would. In the other condition, the subjects were waiting in groups of three. This would allow *diffusion of responsibility* to occur. Each person could ask himself, "Should I take action, or will one of these others do it instead?" If he asked himself that question, he might be less likely to do anything.

Sure enough, fewer subjects took any action, and those who did took longer to act, in the grouped condition.

In their book, the authors report several other experiments like this, with different kinds of emergencies, and the findings remained the same: the mere presence of multiple bystanders made it less likely that any of them would offer help. Moreover, it did indeed depend on how the bystander *interprets* the situation. Further experiments showed that if the bystander *believes* other people are around, even if they are not, that is enough! He or she is less likely to offer help (Darley & Latané, 1968).

Figure 59.1
Results of a bystander-intervention experiment. The presence of other onlookers made it much less likely that a participant would offer help in an emergency.

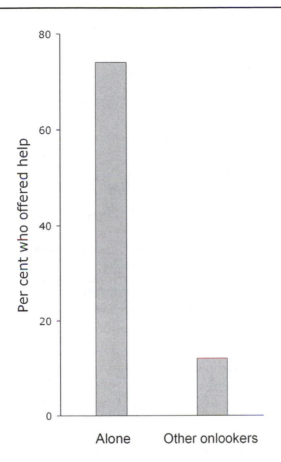

Source: From *Psychological Research: The Ideas behind the Methods* by Douglas G. Mook. Copyright 2001 by W. W. Norton & Company, Inc. Used by permission of W. W. Norton & Company, Inc.

Now, these experiments, it is true, were conducted in an artificial laboratory situation. Would the same sort of thing happen in a natural situation? To find out, Latané and Darley staged some of their experiments in natural settings—in one case, for example, a liquor store.

This experiment was worked out in advance with the proprietor of the store, who agreed to help the experimenters stage an apparent emergency: two men stealing a case of beer while the proprietor's back was turned.

The participants in this experiment were real liquor-store customers, who had no idea that they were in an experiment. The "crimes" were staged sometimes when only one real customer was present, and sometimes when there were two real customers, so again there were two experimental conditions: waiting alone, and waiting with another person. Then the question was whether the real customer(s) would report the theft to the proprietor when he came back.

(Here, by the way, we see one great advantage of experiments: they make things happen at will, so we don't have to wait for the right events to happen naturally. The liquor-store "emergency" was made to happen 96 times in a single week!)

The results were quite consistent with the earlier, smoke-filled-room study. If only one real customer was present, the chances were that he or she would report the theft. But when there were two, it was less likely that *either one* would report it. The multiple-onlooker effect showed up again.

Further follow-up research showed that there are limits to the multiple-onlooker effect. If, for instance, one member of a group has some special expertise that is relevant to the emergency, then it is likely that he or she will take action even if other onlookers are present. Then again, that situation probably occurs only in a minority of real-life emergencies.

The authors sum up the implications of their studies as follows:

> "There's safety in numbers" according to an old adage, and modern city dwellers seem to believe it . . . It may be that people are less likely to find themselves in trouble if there are others present. But if a person does find himself in trouble, safety in numbers may be illusory . . . In fact, the opposite seems to be true. A victim may be more likely to get help or an emergency to be reported, the fewer people who are available to take action. (Latané & Darley, 1970, p. 156)

We say that there is "safety in numbers," and intuitively it seems obvious that this should be so. The more people are around, the more likely it should be that *someone* will intervene. But it appears that our intuition is wrong.

These experiments tell us something more as well. When such a tragedy as the murder of Kitty Genovese occurs, the standard explanations of failures to help will speak about such things as alienation, apathy, indifference, and similar personality characteristics thought to be produced by modern city environments. But in the smoke experiment, subjects were assigned *at random* to wait alone, or to wait with others. Therefore, each group of subjects should have contained about equal numbers of alienated, apathetic, and indifferent people. Still, the two groups behaved very differently. Therefore, it was not the participants' personal characteristics, but the *presence of other onlookers* that made participants so much less likely to help if they were in a group. The external social situation was a much more powerful influence than internal personal or personality factors. Moreover, in some of their studies, Latané and his coworkers measured a whole series of personality variables to see if there were differences between people who helped and people who did not. No such differences were found.

Finally, this research bears on a more general issue. The findings challenge the "safety in numbers" prediction, yes. But they also take their place along with many other findings to suggest a more general conclusion: external, situational factors can be much more powerful influences on our actions than internal personality factors are. We tend to believe the opposite—that a person tends to act as he or she does because he or she is "that kind of person." That may sometimes be true. But the bystander effect, and many other findings, suggest that we should not be too quick to jump to that conclusion. The *situation* can be a powerful influence on the way we behave, and we discount it at our peril.

BIBLIOGRAPHY

Aronson, E. (1999). *The social animal* (8th ed.). New York: Worth Publishers.

Aronson, E., Wilson, T. D., & Akert, R. M. (1994). *Social psychology: The heart and the mind.* New York: Harper Collins College Publishers.

Darley, J., & Latané, B. (1968). Bystander intervention in emergencies: Diffusion of responsibility. *Journal of Personality and Social Psychology, 8,* 377–383.

Latané, B., & Darley, J. (1970). *The unresponsive bystander: Why doesn't he help?* New York: Appleton-Century-Crofts.

Latané, B., & Rodin, J. (1969). A lady in distress: Inhibiting effects of friends and strangers on bystander intervention. *Journal of Experimental Social Psychology, 5*(2), 189–202.

60 BENJAMIN FRANKLIN: MESMER AND ANIMAL MAGNETISM

Most readers will have heard of Benjamin Franklin (1706–90)—statesman, signer of the American colonies' Declaration of Independence from Britain, and a moving force behind the framing of the Constitution, which welded the American colonies into the United States of America. It is less well known that he was also a scientist of international standing, having done fundamental research on electricity.

Still less well known is Franklin's brief career as an experimental psychologist. But he was one, in a single investigation that was a masterpiece of *experimental control*, and as such was a lasting contribution to the methodology of psychological research.

The story begins with Friedrich Anton Mesmer (1734–1815), an Austrian who, as a medical student, was greatly influenced by the writings of Paracelsus, a sixteenth-century physician who sought, among other things, to show the influence of the stars on human health. The influence of the stars was mysterious; electricity was a mystery; so Mesmer may be forgiven for suggesting that astrological effects might be electrical ones. Around 1760, Mesmer saw demonstration of cures apparently produced by the use of magnetized metal plates.

At the time, what we would now call "faith healing" was common in Europe. As a scientist, Mesmer did not accept the popular explanation in terms of exorcising of demons or witches. Instead, he related these mysterious occurrences to other, equally mysterious but natural, forces—like electricity. He supposed that a fluid pervaded the entire universe, and that it could be moved around by such things as gravity (which also could account for astrological influences) and electricity. Remnants of these ideas still survive, by the way, in everyday language; thus a *lunatic* was once thought to be a person under the influence of the moon *(luna)*.

Mesmer argued that diseases, including mental disorders, arose from an imbalance of this universal fluid in the body. Therefore, the task of medicine was to restore balance. There were already some reports that cures for certain disorders might be produced by application of magnets to parts of the body. This, Mesmer proposed, could mean that the universal fluid was subject to magnetic influences that could correct its imbalance.

He tried his "magnet therapy" on patients, with some dramatic successes. An early one is described as follows:

> Success—and fame—came to him with the cure of a certain Fräulein Österlin, who had been afflicted with an extravagance of purportedly severe symptoms, including paralyses, headaches, vomiting, and paroxysms of rage. Mesmer had noticed that her condition exhibited a certain periodic quality, to the point that he could predict its ebb and flow. From this he drew confirmation for his presupposition that planetary motions, with their mathematical periodicities, underlay her condition. He set about correcting the inferred fluid imbalances of her body by inducing, by means of his magnets, a restorative "artificial tide." He attached three magnets to her body; one to her stomach and one to each of her legs. Then, to maximize his magnets' effectiveness, he had her swallow a preparation containing iron. As Mesmer made "passes" over her with a magnet, Fräulein Österlin began experiencing strange bodily perturbations. Streams of fluid, she felt, radiated downward through her body. Her breathing got heavier; she started moaning; her body began trembling and then convulsing uncontrollably, reaching a grand crescendo of spasms and gasps—followed by unaccustomed peace. The high point of excitement, which Mesmer called the *crisis*, was construed by him as the final dramatic phase of fluidic readjustment. (Erdelyi, 1985, p. 14)

As the commentator notes delicately: "He did not apparently explore . . . an alternative hypothesis" (Erdelyi, 1985, p. 14).

Much encouraged by such successes—and there were many—Mesmer went on to explore a kind of forerunner of group therapy: group healing (figure 60.1). Groups of patients would sit around a *baquet*, a vat filled with "magnetized" water. Each patient held on with one hand to a metal rod protruding from the vat. With their free hands, or with ropes, they joined themselves together in a circle through which the "magnetism" could flow. Mesmer would appear, sometimes in magician's dress, and pass around the circle of patients, touching them or making passes with his hands. He might sit before a patient for long periods, while fixing him or her with his eyes.

Some of this mumbo-jumbo might have meant only that Mesmer enjoyed being the star of the show, but it also might have contributed to his successes. Mesmer might have succeeded in inducing in some of his patients the highly suggestible state that came to be called *mesmerism*, after him, but that today we call *hypnosis*. In any case, the effects could be dramatic, sometimes resulting in loss of consciousness or even full-scale convulsions. But the fact is that some dramatic cures occurred.

Mesmerism became very popular in Paris, to which Mesmer had moved in 1778. The physicians of Paris were upset by all this—first, because the physicians of the time were working hard to separate themselves from magic and sorcery; second, because they worried that Mesmer might be doing harm; and third, no doubt, from professional (and financial) jealousy. They persuaded King Louis XVI to establish a royal commission to test Mesmer's claims. This included such prominent scientists as the chemist Anton Lavoisier—and Benjamin Franklin, who was in Paris as representative of America. King Louis appointed him to head the commission.

The commission began by observing what went on at the baquet. There was much to see. Patients, crowded around the baquet in several rings, were "magne-

Figure 60.1
Mesmer's *baquet*. Patients are connected to the tub of "magnetized water" and/or to each other with ropes or with metal rods that they can clasp.

Source: From Foveau de Cormelles (1890).

tized" by contact with the metal rods and with each other. The commission's report says,

> Patients then display a variety of reactions . . . Some are calm, quiet, & feel nothing . . . others are agitated & tormented by convulsions . . . As soon as a convulsion begins, many others follow [and] are characterized by quick, involuntary movements of the limbs & the entire body . . . by piercing shrieks, tears, hiccups & excessive laughter. They are preceded or followed by a state of languor & dreaminess, of a kind of prostration & even sleepiness. (Franklin et al., 1784/2002, p. 801)

Clearly something dramatic was happening.

The commissioners soon convinced themselves that this was not a good research setting. "One sees too many things at once to see particular things clearly" (Franklin et al., 1784/2002, p. 802). The situation lacked control; too many things were varying at once. "Moreover, distinguished patients who come to the treatment for their health could be bothered by the questioning." Then as now, there were matters of ethics to consider.

They therefore set out to experiment on persons who were willing to be "tested" alone. They began with themselves, and a separate room with a baquet vat was set up for them. Mesmer himself did not participate in the resulting experiments. Instead, he appointed one of his students, a M. Charles Deslon, to take his place.

Now, having attached themselves to the vat in the new surroundings, none of the commission members felt anything at all. Nor were there any therapeutic effects on the mild aches and pains that troubled the members.

The commissioners could not help but be struck by the difference between "group treatment & private treatment at the vat. Calm & silence in one, movement and agitation in the other; there, multiple effects, violent crises . . . here, the body without pain, the spirit without trouble" (Franklin et al. 1784/2002, p. 805). The members were already beginning to wonder whether an agitated, excited state might play a role, quite apart from magnetism, in the dramatic responses of the original group.

Other people too were tested in the quieter setting. Only a minority reported any effect at all of being magnetized. There were exceptions. One woman in particular, when a magnet was passed close to her stomach, felt heat there. Magnetized on the back, she felt heat there. Was she perhaps especially sensitive?

No, because when she was blindfolded, as a way of "protecting her from her imagination, or at least of getting it out of the way" (Franklin et al., 1784/2002, p. 809)—then her reports no longer located the warmth where the magnets were. "Magnetized successively over the stomach & the back, the woman felt heat in her head, pain in her right leg, her left eye & left ear" (p. 809). In short, the sensations she had reported had little to do with the magnets, and much to do with her expectations.

> The Commissioners . . . conducted numerous experiments on different subjects whom they magnetized themselves, or whom they led to believe had been magnetized . . . there was not in all these experiments any variation other than that of the degree of imagination. (p. 811)

The committee devised some further tests whereby some subjects were led to think they were being magnetized when they were not, while others did receive the magnetizing treatment but without knowing it. The results were clear: participants who reported effects were those who *thought* they had been magnetized, whether or not they actually had been.

In another kind of experiment, Franklin had M. Deslon magnetize one of the trees in a garden. Then an experimental participant, who was allegedly sensitive to magnetic effects but who was not told which tree was the magnetized one, walked around the garden hugging trees for two minutes each, as prescribed by M. Deslon. At one of the trees, he had a "crisis": he "lost consciousness, his limbs stiffened & he was carried to a nearby lawn where M. Deslon gave him first aid and revived him" (Franklin et al., 1784/2002, p. 812).

Unfortunately, it was the wrong tree.

M. Deslon was unconvinced by that finding, arguing that perhaps all trees are naturally magnetized. The commission's reply bears the Franklin stamp: "In that case, anyone sensitive to magnetism could not chance going into a garden without incurring the risk of convulsions, an assertion contradicted by everyday experience" (Franklin et al., 1784/2002, p. 812).

In another experiment, a woman claimed that she could sense "magnetized" water. Lavoisier filled several cups with water but magnetized only one of them. After touching one of the cups, she collapsed in a convulsion—but it was the wrong cup. Then, when Lavoisier gave her the magnetized water to drink, she drank it quietly without incident.

All of this is reminiscent of the Clever Hans phenomenon and how it was unmasked (chapter 37)—except that here, it is not that the onlookers gave unintended cues to the participants. It is that the participants' own expectations influenced what they felt. If the participants did not know in advance which tree or cup of water was the magnetized one, they could not identify it, nor were they affected by it—though they were affected by trees or cups that they *thought* were magnetized. In a word, the participants felt what they *expected* to feel, when and where they expected to feel it.

This fact was demonstrated simply by not letting the participant know when he or she *should* feel the magnetism. This "blind" control—not letting the participant know in advance what would fit with his or her expectations and what would not—is now a routinely used control procedure in any situation where the participants' expectations or beliefs might affect what they say or do in ways that might lead to wrong conclusions. (Compare the double-blind placebo control, chapter 26.)

One source of Mesmer's effects, then, was the expectations of his patients. But why was the smaller, quiet baquet so different from the original one? This points to some other sources of Mesmer's effects. The rather frenzied atmosphere of the original setting surely produced an aroused state, and we know today that such a state can be interpreted in different ways with different emotions resulting (chapter 16). Perhaps Mesmer's patients *interpreted* the simple discomfort of the situation as the experience of a mysterious flow of energy through their bodies.

Then, too, there may have been social influences (compare chapters 53 and 56). Imitation may have played a part (chapter 25). In modern therapy groups, there may be pressure to report certain symptoms or life experiences; in Mesmer's groups, one may have best fit into the group by expressing the same symptoms as they. The commission recognized this too: the patient may "[believe] that it pleases us more when he says he feels effects" (Franklin et al. 1784/2002, p. 808).

Is it really plausible that such internal factors as expectations, excitement, group pressure, and the like could produce such dramatic symptoms? Let us be clear: *The experimental data from the commission's research show that such things can and do happen.* Think again about the participant who went into spasms and lost conscious in the presence of a tree that he *thought* was magnetized. It wasn't, so it was not an external magnetic force that produced these effects. They could only have come from within.

Franklin's commission reported to the King that "nothing proves the existence of Animal-magnetism fluid; that this fluid with no existence is therefore without utility; that the violent effects observed at the group treatment belong . . . to the imagination set in action" (Franklin et al., 1784/2002, p. 821). The effect, in other words, is not magnetic but psychological—the result of suggestion, excitement, and group influence. We discover this when, and only when, we *control* for the effects of these other influences, and thus isolate the effects of magnetism—if it has effects. In these experiments, it had none.

As a result of all this, Mesmer was forced to leave Paris for Switzerland in disgrace. However, it is not as if there were only one Mesmer. During his time, and before and since, purveyors of quack remedies and benefits have been leaving their workplaces and going not to Switzerland, but straight to the bank.

One can still buy magnets with alleged curative powers, though double-blind controlled studies have shown their utter uselessness. "Subliminal tapes" are offered that will teach us a foreign language or improve our self-esteem while we sleep—though double-blind experiments have repeatedly shown that their "benefits" are illusory. And so on—for the list is long. This flood of pseudoscience cannot be reviewed here. The curious reader will find much to ponder in the pages of two magazines, *The Skeptical Inquirer* and *The Skeptic*, and in many books (e.g., Randi, 1987; Stanovich, 2001).

The parallel between then and now goes further. Today's pseudoscientist often supports his or her claims with exactly the kind of "evidence" by which Mesmer supported his. In our own time, the report of another commission—or rather, a committee of the United States Congress—listed some characteristics of medical quacks and frauds (Stanovich, 2001).

First, medical quacks may offer a "special" or "secret" formula for cures. Mesmer is said to have been offered a substantial sum of money for his "secret," and to have refused—if only because he had no secret to impart.

Second, they advertise, using individual case histories or testimonials ("I lost 60 pounds on Dr. Skinnem's diet!"). These make dramatic reading, and the failures, which do not, are not reported. We have no tally of Mesmer's failures.

Third, they may claim to know the cause of a disorder and talk about "cleansing" the body or about "rebalancing" one's "energy fields." (Compare Mesmer's "animal magnetism.")

Fourth, they may accuse the "medical establishment" of persecuting them—as Mesmer accused the physicians of Paris in his time.

The present author would add another: quack physicians or therapists will make no attempt to *control for the effects of expectation or suggestion*. Mesmer did not—and when Franklin's commission did, it was these factors that turned out to be responsible for his effects. In our own time, patients or clients who use (say) magnets or subliminal tapes may feel very strongly that they have been helped by them—as Mesmer's patients did. However (again as in Mesmer's case) the feeling can be shown, by the double-blind experiments mentioned earlier, to be the result of suggestion only.

The best safeguard against pseudoscience is real science—and research psychologists, as well as other scientists, have been active in challenging the claims of the fraudulent or the honestly self-deluded, as in chapters 33 and 37. Moreover, the use of experimental methods to expose fraud or self-delusion very often use exactly the same experimental technique as was used by Franklin's commission. The key is to *separate what is going on from what the patient or participant thinks is going on*. The participants in the Paris experiment reported effects if they *thought* they were being magnetized, even if they were not. They reported no effects if they were magnetized without knowing it. Clearly, they were experiencing what they *expected* to experience, and the magnets had nothing to do with it.

The blind control, mentioned a moment ago, makes that experimental separation: if one does not know what to expect, then expectations cannot bias what one sees or feels. It is remarkable how often that procedure may be all that is needed to expose a bogus claim. It is what exposed Clever Hans and the Facilitated Communication mistake—and Mesmer—and magnets and subliminal tapes in our own time. When confronted with a dramatic claim, it is usually worth asking, Was it tested blind?

Bringing that powerful technique to bear may not even be difficult, and it is certainly not restricted to professional scientists. To show this, here is a final example, for dessert. This beautiful little experiment was told to the author by an online listmate, on the condition of anonymity. It was not done by a professional researcher, and, indeed, a professional researcher might have faced some ethical problems here. This is what happened:

> I wanted to share with you an experience of mine yesterday that may make you smile. It involves my girlfriend's family, who I feel are very smart people who believe weird things. She has a large immediate family, and they are all firm believers in multiple fringe concepts, including astrology, ghosts, and psychic powers . . . my girlfriend's mother's birthday was yesterday, and they had a huge party at her house. I [tried] a small experiment. I found an astrology website on the Internet, and printed out 30 copies of the full 12 sign horoscope. However, I changed 15 of the copies . . . so that the readings no longer matched up with the Zodiac sign. At the party, I passed all these out and had everyone rate how accurate their own readings were on a scale of 1 to 5 . . . In the end, the average score for the correct horoscopes was 3.7, and for the non-correct 3.9. (personal communication)

In other words, even someone else's horoscope was accepted as accurate if the person *thought* it was his or her own. Given a horoscope, real or bogus, the participants looked within themselves for the characteristics it specified—and saw what they was looking for.

This elegant little demonstration was a full-blown experiment. There was an independent variable (real versus doctored horoscopes), a dependent variable (how accurate the participants rated the horoscope to be), *and*, the focus of the present discussion, *experimental control* for the effects of suggestion and expectation (the participants were blind as to whether the horoscopes were really theirs or not). When this was done, the independent variable turned out to have no effect at all, but the consistently high accuracy ratings suggest that the participants indeed were seeing what they expected to see.

Moreover, like others, this experiment does not stand alone (chapter 1). There is now a substantial literature consisting of experiments much like this one, supporting the same conclusion about astrology.

This kind of informal experiment does have its dangers:

> When it was all over, I told them the truth, and showed them that the doctored horoscopes actually got a slightly higher rating. The response was alarming. I was called a know-it-all by at least two people, overheard someone call me [a bad name], and my girlfriend later informed me that her father was upset, and that I had to apologize. I

found it very ironic that they were upset with me for "tricking" them, but failed to see that the evidence from the experiment showed that it was astrology doing the tricking. (personal communication)

The application of a simple control procedure has its risks! We have seen that people can cling to a belief, even in the face of data that bear a clear message that the belief is false (chapter 57). Now we are reminded that they may also be inclined to shoot the messenger—metaphorically, one hopes. But at least the message is there to be heard.

The real point of this example, and a good note on which to end this book, is just this: The logic of experimentation is by no means confined to professional experimenters. It is available to all of us, if we will use it.

BIBLIOGRAPHY

Boring, E. G. (1950). *A history of experimental psychology* (2nd ed.). New York: Appleton-Century-Crofts.

Darnton, R. (1968). *Mesmerism and the end of the enlightenment in France.* Cambridge, MA: Harvard University Press.

Erdelyi, M. (1985). *Psychoanalysis: Freud's cognitive psychology.* New York: W. H. Freeman.

Foveau de Cormelles, F.-V. (1890). *L'hypnotisme.* Paris: Hachette.

Franklin, B., et al. (2002). Report of the commissioners charged by the King to examine animal magnetism (D. Salas & C. Salas, Trans.). In M. Shermer (Ed.), *The* Skeptic *encyclopedia of pseudoscience* (Vol. 2, pp. 797–823). Santa Barbara, CA: ABC/CLIO. (Original work published 1784)

Randi, J. (1987). *Flim-Flam! Psychics, ESP, unicorns and other delusions.* Buffalo, NY: Prometheus Books.

Sagan, C. (1997). *The demon-haunted world: Science as a candle in the dark.* New York: Ballantine Books.

Stanovich, K. E. (2001). *How to think straight about psychology* (6th edition). Boston: Allyn & Bacon.

INDEX

Index

Index

About the Author

DOUGLAS MOOK is Professor Emeritus of Psychology at the University of Virginia.